WITHDRAWN FROM
TSC LIBRARY

Copyright ©1991 The Creative Black Book, a Division of Macmillan Information Company, Inc.
All rights reserved. We are not responsible for errors or omissions.
The Creative Black Book, 115 Fifth Avenue, New York, NY 10003
(212) 254-1330, Facsimile (212) 598-4497 Telex 230199 SWIFT UR Attn: CBB

Publisher: John P. Frenville
Assistant: Karen Price

S A L E S

Director: Rob Drasin
Assistant: Linda Anne Braunstein
Account Representatives: Sharon Ames, Adrian Hessel, Susan Sgueglia, Shirona Sheffer, Amy Wheeler
Administrative Staff: Corby Barnett, Mark Coffey, Danna Markson, Dana E. White

C R E A T I V E

Director: Joseph S. Napolitano
Assistant: Ellyn Moran
Art Directors: Lori McDaniel, Peter Del Pesce

P R O D U C T I O N

Director: Meggin Chinkel
Coordinators: Jason Taback
Christina Holbrook
Traffic: Terri Jackson
Studio Manager: Paul Turzio
Artists: Laura Hayes, Annette Namaroff

L I S T I N G S   A N D   D I S T R I B U T I O N

Director: Maria Ragusa
Assistant Listings Manager: Me'Shel Riedel
Staff: Kip Azzoni Longinotti-Buitoni, Rosa Munguia

P R O M O T I O N

Director: Mitchell Engelmeyer
Coordinator: Lecia Wood
Art Director: Janet Giampietro

A D M I N I S T R A T I V E

Business Manager: Christopher E. Lenzi
Staff: Judy Chin, Cynthia Riley, Michael Rispoli, Steve Schmidt

Special Thanks for their support and contribution:
Katie Adams, Faye Balestro, Roxanne Brown, Diane Casey, Brian Celiberti, Cathy Citarella, Francoise DuBois,
Lynn Feinberg, Merrit Hartblay, Sue Ellen McMaster, Kirk Oliphant, Carol Schultheiss,
Katharine S. Spadoni, Woody Stevenson, Ginger Wheeler, Juliette Wolf

Jacket and Divider Design by Lesley Ehlers

Advertising Sales Offices:
The Creative Black Book, 212 W. Superior St., Ste. 203, Chicago, IL 60610 (312) 944-5115
The Creative Black Book, 5619 W. Fourth St., #7, Los Angeles, CA 90036 (213) 939-0085

THE CREATIVE ILLUSTRATION BOOK 1991

The Creative Illustration Book is distributed in the US and Canada by:
The Creative Black Book, 115 Fifth Avenue, New York, NY 10003
(212) 254-1330, Telex 230199 SWIFT UR Attn: CBB.
The Creative Illustration Book is distributed outside of the US and Canada by:
Hearst Books International, 105 Madison Avenue, New York, NY 10016, Facsimile: (212) 481-3826.
The Creative Illustration Book is a trademark of The Creative Black Book,
a Division of Macmillan Information Company, Inc. ISBN 0-916098-56-7   ISSN 1049-2232
Much of the artwork contained in this publication is protected by prior copyright in the name of the artist,
and is reproduced here with permission. No art shown in this publication may be reproduced in any form
without first obtaining the permission of the artist.

Printed in Japan by Dai Nippon.

THE CREATIVE ILLUSTRATION BOOK

Welcome to the second edition of *The Creative Illustration Book*.

Last year we set out to create a directory that would capture all the breadth and dynamism of today's illustration market. The response from art directors and art buyers across the country has been overwhelmingly positive. *The Creative Illustration Book* is a uniquely useful sourcebook with a potent mix of talent.

This year you'll find more of everything you liked last year: more quality illustrators, more variety of styles. All in a format that allows you to find your artist easily and quickly.

Above all you'll find an accessible, functional resource that provides a wealth of illustrative solutions to the creative challenges you face every day.

John P. Frenville
John P. Frenville
Publisher

1991

	JANUARY					
S	M	T	W	T	F	S
		1	2	3	4	5
6	7	8	9	10	11	12
13	14	15	16	17	18	19
20	**21**	22	23	24	25	26
27	28	29	30	31		

	FEBRUARY					
S	M	T	W	T	F	S
					1	2
3	4	5	6	7	8	9
10	11	**12**	13	**14**	15	16
17	**18**	19	20	21	22	23
24	25	26	27	28		

	MARCH					
S	M	T	W	T	F	S
					1	2
3	4	5	6	7	8	9
10	11	12	13	14	15	16
17	18	19	20	21	22	23
24	25	26	27	28	**29**	**30**
31						

	APRIL					
S	M	T	W	T	F	S
	1	2	3	4	5	6
7	8	9	10	11	12	13
14	15	16	17	18	19	20
21	22	23	24	25	26	27
28	29	30				

	MAY					
S	M	T	W	T	F	S
			1	2	3	4
5	6	7	8	9	10	11
12	13	14	15	16	17	18
19	20	21	22	23	24	25
26	**27**	28	29	30	31	

	JUNE					
S	M	T	W	T	F	S
						1
2	3	4	5	6	7	8
9	10	11	12	13	14	15
16	17	18	19	20	21	22
23	24	25	26	27	28	29
30						

	JULY					
S	M	T	W	T	F	S
	1	2	3	**4**	5	6
7	8	9	10	11	12	13
14	15	16	17	18	19	20
21	22	23	24	25	26	27
28	29	30	31			

	AUGUST					
S	M	T	W	T	F	S
				1	2	3
4	5	6	7	8	9	10
11	12	13	14	15	16	17
18	19	20	21	22	23	24
25	26	27	28	29	30	31

	SEPTEMBER					
S	M	T	W	T	F	S
1	**2**	3	4	5	6	7
8	**9**	10	11	12	13	14
15	16	17	**18**	19	20	21
22	23	24	25	26	27	28
29	30					

	OCTOBER					
S	M	T	W	T	F	S
		1	2	3	4	5
6	7	8	9	10	11	12
13	**14**	15	16	17	18	19
20	21	22	23	24	25	26
27	28	29	30	**31**		

	NOVEMBER					
S	M	T	W	T	F	S
					1	2
3	4	**5**	6	7	8	9
10	**11**	12	13	14	15	16
17	18	19	20	21	22	23
24	25	26	27	**28**	29	30

	DECEMBER					
S	M	T	W	T	F	S
1	**2**	3	4	5	6	7
8	9	10	11	12	13	14
15	16	17	18	19	20	21
22	23	24	**25**	26	27	28
29	30	31				

HOLIDAYS 1991

New Year's Day January 1
Martin Luther King Jr Day January 21
Lincoln's Birthday February 12
Valentine's Day February 14
President's Day February 18
St. Patrick's Day March 17
Palm Sunday March 24
Good Friday March 29
Passover begins March 30
Easter Sunday March 31
Mother's Day May 12
Memorial Day (Obsvd) May 27
Father's Day June 16
Independence Day July 4
Labor Day September 2
Rosh Hashanah September 9
Yom Kippur September 18
Columbus Day (Obsvd) October 14
Halloween October 31
Election Day November 5
Veterans Day November 11
Thanksgiving Day November 28
Hanukkah December 2
Christmas Day December 25

ILLUSTRATION EVENTS

January 31 Deadline For Entries, The One Show

February 6 Society of Illustrators 33rd Annual Exhibit Opens/NYC
(Editorial & Book)

February 15 Deadline For Entries, A.I.G.A. Book Show

March 1 Deadline For Entries, 8th Annual International Advertising Festival Of
New York (Print)

March 20 Society Of Illustrators 33rd Annual Exhibit Opens/NYC
(Advertising & Institutional)

March 21 Deadline For Entries, Communication Arts Illustration Annual 1991

March 28 Communication Graphics Of The Year Exhibition/NYC

April 15 Deadline For Entries, ADDY Awards

May (First Week) ANDY Awards Presentation/NYC

May 16 A.I.G.A. Book Show/NYC

June (First Week) CLIO Awards: Radio, Print, Package Design,
Specialty Advertising/NYC

1992

	JANUARY					
S	M	T	W	T	F	S
			1	2	3	4
5	6	7	8	9	10	11
12	13	14	15	16	17	18
19	**20**	21	22	23	24	25
26	27	28	29	30	31	

	FEBRUARY					
S	M	T	W	T	F	S
						1
2	3	4	5	6	7	8
9	10	11	**12**	13	**14**	15
16	**17**	18	19	20	21	22
23	24	25	26	27	28	29

	MARCH					
S	M	T	W	T	F	S
1	2	3	4	5	6	7
8	9	10	11	12	13	14
15	16	**17**	18	19	20	21
22	23	24	25	26	27	28
29	30	31				

	APRIL					
S	M	T	W	T	F	S
			1	2	3	4
5	6	7	8	9	10	11
12	13	14	15	16	**17**	18
19	20	21	22	23	24	25
26	27	28	29	30		

	MAY					
S	M	T	W	T	F	S
					1	2
3	4	5	6	7	8	9
10	11	12	13	14	15	16
17	18	19	20	21	22	23
24	**25**	26	27	28	29	30
31						

	JUNE					
S	M	T	W	T	F	S
	1	2	3	4	5	6
7	8	9	10	11	12	13
14	15	16	17	18	19	20
21	22	23	24	25	26	27
28	29	30				

	JULY					
S	M	T	W	T	F	S
			1	2	3	**4**
5	6	7	8	9	10	11
12	13	14	15	16	17	18
19	20	21	22	23	24	25
26	27	28	29	30	31	

	AUGUST					
S	M	T	W	T	F	S
						1
2	3	4	5	6	7	8
9	10	11	12	13	14	15
16	17	18	19	20	21	22
23	24	25	26	27	28	29
30	31					

	SEPTEMBER					
S	M	T	W	T	F	S
		1	2	3	4	5
6	**7**	8	9	10	11	12
13	14	15	16	17	18	19
20	21	22	23	24	25	26
27	**28**	29	30			

	OCTOBER					
S	M	T	W	T	F	S
				1	2	3
4	5	6	**7**	8	9	10
11	**12**	13	14	15	16	17
18	19	20	21	22	23	24
25	26	27	28	29	30	**31**

	NOVEMBER					
S	M	T	W	T	F	S
1	2	**3**	4	5	6	7
8	9	10	**11**	12	13	14
15	16	17	18	19	20	21
22	23	24	25	**26**	27	28
29	30					

	DECEMBER					
S	M	T	W	T	F	S
		1	2	3	4	5
6	7	8	9	10	11	12
13	14	15	16	17	18	19
20	21	22	23	24	**25**	26
27	28	29	30	31		

AND AWARDS 1991

June 3 Deadline For Registration, International Design Conference In Aspen

June 4 The One Show/NYC

June 8 National Advertising Conference Begins/Nashville
ADDY Awards Presentation During Conference

June (Mid-Month) 8th Annual International Advertising Festival
Of New York Begins (Print)

June 16 International Design Conference In Aspen

June 22 Deadline For Entries, Communication Arts Design Annual 1991

June 22 Deadline For Entries, Communication Arts Advertising Annual 1991

October 1 Deadline For Entries, Society of Illustrators 34th Annual Exhibit
(All Categories)

October 3 A.I.G.A. Biennial Design Conference Begins/Chicago

November Deadline For Entries, Communication Graphics Of The Year

December (First Week) Deadline For Entries, ANDY Awards

December 1 Deadline For Entries, CLIO Awards

HOLIDAYS 1992

New Year's Day January 1
Martin Luther King Jr Day January 20
Lincoln's Birthday February 12
Valentine's Day February 14
President's Day February 17
St. Patrick's Day March 17
Palm Sunday April 12
Good Friday April 17
Passover begins April 18
Easter Sunday April 19
Mother's Day May 10
Memorial Day (Obsvd) May 25
Father's Day June 21
Independence Day July 4
Labor Day September 7
Rosh Hashanah September 28
Yom Kippur October 7
Columbus Day (Obsvd) October 12
Halloween October 31
Election Day November 3
Veterans Day November 11
Thanksgiving Day November 26
Hanukkah December 20
Christmas Day December 25

GRAPHIC ARTS GUIDELINES

In an effort to encourage better business relations between design and illustration professionals and art buyers, the CODE OF FAIR PRACTICE for the Graphic Communications Industry has been included in *The 1991 Creative Illustration Book*. The Code is widely accepted and agreed upon within the Graphics Community and serves as a guide for the voluntary conduct of its members. By making this information easily accessible to art buyers as well as to graphic artists, we hope to encourage improved communication between the groups.

In 1948, the Joint Ethics Committee formulated the original CODE OF FAIR PRACTICE in order to provide the graphic communications industry with an accepted standard of ethics and professional conduct. Since then, the Code has been revised twice. The version reprinted here is the most recent revision. Sponsoring organizations of the Committee are the American Institute of Graphic Arts, the American Society of Magazine Photographers, the Art Directors Club, the Graphic Artists Guild, the Society of Illustrators and the Society of Photographers and Artists Representatives.

The Committee's influence is derived from widespread acceptance and, while it has neither judicial nor police powers, its performance has made it an effective and respected tribunal. Judgments and decisions of the Committee are supported by the professions represented in the Committee. For further information, as well as assistance, please contact the local chapter of any of the above-mentioned organizations.

THE JOINT ETHICS COMMITTEE CODE OF FAIR PRACTICE FOR THE GRAPHIC COMMUNICATIONS INDUSTRY

Relations between Artist and Buyer

This Code provides the graphic communications industry with an accepted standard of ethics and professional conduct. It presents guidelines for the voluntary conduct of persons in the industry, which may be modified by written agreement between the parties.

The word "artist" should be understood to include creative people in the field of visual communications such as illustration, graphic design, photography, film, and television.

ARTICLE 1
Negotiations between an artist or the artist's representative and a client should be conducted only through an authorized buyer.

ARTICLE 2
Orders or agreements between an artist or representative and buyer should be in writing and shall include the specific rights which are being transferred, the specific fee arrangement agreed to by the parties, delivery date, and a summarized description of the work.

ARTICLE 3
All changes or additions not due to the fault of the artist or artist's representative should be billed to the buyer as an additional and separate charge.

ARTICLE 4
There should be no charges to the buyer, for revisions or retakes made necessary by errors on the part of the artist or the artist's representative.

ARTICLE 5
If work commissioned by a buyer is postponed or cancelled, a "kill-fee" should be negotiated based on time allotted, effort expended, and expenses incurred.

ARTICLE 6
Completed work shall be paid for in full and the artwork shall be returned promptly to the artist.

ARTICLE 7

Alterations shall not be made without consulting the artist. Where alterations or retakes are necessary, the artist shall be given the opportunity of making such changes.

ARTICLE 8

The artist shall notify the buyer of any anticipated delay in delivery. Should the artist fail to keep the contract through unreasonable delay or non-conformance with agreed specifications, it will be considered a breach of contract by the artist.

ARTICLE 9

Asking an artist to work on speculation is not deemed professionally reasonable because of its potentially exploitative nature.

ARTICLE 10

There shall be no undisclosed rebates, discounts, gifts, or bonuses requested by or given to buyers by the artist or representative.

ARTICLE 11

Artwork and copyright ownership are vested in the hands of the artist.

ARTICLE 12

Original artwork remains the property of the artist unless it is specifically purchased. It is distinct from the purchase of any reproduction rights.* All transactions shall be in writing.

ARTICLE 13

In cases of copyright transfers, only specified rights are transferred. All unspecified rights remain vested with the artist.* All transactions shall be in writing.

ARTICLE 14

Commissioned artwork is not to be considered as "work for hire."

ARTICLE 15

When the price of work is based on limited use and later such work is used more extensively, the artist shall receive additional payment.

ARTICLE 16

If exploratory work, comprehensives, or preliminary photographs from an assignment are subsequently used for reproduction, the artist's prior permission shall be secured and the artist shall receive fair additional payment.

ARTICLE 17

If exploratory work, comprehensives, or photographs are bought from an artist with the intention or possibility that another artist will be assigned to do the finished work, this shall be in writing at the time of placing the order.

ARTICLE 18

If no transfer of copyright ownership* has been executed, the publisher of any reproduction of artwork shall publish the artist's copyright notice if the artist so requests at the time of agreement.

*Artwork ownership, copyright ownership, and ownership and rights transfers after January 1, 1978 are to be in compliance with the Federal Copyright Revision Act of 1976.

ARTICLE 19

The right to remove the artist's name on published artwork is subject to agreement between artist and buyer.

ARTICLE 20

There shall be no plagiarism of any artwork.

ARTICLE 21

If an artist is specifically requested to produce any artwork during unreasonable working hours, fair additional remuneration shall be paid.

ARTICLE 22

All artwork or photography submitted as samples to a buyer should bear the name of the artist or artists responsible for the work. An artist shall not claim authorship of another's work.

ARTICLE 23

All companies and their employees who receive artist portfolios, samples, etc. shall be responsible for the return of the portfolio to the artist in the same condition as received.

ARTICLE 24

An artist entering into an agreement with a representative, studio, or production company for an exclusive representation shall not accept an order from nor permit work to be shown by any other representative or studio. Any agreement which is not intended to be exclusive should set forth the exact restrictions agreed upon between the two parties.

ARTICLE 25

No representative should continue to show an artist's samples after the termination of an association.

ARTICLE 26

After termination of an association between artist and representative, the representative should be entitled to a commission for a period of six months on accounts which the representative has secured, unless otherwise specified by contract.

ARTICLE 27

Examples of an artist's work furnished to a representative or submitted to a prospective buyer shall remain the property of the artist, should not be duplicated without the artist's consent, and must be returned promptly to the artist in good condition.

ARTICLE 28

Contests for commercial purposes are not deemed professionally reasonable because of their potentially speculative and exploitative character.

ARTICLE 29

Interpretation of the Code for the purposes of mediation and arbitration shall be in the hands of the Joint Ethics Committee and is subject to changes and additions at the discretion of the parent organizations through their appointed representatives on the Committee.

Submitting to mediation and arbitration under the auspices of the Joint Ethics Committee is voluntary and requires the consent of all parties to the dispute.

HOW TO GET BOOKED

1. WITH AN AD...

To find out how to buy an ad in the illustration book that'll get you work, call or write to the address nearest you:

THE CREATIVE ILLUSTRATION BOOK
115 FIFTH AVENUE
NEW YORK, NY 10003
(212) 254-1330

THE CREATIVE ILLUSTRATION BOOK
212 WEST SUPERIOR STREET
CHICAGO, IL 60610
(312) 944-5115

THE CREATIVE ILLUSTRATION BOOK
5619 WEST FOURTH STREET, SUITE 7
LOS ANGELES, CA 90036
(213) 939-0085

2. A LISTING...

Listings are free in the following categories: illustration, design, computer graphics, and studio services.

One listing per customer.

Send in a request on your company letterhead before April 1st.

3. OR A BOOK.

We accept MasterCard, Visa and American Express.

Price is $45 plus shipping of $4 per copy. Orders shipped to the following states must include sales tax: CA 6.5%; OH 5.5%; NJ 6%; GA 5%; IN 5%; PA 6%; FL 6%; IL 7%; NY 8.25%; TX 8%.

PLEASE SEND ALL ORDERS TO:
THE CREATIVE ILLUSTRATION BOOK
BOOK SALES DEPARTMENT
115 FIFTH AVENUE
NEW YORK, NY 10003

OR CALL:
BOOK SALES (212) 254-1330;
FAX (212) 598-4497

ILLUSTRATION

LISTINGS

PAGES 10-52

ADS

PAGES 53-432

ILLUSTRATION

A-Art /B. Rasmussen/ Ltd./8828 Pendleton, St. Louis .... (314) 962-1842
Aagaard, Gary/312 Fifth St., Brooklyn .... (718) 499-4687
Abe, Yoshiko/165 Jacoby St., Maple Wood .... (201) 378-9188
Abraham, Daniel/NYC, NY/(718) 499-4006 .... **page 226**
Abrams, Kathie/41 Union Sq. W., NYC .... (212) 741-1333
Accornero, Franco/NYC .... (212) 697-8525
Acuna, Ed/NYC .... (212) 889-8777
Ad Store, Inc./8950 St. Ives Dr., L.A. .... (213) 276-1865
Adams, Jeanette/NYC, NY/(212) 732-3878 .... **page 186**
Adams, Jenny/2120 S. Bentley Ave., L.A. .... (213) 312-1172
Adams, Lisa/100 W. 12th St., NYC .... (212) 691-3238
Adams, Marcia/Culver City .... (213) 558-3325
Adams, Norman/213 Hite Ave. N., Louisville .... (502) 895-4513
Adams, Norman/NYC .... (212) 755-1365
Adelmann, Morton/144-69 28th Ave., Flushing .... (718) 961-5072
Agnello, Nick/Rochester .... (716) 244-6956
Airbrush Ink Studio/Ronkonkoma, NY/(516) 471-2728 .... **page 315**
Ajhar, Brian/NYC, NY/(212) 529-6389 .... **page 431**
Ajin/521 W. 47th St., NYC .... (212) 333-7377
Akimoto, George/6389 Embarcadero Dr., Stockton .... (209) 476-0483
Albahae, Andrea/Brooklyn .... (718) 934-7004
Alcorn, Bob/434 S. Main St., Hightstown .... (609) 448-4448
Alcorn, Stephen/135 E. 54th St., NYC .... (212) 421-0050
Aldridge Reps, Inc./Atlanta, GA/(404) 872-7980 .... **page 339**
Alevezos, Gus/2215 Parmigan Ln., Colorado Springs .... (719) 528-6821
Alexander & Turner/NYC .... (212) 889-8777
Alexander/Pollard/Atlanta, GA/(404) 875-1363 .... **pages 300-304**
Alexander/Pollard/Tampa Bay, FL/(813) 725-4438 .... **pages 300-304**
Alexander, Pat/19 E. 83rd St., NYC .... (212) 288-3345
Alexander, Paul/NYC .... (212) 986-5680
Allaux, Jean Francois/21 W. 86th St., NYC .... (212) 496-8593
Allen, David/18108 Martin Ave., Homewood .... (708) 798-3283
Allen, Gary/Samsonville .... (914) 657-6473
Allen, Julian/NYC .... (212) 925-6550
Allen, Pat/S.F. .... (415) 775-3366
Allen, Terry/164 Daniel Low Ter., Staten Island .... (718) 727-0723
Allied Artist's Studio/2630 Washington St, Alameda .... (415) 523-8796
Allison, Gene/1232 Glen Lake, Brea .... (213) 690-8382
Almquist, Don/NYC .... (212) 682-2462
Alper, A.J./L.A., CA/(213) 666-6036 .... **page 213**
Alper, A.J./NYC, NY/(212) 935-0039 .... **page 213**
Alpert, Olive/9511 Shore Rd., Brooklyn .... (718) 833-3092
Alsop, Mark E./Brewster .... (914) 278-7352
Alterio, Caroline/Boston, MA/(617) 236-1920 .... **page 197**
Amato, Joseph/NYC .... (212) 986-5680
Ameijide, Ray/NYC .... (212) 889-3337
American Artists/NYC, NY/(212) 682-2462/582-0023 .... **pages 115-132, 212, 240**
Amit, Emmanuel/4322 Sunset Ave., Montrose .... (818) 249-1739
Anatoly/Boston .... (617) 266-3858
Anderson, Lori/Weston .... (203) 226-1468
Anderson, Lyman/585 Hoyden's Ln., Fairfield .... (203) 259-8170
Anderson, Richard/490 Bleeker Ave., Mamaroneck .... (914) 381-2682
Anderson, Sara/117 W. Denny Way, Seattle .... (206) 285-1520
Anderson, Toyce/NYC .... (212) 545-9155
Angelini, George/NYC .... (212) 889-8777
Angelo, Peter/500 W. 43 St., NYC .... (212) 724-2800
Ansley, Frank/S.F. .... (415) 956-4750
Anthony, Mitchell/960 Maddux Dr., Palto Alto .... (415) 494-3240

Antonios, Tony/230 W. 79th St., NYC . . . . (212) 682-1490
Anzalone, Ross/17905 Sky Park Cir., Irvine . . . . (714) 250-0943
Apartment 3-D Studios/1009 S. Berry Rd., St. Louis . . . . (314) 961-2303
Apel, Eric/Cleveland . . . . (216) 661-4222
Apice, Michael/3419 Lindbergh Ave., Oceanside . . . . (516) 678-3735
Appleoff, Sandy/4931 Bell St., Kansas City . . . . (816) 753-5421
Archer, Doug/512 S. Oak, Garrett . . . . (913) 448-3841
Arisman, Marshall/314 W. 100th St., NYC . . . . (212) 662-2289
Armes, Steve/Irving, TX/(214) 721-0164 . . . . **page 291**
Armine, Cynthia/240 E. 27th St., NYC . . . . (212) 679-0129
Armstrong, Hugh/1613 College Pkwy, Gulf Breeze . . . . (904) 932-4225
Armstrong, Joel/5521 Greenville, Dallas . . . . (214) 907-0443
Arnot, Christiaan/1349 Fox Run, Willoughby . . . . (216) 942-9208
Arroyo, Fian/7312 S.W. 80th St. Plaza, Miami . . . . (305) 663-1224
Arruda, Richard/S.F. . . . . (415) 225-7393
Art Ala'carte/180 Racine, Memphis . . . . (901) 458-4584
Art Bunch, The/230 N. Michigan, Chicago . . . . (312) 368-8777
Art Director's Studio, The, Inc./419 Park Ave. S., NYC . . . . (212) 689-9888
Art Farm, The Inc./420 Lexington, Ave., NYC . . . . (212) 688-4555
Art Rep,Inc./3525 Mockingbird Ln., Dallas . . . . (214) 521-5156
Art Source, The Diane Barkley/444 Bedford Rd., Pleasantville . . . . (914) 747-2220
Art Staff/1463 Premier, Troy . . . . (313) 649-8630
Artco/232 Madison Ave., NYC . . . . (212) 889-8777
Artists Associates/211 E. 51st St., NYC . . . . (212) 755-1365
Arvelo, Luis/Four Vancourtlandt Park Ave., Yonkers . . . . (914) 965-4262
Asbaghi, Zita/Forest Hills, NY/(718) 275-1995 . . . . **page 76**
Asciutto Art Representatives, Inc./19 E. 48th St., NYC . . . . (212) 838-0050
Atkins, Bill/L.A. . . . . (213) 470-2644
Atkinson, Richard C./Downers Grove . . . . (312) 968-5404
Atkinson, Susan/2111 E. Sprucewood Ln., Lindenhurst . . . . (312) 356-0288
Aubrey, Meg Kelleher/226 Cypress Point Dr.., Palm Beach Gardens . . . . (407) 624-6243
Avila, Mario/NYC . . . . (212) 221-8090
Ayriss, Linda Holt/12477 12th Ave. N.W., Seattle . . . . (206) 368-2451
Azzinarro, Lew/11872 St. Trinians Ct., Reston . . . . (703) 620-5155
B.J. Johnson/540 N. Lake Shore Dr., Chicago . . . . (312) 836-1166
BC Graphics/54 W. 21st St., NYC . . . . (212) 989-7563
Bacall, Aaron/204 Arlene St., Staten Island . . . . (718) 494-0711
Bacchus, Hamid/1370 Carroll St., Brooklyn . . . . (718) 493-6942
Backes, Nick/250 Hazelwood Ave., S.F. . . . . (415) 239-6232
Backus, Michael/286 E. Montecito Ave., Sierra Madre . . . . (818) 355-5501
Badin, Andy & Assocs./Flushing . . . . (212) 532-1222
Bahm, Darwin M. Inc./Six Jane St., NYC . . . . (212) 989-7074
Bailey, Pat/NYC, NY/(212) 682-1490 . . . . **page 71**
Baker, Kolea/1822 N.E. Ravenna Blvd., Seattle . . . . (206) 443-0326
Baker, Skip/Phila., PA/(215) 232-6666 . . . . **page 421**
Baldassini, Paul Co./234 Clarendon St., Boston . . . . (617) 236-0190
Baldwin, Scott/NYC . . . . (212) 741-2539
Balistreri Commercial Art/1410 E. Pinedale Ct., Shorewood . . . . (414) 628-3724
Ballantyne, Joyce/18 S. Magnolia St., Ocala . . . . (904) 732-6833
Bancroft, Carol & Friends/185 Goodhill Rd., Weston . . . . (203) 226-7674
Banek, Yvette/Weston . . . . (203) 266-7674
Banner, Shawn/170 Broadway, NYC . . . . (212) 312-6447
Banthien, Barbara/S.F. . . . . (415) 552-4252
Banyai, Istvan/13220 Valley Heart, Studio City . . . . (818) 906-7748
Baradat, Sergio/NYC, NY/(212) 721-2588 . . . . **page 275**
Baran, Zafer/Brooklyn . . . . (718) 624-1906
Barner, Bob/65 Mt. Vernon St., Boston . . . . (617) 523-0953
Barnes, Suzanne/Boston, MA/(617) 236-1920 . . . . **page 196**
Barr, Ken/NYC . . . . (212) 697-8525
Barracca, Sal & Assoc./381 Park Ave. S., NYC . . . . (212) 889-2400
Barrera, Polo/36 Walden Dr., Natick . . . . (508) 653-8292
Barrett, Andrea/164 Elm St., Kingston . . . . (617) 585-5791
Barrett, Robert/NYC . . . . (212) 369-1925

Barrett, Ron/2112 Broadway, NYC	(212) 874-1370
Barrett, Tom/7118 Wayne Ave., Upper Darby	(215) 352-9530
Barry, Ron/NYC	(212) 686-3514
Bartczak, Peter/Santa Cruz, CA/(408) 426-4247	**page 350**
Bartek-Mitchell, Shelly/608 S. 55th St., Omaha	(402) 554-0656
Bartels, Ceci Assocs./Chicago, IL/(312) 786-1560	**pages 394-395**
Bartels, Ceci Assocs./NYC, NY/(212) 912-1877	**pages 394-395**
Bartels, Ceci Assocs./St. Louis, MO/(314) 241-4014	**pages 394-395**
Bartholomew, Caty/Brooklyn, NY/(718) 636-1252	**page 150**
Baruffi, Andrea/341 Hudson Terrace, Piermont	(914) 359-9542
Baseman, Gary/Brooklyn, NY/(718) 499-9358	**page 113**
Bass, Saul & Yager, Herb Assoc./7039 Sunset Blvd., L.A.	(213) 466-9701
Batcheller, Keith/NYC, NY/(212) 682-2462	**page 120**
Bates, Harry G., Jr./Brooklyn, NY/(718) 693-6304	**page 75**
Batkin, Glenn/140 E. 17th St., NYC	(212) 673-7625
Battles, Brian/L.A.	(213) 937-3414
Bauman, Jill/Jamaica	(718) 886-5616
Baumann, Karen/NYC, NY/(212) 254-4996	**page 253**
Bausman, Mary/Weston	(203) 226-7674
Beach, Lou/1114 S. Citrus Ave., L.A.	(213) 934-7335
Beck, David/5112 W. Winona St., Chicago	(312) 725-8474
Becker, Neesa/241 Monroe St., Phila.	(215) 925-5363
Becker, Ron/NYC	(212) 243-4412
Bedrick, Jeff/Cleveland	(216) 661-4222
Beecham, Greg/NYC	(212) 697-8525
Beerworth, Roger/1723 S. Crescent Hghts., Blvd., L.A.	(213) 933-9692
Begleiter, Marcie/Culver City	(213) 558-3325
Bego, Dolores/NYC	(212) 697-6170
Behum, Cliff/26384 Aaron Ave., Euclid	(216) 261-9266
Bell, Jill/L.A.	(213) 216-0235
Bell, Karen/NYC, NY/(212) 677-9100	**page 427**
Belliveau, Allison/Pasadena, CA/(818) 577-2769	**page 244**
Ben-Ami, Doron/14 Fox Run Ln., Newton	(203) 270-7451
Benas, Jeanne A./54 Alpine Dr., Latham	(518) 783-9556
Bendell, Norm/41 Union Sq. W., NYC	(212) 807-6627
Bendis, Keith/41 Union Sq. W., NYC	(212) 807-6627
Benjamin, Bernard/444 Park Ave. S., NYC	(212) 722-7773
Bennett, Diane/430 S. Fuller Ave., L.A.	(213) 934-6609
Bennett, Gary/Louisville, KY/(502) 458-0338	**page 269**
Benny, Mike/Sacramento, CA/(916) 447-8629	**page 351**
Benoît/NYC, NY/(212) 925-3053	**page 247**
Benson, Gavin/Ten C. Parkview Ln., Bradford	(508) 521-5517
Benson, Linda/NYC	(212) 686-3514
Berendsen & Assocs./2233 Kemper Ln., Cincinnati	(513) 861-1400
Bergendorff, Roger/NYC, NY/(212) 682-2462	**page 123**
Berger, Charles/53 Maplewood Dr., Plainview	(516) 931-5085
Berglund, Cindy/Mpls., MN/(612) 343-0432/0104	**page 154**
Berkey, John/5940 Christmas Lake Rd., Excelsior	(612) 474-3042
Berlin Productions/200 William St., Port Chester	(914) 937-5594
Berlin, Rick/25 Stewart Pl., Mt. Kisco	(914) 666-2347
Berlin, Rose Mary/25 Stewart Pl., Mt. Kisco	(914) 666-2347
Bernal, Richard/St. Louis, MO/(314) 781-8851	**page 384**
Bernstein & Andriulli/NYC, NY/(212) 682-1490	**pages 53-73**
Berrett, Randy/1450 Morning Glory Dr., Petaluma	(707) 763-7254
Berry, Fanny Mellet/NYC	(212) 697-6170
Beylon, Cathy/NYC	(212) 532-0928
Biedrzycki, David/Eight Pilgrim Ln., Medfield	(508) 359-6276
Biegel, Michael David/Allendale, NJ/(201) 825-0084	**page 352**
Biers, Nanette/NYC	(212) 475-0440
Billout, Guy/225 Lafayette St., NYC	(212) 431-6350
Bilmes, Semyon/NYC	(212) 697-8525
Binder, Pat/2713 Prairie Creek Ct., Plano	(214) 596-5275
Birdseye, Colin/L.A.	(213) 470-2644

Birkey, Randal/542 S. Dearborn, Chicago	(312) 939-6766
Birmingham, Lloyd P./500 Peekskill Hollow Rd., Putnam Valley	(914) 528-3207
Birnbaum, Meg/331 Harvard St., Cambridge	(617) 491-7826
Bishop, Randy/6333 Goliad, Dallas	(214) 823-3337
Björkman, Steve/NYC, NY/(212) 490-2450	**page 322**
Blackdog Int'l./85 Liberty Ship Way, Sausalito	(415) 331-3294
Blackshear II, Thomas/1428 Elm Dr., Novato	(415) 897-9486
Blackwell, Garie/NYC	(212) 682-1490
Blake, Marty/Jamesville	(315) 492-1332
Blake, Quentin/NYC	(212) 925-3053
Blake, Robert/251 W. 97th St., NYC	(212) 316-4656
Blake, Tony/1328 E. Kellogg Dr., Wichita	(316) 262-1333
Blakey, Paul/Marietta, GA/(404) 977-7669	**page 342**
Blasutta, Mary Lynn/One Union Sq., NYC	(212) 675-0287
Blechman, R.O./Two W. 47th St., NYC	(212) 869-1630
Bleck, Cathie/NYC	(212) 741-2539
Bleck, Linda/433 E. 80th St., NYC	(212) 879-8052
Blickenstaff, Gina/3050 Baylor Dr., Boulder	(303) 494-4462
Bliss, Harry/1703 S. Tenth, Phila.	(215) 551-0888
Bliss, Jim/Rochester	(716) 244-6956
Bliss, Phil/22 Briggs Ave., Fairport	(716) 377-9771
Blount, Lester/292 First St., Brooklyn	(718) 768-0059
Blubaugh, Susan M./One Union Sq. W., NYC	(212) 463-0904
Blue Sky Studios/95 Richard Ct., Pomona	(914) 354-3085
Blum, Zevi/NYC	(212) 925-3053
Blume, George/101 Cedar Ave., Patchoque	(516) 447-5241
Bobnick, Dick/3412 Barbara Ln., Burnsville	(612) 890-6984
Boehm, Roger/529 Seventh St. S., Mpls.	(612) 332-0787
Boer, Jan Willem/128 E. Golden Lake Ln., Circle Pines	(612) 780-4085
Boggs, Marv/2964 Tomahawk Ln., Eugene	(503) 683-3885
Boguslav, Raphael/52 Thames St., Newport	(212) 570-9069
Boies, Alex/Mpls., MN/(612) 343-0432/0104	**page 156**
Bolinsky, David/Westport	(203) 226-4293
Boll, Maxine/NYC, NY/(212) 873-3797	**page 178**
Bolle, Frank/NYC	(212) 682-2462
Bolling, Bob/2395 N.E. 185th St., N. Miami Beach	(305) 931-0104
Bollinger, Kristine/Weston	(203) 226-7674
Bolton, Suzannah/19585 Grand View Dr., Topanga	(213) 455-2671
Bonavita, Donna/Four Vera Pl., Montclair	(201) 744-7154
Bonhomme, Bernard/NYC	(212) 925-0491
Bono, Peter/114 E. Seventh St., Clifton	(201) 340-1169
Bookmakers Ltd./Westport	(203) 226-4293
Booth, Brenda/104 W. 70th St., NYC	(212) 595-7601
Booth, Claire/NYC, NY/(212) 768-1829	**page 388**
Booth, George/950 Klish Way, Del Mar	(619) 259-5774
Borkenhagen, Susan/4180 Cleveland St., San Diego	(619) 295-6891
Borldelon, Melinda/NYC	(212) 682-2462
Bostic, Alexander/Cleveland	(216) 661-4222
Boswick, Steven/331 Oak Cir., Wilmette	(708) 251-1430
Botts, Steve/Westport	(203) 226-4293
Bowles, Douglas A./Seven W. 70th Ter., Kansas City	(816) 523-6324
Boyer-Pennington, Lyn/3904 Sherwood Forest Dr., Traverse City	(616) 938-1911
Bozzo, Frank/400 E. 85th St., NYC	(212) 535-9182
Bracco, Anthony Art Studio/214 65th St., W. New York	(201) 861-9098
Brachman, Richard/30-44 34th St., Astoria	(718) 204-6879
Bradshaw, James/97 Mt. Tabor Way, Ocean Grove	(201) 775-2798
Brady, Elizabeth Illustration/722 N. Robinson St., L.A.	(213) 664-8024
Bralds, Braldt/135 E. 54th St., NYC	(212) 421-0050
Bramhall, William/NYC, NY/(212) 925-3053	**page 247**
Brandtner, Al/1304 W. Cornelia, Chicago	(312) 975-1154
Braught, Mark/629 Cherry St., Terre Haute	(812) 234-6135
Braun, Kathy/75 Water St., S.F.	(415) 775-3366
Braun, Wendy S./333 W. 86th St., NYC	(212) 873-3312

Brautigam, Don/NYC .... (212) 755-1365
Brazeal, Lee Lee/Dallas .... (214) 521-5156
Brennan, Dan/Chicago, IL/(312) 822-0887 .... **page 389**
Brennan, Neil/NYC, NY/(212) 473-8747 .... **page 355**
Brennan, Steve/NYC .... (212) 986-5680
Brenno, Vonnie/Culver City .... (213) 558-3325
Brent, Mike/Westport .... (203) 226-4724
Brent/Creative Services, John/Westport .... (203) 226-4724
Brevoort, Dick/13444 Moorpark St., Sherman Oaks .... (818) 906-9791
Brickman, Robin/32 Fort Hoosac Pl., Williamstown .... (413) 458-9853
Brickner, Alice/4720 Grosvenor Ave., Bronx .... (212) 549-5909
Bridy, Dan/NYC, NY/(212) 545-9155 .... **page 203**
Brigance, Maurice/NYC .... (212) 673-1600
Brindle, Carolyn & Partner/NYC, NY/(212) 534-4177 .... **pages 168-169**
Bringham, Sherry/El Cerrito .... (415) 621-2992
Britt, Stephanie/Weston .... (203) 226-7674
Britt, Tracy/Dayton .... (513) 433-8383
Brock, Melissa/43 Buena Vista Terrace, S.F. .... (415) 255-7393
Broda, Ron/911 Wonderland Rd., London .... (519) 657-5057
Brodie, Michael/7 Dublin Hill Dr., Greenwich .... (212) 713-5490
Brody, David L. & Assocs., Inc./6001 N. Clark, Chicago .... (312) 761-2735
Brody, Sam/NYC, NY/(212) 758-0640 .... **pages 97, 198**
Brooks, Andrea/11 W. 30th St., NYC .... (212) 695-0824
Brooks, Clare Vanacore/415 W. 55th St., NYC .... (212) 245-3632
Brooks, Hal/20 W. 87th St., NYC .... (212) 595-5980
Brooks, Lou/415 W. 55th St., NYC .... (212) 245-3632
Brooks, Nan/Wilmette, IL/(708) 256-2304 .... **page 187**
Brothers, Barry/1922 E. 18th St., Brooklyn .... (718) 336-7540
Brown, André/784 Snediker Ave., Brooklyn .... (718) 257-3354
Brown, Bill/1531 Pontius Ave., L.A. .... (213) 478-6599
Brown, Bradford/283 S. Tenth St., Newark .... (201) 624-8743
Brown, Dan/NYC .... (212) 889-8777
Brown, Dennis/662 B Shopper's Lane Plaza, Covina .... (818) 339-8289
Brown, Don/20 Bay St. Landing, Staten Island .... (212) 532-1705
Brown, Greg/1025 Conkey St., Hammond .... (219) 931-1164
Brown, Margaret/., NYC .... (212) 673-1600
Brown, Michael David/NYC .... (212) 889-3337
Brown, Peter D./235 E. 22nd St., NYC .... (212) 684-7080
Brown, Rick/NYC, NY/(212) 682-1490 .... **page 59**
Brown, Sue Ellen/3527 Oaklawn Ave., Dallas .... (214) 827-6140
Browne, Pema Ltd./185 E. 85th St., NYC .... (212) 369-1925
Brownwood, Bruce/15402 Saranac Dr., Whittier .... (213) 947-5770
Bru, Salvador/5130 Bradley Blvd., Chevy Chase .... (202) 654-4420
Bruce, Sandra/S.F. .... (415) 775-3366
Bruce, Taylor/NYC, NY/(212) 677-9100 .... **page 426**
Bruck, Nancy/100 Bleeker St., NYC .... (212) 982-6533
Bruckstein, Donald/NYC, NY/(212) 254-4996 .... **pages 248-266**
Bruinsma, Martin/377 Broome St., NYC .... (212) 226-5460
Brun, Robert/Newburyport, MA/(508) 462-1948 .... **page 88**
Brunkus, Denise/Perryville Rd., Pittstown .... (201) 735-2671
Brusca, Jack/NYC, NY/(212) 254-4996 .... **page 251**
Bryan, Mike/NYC .... (212) 697-8525
Bryant, Amy/Dallas, TX/(214) 902-0163 .... **page 314**
Bucalo, Ron/96 Altamont Ave., Tarrytown .... (914) 332-0174
Buchanan, Yvonne/18 Lincoln Pl., Brooklyn .... (718) 783-6682
Buck, Sid & Kane, Barney/NYC, NY/(212) 221-8090 .... **pages 171, 290, 432**
Budwine, Olden/S.F. .... (415) 776-4247
Buerge, Bill/734 Basin Dr., Topanga .... (213) 455-3181
Bull, Michael H./2350 Taylor St., S.F. .... (415) 776-7471
Bulthuis, Henri/W. Covina, CA/(818) 918-0755 .... **page 397**
Burger, Robert/145 Kingwood Stockton Rd., Stockton .... (609) 397-3737
Burgoyne, John/NY .... (212) 570-9069
Burke, Ron/NYC .... (212) 727-2667

Burleson, Joe Illustration/6035 Blvd. E., W. New York . . . . (201) 854-6029
Burn, Ted/Marietta, GA/(404) 977-9246 . . . . **page 347**
Burnett, Lindy/Atlanta, GA/(404) 875-1363 . . . . **pages 300-301**
Burnett, Lindy/Tampa Bay, FL/(813) 725-4438 . . . . **pages 300-301**
Burns, Rhonda/L.A. . . . . (213) 931-7449
Burris, Jimm/NYC . . . . (212) 239-6767
Burton, Caroline/Jersey City, NJ/(201) 656-6502 . . . . **page 316**
Burzynski, Mary/3856 N. Oakley, Chicago . . . . (312) 463-6555
Busaca, Mark/S.F. . . . . (415) 776-4247
Busch, Lon/NYC . . . . (212) 889-3337
Buszka, Kimberly/288 Chestnut Hill Ave., Brighton . . . . (617) 743-4711
Butcher, Jim/NYC . . . . (212) 355-0910
Buterbaugh, Rick/Phila., PA/(215) 232-6666 . . . . **page 420**
Butkus, Michael T./328 Paseo De La Plya, Redondo Beach . . . . (213) 375-8151
Butler, Chris/NYC, NY/(212) 682-2462 . . . . **page 129**
Buttram, Andy/Miamisburg . . . . (513) 859-7428
Buxton, John/Dayton . . . . (513) 433-8383
Byrd, Bob/NYC . . . . (212) 682-2462
Byrd, David/Santa Monica . . . . (213) 392-4877
Cabarga, Leslie/258 W. Tulpehocken St., Phila. . . . . (215) 438-9954
Cable, Annette/Louisville . . . . (502) 561-0737
Cable, Mark/Louisville . . . . (502) 561-0737
Cain, David/200 W. 20th St., NYC . . . . (212) 633-0258
Cain, Thomas/376 Arcadia Pl., Atlanta . . . . (404) 381-5478
Caldwell, Kirk/66 Broadway, S.F. . . . . (415) 398-7553
Call, Ken/Chicago, IL/(312) 489-2323 . . . . **page 290**
Callanan, Maryjane Begin/NYC . . . . (212) 644-2020
Calle, Christopher/316 Old Sib Rd., Ridgefield . . . . (203) 438-5226
Calver, Dave/70 Stoneham Dr., Rochester . . . . (716) 383-8996
Campbell, George/S.F. . . . . (415) 776-4247
Campbell, Jenny/Phila., PA/(215) 232-6666 . . . . **page 420**
Campbell, Jim/NYC . . . . (212) 986-5680
Campbell, Marianne/240 Stewart St., S.F. . . . . (415) 227-0939
Cannella, Vito/224 Avenue B, NYC . . . . (212) 982-5861
Caporale, Wende/NYC, NY/(212) 398-9540 . . . . **page 233**
Carbone, Kye/Brooklyn, NY/(718) 802-9143 . . . . **page 411**
Carbone, Lou/NYC, NY/(212) 874-7074 . . . . **page 237**
Carey, Wayne/Atlanta . . . . (404) 874-2014
Carlson, Frederick H./2335 Meadow Dr., Pittsburgh . . . . (412) 371-8951
Carpenter, Davey/P.O. Box 329, Webster Springs . . . . (304) 847-5112
Carr, Barbara/245 E. 40th St., NYC . . . . (212) 370-1663
Carr, Ted/43 E. Ohio St., Chicago . . . . (312) 467-6865
Carroll, Dick/NYC . . . . (212) 688-4555
Carroll, Justin/1118 Chautaugua Blvd., Pacific Palisades . . . . (213) 459-3104
Carroll, Michael/429 S. Sodville, Oak Park . . . . (312) 752-6262
Carrozza, Cynthia/393 Beacon St., Boston . . . . (617) 437-7428
Carter, Abbey/NYC . . . . (212) 673-1600
Carter, Bob/NYC . . . . (212) 727-2667
Carter, Bunny/NYC . . . . (212) 570-9069
Carter, Penny/430 E. 66th St., NYC . . . . (212) 772-3715
Carver, Steve/NYC, NY/(212) 473-8747 . . . . **page 363**
Cary & Company/666 Banty Ln., Stone Mountain . . . . (404) 296-9666
Cascio, Peter/810 Seventh Ave., NYC . . . . (212) 408-2177
Cashwell, Charles/Atlanta, GA/(404) 874-2014 . . . . **page 280**
Cassler, Carl/NYC . . . . (212) 986-5680
Castellanos, Carlos/Hialeah, FL/(305) 651-9524 . . . . **page 390**
Castellitto, Mark/38 Sixth St., Wood-Ridge . . . . (201) 939-8049
Cat Pak/2400 McKinney Blvd., Dallas . . . . (214) 744-4421
Catalano, Sal/114 Boyce Pl., Ridgewood . . . . (201) 447-5318
Catalanotto, Peter/196 Clinton Ave., Brooklyn . . . . (718) 237-0277
Cathcart, Marilyn/8520 Roanoke Dr., St. Louis . . . . (314) 383-5946
Cavanagh, Tom/119 N.W. 93rd Ter., Coral Spgs. . . . . (305) 753-1874
Cedergren, Carl/225 Gramsie Rd., St. Paul . . . . (612) 481-1429

Cellini, Joseph/NYC . . . . (212) 490-2450
Celsi, David/43 W. 27th St., NYC . . . . (212) 889-6196
Centaur Studios, Inc./310 Mansion House Ctr., St. Louis . . . . (314) 421-6485
Ceribello, Jim/11 W. Cedarview Ave., Staten Island . . . . (718) 317-5972
Cesc/NYC . . . . (212) 925-3053
Chabrian, Deborah/NYC . . . . (212) 986-5680
Chaffee, James/Sacramento, CA/(916) 348-6345 . . . . **page 392**
Chambers, Lindy/Dallas . . . . (214) 521-5156
Chan, Ron/32 Grattan St., S.F. . . . . (415) 681-0646
Chandler, Fay/444 Western Ave, Brighton . . . . (617) 254-0428
Chandler, Karen/80 Lattington Rd., Locust Valley . . . . (516) 671-0388
Chang, Alain/NYC . . . . (212) 889-8777
Chang, Andrew/5160 Van Kleek St., Elmhurst . . . . (718) 426-1844
Chang, Warren/L.A. . . . . (818) 574-0288
Chapman, Bob/1449 N. Pennsylvania St., Indpls. . . . . (317) 637-1931
Chappell, Ellis/Dallas . . . . (214) 521-5156
Charmatz, Bill/25 W. 68th St., NYC . . . . (212) 595-3907
Chau, Tungwai/Nashville, TN/(615) 781-8607 . . . . **page 425**
Chen, Tony/NYC . . . . (212) 713-5490
Cheng, Judith/NYC . . . . (212) 686-3514
Chermayeff, Ivan/NYC . . . . (212) 741-2539
Chernishov, Anatoly/Four Willowbank Ct., Mahwah . . . . (201) 327-2377
Cherry, Jim/Pheonix . . . . (602) 252-5072
Chessare, Michele/25 Compass Ave., W. Milford . . . . (201) 728-9685
Chezem, Douglas R./3613 Cornell Rd., Fairfax . . . . (703) 591-5424
Chichoni, Oscar/NYC, NY/(212) 254-4996 . . . . **page 263**
Chid/55 Desmond Ave., Bronxville . . . . (914) 793-6011
Chirko, Gail/Atlanta, GA/(404) 262-1209 . . . . **page 338**
Chironna, Ron/135 Sturges St., Staten Island . . . . (718) 720-6142
Chislovsky, Carol Inc./NYC, NY/(212) 677-9100 . . . . **pages 426-427**
Chodos-Irvine, Margaret/Seattle, WA/(206) 624-2480 . . . . **page 135**
Christiansen, Lee/12 Kings Ln., Chaska . . . . (612) 448-3912
Christman, Michael/104 S. El Molino Ave., Pasadena . . . . (818) 793-1358
Chui's Studio/2250 Elliot St., Merrick . . . . (516) 223-8474
Chung, Chi/Weston . . . . (203) 266-7674
Chung, Helen/NYC . . . . (212) 221-8090
Chwast, Seymour/NYC . . . . (212) 674-8080
Ciardiello, Joe/2182 Clove Rd., Staten Island . . . . (718) 727-4757
Ciccarelli, Gary/317 Elmwood, Dearborn . . . . (313) 278-3504
Clark, Bradley H./NYC . . . . (212) 929-5590
Clark, Tim/8800 Venice Blvd., L.A. . . . . (213) 202-1044
Clarke, Bob/NYC . . . . (212) 686-3514
Clay, Steve/1340 E. 48th St., Chicago . . . . (312) 624-2497
Clay, Turner/NYC . . . . (212) 682-1490
Clayton, Elaine/NYC, NY/(212) 925-3053 . . . . **pages 246-247**
Clegg, Dave/Cumming, GA/(404) 887-6306 . . . . **page 268**
Clifford, Judy/24 W. 90th St., NYC . . . . (212) 874-9725
Cline, Rob/Boston . . . . (617) 266-3858
Clownbank Studio/Santa Cruz, CA/(408) 426-4247 . . . . **page 350**
CoConis, Ted/ad, Cedar Key . . . . (904) 543-5720
Cobane, Russell/NYC . . . . (212) 677-9100
Cober, Alan E./95 Croton Dam Rd., Ossining . . . . (914) 941-8696
Cober, Leslie/95 Croton Dam Rd., Ossining . . . . (914) 941-8788
Cochran, Bobbye/433 W. Webster St., Chicago . . . . (312) 404-0375
Cochran, Bruce/4921 W. 77th. St., Prairie Village . . . . (913) 381-2510
Codarcea, Daniela/NYC, NY/(212) 254-4996 . . . . **page 265**
Cogbill, Sharon/3138 N. Seminary, Chicago . . . . (312) 348-6541
Cohen, Elaine/Seattle . . . . (206) 443-0326
Cohen, Elisa/L.A. . . . . (213) 933-2500
Cohen, Gil/8-2 Aspen Way, Doylestown . . . . (215) 348-0779
Cohen, Jim/NYC, NY/(212) 677-9100 . . . . **page 427**
Colby, Garry/NYC . . . . (212) 986-5680
Cole, Dick/L.A. . . . . (213) 850-8222

Coleman, Woody Presents, Inc./Cleveland	(216) 661-4222
Collicott, Sharleen/101 California Ave., Santa Monica	(213) 458-6616
Collier, Jan/S.F., CA/(415) 552-4252	**pages 113, 331**
Collier, Roberta/NYC	(212) 532-0928
Collignon, Daniele/NYC, NY/(212) 243-4209	**page 331**
Collins, Britt Taylor/Atlanta, GA/(404) 874-2014	**page 278**
Collins, Ronald/533 Navarre Pl., Modesto	(209) 575-9545
Colon, Raul/NYC	(212) 799-6532
Colvin, Rob/1351 N. 1670 West, Farmington	(801) 451-6858
Combs, Jonathan/Seattle	(206) 447-1600
Comely, Richard/34 Water St. N., Cambridge	(519) 621-7475
Comito, John/24 Sutton St., Brooklyn	(718) 383-2021
Comport, Sally Wern/241 Central Ave., St. Petersburg	(813) 821-9050
Computer Illustration/324 Pearl St., NYC	(212) 571-4444
Comstock, Joe/26096 Adamor Rd., Calabasas	(818) 880-4080
Conahan, Jim/822 Charles Ave., Naperville	(312) 961-1478
Condon, Ken/37 West St., Granby	(413) 467-3792
Conge, Bob/28 Harper St., Rochester	(716) 473-0291
Conine, Steve/3450 W. Central Ave, Toledo	(419) 241-9261
Connelly, Gwen/1005 Brittany, Highland Pk.	(312) 943-4477
Conner, Mona/Brooklyn, NY/(718) 636-1527	**page 294**
Conrad, Jon/12 S. Fair Oaks Ave., Pasadena	(818) 795-6460
Conrad, Liz/Shelbyville	(616) 672-5757
Conrad, Melvin/919½ Market St., Williamsport	(717) 322-2002
Consani, Chris/NYC, NY/(212) 682-2462	**page 115**
Console, Carmen/Eight Gettysburg Dr., Voorhees	(609) 424-8735
Continuity Studios/4710 W. Magnolia Blvd., Burbank	(818) 980-8852
Conway, Michael/NYC	(212) 722-3300
Cook, Anne/232 Madison Ave., NYC	(212) 889-8777
Cook, John/Dallas, TX/(214) 748-8663	**page 337**
Cook, Mark A./7241 Roe Ave., Prairie Village	(913) 362-9223
Cook, William/3804 E. Northern Pkwy., Baltimore	(301) 426-1130
Coons, Byron/L.A.	(213) 850-8222
Cooper, Bob/Atlanta, GA/(404) 874-2014	**page 282**
Cooper, Cheryl/Atlanta, GA/(404) 875-1363	**page 303**
Cooper, Cheryl/Tampa Bay, FL/(813) 725-4438	**page 303**
Cooper, Dan/17346 Chatsworth St., Granada Hills	(818) 368-3919
Cooper, Floyd/NYC	(212) 644-2020
Cooper, Karla Tuma/Dallas	(214) 871-1956
Cooper, Robert/L.A.	(213) 655-0998
Coppin, Steve/Seattle	(206) 447-1600
Corkery, Eddie/Villa Park, IL/(708) 834-3039	**page 172**
Cormier Illustration/911 E. Elizabeth St., Pasadena	(818) 797-7999
Cornelius, Ray-Mel/NYC	(212) 683-1362
Cornell, Jeff/NYC	(212) 889-8777
Cornell, Laura/118 E. 93rd St., NYC	(212) 534-0596
Corvi, Donna/NYC	(212) 682-2462
Cosgrove, Dan/405 N. Wabash, Chicago	(312) 527-0375
Couch, Greg/112 Willow St., Brooklyn	(718) 625-1298
Courtney Studios/NYC, NY/(212) 254-4996	**page 266**
Coveny, Rich/Atlanta, GA/(404) 873-2287	**pages 413-415**
Covington, Neverne/Mpls., MN/(612) 343-0432/0104	**page 157**
Cowdrey, Richard/Boston	(617) 266-3858
Cowdrick, Norma/2919 W. 46th Ave., Kansas City	(913) 677-0784
Cozzolino, Paul/NYC, NY/(212) 969-8680	**page 215**
Craft, Kinuko Y./Litchfield Rd., Norfolk	(203) 542-5018
Craig, Daniel/NYC	(212) 682-1490
Craig, John/Tower Rd., Soldiers Grove	(608) 872-2371
Craig, Robert/3214 Brassfield Rd., Greensboro	(919) 282-2319
Cramer, D.L., Ph.D./Ten Beachwood Dr., Wayne	(201) 628-8793
Cramp Graphics/2162 Mall, Dallas	(214) 352-7894
Craven Design Studios, Inc./234 Fifth Ave., NYC	(212) 696-4680
Crawford, Denise Chapman/Houston, TX/(713) 529-3634	**page 314**

Crawford, Robert/NYC .... (212) 674-8080
Creative Advantage, The/620 Union St., Schenectady .... (518) 370-0312
Creative Capers/NYC, NY/(212) 682-1490 .... **page 58**
Creative Food Promotion/1845 McFarlane St., San Morino .... (213) 255-5574
Creative Freelancers, Inc./NYC, NY/(212) 398-9540 .... **pages 223, 230-236**
Creative Source/Chicago, IL/(312) 649-9777 .... **page 82**
Creative Resource, The/2956 Nicada Dr., L.A. .... (213) 470-2644
Criss, Keith/1005 Camelia St., Berkeley .... (415) 525-8703
Crnkovich, Tony/5706 S. Narragansett, Chicago .... (312) 586-9696
Crockett, David/114 E. 28th St., NYC .... (212) 889-6754
Crockett, Linda & Assocs./23342 Williams Ave., Euclid .... (216) 261-7031
Crofut, Bob/Eight New St., Ridgefield .... (203) 431-4304
Croll, Carolyn/Weston .... (203) 227-1366
Crowe, Trish/3310 N. 23rd Rd., Arlington .... (703) 525-2084
Cruz, José/4810 Cedar Springs, Dallas .... (214) 520-7004
Cruz, Julia/1007 Beach View, Dallas .... (214) 948-9603
Cruz, Ray/194 Third Ave., NYC .... (212) 475-0440
Csatari, Joseph/Two Snapper Ave., South River .... (201) 257-4660
Csicsko, David/Chicago .... (312) 644-8322
Cuan, Sergio/92 Edgemont Pl., Teaneck .... (201) 833-4337
Cumings, Art/Cedar Hill Terrace, Millar Pl. .... (516) 473-1209
Cuneo, John/S.F. .... (415) 255-7393
Cunningham, Robert M./Warren .... (203) 868-2702
Curran, Don/St. Louis, MO/(314) 781-8851 .... **page 386**
Curry, Tom/Austin .... (512) 328-2148
Curtis, Art/2647 S. Magnolia, L.A. .... (213) 749-7347
Cusack, Margaret/124 Hoyt St., Brooklyn .... (718) 237-0145
Cusano, Steven R./80 Talbot Ct., Media .... (215) 565-8829
Cushwa, Tom/303 Park Ave. S., NYC .... (212) 228-2615
Cutler, Dave/Chester .... (914) 469-4013
Czebiniak, Gene/ade, Johnson City .... (607) 729-1984
Czechowski, Alicia/NYC .... (212) 674-8080
D'Andrea, Bernard/50 E. 50th St., NYC .... (212) 355-0910
DaRold, Thierry/NYC .... (212) 682-2462
Dacey, Bob/NYC .... (212) 889-8777
Dadds, Jerry/2220 N. Charles, Baltimore .... (301) 243-0211
Daily, Don/509 Madison Ave., NYC .... (212) 355-0910
Dakini Designs/23661 99th Ave., Burton .... (206) 463-5412
Dale, Robert/NYC, NY/(212) 473-8747 .... **page 365**
Dallasta, Ray/Phila., PA/(215) 232-6666 .... **page 419**
Dallison, Ken/NYC .... (212) 889-3337
Daly, Tom/47 E. Edsel Ave., Palisades Park .... (201) 943-1837
Daniels & Daniels/L.A. .... (213) 655-0998
Daniels, Alan/7811 Waring Ave., L.A. .... (213) 655-0998
Daniels, Dick/6404 Ballentine Ave., Shawnee .... (913) 268-8910
Daniels, Sid/NYC, NY/(212) 673-6520 .... **page 83**
Danila, Deborah/Phila., PA/(215) 232-6666 .... **page 419**
Darrow, David R./9743 Odessa Ave., Sepulveda .... (818) 892-5409
David Brier Design Works, Inc./38 Park Ave., Rutherford .... (201) 896-8476
David, Susan/1010 Willow, Hoboken .... (201) 798-3062
Davidson, Dennis/NYC, NY/(212) 254-4996 .... **page 250**
Davidson, Everett/NYC .... (212) 682-1490
Davidson, Kevin/505 S. Grand, Orange .... (714) 633-9061
Davis, Allen/NYC, NY/(212) 254-4996 .... **page 255**
Davis, Diane K./Dallas .... (214) 369-6990
Davis, Gary/One Cedar Pl., Wakefield .... (617) 245-2628
Davis, Harry R./NYC .... (212) 532-0928
Davis, Jack E./NYC .... (212) 683-1362
Davis, Nelle/20 E. 17 St., NYC .... (212) 807-7737
Davis, Paul Studio/14 E. Fourth St., NYC .... (212) 420-8789
Davis, Susan/1107 Notley Rd., Silver Spg. .... (301) 384-9426
Davisson, Zita/563 Park Ave., NYC .... (212) 223-4949
Dawson, John D./Hilo .... (808) 959-2008

Day, Adrian/San Francisco	(415) 928-0457
Day, Bruce/8141 Fifth Green, Buena Park	(714) 994-0338
Day, Rob/NYC	(212) 490-2450
Dayal Studio/1596 Wright St., Santa Rosa	(707) 526-6935
Dazzeland Studios/NYC	(212) 697-8525
de Barros, A. Martins/NYC, NY/(212) 254-4996	**page 264**
De Berardinis, Olivia/Pt. Dume Station, Malibu	(213) 457-8065
De Cerchio, Joe/NYC, NY/(212) 398-9540	**page 236**
De Graffenreid, Jack/NYC	(212) 221-8090
de Jesus, Jaime/NYC	(212) 799-2231
De Luz, Tony/Boston, MA/(617) 695-0006	**page 288**
de Michiell, Robert/226 W. 78th St., NYC	(212) 769-9192
De Muth Roger T./NYC, NY/(212) 874-7074	**page 237**
de Sève, Peter/25 Park Pl., Brooklyn	(718) 398-8099
De Vito, Grace/Stamford, CT/(203) 967-2198	**page 310**
de la Houssaye, Jeanne/New Orleans, LA/(504) 581-2167	**page 89**
DeAnda, Ruben/890 Entrada Pl., San Diego	(619) 272-8147
DeLapine, Jim/Lindenhurst, NY/(516) 225-1247	**page 144**
DeLouise, Daniel/177 N. Cottage St., Valley Stream	(516) 825-3015
DeMar, Charles/7021 Canoga Ave., Canoga Park	(818) 888-6645
DeNaro, Joe/NYC	(212) 221-8090
DeSpain, Pamela Mannino/344 E. 63rd St., NYC	(212) 486-2315
Deal, Jim/4100 W. Victoria, Chicago	(312) 539-6088
Dean, Bruce/23211 Leonora Dr., Woodland Hills	(818) 716-5632
Dean, Glenn/NYC, NY/(212) 490-2450	**page 327**
Dean, Michael/2001 Sul Ross, Houston	(713) 527-0295
Dearstyne, John/22982 La Cadena Dr., Laguna Hills	(714) 768-5619
Dearth, Greg/4041 Beal Rd., Franklin	(513) 746-5970
Deas, Michael/NYC	(212) 755-1365
Dedell, Jacqueline, Inc./58 W. 15th St., NYC	(212) 741-2539
Deel, Guy/60 E. 42nd St., NYC	(212) 867-8092
Dees, David/NYC	(212) 929-5590
Deeter, Catherine/L.A.	(213) 874-1661
Degen, Paul/NYC, NY/(212) 925-3053	**page 246**
Degroat, Diane/225 Park Ave. S., NYC	(914) 238-4115
Deigan, Jim/NYC	(212) 682-2462
Del Rosso, Richard/Eight Washington St., Hicksville	(212) 779-9499
Delaney, John/14 Castle St., Saugus	(617) 233-1409
Dellorco, Chris/Burbank	(818) 985-8181
Delmonte, Steve/328 W. Delavan Ave., Buffalo	(716) 883-6086
Deloy, Dee/8166 Jellison St., Orlando	(407) 273-8365
Demarest, Chris/NYC, NY/(212) 925-3053	**page 247**
Demarest, Robert J./87 Highview Ter., Hawthorne	(201) 427-9639
Deming, Linda/11 Story St., Cambridge	(617) 576-2861
Deneen, Jim/NYC	(212) 986-5680
Depew, Bob/2755 Rolling Dale, Farmer's Branch	(214) 241-9206
DesCombes, Roland/NYC	(212) 355-0910
Deschamps, Bob/NYC	(212) 889-3337
Design Library, The/1435 Broadway, NYC	(212) 391-1201
Design Ogden/6535 N. Ferguson, Indpls.	(317) 255-2620
Design Plus/156 Fifth Ave., NYC	(212) 645-2686
Detrich, Susan/Brooklyn, NY/(718) 237-9174	**page 289**
Devaud, Jacques/NYC	(212) 682-2462
Dewey, Frank & Assocs./420 Lexington Ave., NYC	(212) 986-1249
Dewey, Ken/NYC	(212) 986-5680
Dey, Lorraine/Toms River	(201) 505-1670
Di Fabio, Jessica/56 Jane St., NYC	(212) 645-3620
Di Fate, Vincent/12 Ritter Dr., Wappingers Falls	(914) 297-6842
DiCianni, Ron/NYC	(212) 949-1843
DiComo, Charles/147 W. 27th St., NYC	(212) 243-2667
DiScenza, Ron/Schenectady	(518) 370-0312
DiSpenza, John/97 Forest Hill Rd., W. Orange	(201) 325-3591
Diamond, Donna/NYC	(212) 986-5680

Name	Contact
Dicesare, Joe/NYC	(212) 697-8525
Diefendori, Cathy/Wellesley Hills	(617) 235-8658
Dierksen, Jane Brunkan/Duarte, CA/(818) 359-7745	**page 245**
Dietz, James/2203 13th Ave. E., Seattle	(206) 325-2857
Dimensional Illustrators, Inc./362 Second St. Pike, Southhampton	(215) 953-1415
Dimock Illustration/330 E. Ninth St., St. Paul	(612) 291-7718
Dininno, Steve/NYC, NY/(212) 398-9540	**page 230**
Dion, Madge/320 Palmer Ter., Mamaroneck	(914) 698-1027
Dior, Jerry/Nine Old Hickory Ln., Edison	(201) 561-6536
Dismukes, John/Burbank	(818) 985-8181
Dittrich, Dennis/NYC	(212) 459-4325
Dodds, Glenn/238 E. 36th St., NYC	(212) 679-3630
Dodge, Susan/Weston	(203) 226-7674
Doheny, Dennis/Santa Monica	(213) 392-4877
Doktor, Patricia/NYC, NY/(212) 645-4452	**page 148**
Dolobowsky, Mena/NYC, NY/(212) 874-7074	**page 237**
Dolphens, Tom/Dallas	(214) 521-5156
Domingo, Ray/NYC	(212) 889-3337
Doney, Todd/NYC	(212) 369-1925
Doniger, Nancy/402A 19th St., Brooklyn	(718) 965-0284
Donner, Carol/NYC	(212) 490-2450
Donovan, Bil/NYC	(212) 697-8252
Doret /Smith Studios/12 E. 14th St., NYC	(212) 928-1688
Dorsey, Bob/107 N. Hoopes Ave., Auburn	(315) 255-2367
Doty, Curt/Four S. Portland Ave., Brooklyn	(718) 797-5115
Doty, Eldon/3435 260th Ave. N.E., Redmond	(206) 868-9540
Dougherty, Mervin/550 Battery St., S.F.	(415) 391-1526
Downs, Bob/Littleton, CO/(303) 971-0033	**page 93**
Drama Merchant Studios/437 Engel Ave., Henderson	(702) 564-3598
Draper, Chad/Dallas	(214) 526-4668
Drawson, Blair/335 Mathers Ave, W. Vancouver	(604) 922-2676
Drayton, Richard/Village Oak Creek	(602) 284-1566
Dressel, Peggy/11 Rockaway Ave., Oakland	(201) 337-2143
Drexler, Sharon/NYC, NY/(212) 768-8072	**page 100**
Drisi, Mohamed/100 W. Main St., Glenwood	(312) 758-5143
Driver, Raymond/26012E Brigadeer Pl., Damascus	(301) 972-0556
Drucker, Mort/42 Juneau Blvd., Woodbury	(516) 367-4920
Dryden, Jim/Mpls., MN/(612) 343-0432/0104	**page 155**
Dryden, Patty/194 Third Ave., NYC	(212) 475-0440
Dubanevich, Arlene/866 UN Plaza, NYC	(212) 644-2020
duCharme, Tracy/Venice, CA/(213) 396-6316	**page 373**
DuPont, Lane/NYC, NY/(212) 682-2462	**page 127**
Dudash, Michael/NYC	(212) 755-1365
Dudley, Don/S.F.	(415) 543-6056
Dudzinski, Andrzej/54 E. 81st St., NYC	(212) 772-3098
Duffy, Pat/Phila., PA/(215) 232-6666	**page 422**
Dugan, Brian/544 W. Meadow Ave., Rahway	(201) 688-4322
Duggan, Lee/3780 Schooner Ridge, Alpharetta	(404) 664-1609
Duillo, Elaine I./146 Dartmouth Dr., Hicksville	(516) 681-8820
Duke, Chris/NYC	(212) 355-0910
Dula, Bill/5 London Ct., Northport	(516) 757-1480
Dunaway, Suzanne Shimek/10333 Chrysanthemum Ln., L.A.	(213) 279-2006
Dunne, Tom/16 Cherry St., Locust Valley	(516) 676-3641
Dunnick, Regan/NYC	(212) 929-5590
Dupuy, Jacques/2666 Vista Laguna Ter., Pasadena	(818) 794-3344
Duran, Nina/NYC	(212) 682-1490
Durfee, Thomas L./25 Hotaling Pl., S.F.	(415) 781-0527
Dvord/Goodspeed/165 Lexington Ave, NYC	(212) 475-4580
Dyekman, James E./51 Grasslands Rd., Vahalla	(914) 946-0255
Dyen, Don/NYC	(212) 727-2667
Dykes, John/Westport, CT/(203) 222-8150	**page 387**
Dynamic Duo Studio, The, Inc./382 Lafayete St., NYC	(212) 254-8242
Dypold, Pat/429 W. Superior, Chicago	(312) 337-6919

Dzedzy, John/NYC, NY/(212) 398-9540 .... **page 235**
Eagle, Bruce/L.A. .... (213) 532-4353
Eagle, Cameron/NYC .... (212) 929-5590
Eastman, Jody/3455 D. St., La Verne .... (714) 593-6501
Eastman, Norm/NYC .... (212) 697-8525
Eastwood, Peter/458 W. Briar Pl., Chicago .... (312) 327-4704
Ebersole, Patricia/White Plains .... (914) 686-0860
Echevarria, Abe/119 W. 23rd St., NYC .... (212) 633-9880
Eckart, Chuck/S.F. .... (415) 552-4252
Ecklund, Rae/S.F. .... (415) 552-4252
Edens, John/2464 Turk Hill Rd., Victor .... (716) 425-3441
Edmonds, Laurie/Madison Sq. Sta. .... (212) 477-5693
Edsey, Steven & Sons, Inc./520 N. Michigan Ave., Chicago .... (312) 527-0351
Edwards, Karl/Nevada City, CA/(916) 265-5666 .... **page 308**
Effler, Jim/NYC, NY/(212) 682-2462 .... **page 119**
Egan, Roberta/Ten Myrtle St., White Plains .... (914) 761-8650
Ehlers, Lesley/NYC, NY/(212) 683-2773 .... **pages 446-447**
Eggert, John F./NYC .... (212) 986-5680
Ehlert, Lois/839 N. Marshall, Milwaukee .... (414) 276-8336
Einsel, Naiad/NYC, NY/(212) 874-7074 .... **page 237**
Einsel, Walter/NYC .... (212) 874-7074
Eisner, George/203 N. Wabash, Chicago .... (312) 726-8750
Eldridge Corp./916 Olive St., St. Louis .... (314) 231-6800
Eldridge, Gary/Shelbyville .... (616) 672-5757
Electric Paint/6335 Homewood Ave., L.A. .... (213) 462-2300
Elins, Michael/4355 Ventura Canyon, Sherman Oaks .... (818) 501-8361
Ella/229 Berkely St., Boston .... (617) 536-8936
Ellescas, Richard/321 N. Martel Ave., L.A. .... (213) 939-7396
Ellis, Dean/30 E. 20th St., NYC .... (212) 254-7590
Ellis, Jon/NYC, NY/(212) 682-1490 .... **page 65**
Ellistrations/Greensboro .... (919) 288-6521
Elmer, Richard/NYC, NY/(212) 598-4024 .... **page 79**
Elmore, Larry/Cleveland .... (216) 661-4222
Eloqui/Mt. Lake Park, MD/(301) 334-4086 .... **page 158**
Elstad, Ron/18253 Solano River Ct., Fountain Valley .... (714) 964-7753
Ely, Creston/74 Glen Rd., Sandy Hook .... (203) 426-8115
Emerson, Carmela/217-11 54th Ave., Bayside .... (718) 224-4251
Emmett, Bruce/509 Madison Ave., NYC .... (212) 355-0910
Emphasis Seven Communications/43 E. Ohio, Chicago .... (312) 951-8887
Endewelt, Jack/50 Riverside Dr., NYC .... (212) 877-0575
Endicott, Jim/3509 N. College, Newburg .... (503) 538-5466
English, Mark/NYC .... (212) 755-1365
Engstrom, Michael/10333 Brookside Ln., Omaha .... (402) 397-5336
Enik, Ted/NYC, NY/(212) 254-4996 .... **page 261**
Entwisle, Mark/Brooklyn .... (718) 624-1906
Epstein, Aaron/2015 Aspen Dr., Plainsboro .... (609) 275-1034
Ericksen, Marc/S.F., CA/(415) 362-1214 .... **page 273**
Erickson, Mary Anne/25 Fifth Ave., NYC .... (212) 979-8246
Erlacher, Bill/NYC .... (212) 755-1365
Erramouspe, David/St. Louis .... (314) 231-6800
Etow, Carole/18224 Herbold St., Northridge .... (818) 772-7501
Eubank, Mary Grace/6222 Northwood Rd., Dallas .... (214) 692-7579
Evans, Jan/L.A. .... (213) 850-8222
Evans, Robert/S.F., CA/(415) 397-5322 .... **page 272**
Evaristo, Pete/4504 36th Street, San Diego .... (619) 284-8339
Evcimen, Al/305 Lexington Ave., NYC .... (212) 889-2995
Evergreen Studio/400 Cemetery Rd., Dayton .... (702) 246-0659
Everitt, Betsy/505 Court St., Brooklyn .... (718) 797-1692
Fabara, Carlos/31-20 54th St., Woodside .... (718) 545-2626
Facklam, Paul/Rochester .... (716) 244-6956
Falcon Advertising Art, Inc./1138 W. Ninth St., Cleveland .... (216) 621-4327
Falkenstern, Lisa/NYC .... (212) 889-8777
Fallin, Ken/25 Windsor Rd., Milton .... (617) 696-2677

Fallon, Douglas Patrick/50 Tein Brooks Ave., Middletown	(201) 671-6064
Familton, Herb/NYC	(212) 254-2943
Faria, Jeff/Hoboken, NJ/(201) 656-3063	**pages 340-341**
Farkas, Gabriella/Culver City	(213) 558-3325
Farley, Malcolm/NYC	(212) 682-2462
Farnham, Joe/25 Fuller St., Magnolia	(508) 525-3735
Farnsworth, Bill/New Milford	(203) 355-1649
Farrell, Russ/NYC, NY/(212) 682-2462	**page 125**
Farris, Joseph/Westport	(203) 227-7806
Farrow, T.C./95 Fifth Ave., NYC	(212) 924-3815
Fasolino, Teresa/NYC	(212) 741-2539
Faulkner, Matt/35 Pineapple St., Brooklyn Heights	(718) 797-2784
Faure, Renee/Atlanta	(404) 266-1070
Faville Graphics/156 5th Ave, NYC	(212) 989-1566
FeBland, David/670 West End Ave., NYC	(212) 580-9299
Febbri, Miriam/S.F.	(415) 255-7393
Feiza, Anne/NYC	(212) 398-9540
Feldkamp-Malloy, Inc./180 N. Wabash, Chicago	(312) 263-0633
Feldman, Ken/Chicago, IL/(312) 337-0447	**page 97**
Fennimore, Linda/NYC	(212) 866-0279
Fernandes, Stanislaw/115 Fourth Ave., NYC	(212) 533-2648
Fernandez, Laura/NYC, NY/(212) 473-8747	**page 357**
Ferris Jones, Susan/NYC	(212) 459-4325
Ferris, Keith/50 Moraine Rd., Morris Plains	(201) 539-3363
Ferrone-Roth, Eileen/6736 N. 11th St., Phoenix	(602) 234-1598
Fetter Graphics Inc./2751 E. Jefferson, Detroit	(313) 259-4190
Field, Lori Nelson/860 W. 181 St., NYC	(212) 795-4281
Filip, Traian Alexandru/NYC, NY/(212) 873-3797	**page 179**
Filippo, Judy/Brookline, MA/(617) 731-4277	**page 114**
Filippucci, Sandra/614-C Larchmont Acres East, Larchmont	(914) 834-4282
Fine, Howard/330 Rolling Rock Rd., Mountainside	(201) 232-5394
Finewood, Bill/605 Main St., E. Rochester	(716) 377-3126
Finney, Lawrence/110 Mercer St., Jersey City	(201) 432-8407
Fione, Dan/206 Mckean Ct., N. Wales	(215) 699-7611
Fiore, Peter/10-11 162nd St. 7D, Whitestowe	(718) 767-9455
Firestone, Bill/4810 Bradford Dr., Annandale	(703) 354-0247
Fischer, Mark S./Framingham	(508) 877-8830
Fischer, Robert/333 N. Michigan Ave., Chicago	(312) 368-1441
Fisher, Jeffrey/NYC, NY/(212) 925-3053	**page 246**
Fisher, Leonard Everett/Seven Twin Bridge Acres Rd., Westport	(203) 227-0133
Fisher, Mark S./15 Colonial Dr., Westford	(508) 392-0303
Fisher, Mike/411 Amethyst St., New Orleans	(504) 288-4860
Fitz-Maurice, Jeff/Phila., PA/(215) 232-6666	**page 423**
Fitzhugh, Gregg/Pheonix	(602) 252-5072
Flaherty, David/449 W. 47th St., NYC	(212) 262-6536
Fleck, Tom/Atlanta, GA/(404) 262-1209	**page 338**
Fleishman, Michael/Yellow Springs, OH/(513) 767-7955	**page 381**
Fleming, Ron/NYC, NY/(212) 682-1490	**page 68**
Flesher, Vivienne/194 Third Ave., NYC	(212) 475-0440
Flood, Richard/Chicago, IL/(312) 565-2701	**page 147**
Florczak, Robert/Burbank	(818) 985-8181
Floyd, Walt/Atlanta, GA/(404) 875-8061	**page 86**
Flynn, James/1930 W. Newport, Chicago	(312) 871-4744
Fogle, David/1257 Virginia Ave., Lakewood	(216) 521-2854
Forbes, Bart/NYC	(212) 490-2450
Forman, James/Two Central Pl., Lynbrook	(516) 599-2046
Foster, Matthew/815 N. First Ave., Phoenix	(602) 257-0097
Foster, Stephen/145 W. 28th St., NYC	(212) 967-2533
Foster, Susan/4800 Chevy Chase Dr., Chevy Chase	(301) 652-3848
Foty, Tom/Minnetonka, MN/(612) 933-5570	**page 200**
Fowler, Eric/417 Beatty St., Trenton	(609) 695-4305
Fox, Ann/NYC	(212) 221-8090
Fox, Barbara/301 W. 53rd St., NYC	(212) 245-7564

Frampton, Bill/NYC .... (212) 243-4209
Frampton, David/NYC .... (212) 741-2539
Francis, Judy/110 W. 96th St., NYC .... (212) 866-7204
Franco/Richmond Hill, NY/(718) 441-0919 .... **page 133**
Frank/95-08 112 St., Richmond Hills .... (718) 441-0919
Franke, Phil/NYC .... (212) 986-5680
Franks, Sylvia/2956 Nicada Dr., L.A. .... (213) 470-2644
Franzen, Dennis/1296 Washington St., Des Plaines .... (708) 296-4609
Fraser, Douglas/S.F. .... (415) 552-4252
Frazee, Marla/Weston .... (203) 226-7674
Frazier, Jillian/Seven Wells Rd., Lincoln .... (617) 259-9380
Fredrickson, Mark A./5285 North Stonehouse Pl., Tuscon .... (602) 749-9257
Freelance Professionals of Chicago, Inc./53 W. Jackson, Chicago .... (312) 427-5077
Freelance Store, The/1501 Broadway, NYC .... (212) 354-5962
Freeman, Nancy/S.F. .... (415) 441-4384
French, Martin/Redmond, WA/(206) 867-3939 .... **page 311**
Fresh, Mark/NYC .... (212) 925-0491
Fried, Janice/459 Ninth St., Brooklyn .... (718) 832-0881
Friederichs, Anni/Ten Bay St., Westport .... (203) 544-8943
Friedman, Barbara/29 Bank St., NYC .... (212) 242-4951
Friel, Bryan/L.A. .... (818) 769-3140
Frisari, Frank/Richmond Hill, NY/(718) 441-0919 .... **page 92**
Fritch, Steve/NYC .... (212) 727-2667
Frost, Ralph/402 Newbury Ave., LaGrange Park .... (708) 482-9060
Fruzyna, Frank/St. Louis .... (314) 241-4014
Fry, Leslie Stevenson/567 St. Paul St., Burlington .... (802) 862-4034
Fuchs, Bernard/14 E. 52nd St., NYC .... (212) 752-8490
Fujisaki, Tuko/San Diego, CA/(619) 484-2211 .... **page 238**
Fuka, Ted/Chicago, IL/(312) 585-2314 .... **page 307**
Fulp, Jim/S.F. .... (415) 775-3366
Funkhouser, Kristen/2431 3rd St. #7, Santa Monica .... (619) 272-8147
Furchgott-Scott, Carol/242 Barren Hill Rd., Spring Mill .... (215) 828-3446
Furukawa, Mel/NYC .... (212) 349-3225
GFI Graphics for Industry, Inc./Eight W. 30th St., NYC .... (212) 889-6202
Gaadt, David/Atlanta, GA/(404) 874-2014 .... **page 285**
Gaadt, George/NYC, NY/(212) 682-2462 .... **page 117**
Gaber, Brad/4946 Glenmeadow, Houston .... (713) 723-0030
Gabriele, Tony/931 Deep Lagoone Ln., Ft. Meyers .... (813) 433-3202
Gadino, Victor/NYC, NY/(212) 682-1490 .... **page 56**
Gaetano, Nick/14 E. 52nd St., NYC .... (212) 752-8490
Gaivis, Ted/NYC .... (212) 986-5680
Gale, Cynthia/229 E. 88th St., NYC .... (212) 860-5429
Galey, Chuck/Dallas .... (214) 369-6990
Galindo, Felipe/NYC .... (212) 477-2485
Gall, Chris/NYC, NY/(212) 677-9100 .... **page 426**
Gallardo, Gervasio/NYC .... (212) 355-0910
Gallipoli, Wayne/12 Belmont St., Milford .... (203) 874-6992
Galloway, Nixon/755 Marine Ave., Manhattan Beach .... (213) 545-7709
Gambale, David/NYC .... (212) 243-4209
Gampert, John/Kew Gardens, NY/(718) 441-2321 .... **page 163**
Garcia, Manuel/4385 Rosebud Ln. #C, La Mesa .... (619) 272-8147
Gardina, Anne Marie/95 Richard St., Pomona .... (914) 354-3085
Garé, m./Mastic Beach, NY/(516) 399-5531 .... **page 243**
Garé, m./NYC, NY/(212) 947-1054 .... **page 243**
Garland, Michael/19 Manor Rd., Patterson .... (914) 878-4347
Garner, David Design & Illustration/301 W. 110th St., NYC .... (212) 663-5625
Garns, Allen/NYC, NY/(212) 473-8747 .... **page 360**
Garrick, Jacqueline/333 E. 75th St., NYC .... (212) 628-1018
Garrido, Hector/NYC .... (212) 986-5680
Garrison, Barbara/Weston .... (203) 226-7674
Garrow, Dan/NYC, NY/(212) 490-2450 .... **page 326**
Gatto, Chris/Stamford .... (203) 264-2400
Gavin, Bill/268 Orchard St., Millis .... (508) 376-5727

Gavin, Kerry/591 Bolton Rd., Vernon	(203) 871-6438
Gay-Kassel, Doreen/24a Chestnut Ct., Princeton	(609) 497-0783
Gazsi, Edward/84 Evergreen Rd., New Eygpt	(609) 758-9466
Gebert, Warren/12 Stoneham Ln., New City	(914) 354-2536
Gehm, Charles/NYC	(212) 697-8525
Gem Studio, Inc./420 Lexington Ave., NYC	(212) 687-3460
Geng, Maud/Boston, MA/(617) 236-1920	**pages 196-197**
Genigraphics Corp./215 Lexington Ave., NYC	(212) 532-5930
Genova, Joe/NYC	(212) 682-1490
Genzo, John Paul/Phila., PA/(215) 232-6666	**page 422**
George, Jeff/Culver City	(213) 204-1771
George, Nancy/302 N. La Brea, L.A.	(213) 655-0998
Georgio, Nate/NYC	(212) 221-8090
Gerber, Mark & Stephanie/18 Oak Grove Rd., Brookfield	(203) 775-3658
Gergely, Peter/Highland Falls, NY/(914) 446-2367	**page 167**
Gerns. Laurie/L.A.	(213) 931-7449
Gerrie, Dean/515 N. Main, Santa Ana	(213) 647-9488
Gersten, Gerry/1380 Riverside Dr., NYC	(212) 928-7957
Gerwitz, Rick/93 Perry St., NYC	(212) 989-9342
Gettier-Street, Renee/1414 S. Pollard St., Arlington	(703) 521-6227
Geyer, Jackie/NYC	(212) 682-2462
Giambarba, Paul/5851 Vine Hill Rd., Sebastopol	(707) 829-8921
Giardina, Anne Marie/95 Richard Ct., Pomona	(914) 354-3085
Gignilliat, Elaine/NYC	(212) 986-5680
Giguere, Ralph/NYC, NY/(212) 473-8747	**page 362**
Gilbert, Jim/Toledo, OH/(419) 243-7600	**page 329**
Gillies, Chuck/NYC	(212) 986-5680
Gillot, Carol/NYC	(212) 353-1174
Gilmour, Joni/Ten Dane St., Boston	(617) 524-6556
Gin, Ron/Chicago	(312) 935-1707
Girvin, Tim Design Inc./1601 Second Ave., Seattle	(206) 623-7808
Gist, John & Linda/224 Madison Ave., Ft. Washington	(215) 643-3757
Giusti, Robert/340 Long Mt. Rd., New Milford	(203) 354-6539
Glad, Deanna/San Pedro	(213) 831-6274
Gladstone, Dale/128 N. First St., Brooklyn	(718) 782-2250
Glasbergen, Randy/Sherburne	(607) 674-9492
Glasgow & Assocs./Woodbridge, VA/(703) 590-1702	**pages 276-277**
Glasgow, Dale/Woodbridge, VA/(703) 590-1702	**pages 276-277**
Glass, Damian/NYC	(212) 682-2462
Glass, Randy/2706 Creston Dr., L.A.	(213) 462-2706
Gleason, Bob/S.F.	(415) 956-4750
Glick, Ivy & Associates/S.F., CA/(415) 543-6056	**pages 311-313**
Glick, Judith Medical Art, Inc./301 E. 79th St., NYC	(212) 734-5268
Glover, Gary/75 Brookview, Dana Pt.	(714) 248-0232
Gnan, Patrick/Phila., PA/(215) 232-6666	**page 421**
Gnidziejko, Alex/Alna	(207) 586-5247
Godfrey, Dennis/95 Horatio St., NYC	(212) 807-0840
Goetz, John/Irvine	(714) 250-0943
Goffe, Toni/Weston	(203) 226-7674
Gold, Albert/6814 McCallum St., Phila.	(215) 848-5568
Gold, Ethel/Weston	(203) 226-7674
Gold, Marcy/200 E. 28th St., NYC	(212) 685-4974
Goldammer, Ken/Chicago	(312) 836-0143
Goldberg, Richard A./Framingham	(508) 877-8830
Goldman, Caren/4504 36th St., San Diego	(619) 284-8339
Goldman, Dara/NYC	(212) 644-2020
Goldman, David Agency/41 Union Sq. W., NYC	(212) 807-6627
Goldstein, Gwen Jo/91 Hundreds Rd., Wellesley Hills	(617) 235-8658
Goldstrom, Robert/NYC	(212) 421-0050
Gomberg, Susan/NYC, NY/(212) 473-8747	**pages 353-367**
Gomez, Ignacio/S.F.	(415) 776-4247
Gonnella, Rick/225 N. Michigan Ave., Chicago	(312) 565-2580
Gonzalez, Danilo/1760 State St., S. Pasedena	(818) 441-2787

Gonzalez, Ray/1099 Rosse Ave., New Milford . . . . (201) 304-0903
Gonzalez, Thomas/Atlanta, GA/(404) 872-7980 . . . . **page 339**
Goodman, Joan Elizabeth/684 Washington St., NYC . . . . (212) 255-3134
Goodrich, Carter/137 Water St., Stonington . . . . (203) 535-1141
Goodwin & Friends, Inc./Ashland, OR/(503) 488-2355 . . . . **page 305**
Goodwin, David Scott/Ashland, OR/(503) 488-2355 . . . . **page 305**
Gordley, Scott/NYC . . . . (212) 243-4412
Gordon, Barbara & Assocs./165 E. 32nd St., NYC . . . . (212) 686-3514
Gordon, Emily/San Francisco . . . . (415) 928-0457
Gorman, Martha/3057 Pharr Ct. N., Atlanta . . . . (404) 261-5632
Gorman, Stan/15117 Ventura Blvd., Sherman Oaks . . . . (818) 981-3525
Gorton /Kirk Studio/85 South St., NYC . . . . (212) 825-0190
Gorton, Julia/85 South St., NYC . . . . (212) 825-0190
Gothard, David/Bangor . . . . (215) 588-4937
Gottlieb, Dale/2821 Victor St., Bellingham . . . . (206) 647-2598
Gottlieb, Penelope/L.A. . . . . (213) 655-0998
Graber, Jack/Schenectady . . . . (518) 370-0312
Grace, Alexa/70 University Pl., NYC . . . . (212) 254-4424
Grace, Robert/7516 Lamar, Prairie Village . . . . (913) 341-9135
Graef, Renee/403 W. Washington Ave., Madison . . . . (608) 256-7796
Graham, Cory Represents/Pier 33 North, S.F. . . . . (415) 956-4750
Graham, Jack/4160 n. Craftsman Ct., Scottsdale . . . . (602) 432-1500
Graham, Mariah Studio/670 West End Ave., NYC . . . . (212) 580-8061
Graham, Mark/Weston . . . . (203) 226-7674
Graham, Tom/Brooklyn, NY/(718) 680-2975 . . . . **page 241**
Grajek, Tim/184 E. Second St., NYC . . . . (212) 995-2129
Grandstaff, Chris/Woodridge, VA/(703) 494-0422 . . . . **page 164**
Graning, Ken/1975 Cragin Dr., Bloomfield Hills . . . . (313) 851-3665
Grant, Mel/NYC, NY/(212) 254-4996 . . . . **page 252**
Grant, Stan/L.A. . . . . (213) 934-9420
Grant, William/119 Amherst St., Brooklyn . . . . (718) 891-4936
Graphic Chart & Map Co.,Inc./236 W. 26th St., NYC . . . . (212) 463-0190
Graphic Design & Advertising/102 Twin Oak Ln., Wilton . . . . (203) 762-8961
Graphics Illustrated/5720-E Capital Blvd., Raleigh . . . . (919) 878-7883
Grashow, James/NYC . . . . (212) 929-5590
Grau, Julie (Yaél)/3235 Cambridge Ave., Riverdale . . . . (212) 601-4705
Graves, David/133 RR Wheeler St., Gloucester . . . . (508) 283-2335
Graves, Linda/Weston . . . . (203) 226-7674
Gray, Barbara/150 E. 69th St., NYC . . . . (212) 288-3938
Gray, Doug/NYC . . . . (212) 799-2231
Gray, George/236 W. 26th St., NYC . . . . (212) 989-1707
Gray, Steve/NYC, NY/(212) 677-9100 . . . . **page 426**
Gray, Susan/42 W. 12th St., NYC . . . . (212) 675-2243
Greathead, Ian/1591 Sandpoint Dr., Roswell . . . . (404) 640-6517
Green, Norman/119 W. 23rd St., NYC . . . . (212) 633-9880
Greenberg, Sheldon/NYC, NY/(212) 873-3797 . . . . **page 180**
Greenstein, Susan/4915 Surf Ave., Brooklyn . . . . (718) 373-4475
Greenwald, Joe/650 Inca Ln., New Brighton . . . . (612) 631-3355
Gregoretti, Rob/240-13 Hanford St., Douglaston . . . . (718) 229-5647
Gregori, Lee/400 E. 56th St., NYC . . . . (212) 758-1662
Gregory, Lane/Wellesley Hills . . . . (617) 235-8658
Grien, Anita/155 E. 38th St., NYC . . . . (212) 697-6170
Griesbach, Cheryl /Martucci, Stanley/NYC . . . . (212) 741-2539
Griffel, Barbara/23-45 Bell Blvd., Bayside . . . . (718) 631-1753
Griffin, David/2706 Fairmount, Dallas . . . . (214) 742-6746
Griffo, Joseph/54 North Ave., New Rochelle . . . . (914) 633-5734
Grimes, Melissa/901 Cumberland Rd., Austin . . . . (512) 445-2398
Grimes, Rebecca/936 Stone Rd., Westminster . . . . (301) 857-1657
Grimes, Rick/20 W. Ontario St., Chicago . . . . (312) 944-2017
Grinnell, Derek/S.F., CA/(415) 221-2820 . . . . **page 313**
Groff, David/Dayton . . . . (513) 433-8383
Gross, Mort/Two Park Ave., NYC . . . . (212) 686-4788
Grossman, Bobby/310 W. 93rd St., NYC . . . . (212) 666-1420

Grossman, Myron/NYC, NY/(212) 874-7074	**page 237**
Grossman, Robert/19 Crosby St., NYC	(212) 925-1965
Grossman, Wendy/355 W. 51th St., NYC	(212) 262-4497
Grote, Rich/21 Tyndale Rd., Hamilton Sq.	(609) 586-5896
Grove, David/S.F., CA/(415) 433-2100	**pages 160-161**
Grubaugh, Kurt/1239 Waterview, Mill Valley	(415) 381-3038
Guarnaccia, Steven/430 W. 14th St., NYC	(212) 645-9610
Guinn, David/NYC	(212) 673-1600
Guitteau, Jud/NYC, NY/(212) 490-2450	**page 323**
Gulick, Dorothy/Whittier, CA/(213) 695-3490	**page 319**
Gullatt, Lou/500 Fifth Ave., NYC	(212) 768-3441
Gullerud, Peter/Burbank	(213) 660-2045
Gumen, Sururi/NYC	(212) 688-4555
Gunn Assoc./275 Newbury, Boston	(617) 267-0618
Gunn, Robert/229 Berkely St., Boston	(617) 266-3858
Gunning, Kevin/37 Denison Rd., Middletown	(203) 347-0688
Gunsaullus, Marty/601 S. St. Andrews Pl., LA	(619) 272-8147
Gurney, James/Rhinebeck	(914) 876-7746
Gurney, John/261 Marlborough Rd., Brooklyn	(718) 462-5073
Gurvin, Abe/31341 Holly Dr., Laguna Beach	(714) 499-2001
Gustafson, Dale/NYC	(212) 986-5680
Gustafson, Glenn/Westmont, IL/(708) 810-9527	**page 106**
Gustavson, Mats/NYC	(212) 206-0737
Guzzi, George/11 Randlett Pk., W. Newton	(617) 244-2932
H K Portfolio/458 Newtown Tpke., Weston	(203) 454-4687
Haas, Ken/Oley	(215) 987-3711
Hackett, Pat/Seattle, WA/(206) 447-1600	**page 311**
Haefele, Steve/NYC, NY/(212) 254-4996	**page 260**
Haeffele, Deborah/Weston	(203) 226-7674
Hagel, Mike/Arlington Heights	(708) 253-0638
Hagio, Kunio/6151 N. Sauganash Ave., Chicago	(312) 725-8212
Hagner, Dirk/San Diego	(619) 272-8147
Hahn, Marika/11 Riverside Dr., NYC	(212) 580-7896
Hahn, Holly/Chicago, IL/(312) 973-0410	**page 187**
Haimowitz, Steve/67-40 Yellowstone Blvd., Forest Hills	(718) 520-1461
Halbert, Michael/St. Louis, MO/(314) 241-4014	**page 395**
Hale, John Winter/329 E. 13th St., NYC	(212) 254-6665
Hall, Bill/1235-B Colorado Ln., Arlington	(817) 467-1013
Hall, Deborah Ann/105-28 65th Ave., Forest Hills	(718) 896-3152
Hall, H. Tom/Warwick Furnace Rd., Pottstown	(215) 469-9744
Hall, Joan/155 Bank St., NYC	(212) 243-6059
Hall, Kate Brennan/St. Paul	(612) 698-7858
Hallenbeck, Pomona/3737 EGP Rd., Roswell	(505) 625-2643
Hallgren, Gary/Mastic Beach, NY/(516) 399-5531	**page 243**
Hallgren, Gary/NYC, NY/(212) 947-1054	**page 243**
Hallman, Tom/38 S. 17th St., Allentown	(215) 776-1144
Hamagami, John/NYC, NY/(212) 682-2462	**page 126**
Hamann, Brad/330 Westminster Rd., Brooklyn	(718) 287-6086
Hamblin, George/944 Beach Ave., La Grange Park	(708) 352-1780
Hambly, Bob/33 Sumach St., Toronto	(416) 361-3272
Hamilton, Ken C./405 E. 56th St., NYC	(212) 758-8985
Hamilton, Laurie/Brooklyn	(718) 797-0413
Hamilton, Marcus/12225 Ranburne Rd., Charlotte	(704) 545-3121
Hamilton, Pam/NYC	(212) 682-2462
Hamilton, William/950 Klish Way, Del Mar	(619) 259-5774
Hamlin, Janet/Brooklyn, NY/(718) 492-4075	**page 417**
Hamlin, Mary Jo/8024 Henry Clay Blvd., Liverpool	(315) 652-7236
Hampton, Blake/NYC	(212) 398-9540
Hampton, Gerry/4792 Tiara Dr., Huntington Beach	(714) 840-8239
Hamrick, Chuck/NYC	(212) 986-5680
Hamrick, Ron/Smiths	(205) 297-7435
Hankins & Tegenborg/60 E. 42nd St., NYC	(212) 867-8092
Hannah, H. C./2547 Eighth St., Berkeley	(415) 841-2273

Hannan, Peter/1341 W. Melrose, Chicago	(312) 883-9029
Hansen-Cole, Robin/Four Marie Dr., Andover	(508) 470-0609
Hanson, Eric/Mpls.	(612) 374-3169
Hanson, Jim and Talent/Chicago, IL/(312) 337-7770	**pages 107, 331, 418**
Hanzon-Kurrasch, Toni/L.A., CA/(213) 474-7687	**page 404**
Hardiman, Miles W./Littleton, CO/(303) 798-9143	**page 221**
Hardwood, John/NYC	(212) 682-1490
Hardy, Neil O./Two Woods Grove Rd., Westport	(203) 226-4446
Harper, Patrick/Culver City	(213) 558-3325
Harrington, Glenn/329 Twin Lear Rd., Pipersville	(215) 294-8104
Harrington, Stephen/Norwalk, CT/(203) 847-6430	**page 274**
Harris, Diane Teske/342 Madison Ave., NYC	(212) 719-9879
Harris, Gretchen/5230 13th Ave. S., Mpls.	(612) 822-0650
Harris, James/2310 E. 101st Ave., Crown Pt.	(219) 769-4460
Harris, Jennifer/6723 Meadow Ln., Dallas	(214) 750-4669
Harris, Leslie/Atlanta, GA/(404) 872-7163	**page 330**
Harris, Ralph/Sun Valley	(208) 726-8077
Harris, Scott/820 Gaffield Pl., Evanston	(708) 864-7781
Harrison, Bill/NYC	(212) 206-0322
Harrison, Mark/NYC	(212) 682-2462
Harrison, Sean/1349 Lexington Ave., NYC	(212) 369-3831
Harrison, William/NYC, NY/(212) 490-2450	**page 321**
Harsh, Fred/Weston	(203) 226-7674
Harston, Jerry/5732 Skyline Dr., Seven Hills	(216) 741-4722
Hart, John/494 State St., Brooklyn	(718) 852-6708
Harto, David/713 Highland Dr., Seattle	(206) 286-8534
Harvey, Paul/475-B Commanche Ln., Stratford	(203) 381-9836
Harwood, John/NYC, NY/(212) 682-1490	**page 61**
Haselbacher, Nancy Jo/109 Queensberry St., Boston	(617) 267-3728
Hasz, Judith Ann/89 Delmore Ave., Berkeley Hts.	(201) 464-2466
Hathaway, Norman/Seattle	(206) 447-1600
Hauser, Barb/S.F., CA/(415) 339-1885	**pages 97, 212**
Haverfield, Mary/3104 Cornedd Ave., Dallas	(214) 520-2548
Havlicek, Karel/NYC, NY/(212) 682-2462	**page 130**
Haworth, Jerry/3428 S.E. Ninth, Portland	(503) 231-9012
Hayes, John/1922 N. Orchard, Chicago	(312) 266-0531
Healy, Deborah/72 Watchung Ave., Upper Montclair	(201) 746-2549
Heath, Alyce/5000 Van Nuys, Sherman Oaks	(818) 784-0588
Heath, Mark R./4338 Roland Springs Dr., Baltimore	(301) 366-4633
Heck, Cathy/NYC	(212) 679-1358
Hedge, Joanne/1838 El Cerrito Pl., L.A.	(213) 874-1661
Heffron Graphic Art/1409 Willow St., Mpls.	(612) 870-8334
Heffron, Joe/Mpls.	(612) 729-1774
Heimann, Steve/196 Stefanic Ave., Elmwood Park	(201) 345-9132
Heindel, Robert/NYC	(212) 755-1365
Heiner, Joe/850 N. Grove Dr., Alpine	(801) 756-6444
Heiner, Kathy/850 Grove Dr., Alpine	(801) 756-6444
Hejja, Attila/NYC	(212) 986-5680
Henderling, Lisa/NYC	(212) 889-8777
Henderson, David F./32 James Rd., Boonton	(201) 402-1461
Henderson, Louis/1140 S. Pasadena Ave., Pasadena	(818) 441-7703
Hendler, Sandra/1823 Spruce St., Phila.	(215) 735-7380
Hendricks, Steve/NYC	(212) 682-2462
Henrie, Cary/310 E. 46th St., NYC	(212) 986-0299
Henriquez, Celeste/NYC, NY/(212) 673-1600	**page 407**
Henry, Doug/NYC	(212) 682-2462
Henselmann, Caspar/21 Bond St., NY	(718) 522-0129
Herbert, Jonathan/NYC, NY/(212) 571-4444	**pages 94-95**
Herman, Mark/826 S. Tenth St., Mpls	(612) 339-5083
Hernandez, Oscar/5708 Case Ave., N. Hollywood	(818) 506-4541
Hersey, John Sherlock/245 San Anselmo Ave., San Anselmo	(415) 454-0771
Hess, Mark/135 E. 54th St., NYC	(212) 421-0050
Hess, Richard/135 E. 54th St., NYC	(212) 421-0050

Hewitson, Jennifer/859 Sandcastle Dr., Cardiff	(619) 944-6154
Hewitt/Low Studios/31 Ocean Pkwy., Brooklyn	(718) 436-2039
Hickey, John/NYC	(212) 221-8090
Hicks, Richard/3667 Vanet Rd., Atlanta	(404) 457-8928
Hickson, Bob/NYC	(212) 475-0440
Hidy, Lance/56 Milk St., Newburyport	(508) 465-1346
Hierro Studio/1099 Rosse Ave., New Milford	(201) 907-0423
Hildebrandt, Greg/120 American Rd., Morris Plains	(201) 292-6857
Hildebrandt, Tim/NYC	(212) 355-0910
Hill, Amy/NYC	(212) 925-0491
Hillenbrand, William/3417 Erie Ave., Cincinnati	(513) 871-5891
Hilliard, Fred/Bainbridge Is., WA/(206) 842-6003	**page 97**
Hillman, Betsy/S.F., CA/(415) 391-1181	**page 432**
Hilton-Putnam, Denise/San Diego	(619) 272-8147
Himsworth, Jim III/Phila., PA/(215) 232-6666	**page 419**
Hines, Norman/W. Sacramento, CA/(916) 373-0466	**page 372**
Hinlicky, Gregg/Toms River	(201) 269-4867
Hinton, Hank/L.A.	(213) 935-4696
Hirashima, Jean/166 E. 61st St., NYC	(212) 593-9778
Hitch, Jeffrey/211 E. Columbine, Santa Anna	(714) 432-1802
Hoch, Joan/2956 Nicada Dr., L.A.	(213) 470-2644
Hodges, Jeanette/12401 Bellwood Rd., Los Alamitos	(213) 431-4343
Hodges, Mike/3613 Noble Ave., Richmond	(804) 321-0100
Hoff, Ken/Culver City	(213) 558-3325
Hoff, Terry/1525 Grand Ave., Pacifica	(415) 359-4081
Hoffman, Martin/NYC	(212) 355-0910
Hofkin, Bonnie/Rowayton	(212) 581-8338
Hofmann, Ginnie/NYC	(212) 889-3337
Hogan, Barb/Atlanta, GA/(404) 255-1430	**page 344**
Hogan, Shannon/Culver City	(213) 558-3325
Hogarth, Paul/NYC, NY/(212) 925-3053	**pages 246-247**
Hogenkamp, Johanna/1151 W. Peachtree St. N.W., Atlanta	(404) 881-0087
Hokanson, Lars/Hopeland	(717) 733-9066
Holladay, Reggie/Lauderhill, FL/(305) 749-9031	**page 82**
Holland, Brad/96 Greene St., NYC	(212) 226-3675
Holland, Mary & Co./6638 N. 13th St., Phoenix	(602) 263-8990
Holm, John/NYC	(212) 682-2462
Holmberg, Irmeli/NYC, NY/(212) 545-9155	**pages 166, 202-207, 349**
Holmes, Matthew/Carmichael, CA/(916) 944-7270	**page 312**
Holter, Al/422 E. 81st St., NYC	(212) 744-7870
Hom & Hom/NYC	(212) 242-6367
Homad, Jewell Jan/1259 Long Beach Ave., San Diego	(619) 272-8147
Hong, Min Jae/NYC, NY/(212) 674-4320	**pages 80-81**
Hooks, Mitchell/NYC	(212) 986-5680
Hoover, Gary/L.A.	(213) 655-0998
Hoover, Sherry/NYC, NY/(212) 254-4996	**page 258**
Hopkins, Chris/5018 Sound Ave., Everett	(206) 447-1600
Hopper, Pegge/1164 Nuuanu Ave., Honolulu	(808) 524-1160
Horn, Robert/Chicago, IL/(312) 644-0058	**page 445**
Horne, Daniel/Weston	(203) 226-7674
Hosner, William/20500 Civic Center Dr., Southfield	(313) 354-4567
Hoston, Jim/420 Clinton Ave., Brooklyn	(718) 230-7908
Hostovich, Michael/Phila., PA/(215) 232-6666	**page 422**
Houlé, Harrison/S.F., CA/(415) 871-9163	**page 112**
Houlé, Harrison/Sherman Oaks, CA/(818) 783-6563	**page 112**
Houlihan, Joyce/Pheonix	(602) 252-5072
Hovland, Gary/3408 Crest Dr., Manhattan Beach	(213) 545-6808
Howard, Deborah/1800 N. McCord Rd., Toledo	(419) 867-0249
Howard, John H./NYC	(212) 421-0050
Howe, Philip/Seattle	(206) 443-0326
Howe, Robert Charles/Three Cottage Ln., Midlothian	(312) 371-6126
Howell, Van/Huntington	(516) 424-6499
Hoyos, Andy/NYC	(212) 682-2462

Hrabe, Curt/2944 Greenwood Ave., Highland Park	(708) 432-4632
Hranilovich, Barbara/1200 N. Jenison, Lansing	(517) 487-6474
Hudgins, Paul/San Antonio	(512) 558-8236
Huerta, Gerard/45 Corbin Dr., Darien	(203) 656-0505
Huffaker, Sandy/23D Norwood Ct., Princeton	(609) 924-2883
Huffman, Tom/130 W. 47th St., NYC	(212) 819-0211
Hughes, Charlie/172 Eugenie St., Chicago	(312) 664-3184
Hughes, Marianne/Phila., PA/(215) 232-6666	**page 422**
Hughes, Neal/Phila., PA/(215) 232-6666	**page 423**
Huhn, Tim/Santa Monica, CA/(213) 394-5031	**page 192**
Hul, Jon Jr./N. Hollywood, CA/(818) 508-8228	**page 332**
Hull, Cathy/165 E. 66th St., NYC	(212) 772-7743
Hull, John/NYC, NY/(212) 682-2462	**page 131**
Hull, Scott/68 E. Franklin, Dayton	(513) 433-8383
Humor Assoc./175 Fifth Ave., NYC	(212) 459-4325
Humphries, Michael/Santa Monica, CA/(213) 394-5031	**page 194**
Hungry Dog Studio/1361 Markan Ct., Atlanta	(404) 872-7496
Hunt, Robert/S.F.	(415) 552-4252
Hunt, Walter/Roswell	(404) 642-9680
Hunter, Nadine/80 Wellington Ave., Ross	(415) 456-7711
Hunter, Stan/509 Madison Ave., NYC	(212) 355-0910
Hurd, Jane/NYC	(212) 490-2450
Husley, Kevin/NYC	(212) 682-1490
Huston, Steve/L.A.	(213) 933-2500
Hutchison, Bruce/192 Southville Rd., Southboro	(508) 872-4549
Huxtable, John/S.F.	(415) 775-3366
Huyssen, Roger/Darien	(203) 656-0200
Hyatt, John/2217 Canyon Dr., L.A.	(213) 463-0868
Hyatt, Mitch/NYC	(212) 682-2462
Hynes, Robert/5215 Muncaster Mill Rd., Rockville	(301) 926-7813
Ianacone, Mark/813 N. Wahsatch, Colorado Spgs.	(719) 635-4130
Ibusuki, James/13053 Beaver St., Sylmar	(818) 362-9899
Ilic, Mirko/NYC	(212) 486-9644
Image Factory/19 W. Flagler St., Miami	(305) 372-9992
Incandescent Ink/111 Wooster St., NYC	(212) 925-0491
Independent Pencil, Co./Newburyport, MA/(508) 462-1948	**page 88**
Ingraham, Erick/66 Old Jeffrey Rd., Peterborough	(603) 924-6785
Inoue, Izumi DesignPlus/325 W. 37th St., NYC	(212) 643-9079
Inouye, Carol/NYC, NY/(212) 873-3797	**page 184**
Iosa, Ann/Weston	(203) 226-7674
Irish, Gary Graphics/45 Newbury St., Boston	(617) 247-4168
Ishioka, Harou/L.A.	(213) 931-7449
Italia, Marc/The Freelane Stone, NYC	(212) 354-5962
Italiano, Joe G./9221 Wissinoming St., Phila.	(215) 824-2808
Ivens, Peter/8515-92 Ave., Edmonton	(403) 465-2037
Ivens, Rosalind/483 13th St., Brooklyn	(718) 499-8285
Ivy League of Artists, The, Inc./156 Fifth Ave., NYC	(212) 243-1333
Iwasaki, Glen/L.A.	(213) 937-3414
Izold, Donald/20475 Bunker Hill Dr., Cleveland	(216) 333-9988
Jackson, Barry/NYC, NY/(212) 645-4452	**page 149**
Jacbson/Fernandez/NYC	(212) 473-8747
Jack, Tom/80 Varick St., NYC	(212) 941-1860
Jackson, Barry E./95 Horatio St., NYC	(212) 645-4452
Jacobs, Jim/Dallas	(214) 521-5156
Jacobsen, Gary/3636 Woodland Park Ave. N., Seattle	(206) 634-2264
Jacobson, Rick/NYC, NY/(212) 473-8747	**page 356**
Jaffee, Al/140 E. 56th St., NYC	(212) 371-5232
Jakesevic, Nenad/NYC	(212) 686-3514
James, Bill/15840 S.W. 79th Ct., Miami	(305) 238-5709
Jamieson, Doug/42-20 69th St., Woodside	(718) 565-6034
Janovsky, Paul/Santa Monica, CA/(213) 394-5031	**page 193**
Jareaux, Robin/28 Eliot St., Boston	(617) 524-3099
Jarvis, David/Cocoa Beach, FL/(407) 784-6263	**page 171**

Jarvis, Nathan Y./708a Main St., Grandview .... (816) 765-0617
Jasper, Jackie/NYC .... (212) 686-3514
Jay/17858 Rose St., Lansing .... (708) 474-9704
Jaynes, Bill/Long Beach .... (213) 495-0134
Jaz & Jaz/Seattle, WA/(206) 783-5373 .... **page 135**
Jazwiecki, Leonard/18 Main St., Amherst .... (413) 256-0321
Jig, Harold/8421 Spruce Dr., Bonnie .... (301) 652-5485
Jeffers, Kathy/106 E. 19th St., NYC .... (212) 475-1756
Jeffries, Shannon/Brooklyn, NY/(718) 638-1132 .... **page 410**
Jenne, E.R./1534 Maurice Ave., Missoula .... (406) 543-5535
Jensen, Dave/1641 Merriton Ct., San Jose .... (408) 266-5645
Jessell, Tim/NYC .... (212) 682-1490
Jett, Clare/21 Theater Sq., Louisville .... (502) 561-0737
Jezierski, Chet/NYC .... (212) 398-9540
Jinks, John/690 Greenwich St., NYC .... (212) 675-2961
Jobe, Jody/875 W. 181st St., NYC .... (212) 795-4941
Johnson, David/NYC .... (212) 683-1362
Johnson, Diane/Chicago .... (312) 527-2128
Johnson, Doug/45 E. 19th St., NYC .... (212) 260-1880
Johnson, Evelyne Assoc./201 E. 28th St., NYC .... (212) 532-0928
Johnson, Irskra/NYC .... (212) 682-2462
Johnson, Joel Peter/NYC .... (212) 980-8061
Johnson, Julie/NYC .... (212) 697-6170
Johnson, Lanie/NYC .... (212) 532-0928
Johnson, Lonni Sue/NYC, NY/(212) 873-7749 .... **page 102**
Johnson, Lonni Sue/New Milford, CT/(203) 355-9359 .... **page 102**
Johnson, Steve/440 Sheridan Ave. S., Mpls. .... (612) 377-8728
Johnston, David McCall/NYC .... (212) 355-0910
Johnston, W.B./572 Mountain Ave., Winnipeg .... (204) 582-1686
Jonason, Dave/NYC .... (212) 674-8080
Jones, Barry/2725 Mary St., Easton .... (215) 253-3709
Jones, Bob/47 W. Stewart Ave., Lansdowne .... (215) 626-1245
Jones, Bob/NYC .... (212) 986-5680
Jones, Danielle/Toronto .... (416) 968-6277
Jones, Don/695 Sayne Ave., Perth Amboy .... (201) 324-1096
Jones, Jack/Atlanta, GA/(404) 873-2287 .... **page 414**
Jones, Michael Scott/400 W. Erie #405, Chicago .... (312) 281-0462
Jones, Randy/NYC .... (212) 459-4325
Jones, Ron/67 Ore Hill Rd., S. Kent .... (203) 927-3996
Jones, Rusty/Dallas .... (214) 871-1956
Jorgensen, Donna/Seattle, WA/(206) 284-5080 .... **page 97**
Joyce, Tony/18588 Fieldbrook St., Rowland Heights .... (818) 964-2918
Joyner, Eric/425 The Alemeda, San Anselmo .... (415) 821-2641
Juhasz, Victor/135 E. 54th St., NYC .... (212) 421-0050
Juniper, David/NYC .... (212) 268-1788
Just, Hal/NYC .... (212) 697-6170
Kôerber, Nora/125 Fair Oaks, Pasadena .... (818) 793-1570
Kabaker, Gayle/Rowayton .... (203) 866-3734
Kabaker, Gayle/NYC, NY/(212) 581-8338 .... **page 380**
Kacicek, Barbara/Dallas .... (214) 369-6990
Kaciek, Barbara/Oley .... (215) 987-3711
Kaczman, James/Watertown, MA/(617) 923-4605 .... **page 152**
Kahn, Harvey/14 E. 52nd St., NYC .... (212) 752-8490
Kalish, Lionel/NYC .... (212) 889-3337
Kaloustian, Rosanne/Bayside .... (718) 428-4670
Kanayama, Nobee/Santa Monica .... (213) 392-4877
Kane & Buck/NYC .... (212) 221-8090
Kane, John/New Hope, PA/(215) 862-0392 .... **page 96**
Kaneda, Shirley/NYC .... (212) 925-0491
Kanelous, George/NYC, NY/(212) 688-1080 .... **page 328**
Kanner, Catherine/L.A. .... (818) 574-0288
Kaplan, Karl/1507 West Lynn St., Austin .... (617) 476-6876
Kaplan, Mark/374 Fifth St., Brooklyn .... (718) 832-2317

Kappes, Werner	(914) 654-1669
Karalexis, Ginger/Culver City	(213) 558-3325
Karas, G. Brian/4126 N. 34th St., Phoenix	(602) 956-5666
Karchin, Steve/NYC	(212) 755-1365
Karl, Kevin/3301 S. Jefferson Ave., St. Louis	(314) 773-9989
Karn, Murray/120 E. 86th St., NYC	(212) 289-9124
Karpinski Studio/210 E. Michigan St., Milwaukee	(414) 276-7990
Karwin, Johnny/1430 Walter St., S.F.	(415) 552-3299
Kasak, Harriet/458 Newtown Tpke., Weston	(203) 454-4687
Kasnot, Keith/St. Louis	(314) 241-4014
Kasper, Robert/Boston, MA/(617) 236-1920	**page 196**
Kastaris, Rip/3301 S. Jefferson Ave., St. Louis	(314) 773-2600
Katayama, Mits/1904 Third Ave., Seattle	(206) 625-6946
Katsin, Nancy/17 E. 31st St., NYC	(212) 213-0709
Katz, Les/451 Westminster Rd., Brooklyn	(718) 284-4779
Katz, Les/NYC, NY/(212) 768-8072	**page 100**
Keating, Peggy/30 Horatio St., NYC	(212) 691-4654
Kecman, Milan/4736 W. 20th St., Cleveland	(216) 741-8755
Kelen, Linda/Chicago	(312) 664-8322
Keleny, Earl/NYC	(212) 486-9644
Keller, Merle/Culver City	(213) 558-3325
Kelley, Barbara/555 Tenth St., Brooklyn	(212) 788-2465
Kelley, Gary/NYC	(212) 683-1362
Kemper, Bud/St. Louis	(314) 231-6800
Kendrick, Dennis/99 Bank St., NYC	(212) 924-3085
Kenyon, Liz/NYC	(212) 686-3514
Kernan, Patrick/168 Fifth Ave., NYC	(212) 924-7800
Kettler, Al/1420 Prince St., Alexandria	(703) 548-8040
Kibbee, Gordon/NYC	(212) 989-7074
Kiefer, Alfons/NYC	(212) 986-5680
Kilgore, Susi/2905 Bay Villa, Tampa	(813) 837-9759
Killein, Tom/St. Louis	(314) 231-6800
Kilmer, David/NYC	(212) 986-5680
Kimura, Hiro/Brooklyn	(718) 638-0372
Kincade, John/NYC	(212) 727-2667
King, Greg/Dallas	(214) 521-5156
Kingsbery, Guy/305 High St., Milford	(203) 878-8939
Kirchoff/Wohlberg, Inc./866 United Nations Plaza, NYC	(212) 644-2020
Kirk, Daniel/NYC	(212) 825-0190
Kirkman, Rick/4160 N Craftsman Ave, Scotsdale	(602) 423-1500
Kitchell, Joyce/2755 Eagle St., San Diego	(619) 291-1378
Klanderman, Leland/St. Louis	(314) 241-4014
Klavins, Uldis/30 Topcrest Ln., Ridgefield	(212) 867-8092
Kleber, John/Chicago	(312) 664-8322
Klein, David G./Brooklyn, NY/(718) 788-1818	**page 229**
Klein, Hedy/Forest Hills, NY/(718) 793-0246	**page 398**
Klementz-Harte, Lauren/Meriden	(203) 235-6145
Klimt, Bill & Maurine/NYC, NY/(212) 799-2231	**page 211**
Klippenstein, Stephen/Santa Monica	(213) 394-5031
Kliros, Thea/313 E. 18th St., NYC	(212) 254-2574
Knaff, Jean-Christian/Boston, MA/(617) 236-1920	**page 196**
Knee, Carol/451 Mountian Ave, N. Caldwell	(201) 228-8535
Knettell, Sharon/NYC	(212) 889-3337
Knutsen, Jan/Bloomington, MN/(612) 884-8083	**pages 137-139**
Koda-Callan, Elizabeth/NYC	(212) 683-1362
Kodama, Hidlaki/NYC	(212) 490-2450
Koeffler, Ann Represents/1425 N. Alta Vista Blvd., L.A.	(213) 850-8222
Koehli, Urs/156 Fifth Ave., NYC	(212) 645-2686
Koester, Michael/Cleveland	(216) 661-4222
Kolea Artist's Representative/2815 Alaskan Way, Pier 70, Seattle	(206) 443-0626
Kopecky, Robert/S.F.	(415) 255-7393
Kordic, Vladimir/Cleveland	(216) 661-4222
Korman, Ira M./232 S. Rexford Dr., Beverly Hills	(212) 533-1569

Korn, Pamela & Associates/NYC, NY/(212) 529-6389 .... **pages 429-431**
Koslow, Howard/26 Highwood Rd., E. Norwich .... (516) 922-7427
Koster, Aaron/Two Yeoman Way, Manalapan .... (201) 536-2815
Kotzky, Brian/NYC .... (212) 799-2231
Kovalcik, Terry/124 W. 18th St., NYC .... (212) 620-7772
Kozlowski, Martin/141 Southside Ave., Hastings-on-the-Hudson .... (914) 478-7445
Kozmiuk, Michael/NYC, NY/(212) 682-2462 .... **page 116**
Kraemmer, Gary/1724 Ogden, Denver .... (303) 832-1579
Krafcheck, Kenneth/815 S. Lincoln St., Arlington .... (703) 553-0469
Krainik, Dave/4719 Center, Lisle .... (708) 963-4614
Kramer, Moline/Venice .... (818) 884-1361
Krantz, Kathy/NYC .... (212) 369-1925
Kreffel, Mike/145 E. 14th St., Indpls. .... (317) 636-4891
Krejca, Gary/Tempe, AZ/(602) 829-0946 .... **page 307**
Krepel, Dick/NYC .... (212) 755-1365
Kressley, Michael/67 Brookside Ave., Boston .... (617) 522-5132
Kretschmann, Karin/323 W. 75th St., NYC .... (212) 724-5001
Kretzschmar, H. Studio/211 W. Broadway, NYC .... (212) 431-8517
Kriegler, Richard/NYC .... (212) 682-2462
Kriss, Mariko/194 Third Ave., NYC .... (212) 475-0440
Kritz, Jim/Weston .... (203) 226-7674
Krug, Ken/60 Second Ave., NYC .... (212) 677-1572
Kubinyi, Laszlo/NYC .... (212) 889-3337
Kueker, Don/829 Ginger Wood Ct., Manchester .... (314) 225-1566
Kuhlman, William A./11010 Lakeview Dr., Whitehouse .... (419) 877-0786
Kuhn, Grant M./233 Bergen St., Brooklyn .... (718) 596-7808
Kukalis, Romas/NYC .... (212) 986-5680
Kunsler, Mort/NYC .... (212) 335-0910
Kunz, Anita/230 Ontario St., Toronto .... (416) 364-3846
Kuper, Peter/250 W. 99th St., NYC .... (212) 864-5729
Kupper, Ketti/Three Evergreen Ave., Wilton .... (203) 761-9454
Kurtz, Mike Design/10706 E. 28th, Tulsa .... (918) 622-0193
La Driere, Inc./77 E. Long Lake Rd., Bloomfield Hills .... (313) 644-3932
LaFleur, Dave/Derby, KS/(316) 788-0253 .... **page 383**
LaPadula, Tom/NYC .... (212) 532-0928
LaPorte, Michele/NYC, NY/(212) 673-1600 .... **page 401**
Lackow, Andy/Guttenburg .... (201) 854-2770
Ladas, George/157 Prince St., NYC .... (212) 673-2208
Laden, Nina/Atlanta, GA/(404) 371-0052 .... **pages 208-209**
Laefever, Greg/Dayton .... (513) 433-8383
Lagerstöm, Wendy/L.A. .... (213) 470-2644
Laisson, Murian/410 Riverside Dr., NYC .... (212) 713-5765
Lamb, Jim/Chicago .... (312) 222-0337
Lambert, Saul/NYC .... (212) 221-8090
Lamut, Sonja/NYC .... (212) 686-3514
Lander, Jane Assoc./333 E. 30th St., NYC .... (212) 679-1358
Landis, Joan/NYC .... (212) 627-0863
Landor Associates/1001 Front St., SF .... (415) 955-1200
Lane, Sherry Caricatures/155 Bank St., NYC .... (212) 675-6224
Laney, Ron/St. Louis, MO/(314) 361-4484 .... **page 369**
Lang, Gary/86 Headquarters Rd., Litchfield .... (203) 567-8148
Langenbacher, Linda/824 Bonnie Brae St., L.A. .... (213) 388-3415
Langeneckert, Don/4939 Ringer Rd., St. Louis .... (314) 487-2042
Langer, DC/662 Massachusetts Ave., Boston .... (617) 536-6651
Langley, Sharon/Chicago, IL/(312) 527-2128 .... **pages 172-173**
Lanza, Barbara/Weston .... (203) 226-7674
Lapinski, Joe/NYC .... (212) 677-9100
Lapsley, Robert/NYC .... (212) 221-8090
Lasher, Mary Ann/NYC, NY/(212) 682-1490 .... **page 54**
Laurent, Richard/531 S. Plymouth Ct., Chicago .... (312) 472-6550
Lautenslager, Peter/Rochester .... (716) 244-6956
Lavaty, Frank & Jeff/509 Madison Ave., NYC .... (212) 355-0910
Lavigne, Dan/NYC .... (212) 221-8090

Law, Polly M./305-A President, Brooklyn	(718) 875-4425
Lawson, Robert/1523 Seminole, Kalamazoo	(616) 345-7607
Le-Tan, Pierre/NYC, NY/(212) 925-3053	**page 246**
LeBlanc, Terry/425 Watertown St., Newton	(617) 989-4886
LeBrun, Denise/156 Fifth Ave., NYC	(212) 691-7133
Leary, Catherine/Culver City	(213) 204-1771
Leary, T. Pat/20707 Timberline Ln., Walnut	(714) 598-7221
Lebo, Narda/NYC, NY/(212) 873-3797	**pages 182-183**
Leder, Dora/NYC	(212) 644-2020
Lederman, Marsha/107 N. Columbus St., Arlington	(703) 243-5636
Ledwidge, Natacha/Brooklyn	(718) 624-1906
Lee, Bill/792 Columbus Ave., NYC	(212) 866-5664
Lee, Bryce/126 77th St., N. Bergen	(201) 662-9106
Lee, Jared D./2942 Hamilton Rd., Lebanon	(513) 932-2154
Lee, Michael/Culver City	(213) 558-3325
Lee, Robert J./Seminary Hill, Carmel	(914) 225-4934
Lee, Tim/11 Cherry Tree Farm Rd., Middletown	(201) 706-0780
Lee, Walter W./85 N. Chester Ave., Pasadena	(818) 792-8770
Leeds, Beth Whybrow/S.F.	(415) 928-0457
Leedy, Jeff/NYC, NY/(212) 473-8747	**page 367**
Leff, Jerry Assocs., Inc./NYC, NY/(212) 697-8525	**page 370**
Lefkowitz, Mark/94 Fox Meadow Ln., Dedham	(617) 326-2615
Legrand, Jean-Yves/41 W. 84th St., NYC	(212) 724-5981
Lehr, Paul/NYC	(212) 355-0910
Leigh, LeeAnn/2304 Rosemary, Simi Valley	(805) 527-8955
Leiner, Alan/NYC, NY/(212) 682-2462	**page 124**
Lengyel, Kathy/Atlanta, GA/(404) 875-1363	**page 304**
Lengyel, Kathy/Tampa Bay, FL/(813) 725-4438	**page 304**
Lennard, Elizabeth/NYC	(212) 925-0491
Leon, Karen/Flushing, NY/(718) 461-2050/463-3159	**page 399**
Leonard, Richard/NYC, NY/(212) 254-4996	**page 254**
Leonard, Tom/NYC	(212) 644-2020
Lesh, David/Indpls., IN/(317) 253-3141	**pages 376-377**
Lesli Art, Inc./Woodland Hills	(818) 999-9228
Lesser, Ron/NYC	(212) 949-1843
Lester, Mike/Atlanta, GA/(404) 447-5332	**pages 188-189**
Letostak, John/Cleveland	(216) 661-4222
Levikova-Neyman, Marina/3527 Summerfield Dr., Sherman Oaks	(818) 501-6027
Levin, Arnie/342 Madison Ave., NYC	(212) 719-9879
Levine, Andy/30-85 36th St., L.I.C.	(718) 956-8539
Levine, Arlene/1107 S. Peters St., New Orleans	(504) 522-1520
Levine, Bette/NYC, NY/(212) 682-1490	**page 64**
Levine, Ned/NYC	(212) 682-2462
Levinson, David/219-D Richfield Ter., Clifton	(201) 614-1627
Levy, Robert S./NYC	(212) 986-8833
Lewis, Chris/131 Ponce de Leon Ave., Atlanta	(404) 876-0280
Lewis, Howard B./NYC	(212) 243-3954
Lewis, Maurice/Houston, TX/(713) 664-1807	**page 240**
Lewis, Nancy/4210 Hawthorne, Dallas	(214) 520-2185
Lewis, Tim/184 St. Johns Pl., Brooklyn	(718) 857-3406
Leyonmark, Roger/Boston	(617) 266-3858
Liao, Sharmen/914 Arroyo Ter., Alhambra	(818) 458-7699
Liberman, Joni Levy/14 Hill Park Terrace, Randolph	(617) 986-4657
Lickona, Cheryl/NYC	(212) 688-2562
Lieberman, Ron/NYC	(212) 947-0653
Liepke, Malcolm/NYC	(212) 755-1365
Liepke, Skip/NYC	(212) 755-1365
Ligresti, Roberto/NYC, NY/(212) 697-0650	**pages 298-299**
Lilie, Jim/251 Kearny St., S.F.	(415) 441-4384
Lilly, Charles/Elmhurst	(718) 803-3442
Lindeman, Nicky/548 Hudson St., NYC	(212) 645-8180
Linden, Tamara/Atlanta, GA/(404) 262-1209	**page 338**
Lindgren & Smith/41 Union Sq. W., NYC	(212) 929-5590

Lindlof, Ed/Austin, TX/(512) 472-0195 .... **page 212**
Line, Lemuel/NYC .... (212) 355-0910
Linley, Michael/Columbus, OH/(614) 486-2921 .... **page 428**
Lionsgate/NYC .... (212) 980-8061
Lipman, Deborah Representative/506 Windsor Dr., Framingham .... (508) 877-8830
Lippman, Miriam/Seven Pontiac Ct., Selden .... (516) 698-0296
Litman, Bruce/1514 Magee Ave., Phila. .... (215) 744-7442
Little Apple Art/Brooklyn .... (718) 499-7045
Little, Ed/Bridgewater, CT/(203) 350-6523 .... **pages 190-191**
Littmann, Barry/Hackettstown, NJ/(201) 850-4405 .... **page 375**
Livingston, Francis/San Anselmo, CA/(415) 456-7103 .... **page 370**
Llewellyn, Sue/NYC, NY/(212) 545-9155 .... **page 202**
Lloyd, Jeff/NYC, NY/(212) 874-7074 .... **page 237**
Lloyd, Peter/NYC .... (212) 221-8090
Lo Bue, Keith/Westport .... (203) 226-4293
Lo Grippo, Robert/NYC .... (212) 355-0910
Locciasano, Karen/Weston .... (203) 226-7674
Lochray, Tom/3225 Oakland Ave. S., Mpls. .... (612) 823-7630
Lockwood, Todd/NYC .... (212) 682-1490
Lodigensky, Ted/NYC .... (212) 221-8090
Loehle, Don/Atlanta, GA/(404) 255-1430 .... **page 346**
Loehle, Don/Chicago, IL/(312) 935-1707 .... **page 346**
Lofaro, Jerry/353 W. 53rd St., NYC .... (212) 682-2462
Lohstoeter, Lori/NYC .... (212) 929-5590
Lombardi, Judith/Westpot .... (203) 226-4293
Longacre, Jimmy/5405 Salem Walk, Austin .... (512) 444-2202
Longtemps, Kenneth/362 Clinton St., Brooklyn .... (718) 852-2178
Lord, David/1449 N. Pennsylvania St., Indpls. .... (317) 634-1244
Lorenz, Al/49 Pine Ave., Floral Park .... (516) 354-5530
Lorenz, Lee/NYC .... (212) 889-3337
Löse, Hal/19 E. 48th St., NYC .... (212) 838-0050
Losey, Brenda/Atlanta, GA/(404) 874-2014 .... **page 279**
Lott, Peter & George/60 E. 42nd St., NYC .... (212) 953-7088
Loveless, Jim/4137 San Francisco Ave., St. Louis .... (314) 533-7914
Loveless, Roger/1199 S. Main St., Centerville .... (801) 292-0943
Lovell, Rick/Atlanta, GA/(404) 873-2287 .... **page 413**
Low, William/31 Ocean Pkwy., Brooklyn .... (718) 436-2039
Lowey, Curt & Assocs., Inc./925 Westchester Ave., White Plains .... (914) 948-6500
Lubey, Dick/726 Harvard St., Rochester .... (716) 442-6075
Luce, Ben/Five E. 17th St., NYC .... (212) 255-8193
Lui, David/NYC .... (212) 925-0491
Luiggi, Mark/80 Walnut St., Winchester .... (617) 729-0081
Lukens, Jan/Chaucer Lane Studio, Winston-Salem .... (919) 788-5451
Lulevitch, Tom/101 W. 69th St., NYC .... (212) 362-3318
Lund, Gary/L.A. .... (213) 655-0998
Lundeen, Cathy/Mpls., MN/(612) 343-0432/0104 .... **page 153**
Lundgren-Ellis, Alvalyn/5250 Colodny Dr., Agoura Hills .... (818) 707-0635
Lungstrom, Tom/118 E. 26th St., Mpls. .... (612) 871-9275
Lunia Blue Graphics/Sacramento, CA/(916) 488-3425 .... **page 165**
Lustig, Loretta/330 Clinton Ave., Brooklyn .... (718) 789-2496
Lutzow, Jack A./240 Dolores, S.F. .... (415) 863-6628
Lyall, Dennis/NYC .... (212) 986-5680
Lydecker, Laura/Weston .... (203) 226-7674
Lynaugh, Matthew/410 Ashmont St., Dorchester .... (617) 436-8971
Lynch, Jeffrey/NYC .... (212) 986-5680
Lynch, Larry & Andrea/Dallas, TX/(214) 369-6990 .... **pages 106, 314**
Lynn, Janet/2050 Meadow View, Costa Mesa .... (714) 722-1364
Lyons, Steve/320 Cypress Dr., Fairfax .... (415) 459-7560
Lytle, John/17130 Yosemite Rd., Sonora .... (209) 928-4849
Maas, Julie/Moody .... (207) 646-2764
Macanga, Steve/Roseland, NJ/(201) 403-8967 .... **page 87**
MacCombie, Turi/NYC .... (212) 532-0928
MacDonald, Ross/NYC .... (212) 967-7699

MacDougall, Rob/2049 Lakeshore Rd., W., Oakville	(416) 847-7663
MacNair, Greg/St. Louis	(314) 241-4014
Macanga, Steve/20 Morgantine Rd., Roseland	(201) 403-8967
Mach, Steven/515 N. Halsted Ave., Chicago	(312) 243-4239
Machamer, Gene/Mechanicsburg	(717) 697-1642
Madden, Don/NYC	(212) 644-2020
Madison, Glen/NYC	(212) 986-5680
Magdich, Dennis/Santa Fe	(505) 984-8534
Maggard, John/Dayton	(513) 433-8383
Magovern, Peg/S.F.	(415) 956-4750
Mahan, Benton/Chesterville, OH/(419) 768-2204	**page 368**
Mahler, Joseph/3905 S. Fisher Rd., Indpls	(317) 862-2939
Mahoney, Katherine/60 Hurd Rd., Belmont	(617) 489-0406
Mahoney, Pat/S.F.	(415) 956-4750
Mahoney, Ron/NYC, NY/(212) 682-2462	**page 121**
Maile, Bob/L.A.	(213) 931-7449
Maioresco Deca, Wanda/NYC, NY/(212) 838-2509	**page 185**
Maisner, Bernard/41 Bleecker St., NYC	(212) 477-6776
Makris, Nancy Lou Studio/45 Seeley Rd., Wilton	(203) 762-5921
Manasse, Michèle/NYC, NY/(212) 873-3797	**pages 174-184**
Mandel, Bette/265 E. 66th St., NYC	(212) 737-5062
Mandel, Saul/163 Maytime Dr., Jericho	(516) 681-3530
Mangal/NYC	(212) 697-6170
Mangiat, Jeffrey/NYC	(212) 986-5680
Manning, Michele/894 Chestnut St., S.F.	(415) 771-3088
Mantel, Richard/NYC	(212) 929-5590
Manus, Charles/Cleveland	(216) 661-4222
Manyum, Wallop/NYC, NY/(212) 873-3797	**page 174**
Manzo/Finalborgo Assoc., Inc./150 Fifth Ave., NYC	(212) 645-5770
Marchesi, Stephen/Weston	(203) 266-7674
Marchetti, Lou/NYC	(212) 986-5680
Marciuliano, Frank/NYC	(212) 697-8525
Marconi, Gloria/2525 Musgrove Rd., Silver Spg.	(301) 890-4615
Marcus, Eric/386 Waverly Ave., Brooklyn	(718) 789-1799
Marden, Phil/NYC, NY/(212) 260-7646	**page 104**
Mardon, Allan/NYC	(212) 889-3337
Mardon, John/Weston	(203) 226-7674
Marek, Mark/42 Erie St., Dumont	(201) 384-1791
Margolis, Al/Cleveland	(216) 661-4222
Margolis, Don/Chicago	(312) 527-2128
Margulies, Robert/NYC, NY/(212) 219-9621	**page 195**
Marie, Rita & Friends/183 N. Martel Ave., L.A.	(213) 934-3395
Marie, Rita & Friends/405 W. Walbash, Chicago	(312) 222-0337
Marion, John/24 E. Birch, Three Forks	(818) 241-8229
Mark, Roger/Lenexa	(913) 492-4444
Mark, Steve/Bloomington, MN/(612) 884-8083	**page 138**
Marsh Inc./12 E. Ninth St., Cincinnati	(513) 421-1234
Martha Productions/4445 Overland Ave., Culver City	(213) 204-1771
Martin, Don/Miami	(305) 665-2376
Martin, Gregory S./1307 Greenlake Dr., Cardiff	(619) 753-4073
Martin, Henry/Westport	(203) 227-7806
Martin, John/NYC	(212) 490-2450
Martin, Lyn/Knoxville, TN/(615) 588-1760	**page 218**
Martin, Richard/485 Hilda St., E. Meadow	(516) 221-3630
Martinez, Ed/NYC	(212) 986-5680
Martinez, John/280 Madison Ave., NYC	(212) 545-9155
Martinez, Sergio/NYC, NY/(212) 254-4996	**page 248**
Martinot, Claude/145 Second Ave., NYC	(212) 473-3137
Martins de Barros, A./NYC	(212) 254-4996
Maruca, Francisco/Pheonix	(602) 252-5072
Maruyama, Sen/1307 Scott Rd., Burbank	(818) 846-0369
Marx, Laurel/33 Gold St., NYC	(212) 393-9264
Marziali, Sandra/NYC	(212) 874-7074

Maschler, Lorraine/1310 Brenda Ct., Upland	(714) 981-2631
Masiello, Ralph Peter/17 Tampa St., Worcester	(508) 752-9871
Mason, Brick/NYC	(212) 777-4297
Mason, Marietta/Mpls., MN/(612) 729-1774	**page 106**
Massé, David/81 Seward Ln., Aston	(215) 494-7525
Masuda, Coco/NYC, NY/(212) 727-1599	**page 105**
Mateu, Franc/NYC, NY/(212) 254-4996	**page 257**
Matheis, Shelley/534 Passaic Ave., Bloomfield	(201) 338-9506
Mather, Bill/L.A.	(213) 653-6484
Mathieu, Joseph/64 Pheasant Ln., Brooklyn	(203) 774-5550
Matsick, Anni/345 Oakley Dr., State College	(814) 234-4752
Matson, Marla Represents/74 W. Culver St., Pheonix	(602) 252-5072
Mattelson, Judy/37 Cary Rd., Great Neck	(212) 684-2974
Mattelson, Marvin/NYC	(212) 684-2974
Matthews, Lu/NYC, NY/(212) 545-9155	**page 205**
Mattingly, David B./Hoboken, NJ/(201) 659-7404	**page 134**
Mattos, John/1546 Grant Ave., S.F.	(415) 397-2138
Mauro, Ray/228 Second St., Clifton	(201) 546-8750
Max, Deborah D./157 Newbrook Lane, Bayshore	(516) 968-5918
May, Melinda/834 Moultrie St., S.F.	(415) 648-2376
Mayer, Bill Inc./Decatur, GA/(404) 378-0686	**pages 108-109**
Mayerowitz, Rich/NYC	(212) 989-7074
Mayforth, Hal/121 Rockingham Rd., Londonderry	(617) 432-2873
Mayo, Frank/265 Briar Brae Rd., Stamford	(203) 322-3650
Mayse, Steve/7515 Allman, Lenexa	(913) 962-2285
Mazarin, C.S./Yorkville Station	(212) 410-9628
Mazut, Mark/Hoboken	(201) 656-0657
Mazzetti, Alan/S.F.	(415) 541-0238
McAllister, Chris/7181 N. Hidden Pine Dr., San Gabriel	(619) 272-8147
McCaffrey, Peter/NYC, NY/(212) 673-1600	**page 402**
McCall, Louise & Robert T./4816 Moonlight Way, Paradise Valley	(602) 991-0759
McCarthy, Kathleen Dunne/3191 Deronda Dr., L.A.	(213) 461-1631
McClain, Julia/111 Wooster St., NYC	(212) 925-0491
McClelland, John/21 Coventry Close, Savannah	(912) 598-0322
McClure, Royce/L.A.	(213) 651-3706
McClure, Tim/Dallas, TX/(214) 748-8663	**page 336**
McCollum, Rick/L.A.	(213) 874-1661
McConnell, James/10921 Live Oak Blvd., Bangor	(916) 679-2282
McConnell, Keith A./2131 Bonita Dr., Glendale	(818) 243-2042
McCord, Kathy/Westport	(203) 226-4293
McCormack, Geoffrey/NYC	(212) 986-5680
McDaniel, Jerry/NYC	(212) 697-6170
McDarby, Patrick/17 W. 45th St., NYC	(212) 840-8516
McDermott, Michael/Weston	(203) 226-7674
McDonald, Jerry/180 Clipper St., S.F.	(415) 824-1377
McDonald, Mercedes/1459 Athenour Ct., San Jose	(408) 268-0662
McDonnell, Patrick/11 Laureldale Ave., Metuchen	(201) 549-9341
McElrath-Eslick, Lori/5236 N. Kensington, Kansas City	(816) 453-5304
McElroy, Darlene/2915 Redhill Ave., Costa Mesa	(714) 434-7220
McEntire, Larry/2258 Shakespeare, Houston	(713) 668-5477
McGarry, Richard M., Inc./450 N.E. 52nd Ter., Miami	(305) 757-5720
McGinty, Mick/9909 Rancho Caballo, Shadow Hills	(818) 353-1422
McGovern, Michael/27 Laurel Ave., Bradford	(508) 373-4877
McGovern, Preston/NYC, NY/(212) 982-8595	**page 318**
McGowan, Dan/NYC, NY/(212) 473-8747	**page 364**
McGurl, Michael/Brooklyn, NY/(718) 857-1866	**page 101**
McIntosh, Jon/Boston, MA/(617) 236-1920	**page 197**
McIntosh, Mark/1601 E. 15th St., Newport Beach	(213) 642-7445
McInturff, Steve/Mechanicsburg, OH/(513) 834-3539	**page 412**
McIver, Cary/NYC	(212) 673-1600
McKeever, Michael/1240 NE 171 Terrace, N. Miami Beach	(305) 652-6668
McKelvey, David/Atlanta, GA/(404) 873-2287	**page 415**
McKie, Roy/NYC	(212) 686-3514

McKissick, Randall/1238 Arrowwood Rd., Columbia . . . . (803) 798-3688
McKissick, Stewart/Columbus, OH/(614) 262-3262 . . . . **page 159**
McLain, Julia/NYC . . . . (212) 925-0491
McLaughlin, Gary/NYC . . . . (212) 697-8525
McLean, Wilson/902 Broadway, NYC . . . . (212) 473-5554
McLennan, Constance/Rocklin, CA/(916) 624-1957 . . . . **page 271**
McLoughlin, Wayne/NYC, NY/(212) 490-2450 . . . . **page 325**
McMacken, David/L.A. . . . . (213) 874-1661
McMahon, Bob/6820 Independance Ave., Canoga Park . . . . (818) 999-4127
McMahon, Franklin/1665 W. Devonshire, Lake Forest . . . . (312) 234-9108
McMahon, Mark/321 S. Ridge Rd., Lake Forest . . . . (312) 295-2604
McMullan, James/222 Park Ave. S., NYC . . . . (212) 473-5083
McNamara Associates, Inc./1250 Stephenson Hwy., Detroit . . . . (313) 583-9200
McNeel, Richard/Upper Montclair, NJ/(201) 509-2255 . . . . **page 424**
McVicker, Charles/Rocky Hill . . . . (609) 924-2660
Medical & Legal Visuals, Inc./708 First St. N., Mpls. . . . . (612) 338-1270
Mehalko, Donna/NYC, NY/(212) 534-4177 . . . . **page 169**
Mehlman, Elwyn/NYC . . . . (212) 889-3337
Meisel, Ann/NYC . . . . (212) 986-5680
Meisel, Paul/NYC, NY/(212) 925-3053 . . . . **pages 246-247**
Meisler, Meryl/553 Eighth St., Brooklyn . . . . (718) 768-3991
Melendez, Robert/NYC . . . . (212) 221-8090
Melrath, Susan/W. Palm Beach, FL/(407) 790-1561 . . . . **page 223**
Mendheim Illustrations, LTD/6619 N. Sheridan, Chicago . . . . (312) 338-0773
Mendola, Ltd./NYC, NY/(212) 986-5680 . . . . **page 371**
Merchan, Richard/100 Bella Vista Way, S.F. . . . . (415) 586-8644
Merrell, Patrick/124 W. 18th St., NYC . . . . (212) 620-7777
Merrill, Abby/400 E. 70th St., NYC . . . . (212) 772-6853
Merritt, Norman/621 Paseo de los Reyes, Redondo Beach . . . . (213) 378-4689
Messi, Enzo/NYC, NY/(212) 473-8747 . . . . **page 358**
Metcalf, Paul/Webber Rd., Brookfield . . . . (508) 867-7754
Meyer, Gary/Woodland Hills, CA/(818) 992-6974 . . . . **page 270**
Meyer, Jeff/Mpls. . . . . (612) 729-1774
Meyerowitz, Rick/NYC . . . . (212) 989-7074
Michal, Marie/NYC . . . . (212) 889-3337
Michel, Jean Claude/NYC . . . . (212) 682-2462
Michener, Ted/NYC . . . . (212) 986-5680
Midnight Oil Studios/51 Melcher St., Boston . . . . (617) 350-7970
Mikos, Mike/NYC . . . . (212) 986-5680
Miles, Elizabeth J./Weston . . . . (203) 226-7674
Miller, Dave/NYC, NY/(212) 682-2462 . . . . **page 118**
Miller, Frank/NYC . . . . (212) 674-8080
Miller, Verlin/Phila., PA/(215) 232-6666 . . . . **page 419**
Mills, Elise/150 E. 79th St., NYC . . . . (212) 794-2042
Milnazik, Kimmerle/Drexel Hill, PA/(215) 259-1565 . . . . **page 146**
Milne, Jonathan/NYC . . . . (212) 986-5680
Minor, Wendell/277 W. Fourth St., NYC . . . . (212) 691-6925
Mintz, Less/111 Wooster St., NYC . . . . (212) 925-0491
Mintz, Margery/9 Cottage Ave., Sommerville . . . . (617) 623-2291
Mistretta, Andrea/NYC . . . . (212) 874-7074
Mitchell, Celia/NYC . . . . (212) 697-8525
Mitchell, Dean/420 E. Armour, Kansas City . . . . (816) 531-1384
Mitra, Annie/15 W. 12th St., NYC . . . . (212) 255-2704
Mitsuhashi, Yoko/25 E. 20th St., NYC . . . . (212) 979-1266
Mizzi, Savio/34-50 29th St., L.I.C. . . . . (718) 786-2517
Moede, Jade/96 S. Main St., Lodi . . . . (201) 778-4090
Molano, Gabriel/Catskill . . . . (518) 945-2999
Moldoff, Kirk/Rowayton . . . . (203) 866-3734
Molina, Luis/Culver City . . . . (213) 558-3325
Mollering, Dave/3772 Curtis St., San Diego . . . . (619) 272-8147
Mollica, Pat/Atlanta, GA/(404) 873-2287 . . . . **page 414**
Monahan, Leo & Assocs., Inc./1912 Hilton Dr., Burbank . . . . (818) 843-8934
Monohan, Leo/Santa Monica . . . . (213) 392-4877

Monteleone, John/127 Hunnewell Ave., Elmont . . . . (516) 437-1879
Montgomerg, Marilyn/NYC . . . . (212) 545-9155
Montgomery, Michael G./Atlanta . . . . (404) 478-2929
Montiel, David/115 W. 16th St., NYC . . . . (212) 929-3659
Moody, Eric/1158 Shore Rd., Cape Elizabeth . . . . (207) 767-4541
Moonlight Press Studio/362 Cromwell Ave., Ocean Breeze . . . . (718) 979-9695
Moore, Chris/NYC, NY/(212) 682-1490 . . . . **page 55**
Moore, Cyd/3465 Fernway Dr., Montgomery . . . . (205) 281-4818
Moore, Larry/Orlando, FL/(407) 648-0832 . . . . **page 374**
Moore, Steven/Weston . . . . (203) 226-7674
Moores, Jeff/NYC, NY/(212) 529-6389 . . . . **page 430**
Moraes, Greg/203 Anzona Ave., Santa Monica . . . . (213) 395-4542
Morales Studio/PO Box 1763, Bloomfield . . . . (201) 676-8187
Moran, Michael/21 Keep St., Madison . . . . (201) 966-6229
Mordan, C.B./NYC, NY/(212) 673-1600 . . . . **page 405**
Morgan, Craig/966 Highland View N.E., Atlanta . . . . (404) 874-0743
Morgan, Jacqui/NYC, NY/(212) 463-8488 . . . . **page 110**
Morgan, Leonard E./Chicago . . . . (708) 739-7705
Morgan, Vicki Assocs./194 Third Ave., NYC . . . . (212) 475-0440
Morgan, Wendy/Northport, NY/(516) 757-5609 . . . . **pages 308-309**
Morgen, Barry/253 W. 73rd St., NYC . . . . (212) 595-6835
Morkywas, Mike/Dallas . . . . (214) 254-9517
Moroney, Christopher/12107 Magnolia Blossom, San Antonio . . . . (512) 490-6801
Morris, Ann/140 E. 56th St., NYC . . . . (212) 355-1603
Morris, Frank/NYC . . . . (212) 799-2231
Morrison, Bill/68 Glandore Rd., Westwood . . . . (617) 329-5288
Morrison, Don/NYC . . . . (212) 697-6170
Morrow, J.T./Pacifica, CA/(415) 355-7899 . . . . **page 84**
Morrow, Skip/PO Box 123 Ware Road, Wilmington . . . . (802) 464-5523
Morse, Bill/NYC, NY/(212) 682-1490 . . . . **page 73**
Morser, Bruce/401-Second Ave. S., Seattle . . . . (206) 292-8934
Morykwas, Michael/Dallas . . . . (214) 369-6990
Moscarillo, Mark/90 W. Broadway, NYC . . . . (212) 406-7217
Moses, David/Atlanta, GA/(404) 874-2014 . . . . **page 283**
Moss, Eileen/333 E. 49th St., NYC . . . . (212) 980-8061
Mowry, Scott/Charlestown, MA/(617) 242-2419 . . . . **page 293**
Mueller, Pete/NYC, NY/(212) 682-1490 . . . . **page 70**
Mukai, Dennis/200 W. 15th St., NYC . . . . (212) 391-1830
Mull, Christy/Atlanta, GA/(404) 255-1430 . . . . **page 345**
Mulligan, Donald/418 Central Park W., NYC . . . . (212) 666-6079
Munck, Paula/NYC . . . . (212) 741-2539
Munger, Nancy/Weston . . . . (203) 266-7674
Murakami, Tak/Chicago . . . . (312) 368-8777
Murawski, Alex/NYC . . . . (212) 889-3337
Muzick, Terra/1805 Pine St., S.F. . . . . (415) 346-6141
Myer, Andy/Phila., PA/(215) 232-6666 . . . . **page 420**
Myers, David/228 Bleecker St., NYC . . . . (212) 989-5260
Myers, Lou/NYC . . . . (212) 889-3337
Myers, Robert/Santa Monica, CA/(213) 396-7303 . . . . **page 409**
Myers, Sherwood/9770 Sterling Dr., Miami . . . . (305) 238-0488
Myers, V. Gene/41 Douglas Rd., Glen Ridge . . . . (201) 429-8131
Nacht, Merle/374 Main St., Wethersfield . . . . (203) 563-7993
Nahas, Margo/MZN/11833 Brookdale, Studio City . . . . (213) 654-4771
Najaka, Marlies Merk/NYC, NY/(212) 580-0058 . . . . **page 91**
Nakai-Crowell/218 Madison Ave., NYC . . . . (212) 213-5333
Nakamura, Carl/L.A., CA/(213) 936-2620 . . . . **page 224**
Nakamura, Joel/S.F. . . . . (415) 956-4750
Nakamura, Tak/411 N. Benton Way, L.A. . . . . (213) 383-6991
Nathan, Charlott/600 Lyndhurst Ave., Roseville . . . . (916) 786-2082
Navratil, Sid/1305 Clark Bldg., Pittsburgh . . . . (412) 471-4322
Neail, Pamela Assocs./NYC, NY/(212) 673-1600 . . . . **pages 401-407**
Needham, Jim/NYC . . . . (212) 682-2462
Neibart, Allan D./1715 Walnut St., Phila. . . . . (215) 564-5167

Neider, Alan/NYC	(212) 799-2231
Neider, Alan/Westport	(203) 226-4724
Nels Group, The/11440 Oak Dr., Shelbyville	(616) 672-5757
Nelson Studio, Inc./14849 W. 95th St., Lenexa	(913) 492-4444
Nelson, Bill/107 E. Cary St., Richmond	(804) 783-2602
Nelson, Craig/NYC, NY/(212) 682-1490	**page 69**
Nelson, Fred/Chicago	(312) 222-0504
Nelson, Kenton R./12 S. Fairoaks Ave., Pasadena	(818) 792-5252
Nemirov, Meredith/Ridgway	(303) 626-3972
Neski, Peter/NYC, NY/(212) 737-2521	**page 317**
Network Studios/Northport, NY/(516) 757-5609	**pages 308-309**
Neuhaus, David/Westport	(203) 226-4293
Neumann, Ann/78 Franklin St., Jersey City	(201) 420-1137
New Work/NYC	(212) 873-3797
New York Airbrush/E. Northport, NY/(516) 499-7575	**page 141**
Newborn, Milton, Associates/135 E. 54th St., NYC	(212) 421-0050
Newman, Carole & Assocs./Santa Monica, CA/(213) 394-5031	**pages 190-194**
Newson, Tom/NYC	(212) 986-5680
Newton, Richard/NYC	(212) 490-2450
Ng, Michael/NYC, NY/(212) 398-9540	**page 231**
Nicholass, Jess/NYC	(212) 221-8090
Nicklaus, Carol/NYC	(212) 644-2020
Nicotra, Roseann/NYC	(212) 697-8525
Niklewicz, Adam/St. Louis	(314) 241-4014
Niles, Nancy/9220 W. 73rd St., Merriam	(913) 432-6905
Nishimura, Masato/2630 Washington St., Alameda	(415) 523-8796
Nishinaka, Jeff/NYC, NY/(212) 682-1490	**page 66**
Nixon, Tony/6025 Lamar, Mission	(913) 384-5444
Noi Viva Design/220 Ferris Ave., White Plains	(914) 946-1951
Nolte, Larry/4021 Nebraska, St. Louis	(314) 481-6983
Noonan, Julia/NYC	(212) 243-4412
Norby, Carol H./Atlanta	(801) 756-1096
Norcia, Ernest/Cleveland	(216) 661-4222
Norman, Gary/7120 Fillmore Dr., Buena Park	(714) 761-9731
Norman, Marty/Five Radcliff Blvd., Glen Head	(516) 671-4482
Notarile, Chris/Cranford	(201) 272-1696
Novak, Bob/6878 Fry Rd., Middleburg Hts.	(216) 234-1808
Noyes, David/NYC	(212) 682-2462
Nugent, Denise/23725 99th Ave. S.W., Burton	(206) 463-5412
Nunez, Manuel/NYC	(212) 673-1600
O'Brien, John/NYC	(212) 532-0928
O'Brien, Tim/NYC	(212) 953-7088
O'Connell, Frank/3700 Paula Dr., Richfield	(216) 659-6923
O'Connell, Mitch/6425 N. Newgard, Chicago	(312) 743-3848
O'Connor, Cathy Christy/NYC, NY/(212) 873-3797	**page 181**
O'Donnell, Billy/St. Louis, MO/(314) 781-8851	**page 385**
O'Keefe Young, Mary/NYC	(212) 398-9540
O'Neil, Sharron/409 Alberto Way, Los Gatos	(408) 354-3816
O'Neill, Fran/Boston, MA/(617) 267-9215	**page 222**
O'Shaughnessy, Stephanie/Weston	(203) 454-4687
O'Young, Leoung/36 Woodycrest Ave., Toronto	(416) 462-3388
Oakes, Jim/936 N. Hudson, Chandler	(602) 899-5456
Oakley, Fred/Thornbury	(519) 599-2164
Obrero, Rudy Illustration, Inc./3400 Barham Blvd., L.A.	(213) 850-5700
Ochagavia, Carlos/50 E. 50th St., NYC	(212) 355-0910
Ochsner, Dennis/Seattle	(206) 448-7992
Ohlsson, Eskil Assoc., Inc./767 Third Ave., NYC	(212) 758-4412
Okamoto, Alan H./550 Lake St., S.F.	(415) 626-2501
Okuyan, Selime/69-01 Northern Blvd., Woodside	(718) 476-1456
Olbinski, Rafal/NYC	(212) 242-6367
Olitsky, Eve/235 W. 102nd St., NYC	(212) 678-1045
Olsen, Greg/Stone Mountain	(404) 296-9666
Olson, Richard A./NYC, NY/(212) 925-1820	**page 78**

Olson, Erik/634 W. Sierra Madre Blvd., Sierra Madre ... (818) 355-5235
Olson, Maribeth/NYC ... (212) 727-2667
Olson, Richard/85 Grand St., NYC ... (212) 925-1820
Olson, Rik/L.A. ... (213) 850-8222
Olson, Stan/1084 Carmel Ct., Shoreview ... (612) 482-9862
Oreman, Linda/22 Nelson St., Rochester ... (716) 244-6956
Organisation, The/267 Wyckoff St., Brooklyn ... (718) 624-1906
Ormond, Rick/NYC ... (212) 697-8525
Ortega, José/NYC, NY/(212) 772-3329 ... **page 103**
Orvidas, Ken/832 Evelyn Ave., Albany ... (415) 525-6626
Osaka, Richard/14-22 30th Dr., L.I.C. ... (718) 956-0015
Osborn, Jackie/S.F. ... (415) 775-3366
Osborn, Stephen/S.F. ... (415) 775-3366
Ossip, Jay/2020 S.W. 13th Ave., Miami ... (305) 854-2983
Ostan•Prentice•Ostan, Inc./L.A., CA/(213) 826-1332 ... **page 397**
Otnes, Fred/NYC ... (212) 755-1365
Oudekerk, Doug/Bloomington, MN/(612) 884-8083 ... **page 137**
Oughton, Taylor/Jamison ... (215) 598-3246
Overacre, Gary/Marietta ... (404) 973-8878
Ovies, Joseph M./Atlanta, GA/(404) 262-1209 ... **page 338**
Owen, Kimberly/2071A Beretania St., Honolulu ... (808) 943-6936
Pace, Julie/L.A. ... (213) 655-0998
Palencar, John Jude/6763 Middlebrook Blvd., Middleburg Hts. ... (216) 845-8163
Palladini, David/NYC ... (212) 683-1362
Palmer, Tom/40 Chicasaw Dr., Oakland ... (201) 337-8638
Palombo, Lisa A./226 Willow Ave, Hoboken ... (201) 653-1501
Palulian, Dickran/Rowayton, CT/(203) 866-3734 ... **page 378**
Palulian, Joanne/NYC, NY/(212) 581-8338 ... **pages 376-380**
Palulian, Joanne/Rowayton, CT/(203) 866-3734 ... **pages 376-380**
Paperny, Vladimir/Santa Monica, CA/(213) 394-5031 ... **page 194**
Paquette, Andrew/NYC ... (212) 545-9155
Paraskevas, Michael/NYC ... (212) 929-5590
Pardue, Jack/2307 Sherwood Hall Ln., Alexandria ... (703) 765-2622
Pardy, Cindy/NYC ... (212) 243-4209
Park, W.B./110 Park Ave. S., Winter Park ... (407) 644-1553
Parker, Curtis/4160 N. Craftsman Ct, Scotsdale ... (602) 423-1500
Parker, Edward/NYC ... (212) 741-2539
Parker, Robert Andrew/General Delivery Box 114, West Cornwall ... (203) 672-0152
Parkinson, Jim Lettering/NYC, NY/(212) 925-3053 ... **pages 246-247**
Parrish, George I. Jr./NYC, NY/(212) 688-1080 ... **page 328**
Parry, Ivor/Eastchester, NY/(914) 961-7338 ... **page 267**
Parry, Ivor/NYC, NY/(212) 779-1554 ... **page 267**
Parry, Karl/L.A. ... (213) 931-7449
Parson, Nan/NYC ... (212) 682-2462
Parsons, John/NYC ... (212) 697-8525
Parton, Steve/NYC, NY/(212) 254-4996 ... **page 262**
Passerelli, Charles A./Atlanta, GA/(404) 262-1209 ... **page 338**
Pasternak, Robert/NYC, NY/(212) 675-0002 ... **page 320**
Pastucha, Ron/Irvine ... (714) 250-0943
Pate, Randy/3408 W. Burbank Blvd., Burbank ... (818) 985-8181
Patti, Joyce/NYC ... (212) 475-0440
Paul, Arthur/175 E. Delaware Pl., Chicago ... (312) 266-0621
Pavesich, Vida/L.A. ... (213) 874-1661
Pavey, Jerry Design & Illustration/507 Orchard Way, Silver Spg. ... (301) 384-3377
Pavia, Cathy/Weston ... (203) 266-7674
Payne, C.F./NYC ... (212) 683-1362
Payne, Thomas ... (212) 243-4412
Peak, Bob/14 E. 52nd St., NYC ... (212) 752-8490
Peck, Everett/1344 Blue Heron Ave., Leucadia ... (619) 272-8147
Peck, G. Byron/Wash. D.C. ... (202) 331-1966
Peck, Virginia/NYC ... (212) 683-1362
Pederson, Judy/96 Greene St., NYC ... (212) 226-3675
Pelavin, Daniel/NYC ... (212) 941-7418

Pelosi, Mary Jane/P.O. Box 677, Bronx . . . . (212) 792-4263
Pembroke, Richard/NYC, NY/(212) 682-2462 . . . . page 122
Penca, Gary/Coral Springs, FL/(305) 752-4699 . . . . page 211
Pendleton, Nancy/4160 N. Craftman Ct, Scotsdale . . . . (602) 423-1500
Pendleton, Roy/NYC . . . . (212) 674-8080
Penelope/NYC . . . . (212) 697-8525
Pennington, Lyn Boyer/4281 Baywood Dr., Traverse City . . . . (616) 938-1911
Penny & Stermer Group, The/31 W. 21st St., NYC . . . . (212) 243-4412
Pentleton, Carol/685 Chestnut Hill Rd., Chepachet . . . . (401) 568-0275
Pepera, Fred/405 N Wabash St., Chicago . . . . (312) 329-1370
Pepper, Bob/157 Clinton St., Brooklyn . . . . (718) 875-3236
Pepper, Brenda/NYC . . . . (212) 673-1600
Percivalle, Rosanne/430 W. 14th St., NYC . . . . (212) 633-2480
Perez, Alex/Santa Monica . . . . (213) 394-5031
Perez, Perry/Dallas . . . . (214) 369-6990
Perez, Vincent/Cleveland . . . . (216) 661-4222
Peringer, Stephen/17808 184th St. N.E., Woodinville . . . . (206) 788-5767
Perini, Ben/1113 Clayton Ct., Novato . . . . (415) 892-6535
Perry, Phil/968 Homewood Court, Decatur . . . . (404) 634-2499
Pershing, Stephanie/Pheonix . . . . (602) 252-5072
Personality Inc./NYC . . . . (212) 490-2450
Peters, Bob/NYC . . . . (212) 889-3337
Peterson, Bryan/Milwaukee . . . . (414) 291-0300
Peterson, Cheryl/NYC, NY/(212) 925-3053 . . . . pages 246-247
Petruccio, Steven James/NYC . . . . (212) 532-0928
Phillips, Laura/NYC, NY/(212) 682-1490 . . . . page 60
Phoenix Studio/642 N. Clark St., Chicago . . . . (312) 649-9144
Picasso, Dan/1645 Hennipen, Mpls. . . . . (612) 371-0425
Pickard, Maggie/Two Locust Grove Rd., Rhinebeck . . . . (914) 876-2358
Pickard, Morgan/6855 Coral Gum Court, Garden Grove . . . . (213) 954-0494
Pierce, Michael/S.F. . . . . (415) 776-4247
Pincus, Harry/160 Ave. of the Americas, NYC . . . . (212) 925-8071
Pinkney, Deborah/NYC, NY/(212) 545-9155 . . . . page 204
Pinkney, J. Brian/NYC . . . . (212) 644-2020
Pinkney, Jerry/NYC . . . . (212) 889-3337
Pisano, Al/22 W. 38 St., NYC . . . . (212) 730-7666
Pitt, Bob/503 Emory Cir., Atlanta . . . . (404) 378-0694
Pittman, Jack/Atlanta, GA/(404) 874-2014 . . . . page 284
Pitts, Ted/Dayton . . . . (513) 433-8383
Pizzo, Robert/333 E. 49th St., NYC . . . . (212) 980-8061
Pizzo, Susan/288 E. Devonia Ave., Mount Vernon . . . . (914) 644-4423
Pizzo, Valerie/425 W. 57th St., NYC . . . . (212) 333-5402
Platz III, H. "Rusty"/15922 118th Pl. N.E., Bothell . . . . (206) 488-9171
Plotkin, Barnett/126 Wooleys Ln., Great Neck . . . . (516) 487-7457
Podevin, Jean-Francois/5812 Newlin Ave., Whittier . . . . (213) 945-9613
Podwil, Jerry/108 W. 14th St., NYC . . . . (212) 255-9464
Pogue, Deborah Bazzel/NYC . . . . (212) 243-4412
Poladian, Elena/42 E. 23rd St., NYC . . . . (212) 529-7878
Poladian, Girair/139 E. 33rd St., NYC . . . . (212) 213-3460
Polenghi, Evan/Brooklyn, NY/(718) 499-3214 . . . . page 227
Police, Lou/Culver City . . . . (213) 558-3325
Pollack, Scott/NYC . . . . (212) 980-8061
Pollie, Lissa/609 S. Leroy St., Fenton . . . . (313) 629-5340
Polonsky, Gabriel/274 LaGrange St., Chestnut Hill . . . . (617) 965-3035
Polston, Deb/9165 Prestwick Club Dr., Duluth . . . . (404) 729-8916
Pomerantz, Lisa/Phila., PA/(215) 232-6666 . . . . page 420
Pomilla, Joseph/Ronkonkoma, NY/(516) 471-2728 . . . . page 315
Popadics, Joel/242 Manchester Ave., N. Haledon . . . . (201) 304-0242
Pope, Kevin/1913 Park Ave., St. Louis . . . . (314) 241-4014
Porazinski, Rob/Chicago, IL/(312) 745-9005 . . . . page 107
Porfirio, Guy/St. Louis, MO/(314) 241-4014 . . . . page 394
Porter, Pat Grant/28 W. 69th St., NYC . . . . (212) 799-8493
Potts, Carolyn & Assoc./Chicago, IL/(312) 944-1130 . . . . page 346

Powell, Rick/NYC	(212) 221-8090
Powell, Terrell/1810 Blue Bell Dr., Cedar Park	(512) 335-0253
Powers, Teresa/L.A.	(213) 931-7449
Prato, Rodica/154 W. 57th St., NYC	(212) 683-1362
Pratt, Russell E./NYC, NY/(212) 685-7955	**page 140**
Prentice, Lynne/2691 Hurricane Cove, Port Hueneme	(805) 984-0013
Prentice, Nancy/919 Collier Rd., Atlanta	(404) 266-1070
Prey, Barbara Ernst/Prosperity	(412) 225-2996
Pribble, Laurie/1427 E. Fourth St., L.A.	(818) 574-0288
Price, John Studio/11 N. Franklin St., Chagrin Falls	(216) 247-4228
Pritchett, Karen/NYC, NY/(212) 545-9155	**page 207**
Pritchett, Tom/NYC, NY/(212) 688-1080	**page 328**
Product Illustration Inc./520 N. Michigan Ave., Chicago	(312) 943-7311
Przewodek, Camille/522 E. D St., Petaluma	(415) 826-3238
Pslulian, Dickran/18 McKinley St., Rowayton	(203) 866-3734
Puhalski, Rod/1133 Broadway, NYC	(212) 242-2860
Pullen, Pip/2032 Lakeside Dr., Louisville	(502) 459-7968
Pulver Jr., Harry E./605 S. Cedar Lake Rd., Mpls.	(612) 377-1797
Punchatz, Don Ivan/NYC	(212) 989-7074
Punin, Nikolai/NYC, NY/(212) 727-7237	**page 166**
Purdom, Bill/780 Madison Ave., NYC	(212) 988-4566
Puro, Norina/17-19 S. Village Ave., Rockville Ctr.	(516) 764-2171
Pushpin Assocs./215 Park Ave. S., NYC	(212) 674-8080
Putnam, Denise/San Diego	(619) 272-8147
Pyle, Charles S./S.F.	(415) 255-7393
Quang, Ho/1553 Platte St., Denver	(303) 477-4574
Queen of Arts/12325 S. 90th Ave., Palos Park	(312) 361-0679
Quon, Mike/NYC, NY/(212) 226-6024	**page 225**
RKB Studio, Inc./420 N. Fifth Ave., Mpls.	(612) 339-7055
RadenStudio/3016 Cherry, Kansas City	(816) 756-1992
Radigan, Bob/Atlanta, GA/(404) 255-1430	**page 349**
Ragland, Greg/258 Broadway, NYC	(212) 513-7218
Raglin, Tim/NYC	(212) 929-5590
Ramage, Alfred/Winthrop	(617) 846-5955
Ramin, Linda/St. Louis, MO/(314) 781-8851	**pages 384-386**
Ramsay/In The Black, Inc./119 Merchant St., Honolulu	(808) 537-2787
Ramsey, Carl/825 S. Ogden Dr., L.A.	(213) 934-3150
Randazzo, Anthony/16220 Cambell, Utica	(313) 583-9200
Raphael & Bolognese/53 Irving Pl., NYC	(212) 228-5219
Rapp, Gerald & Cullen, Inc./108 E. 35th St., NYC	(212) 889-3337
Rasmussen, Bonnie/8828 W. Pendleton, St. Louis	(314) 962-1842
Rauch, Peter/1136 Fifth Ave., NYC	(212) 831-0136
Rauchman & Assocs., Inc./5210 S.W. 60th Pl., Miami	(305) 663-9432
Rauffenbart, Bruce/NYC	(212) 688-4555
Raymond, Larry/Weston	(203) 226-7674
Reactor Artists' Representatives/227 W. 29th St., NYC	(212) 967-7699
Recchia, Janet/NYC	(212) 673-1600
Reed, Judy/LA	(213) 290-1430
Reed, Lynn Rowe/Dallas	(214) 871-1956
Reed, Mike/Mpls., MN/(612) 374-3164	**page 306**
Reed, Susie/123 Townsend St., S.F.	(415) 974-5767
Reed, William/2438 W. Tenth, Dallas	(214) 333-2884
Regester, Sheryl/511 Main St., Silver Plume	(303) 569-3374
Reid, Glenn Robert/Boston, MA/(617) 236-1920	**page 196**
Reigle, Todd/St. Louis	(314) 781-3757
Reilly, Donald/211 Newtown Tpk., Wilton	(203) 834-0067
Reim, Melanie/214 Riverside Dr., NYC	(212) 749-0177
Reinbold, David/Oley	(215) 987-3711
Reiner, John/27 Watch Way, Lloyd Neck	(516) 385-4261
Reingold, Alan/NYC	(212) 697-6170
Renard Represents/NYC, NY/(212) 490-2450	**pages 312, 321-327**
Renaudin, Philippe/NYC	(212) 221-8090
Repertory/6010 Wilshire Blvd., L.A.	(213) 931-7449

Repertoire/Dallas, TX/(214) 369-6990 . . . . **pages 106, 314**
Reyes, Eduardo/300 W. Raymond St., Phila. . . . . (215) 455-9176
Reynolds, Bill/Bloomington, MN/(612) 884-8083 . . . . **page 139**
Reynolds, Donna/120 W. Illinois, Chicago . . . . (312) 549-0947
Reynolds, Gene/NYC, NY/(212) 431-3072 . . . . **page 408**
Reynolds, Keith L./RR 2 Box 387, Sanbornville . . . . (603) 522-8765
Reynolds, Mark Andrew/Stinson Beach . . . . (415) 868-9048
Riccio, Frank/33 Eames Blvd., Black Rock . . . . (203) 336-5437
Rice, Rich/420 Clinton Ave., Brooklyn . . . . (718) 230-7908
Rich Art Graphics/1309 Vine St., Phila. . . . . (215) 922-1539
Rich, Anna/NYC . . . . (212) 874-7074
Richard High Design/NYC . . . . (212) 697-8525
Richards, Barbara/10607 Kennel Ln., Charlotte . . . . (704) 846-3944
Richards, Irene/200 E. 36th St., NYC . . . . (212) 679-7436
Richards, Kenn/E. Northport, NY/(516) 499-7575 . . . . **page 141**
Richards, Linda/NYC, NY/(212) 673-1600 . . . . **page 403**
Richens, Keith/NYC . . . . (212) 741-2539
Rickerd, David/22 Canvas Back, Manalapan . . . . (201) 446-2119
Rieser, William/NYC . . . . (212) 545-9155
Rigié, Mitch/41 Union Sq. W., NYC . . . . (212) 807-6627
Rigie, Mitchell/NYC . . . . (212) 807-6627
Riley Illustration/NYC, NY/(212) 925-3053 . . . . **pages 246-247**
Riley, Frank/108 Bamford Ave, Howthorn . . . . (201) 423-2659
Risko/201 W. 11th St., NYC . . . . (212) 989-6987
Ritta, Kurt Studio/632 Park Ave., Hoboken . . . . (201) 792-7422
Ritter Enterprises/444 S. Union St., Burlington . . . . (802) 864-0545
Rivera, Ambrose/4523 Motley Dr., Mesquite . . . . (214) 613-9426
Rivers, Ruth/Brooklyn . . . . (718) 624-1906
Rixford, Ellen/308 W. 97th St., NYC . . . . (212) 865-5686
Roberts, Cheryl/Boston . . . . (617) 266-3858
Roberts, Eva/540 Erbes Rd., Thousand Oaks . . . . (805) 495-2266
Roberts, Ray/NYC . . . . (212) 682-1490
Roberts, Ray & Peggy Illustration/13075 N. 75th Pl., Scottsdale . . . . (602) 991-8568
Robinette, John/Atlanta, GA/(404) 873-2287 . . . . **page 414**
Robins, Lili Petrov/703 Forest Glen Rd., Silver Spring . . . . (301) 593-8228
Robins, Mike/Houston . . . . (713) 522-1862
Robinson, Lenor/201 E. 69th St., NYC . . . . (212) 734-0944
Rocco, Joe/Brooklyn, NY/(718) 492-4776 . . . . **page 416**
Rodericks, Mike/129 Lounsbury Rd., Trumbull . . . . (203) 268-1551
Rodney, Ray/Chicago . . . . (312) 222-0337
Rodriguez, Jon Anthony/172 W. 79th Street, NYC . . . . (212) 787-6518
Rodriguez, Robert/NYC . . . . (212) 490-2450
Roffo, Sergio/42 Shepard St., Boston . . . . (617) 787-5861
Rogers, Joel/2583 Victoria Pwy., Hudson . . . . (216) 656-3129
Rogers, Lilla/33 Bond St., NYC . . . . (212) 529-0193
Rogers, Paul/1 S. Fair Oaks, L.A. . . . . (213) 934-3395
Roman, Barbara J./345 W. 88th St., NYC . . . . (212) 362-1374
Roman, Helen Assocs., Inc./NYC, NY/(212) 874-7074 . . . . **page 237**
Roman, Irena/369 Thomas Clapp Rd., Scituate . . . . (617) 545-6514
Romano Studios/Three E. Ontario St., Chicago . . . . (312) 642-0597
Romas/66 Dale Dr., Keene . . . . (603) 357-7306
Rombola, John/NYC . . . . (212) 645-8000
Romeo Studio, The/1066 N.W. 96th Ave., Fort Lauderdale . . . . (305) 472-0072
Romer, Dan V./125 Prospect Park W., Brooklyn . . . . (718) 965-2524
Root, Barrett/NYC . . . . (212) 741-2539
Root, Kimberely Bulken/NYC . . . . (212) 741-2539
Roper, Marty/14849 W. 95th St., Lenexa . . . . (913) 492-4444
Rosales, Melodye/NYC, NY/(212) 254-4996 . . . . **page 256**
Rosco, Delro/1420 E. Fourth St., National City . . . . (619) 477-9324
Rose, Drew/Atlanta, GA/(404) 874-2014 . . . . **page 281**
Rosenbaum, Tina/Dallas, TX/(214) 748-8663 . . . . **page 334**
Rosenfeld, Mort/35 Evergreen Pky., Westport . . . . (203) 227-7761
Rosenthal Represents/L.A., CA/(213) 390-9595 . . . . **pages 82, 295, 349**

Rosenthal, Elise/L.A., CA/(213) 390-9596	**page 295**
Rosenthal, Marc/Malden Bridge, NY/(518) 766-4191	**page 151**
Rosner, Meryl/NYC, NY/(212) 398-9540	**page 234**
Ross, Barry/12 Fruit St., Northampton	(413) 585-8993
Ross, Ian/NYC	(212) 683-1362
Ross, Larry/53 Fairview Ave., Madison	(201) 377-6859
Ross, Richard/80 Eighth Ave., NYC	(212) 242-3900
Rossi, Pamela/Chicago	(312) 222-0504
Roth, Arnold, Inc./157 W. 57th St., NYC	(212) 333-7606
Roth, Larry I./3843 N. Hermitage, Chicago	(312) 880-0182
Roth, Robert G./Kings Park, NY/(516) 544-4232	**pages 216-217**
Roth, Roger/NYC, NY/(212) 873-3797	**pages 176-177**
Rother, Sue/NYC	(212) 697-8525
Rotoloni, Dave/Chicago, IL/(312) 644-6499	**page 173**
Rowe, Charles/133 Aronimink Dr., Newark	(302) 738-0641
Rowe, John/11718 Garrick Ave., Lake View Ter.	(818) 897-0004
Rownd, Jim/Mpls.	(612) 822-0650
Roy, Joanna/549 W. 123rd St., NYC	(212) 663-7876
Rubess, Balvis/260 Brunswick Ave., Toronto	(416) 927-7071
Ruddell, Gary/L.A.	(213) 934-3395
Rudnak, Theo/NYC, NY/(212) 490-2450	**page 324**
Ruff, Donna/15 Vincent Pl., Rowayton	(203) 866-8626
Ruffins, Reynold/15 W. 20th St., NYC	(212) 627-5220
Ruiz, Art/NYC, NY/(212) 254-4996	**page 249**
Ruppel, Rob/NYC	(212) 697-8525
Rush, John/Evanston, IL/(708) 869-2078	**page 77**
Russell, Bill/NYC	(212) 967-6443
Russo, Anthony/373 Benefit St., Providence	(401) 351-1568
Russo, David Anson/427 Gregory Ave.., Weehawken	(201) 330-8463
Ryan, Terry/NYC, NY/(212) 688-1080	**page 328**
Rybka, Stephen/3119 W. 83rd St., Chicago	(312) 737-1981
S.I. International/NYC, NY/(212) 254-4996	**pages 248-266**
Sabella, Jill/2607 Ninth Ave. W., Seattle	(206) 285-4794
Sacco, Kevin/NYC	(212) 779-9290
Sacks, Cal/721-B Heritage Village, Southbury	(803) 785-8570
Saffold, Joe/Atlanta, GA/(404) 231-2168	**page 145**
Saito, Masao/NYC	(212) 490-2450
Sakahara, Dick/Rancho Palos Verdes	(213) 541-8187
Saksa Art & Design, Inc./41 Union Sq. W., NYC	(212) 255-5539
Salentine, Katherine/L.A.	(213) 850-8222
Salerno, Steve/1020 E. John St., Seattle	(206) 324-4588
Salinas, Bruno, Assocs./NYC	(212) 925-3053
Salk, Larry/L.A., CA/(213) 934-1975	**page 228**
Salvati, Jim/L.A.	(213) 874-1661
Sams, B.B./225 E. Hightower Tr., Social Cir.	(404) 464-2956
Samuels, Mark/25 Minetta Ln., NYC	(212) 777-8580
Sanchez, Pat/6603 Baumgarten Dr., Dallas	(214) 328-2942
Sandford, John/NYC	(212) 369-1925
Sandler, Neil/L.A., CA/(213) 390-9596	**page 295**
Sandoz Studios/118 W. Kinzie St., Chicago	(312) 527-1800
Sands, Trudy/Dallas, TX/(214) 748-8663	**pages 334-337**
Sano, Kazuhiko/NYC	(212) 490-2450
Santa-Donato Studios, Inc./NYC	(212) 921-1550
Santore, Charles/NYC	(212) 889-3337
Saputo, Joe/4024 Jasper Rd., Springfield	(503) 746-1737
Saputo, Joe/L.A.	(213) 874-1661
Saran/S.F.	(415) 956-4750
Sasaki, Goro/NYC, NY/(212) 682-1490	**page 57**
Sasaki, Yutaka/Seattle	(206) 447-1600
Saso, Frank/1841 Lake Cypress Dr., Tampa Bay	(813) 725-4438
Sauriol, Brian/NYC	(212) 986-5680
Sawka, Jan/NYC	(212) 682-2462
Saxon, Charles/Westport	(203) 227-7806

Scarisbrick, Ed/NYC	(212) 677-9100
Schaefer, Robert/L.A.	(213) 931-7449
Schaffer, Amanda/Ramona, CA/(619) 788-0388	**page 382**
Schaller, Tom/2112 Broadway, NYC	(212) 362-5524
Scharf, Linda/240 Heath St., Boston	(617) 738-9294
Scheckman/Ferguson/NYC	(212) 473-8747
Scheffer Studios, Inc./Clearwater	(813) 736-6777
Scherman, John/310 E. 12th St., NYC	(212) 473-7237
Schermer-Gramm, Kathy/Sherman Oaks	(714) 247-6220
Scheuer, Philip A./126 Fifth Ave., NYC	(212) 620-0728
Schields, Gretchen/S.F.	(415) 956-4750
Schier, Fred/Northport	(516) 757-5609
Schiwall-Gallo, Linda/Ashfield	(413) 628-4735
Schleinkofer, David/NYC	(212) 986-5680
Schmidt, Chuck/NYC	(212) 677-9100
Schmidt, John F./Springfield, VA/(703) 750-0927	**page 239**
Schmidt, Urs/NYC, NY/(212) 473-8747	**page 358**
Schneider, Jonathan/NYC	(212) 459-4325
Schneider, R.M./NYC, NY/(212) 677-9100	**page 427**
Schofield, Glen A./Four Hillside Ave., Roseland	(201) 226-5597
Schorr, Kathy Staico/NYC	(212) 682-2462
Schorr, Todd/NYC	(212) 682-2462
Schottland, M./NYC	(212) 242-6367
Schreiber, Dana/36 Center St., Collinsville	(203) 693-6688
Schrier, Fred/Northport, NY/(516) 757-5609	**page 309**
Schroeder, Mark/66 Broadway, S.F.	(415) 421-3691
Schuchman, Bob/L.A.	(213) 937-3414
Schuler, Mark/5410 W. 68th St., Prairie Village	(913) 384-0646
Schumacher, Michael/Seattle	(206) 447-1600
Schumaker, Ward/466 Green St., S.F.	(415) 398-1060
Schumer, Arlen/382 Lafayete St., NYC	(212) 254-8242
Schuna, Frank/Mpls., MN/(612) 343-0104	**pages 153-157, 306**
Schuna, JoAnne/Mpls., MN/(612) 343-0432	**pages 153-157, 306**
Schwab, Michael/NYC	(212) 490-2450
Schwartz, Joanne/NYC	(212) 475-0440
Schwartz, Nancy/NYC	(212) 674-8080
Schweigert, Carol/Boston, MA/(617) 262-8909	**page 136**
Schweitzer, Dave/L.A.	(213) 874-1661
Schwinger, Larry/NYC	(212) 986-5680
Sciacca, Tom/NYC	(212) 421-0050
Scott, Bob/106 Lexington Ave., NYC	(212) 684-2409
Scott, Freda/S.F., CA/(415) 621-2992	**page 370**
Scott, Jack/899 S. Plymouth Ct., Chicago	(312) 922-1467
Scott, Jerry/152 W. Wisconsin Ave., Milwaukee	(414) 271-5210
Scott, Steven/L.A.	(213) 874-1661
Scott, Steven/S.F.	(415) 552-4252
Scrofani, Joseph/Two Akers Ave., Montvale	(201) 391-3956
Searle, Ronald/15 E. 76th St., NYC	(212) 288-8010
Seaver, Jeff/130 W. 24th St., NYC	(212) 741-2279
Seckler, Judy/12 S. Fair Oaks Ave., Pasadena	(818) 792-7358
Seiffert, Claire/NYC	(212) 398-9540
Seigel, Fran/515 Madison Ave., NYC	(212) 486-9644
Sell, Inc./Chicago, IL/(312) 565-2701	**page 147**
Sellers, Joseph/NY	(212) 221-8090
Seltzer, Isadore/NYC	(212) 741-2539
Sempé, J.J./NYC, NY/(212) 925-3053	**page 246**
Serafin, Marsha/Westport	(203) 226-4293
Severn, Jeff/Lafayette	(415) 283-7793
Sharp, Sandra/NYC	(212) 677-9100
Sharpe, Jim/21 Ten O'Clock Ln., Weston	(203) 226-9984
Sharpe, John/3952 W. 59th St., L.A.	(213) 290-1430
Shaw, Barclay/NYC	(212) 986-5680
Shaw, Ned/Bloomington, IN/(812) 333-2181	**page 170**

Shay, R.J./3301 S. Jefferson Ave., St. Louis . . . . (314) 773-9989
Shed, Greg/San Diego . . . . (619) 272-8147
Sheehan, Elizabeth/7928 Ruxway Rd., Baltimore . . . . (301) 828-4020
Shega, Marla/Cleveland . . . . (216) 661-4222
Sherwood, Stewart/625 Yonge St., Toronto . . . . (416) 925-8528
Shields, William/14 Wilmot, S.F. . . . . (415) 346-0376
Shiff, Andrew/153 Clinton St., Hopkinton . . . . (508) 435-5625
Shigley, Neil/427 72nd St., N. Bergen . . . . (201) 854-3737
Shirak, Stephen/32 S. Fairview Ave., Bayport . . . . (516) 472-6762
Shoemaker, Doug/206 N. First St., Mpls. . . . . (612) 332-2361
Shohet, Marti/NYC, NY/(212) 473-8747 . . . . **page 366**
Shoopack, Joseph/San Diego . . . . (619) 560-5824
Shore, Robert/41 Union Sq. W., NYC . . . . (212) 989-2396
Short, Kevin A./Mission Viejo . . . . (714) 472-1035
Short, Robbie/Atlanta . . . . (404) 266-1070
Shrier, Fred/Northport . . . . (516) 757-5609
Shumaker, Ward/S.F. . . . . (415) 552-4252
Siboldi, Carla/141 Bronte St., S.F. . . . . (415) 285-7472
Siciliano, Gerald/Nine Garfield Pl., Brooklyn . . . . (718) 636-4561
Siebel, Max/NYC . . . . (212) 986-5680
Siegel, Tema/NYC . . . . (212) 696-4680
Sienkowski, Laurie/199 Deer Run, Ada . . . . (616) 784-4003
Sigwart, Forrest L./1033 S. Orlando Ave., L.A. . . . . (213) 655-7734
Sikorski, Tony/2304 Clark Bldg., Pittsburgh . . . . (412) 391-8366
Silber, Maurice/183-07 69th Ave., Fresh Meadows . . . . (718) 969-7744
Silverman, Burton/324 W. 71st, NYC . . . . (212) 799-3399
Simon, Arline/Yonkers . . . . (914) 963-6906
Simonetti, Sally/1541 N. Laurel, L.A. . . . . (213) 654-3729
Simpson, Jerry/825 E. Arkansas Ave., Denver . . . . (303) 722-9593
Sims, Blanche/Weston . . . . (203) 226-7674
Simson, David/NYC . . . . (212) 807-0840
Sipp, Geo/Atlanta, GA/(404) 876-0312 . . . . **page 214**
Siracusa, Catherine/112 W. 74th St., NYC . . . . (212) 580-8084
Sirrell, T./Bartlett, IL/(708) 213-9003 . . . . **page 199**
Sisti, Jerry/34 Wiedemann Ave., Clifton . . . . (201) 478-7488
Sketchpad Studio/2605 Westgate, Arlington . . . . (817) 469-8151
Skidmore-Sahratian, Inc./2100 W. Big Beaver Rd., Troy . . . . (313) 643-6000
Skillins, Gunar/NYC, NY/(212) 682-1490 . . . . **page 72**
Slack, Chuck/NYC . . . . (212) 682-1490
Slackman, Chas. B./320 E. 57th St., NYC . . . . (212) 758-8233
Slater, Joann/1608 Via Machado, Palos Verdes Estates . . . . (213) 373-9090
Sloan, William A./NYC . . . . (212) 463-7025
Slonim, David/946 Central Ave., Plainfield . . . . (201) 561-1576
Small, David/NYC, NY/(212) 925-3053 . . . . **page 247**
Smallish, Craig/Chicago, IL/(312) 337-7770 . . . . **page 418**
Smallwood, Steve/Fort Lee, NJ/(201) 585-7923 . . . . **page 143**
Smeraldo, Ray/S.F. . . . . (415) 755-3366
Smith, Douglas/NYC . . . . (212) 683-1362
Smith, Jeffrey/710 Lakeshore Dr., Hewitt . . . . (201) 853-2262
Smith, Jere/Seattle . . . . (206) 443-0326
Smith, John C./Seattle . . . . (206) 447-1600
Smith, Kelly/500 Aurora Ave. N., Seattle . . . . (206) 623-2000
Smith, Laura/12 E. 14th St, NYC . . . . (212) 206-9162
Smith, Mark/San Diego . . . . (619) 284-8339
Smith, Pete/Rochester . . . . (716) 244-6956
Smith, Roy/St. Louis, MO/(314) 781-8851 . . . . **page 386**
Smith, Susan/66 Clarendon St., Boston . . . . (617) 266-4441
Smith, Vicki/Boston, MA/(617) 236-1920 . . . . **page 197**
Smollin, Michael J./NYC . . . . (212) 986-5680
Smythe, Danny/Atlanta, GA/(404) 873-2287 . . . . **page 414**
Snyder, Emilie/Oley . . . . (215) 987-3711
Sockwell, Helen/9921 Sockwell Dr. S.W., Huntsville . . . . (205) 881-8828
Soileau, Hodges/350 Flax Hill Rd., Norwalk . . . . (203) 852-0751

Sola, Luis/109 S. Mansfield Ave., L.A.	(213) 939-2770
Soldwedel, Kip/NYC	(212) 986-5680
Solie, John/NYC	(212) 986-5680
Soliski, Tom/NYC	(212) 925-0491
Solomon, Debra/536 W. 111st St., NYC	(212) 662-5619
Solomon, Richard/NYC	(212) 683-1362
Solway, Chuck/14526 Interlake Ave. N., Seattle	(206) 365-6139
Sonntag, Ned/51 Leroy St., NYC	(212) 924-1571
Sopin, Nan Grover/Nine Bradley Dr., Freehold	(201) 462-7154
Sorel, Edward/NYC	(212) 929-5590
Sormanti, Carla/NYC	(212) 799-2231
Sottung, George/111 Tower Rd., Brookfield Ctr.	(203) 775-6708
Soukup, James/Seward	(402) 643-2339
Soules, Dick/897 University, Grosse Pte.	(313) 881-0094
Sours, Michael/Dallas, TX/(214) 748-8663	**page 335**
South, Randy/2000 Clybourn Ave., Burbank	(818) 567-0863
Southerland, Kirstin/NYC	(212) 925-0491
Southern Belle/305 Peachtree Ave. N.E., Atlanta	(404) 266-1070
Souza, Diana/115 N. Cayuga, Ithaca	(607) 272-8388
Spacek, Peter/611 Broadway, NYC	(212) 505-6802
Spalenka, Greg/165 Perry, NYC	(212) 741-9064
Spaulding, Kevin/Chatsworth, CA/(818) 998-6091	**page 432**
Spear, Charles/Hoboken, NJ/(201) 798-6466	**page 74**
Spear, Jeffrey A./2590 Centinela Ave., L.A.	(213) 395-3939
Spector, Joel/NYC, NY/(212) 254-3527	**page 201**
Spectrum Studio, Inc./Mpls.	(612) 332-2361
Speer, Terry/St. Louis	(314) 961-1670
Speidel, Sandra/L.A.	(213) 850-8222
Speir, Nancy/181 Orchard Ave., Boyes Hot Springs	(707) 996-1703
Spellman, Susan/Wellesley Hills	(617) 235-8658
Spencer, Cindy/Weston	(203) 266-7674
Spengler, Ken/NYC, NY/(212) 673-1600	**page 406**
Spiece, Jim/1811 Woodhaven, Fort Wayne	(219) 747-3916
Spiers, Herbert/NYC, NY/(212) 254-4996	**pages 248-266**
Spohn, Cliff/59 Princess Wenonah Dr., Shelton	(203) 929-3239
Sposato, John/43 E. 22nd St., NYC	(212) 477-3909
Springer, Sally/317 S. Lawrence Ct., Phila.	(215) 925-9697
Stabin, Victor/100 W. 15th St., NYC	(212) 243-7688
Stahl, Nancy/194 Third Ave., NYC	(212) 475-0440
Stallard, Peter/NYC, NY/(212) 682-1490	**page 62**
Starace, Tom/54 W. 21st. St., NYC	(212) 633-1079
Starr, David/NYC, NY/(212) 254-0321	**page 104**
Starrett, Terri/NYC	(212) 243-4412
Staunton, James/3949 Third Ave., San Diego	(619) 272-8147
Steadman, Barbara/NYC	(212) 532-0928
Steadman, E.T./NYC	(212) 242-6367
Steam Inc./NYC	(212) 475-0440
Stearney, Mark/405 N. Wabash, Chicago	(312) 644-6669
Steele, Robert G./S.F.	(415) 552-4252
Stefanski, Janice Represents/2022 Jones St., S.F.	(415) 928-0457
Steiner, Joan/Bate Rd., Craryville	(518) 851-7199
Steirnagle, Michael/NYC	(212) 682-2462
Stephens, Craig/Culver City	(213) 558-3325
Stermer, Dugald/1844 Union St., S.F.	(415) 921-8281
Sternglass, Arno/NYC	(212) 989-7074
Sterrett, Jane/NYC, NY/(212) 929-2566	**page 393**
Steuer, Sharon/Westport	(203) 226-4293
Stevens, James R./5750 Fontenelle, Houston	(713) 723-1373
Stevens, John/53 Clearmeadow Dr., E. Meadow	(516) 735-6535
Stevens, Lynn/NYC	(212) 221-8090
Stevenson, James/Westport	(203) 227-7806
Stewart, Pat/NYC	(212) 532-0928
Stieferman, Guy/488 W. Regis Pl., Cordova	(901) 753-3729

Stillman, Susan/126 W. 71st St., NYC	(212) 724-5634
Stillman, Whit & Iréné/NYC, NY/(212) 925-3053	**pages 246-247**
Stine, Debra/6561 Greengable Ave., San Diego	(619) 272-8147
Stock, Michael/11951 Rothbury Dr., Richmond	(804) 794-6249
Stockman, Jack/Dallas	(214) 369-6990
Stokes, Fiona/Santa Monica, CA/(213) 394-5031	**page 193**
Storey, Barron/852 Union St., S.F.	(415) 776-3857
Story, Michael/Columbia, SC/(803) 256-8813	**page 99**
Strandquest, Shelly/NYC	(212) 727-2667
Street, David/1414 S. Pollard St., Arlington	(703) 521-6227
Streff, Michael/2766 Wasson Rd., Cincinnati	(513) 731-0360
Strogart, Alexander/NYC	(212) 697-8525
Stroster, Maria/2057 N. Sheffield, Chicago	(312) 525-2081
Stroud, Steve/Westport	(203) 226-4724
Struthers, Doug/NYC	(212) 490-2450
Struzan, Drew/Glendale	(714) 337-8847
Stubbs, Tommy/Atlanta, GA/(404) 255-1430	**page 348**
Studio/12 S. Fair Oaks, Pasadena	(818) 792-5252
Studio West/1005 W. Franklin Ave., Mpls.	(612) 871-2900
Stutzman, Mark/Mt. Lake Park, MD/(301) 334-4086	**page 158**
Suares, J.C./NYC	(212) 682-1490
Suchit, Stewart G./88 Summit Ave., Jersey City	(201) 860-9177
Sugarman, Tracy/21 Owenoke Park, Westport	(203) 227-2268
Sullivan, Steve/NYC	(212) 398-9540
Sullivan, Suzánne Hughes/NYC, NY/(212) 581-6112	**page 142**
Suma Design/448 Bryant St., S.F.	(415) 777-2120
Sumichrast, Józef/NYC	(212) 490-2450
Summers, Mark/NYC	(212) 683-1362
Sumpter, Will & Assocs./Atlanta, GA/(404) 874-2014	**pages 278-287**
Supley, Walter/620 Union St., Schenectady	(518) 370-0312
Sutton, Judith/NYC	(212) 925-0491
Swan, Sara/L.A., CA/(213) 935-4781	**page 396**
Swan, Susan/83 Saugatuck Ave., Westport	(203) 226-9104
Swanson, James/815 N. Marion, Oak Park	(312) 383-0141
Swanson, Michael/32 Skyacres Dr., Ontario	(519) 752-1116
Swanson, Robert/17 W. 45th St., NYC	(212) 840-8517
Sweet Represents/716 Montgomery St., S.F.	(415) 433-1222
Swendsen, Paul/4630 Fulton St., S.F.	(415) 668-1077
Sweny, Stephen/39 Davis Ave., White Plains	(914) 683-5653
Swimm, Tom/24241 Porto Bello, Laguna Niguel	(714) 496-6349
Sy, Thomas/NYC	(212) 398-9540
Sykes, Susan/NYC	(212) 727-2667
Szabo, Leslie/NYC	(212) 889-8777
Szumowski, Tom/NYC	(212) 682-1490
Taback, Simms/NYC	(212) 421-0050
Taffet, Marc/1638 James St., Merrick	(516) 623-9075
Takenaga, Steve/NYC	(212) 682-2462
Talaro, Lionel/NYC, NY/(212) 398-9540	**page 232**
Talcott, Julia/38 Linden St., Brookline	(617) 232-7306
Taleporos, Plato/NYC, NY/(212) 689-3138	**page 333**
Tamara, Inc./Atlanta, GA/(404) 262-1209	**page 338**
Tamura, David/153 E. 26th St., NYC	(212) 686-4559
Tanenbaum, Robert/5505 Corbin Ave., Tarzana	(818) 345-6741
Tarbox, Marla/4920 W. 123rd Pl., Hawthorne	(213) 644-0361
Tate, Clarke/Atlanta, GA/(404) 874-2014	**page 287**
Tatko, Thom/L.A.	(213) 470-2644
Taylor, B.K./24940 S. Cromwell, Franklin	(313) 626-8698
Taylor, C. Winston/Granada Hills, CA/(818) 363-5761	**page 111**
Taylor, Dahl/194 Third Ave., NYC	(212) 475-0440
Taylor, David/Indpls., IN/(317) 634-2728	**page 292**
Taylor, Joseph/2117 Ewing Ave., Evanston	(312) 328-2454
Taylor, Ken/22516 Meadow Brook Rd., Novi	(313) 963-8240
Taylor, Tim/Roseland	(201) 228-6869

Taylor, Toni L./1560 Leland Ave., Bronx	(212) 824-9252
Teach, Buz Walker/Sacramento, CA/(916) 454-3556	**page 220**
Tedesco, Michael/Brooklyn, NY/(718) 237-9164	**page 296**
Ten, Arnie/37 Forbus St., Poughkeepsie	(914) 485-8419
Tennant, Craig/NYC	(212) 688-4555
Tenud, Tish/Sacramento, CA/(916) 455-0569	**page 210**
Terreson, Jeffrey/NYC	(212) 986-5680
Tessler, John/Sacramento, CA/(916) 488-3425	**page 165**
Thelen, Mary/5907 Liano, Dallas	(214) 827-8073
Thomas, Maryann/L.A.	(213) 931-7449
Thomas, Sy/5011 Los Robles St., L.A.	(213) 254-3166
Thompson, Arthur/39 Prospect Ave., Pompton Plains	(201) 835-3534
Thompson, William D./15 Greenview Ave., Jamaica Plains	(617) 524-1805
Thomson, Bill/NYC	(212) 221-8090
Thomssen, Kate/1336 Scheffer Ave., St. Paul	(612) 698-9129
Thorn, Dick/NYC, NY/(212) 682-2462	**page 128**
Thornburgh, Bethann/1673 Columbia Rd., N.W., Wash. D.C.	(202) 667-0147
Thornton, Shelley/NYC	(212) 683-1362
Thorpe, Peter/254 Park Ave. S., NYC	(212) 477-0131
Tiani, Alex/Greenwich	(212) 243-4209
Tilley, Debbie/2051 Shadetree Ln., Escondido	(619) 432-6282
Tillinghast, David/4836 Via Colina, L.A.	(213) 258-4563
Timmons, Bonnie/Phila., PA/(215) 247-3556	**page 379**
Tise, Katherine/200 E. 78th St., NYC	(212) 570-9069
Toelke, Cathleen/NYC	(212) 929-5590
Toelke, Ron/Boston	(617) 266-3858
Tokyo, Max/236 W. 26th St., NYC	(212) 463-7025
Tom, Ket/1810 Sunset, Santa Barbara	(805) 689-0249
Torp, Cynthia/S.F.	(415) 552-4252
Torrisi, Gary/80 Elm St., Methuen	(508) 683-0877
Trachok, C.A./NYC	(212) 677-9100
Traynor, Elizabeth/Atlanta, GA/(404) 875-1363	**page 302**
Traynor, Elizabeth/Tampa Bay, FL/(813) 725-4438	**page 302**
Treatner, Meryl/Phila.	(215) 627-2297
Trondsen, Bob/NYC	(212) 727-2667
Trousil, Danna/371 Imperial Way, Daly City	(415) 755-8568
Truxaw, Dick/1709 W. 97th St., Overland Park	(913) 383-1555
Tsui, George & Selena/2250 Elliot St., Merrick	(516) 223-8474
Tucker, Ezra/1865 Old Mission Dr., Solvang	(805) 686-1210
Tughan, James/NYC, NY/(212) 473-8747	**page 361**
Tull, Bobbi/1210 N. Chambliss, Alexandria	(703) 354-4322
Tunstull, Glenn/NYC	(212) 673-1600
Turchyn, Sandie/L.A.	(213) 652-9561
Turk, Stephen/962 Hilgard Ave., L.A.	(213) 208-1620
Turner, Clay/NYC, NY/(212) 682-1490	**page 67**
Uhl, David/2536 Gilpin, Denver	(303) 860-7070
Ulay, Ayse/109 S. Grand Oaks Ave., Pasadena	(818) 796-4615
Underhill, Gary/366 Bellville Ave., Bloomfield	(201) 680-9554
Unruh, Jack/Atlanta, GA/(404) 255-1430	**page 343**
Uram, Lauren/251 Washington Ave., Brooklyn	(718) 789-7717
Urbanovic, Jackie/3249 Hennepin Ave. S., Mpls.	(612) 822-5709
Utley, Tom/Cleveland	(216) 661-4222
Vaccarello, Paul/400 E. Ohio, Chicago	(312) 664-2233
Vahaid/S.F.	(415) 552-4252
Vainisi, Jenny/NYC	(212) 673-1600
Valdez, Patti/1246 E. Cambridge Ave., Phoenix	(602) 277-3845
Valen Associates/950 Klish Way, Del Mar	(619) 259-5774
Van Munching, Paul/104 W. 70th St., NYC	(212) 496-2097
Van Schelt, Perry/L.A.	(213) 851-8262
Van Seters, Kim/Wayne, NJ/(201) 694-5502	**page 90**
VanKanegan, Jeff/Camp Point	(217) 455-4171
VanSchelt, Perry/4495 Balsam Ave., Salt Lake City	(801) 266-7097
Vance, Steve/1955 Cerro Gordo St., L.A.	(213) 662-3441

Vance, Wright, Adams & Assocs./930 N. Lincoln Ave., Pittsburgh ... (412) 322-1800
Vanderbeek, Don/Dayton ... (513) 433-8383
Vann, Bill Studio/1706 S. Eighth St., St. Louis ... (314) 231-2322
Vargö, Kurt/NYC, NY/(212) 529-6389 ... **page 429**
Varner, Charles/3100 Carlisle, Dallas ... (214) 871-2779
Vaughan, Martha/3751 W. St., N.W., Wash. D.C. ... (202) 333-1299
Vaughn, Rob/600 Curtiss Pkwy., Miami Spgs. ... (305) 885-1292
Vaux, Jacquie/NYC ... (212) 686-3514
Ventura, Marco/16 Crooked Tree Ln., Princeton ... (609) 683-5217
Verkaaik, Ben/NYC ... (212) 355-0910
Verkouteren, Dana/4801 Essex Ave., Chevy Chase ... (301) 652-4492
Vernaglia, Michael/1251 Bloomfield St., Hoboken ... (201) 792-4894
Vernon, Don/29320 Poppy Meadows, Canyon County ... (805) 251-8078
Verougstraete, Randy/Santa Monica ... (213) 451-1910
Verzaal, Danny/NYC ... (212) 799-6532
Viannias, Vicki/NYC ... (212) 673-1600
Vibbert, Carolyn/3911 Bagley Ave. N, Seattle ... (206) 634-3473
Vidro, Michelle/100 Bella Vista Way, S.F. ... (415) 586-8644
Viglione, Dawn/384 Elm St., Monroe ... (203) 452-7962
Vigon, Jay/11833 Brookdale Ln., Studio City ... (213) 654-4771
Vigon, Larry/L.A. ... (213) 931-7449
Villani, Ron/Chicago ... (312) 329-1370
Vissichelli, Joe/45 Queen St., Freeport ... (516) 546-0310
Viviano, Sam/NYC, NY/(212) 242-1471 ... **page 98**
Vizbar, Milda/NYC ... (212) 675-6293
Von Haeger, Arden/NYC ... (212) 354-5962
Von Schmidt, Eric/Glendale, CA/(818) 246-7893 ... **page 242**
Voo, Rhonda/8800 Venice Blvd., L.A. ... (213) 839-1532
Vuksanovich, Fran/3224 N. Nordica, Chicago ... (312) 283-2138
Wacholder, Lisa Roma/2613 Ave. J, Brooklyn ... (718) 951-7218
Wack, Jeff/L.A. ... (213) 651-3706
Waggoner, Dug/740 Gilman St., Berkeley ... (415) 524-6288
Wagner, Brett/L.A. ... (213) 470-2644
Wagoner, Jae/L.A., CA/(213) 392-4877 ... **page 331**
Waitzman, William/265 Riverside Dr., NYC ... (212) 662-2645
Wald, Carol/Detroit ... (212) 737-4559
Waldman, Bryna & Neil/47 Woodlands Ave., White Plains ... (914) 693-2782
Waldrep, Richard L./Baltimore ... (301) 243-0211
Waldron, Sarah/NYC ... (212) 925-0491
Walker, Ken/19 W. Lenwood St., Kansas City ... (816) 931-7975
Walker, Norman/NYC ... (212) 755-1365
Wall, Pam/NYC, NY/(212) 682-1490 ... **page 63**
Wallman, Paul/NYC ... (212) 682-1490
Walsh, Terry/NYC ... (212) 243-4412
Walter, Nancy Lee/Elmhurst ... (708) 833-3898
Walters, Steve/L.A. ... (213) 931-7449
Wanamaker, Jo Ann/225 W. 86th St., NYC ... (212) 724-1786
Wander, David/156 Bowery, NYC ... (212) 431-7636
Wangro, Gaynor/NYC ... (212) 727-2667
Ward, John/Freeport, NY/(516) 546-2906 ... **page 400**
Wariner, David/Louisville ... (502) 561-0737
Warnick, Elsa/Portland, OR/(503) 228-2659 ... **page 198**
Warter, Fred/Sherman Oaks, CA/(818) 995-1935 ... **page 219**
Wasserman, Amy L./Framingham ... (508) 879-7679
Wasserman, Randie/NYC, NY/(212) 545-9155 ... **page 206**
Wasson, Cameron/Four S. Portland Ave., Brooklyn ... (718) 875-8277
Watkinson, Brent/L.A. ... (213) 874-1661
Watson, Karen/100 Churchill Ave., Arlington ... (617) 641-1420
Watson, Richard Jesse/Murphys ... (209) 728-2701
Watts, Mark ... (215) 343-8490
Watts, Sharon/NYC, NY/(212) 534-4177 ... **page 168**
Watts, Stan/NYC, NY/(212) 682-2462 ... **page 132**
Weakley, Mark/NYC, NY/(212) 473-8747 ... **page 359**

Weaver, Robert/NYC	(212) 989-7074
Webber, Rosemary/644 Noank Rd., Mystic	(203) 536-3091
Weber, Robert/950 Klish Way, Del Mare	(619) 259-5774
Weber, Tricia/NYC, NY/(212) 779-6532	**pages 413-415**
Wehrman, Richard/247 N. Goodman St., Rochester	(716) 359-1492
Wehrman, Vicki/22 Nelson St., Rochester	(716) 244-6956
Weiland, Garison/61 Pershing Rd., Jamaica Plain	(617) 983-9251
Weiman, Jon/NYC, NY/(212) 787-3184	**page 391**
Weisbecker, Philippe/476 Broadway, NYC	(212) 966-6051
Weisser, Carl Silhouettes/38 Livingston St., Brooklyn	(718) 834-0952
Welker, Gaylord/NYC	(212) 673-1600
Weller, Don/Park City, UT/(801) 649-9859	**page 331**
Weller, Linda/Weston	(203) 226-7674
Wells, Peter/Milwaukee	(414) 272-5525
Wells, Susan/Atlanta, GA/(404) 255-1430	**pages 342-349**
Wende, Philip/Atlanta, GA/(404) 874-2014	**page 286**
Wenzel, Paul/NYC, NY/(212) 254-4996	**page 259**
Werblun, Steve/Culver City	(213) 558-3325
Westerberg, Rob/34-64 Hillside Ave., NYC	(212) 567-1884
Weston, Al/Westport	(203) 226-4724
Weston, Will/NYC	(212) 682-2462
Westphal, Ken/7616 Fairway, Prairie Village	(913) 381-8399
Wetzel, Marcia/Atlanta	(404) 872-7980
Wexler, Ed/1351 Ocean Front Walk, Santa Monica	(213) 451-1910
Whipple, Rick/6934 Mistletoe Dr., Dallas	(214) 327-7889
White III, Charlie/NYC	(212) 929-5590
White, Debra/Four S. Portland Ave., Brooklyn	(718) 797-5115
Whitehead, S.B./304 Seventh Ave., Brooklyn	(718) 768-0803
Whitesides, Kim/NYC	(212) 490-2450
Whitney, Jack/St. Louis, MO/(314) 781-8851	**page 386**
Whitney, Mike/St. Louis, MO/(314) 781-8851	**page 386**
Whitver, Harry K./Nashville	(615) 320-1795
Wickart, Mark A./Lisle	(708) 369-0164
Wickart, Terry/3881 64th St., Holland	(616) 335-3511
Wickenden, Nadine/Brooklyn	(718) 624-1906
Wicks, Ren/L.A.	(213) 937-4472
Wickstrom, Steve/Culver City	(213) 558-3325
Widener, Terry/NYC, NY/(212) 873-3797	**page 175**
Wiemann, Roy/55 E. Houston St., NYC	(212) 431-3793
Wilcox, David/135 E. 54th St., NYC	(212) 421-0050
Wiley, David/1535 Green St., S.F.	(415) 441-1623
Willey, Chris/3202 Windsor, Kansas City	(816) 483-1475
Williams Group, The/Atlanta, GA/(404) 837-2287	**pages 413-415**
Williams Group, The/NYC, NY/(212) 779-6532	**pages 413-415**
Williams, Dean/Seattle	(206) 447-1600
Williams, Phillip/Atlanta, GA/(404) 873-2287	**pages 413-415**
Williams, Jack/Richmond	(804) 272-8271
Williams, Oliver/66 Madison Ave., NYC	(212) 545-0274
Williams, Richard/NYC	(212) 741-2539
Williams, Tim/Alpharetta, GA/(404) 475-3146	**page 162**
Williams-Foster/1149 Dannell, St. Louis	(314) 436-1121
Wilson, Amanda/346 E. 20th St., NYC	(212) 260-7567
Wilson, Ann/Weston	(203) 226-7674
Wilson, Linden/St. Louis	(314) 241-4014
Wilson, Rowland B./Ranco LaCosta	(619) 944-3631
Wimmer, Chuck/Cleveland	(216) 526-2820
Wimmer, Mike/Norman, OK/(405) 329-0478	**page 371**
Winborg, Larry/NYC	(212) 221-8090
Winchester, Linda/228 Clinton St., Brooklyn Heights	(718) 625-1930
Wink, David/864 Charles Allen Dr., Atlanta	(404) 874-3389
Winston, Jeannie/8800 Venice Blvd., L.A.	(213) 655-0998
Winterbauer, Michael-James/280 S. Euclid Ave., Pasadena	(818) 799-4998
Winters, Greg/2139 Pinecrest Dr., Altadena	(818) 798-7666

Wisenbaugh, Jean/NYC	(212) 929-5590
Witte, Michael/NYC	(212) 889-3337
Wolf, Elizabeth/3717 Alton Pl., N.W., Wash. D.C.	(202) 686-0179
Wolf, Leslie/Chicago	(312) 988-4234
Wolf, Paul/900 First Ave. S., Seattle	(206) 623-1459
Wolfe, Bruce/NYC	(212) 475-0440
Wolfe, Deborah Represents/Phila., PA/(215) 232-6666	**pages 419-423**
Wolff, Punz/151 E. 20th St., NYC	(212) 254-5705
Womersley, David/NYC	(212) 986-5680
Wong, Benedict Norbert/333 Broadway, S.F.	(415) 781-7590
Wong, Jean/4160 N. Craftsman Ct, Scotsdale	(602) 423-1500
Wood, Clare/54 Berkeley Pl., Brooklyn	(718) 783-3734
Woodend, Jim/NYC	(212) 697-8525
Woodman, Bill/Westport	(203) 227-7806
Woods, Perry/3343 E. Fairmont, Tucson	(602) 323-1615
Worcester, Mary/Mpls.	(612) 822-0650
Wray, Greg/L.A.	(213) 934-3395
Wray, Wendy/194 Third Ave., NYC	(212) 475-0440
Wright & Co./32 Eugene, Mill Valley	(415) 389-6404
Wright, Jonathan/405 N. Wabash, Chicago	(312) 329-1370
Wright, Ted/St. Louis	(314) 241-4014
Write Direction, The/110 Alpine Way, Athens	(404) 546-5058
Wrobel, Cindy/415 Alta Dena, St. Louis	(314) 721-4467
Wu, Kong/NYC	(212) 688-4555
Wynne, Bob/815 S. Central Ave., Glendale	(818) 241-9903
Wynne, Patricia J./446 Central Park W., NYC	(212) 865-1059
Xavier, Roger/3227 Del Amo Blvd., Lakewood	(213) 531-9531
Y. Arts Illustration/18888 Hwy. 299, Blue Lake	(707) 668-5582
Yadin, Hanan/L.A., CA/(213) 826-1332	**page 397**
Yamada, Kenny/Berkeley, CA/(415) 841-4415	**page 295**
Yaniger, Derek/Atlanta	(404) 266-1070
Yanish, Mary/3887 Bostwick St., L.A.	(213) 263-6040
Yankus, Marc/570 Hudson St., NYC	(212) 242-6334
Yavorsky, Frederick Creative Services/2300 Walnut St., Phila.	(215) 564-6540
Yealdhall, Gary/Pheonix	(602) 252-5072
Yee, Josie/211 W. 20th St., NYC	(212) 206-1260
Yee, Terry/Mesa, AZ/(602) 962-7781	**page 85**
Yesawich & Welsh/Orlando, FL/(407) 647-3001	**page 82**
Yip, Eddie/85 N. Raymond Ave., Pasadena	(818) 793-4120
Yip, Jennie/625 E. 82nd St., Brooklyn	(718) 236-0349
York, Judy/NYC	(212) 697-8525
Youmans, Jill Represents/4040 Lyceum Ave., L.A.	(213) 850-0995
Young, Bruce/Atlanta	(404) 266-1070
Young, Eddie/Santa Monica, CA/(213) 394-5031	**page 192**
Young, Lisa/23003 Lakeview Dr., Mountlake Ter.	(206) 778-7114
Yourke, Oliver/525A Sixth Ave., Brooklyn	(718) 965-0609
Zann, Nicky/155 W. 68th St., NYC	(212) 724-5027
Zavell, Bonnie/1007 Gulf Rd., Elyria	(216) 365-3477
Zeldich, Arieh/NYC	(212) 644-2020
Zick, Brian/194 Third Ave., NYC	(212) 475-0440
Ziegler, Jack/Westport	(203) 227-7806
Ziemienski, Dennis/NYC	(212) 925-0491
Ziering, Bob/151 W. 74th St., NYC	(212) 873-0034
Zimmerman, Bob/530 First St., NYC	(718) 768-2664
Zimmerman, Jerry/124 W. 18th St., NYC	(212) 620-7774
Zink, Deborah/Tahoe City	(916) 583-7346
Zinn, Ron/117 Village Dr., Jericho	(516) 822-3755
Zito, Andy/135 S. La Brea, L.A.	(213) 931-1182
Zudeck, Darryl/35 W. 92nd St., NYC	(212) 663-9454
Zumbo, Matt/NYC	(212) 682-1490
Zurcher, Micki/6124½ Buena Vista Ter., L.A.	(213) 256-0135
Zwarenstien, Alex/NYC	(212) 697-6170
Zwolak, Paul/Toronto, Ontario/(416) 531-6253	**page 297**

We put our artists on a pedestal.

We put our clients on a pedestal.

Then we run like hell between the pedestals.

© Copyright 1991 BERNSTEIN & ANDRIULLI, INC.

BERNSTEIN &
ANDRIULLI INC
REPRESENTATIVES
60 EAST 42ND STREET
NEW YORK NY 10165
FAX [212] 286-1890
TEL [212] 682-1490

MARY ANN LASHER

BERNSTEIN &
ANDRIULLI INC
REPRESENTATIVES
60 EAST 42ND STREET
NEW YORK NY 10165
FAX [212] 286-1890
TEL [212] 682-1490

© Copyright 1991 BERNSTEIN & ANDRIULLI, INC.

CHRIS MOORE

© Copyright 1991 BERNSTEIN & ANDRIULLI, INC.

BERNSTEIN &
ANDRIULLI INC
REPRESENTATIVES
60 EAST 42ND STREET
NEW YORK NY 10165
FAX [212] 286-1890
TEL [212] 682-1490

VICTOR GADINO

© 1990 LUCASFILM LTD.
© Copyright 1991 BERNSTEIN & ANDRIULLI, INC.  

**BERNSTEIN &
ANDRIULLI INC** REPRESENTATIVES
60 EAST 42ND STREET
NEW YORK NY 10165
FAX [212] 286-1890
TEL [212] 682-1490

GORO SASAKI

© Copyright 1991 BERNSTEIN & ANDRIULLI, INC.

BERNSTEIN &
ANDRIULLI INC
REPRESENTATIVES
60 EAST 42ND STREET
NEW YORK NY 10165
FAX (212) 286-1890
TEL (212) 682-1490

LAURA PHILLIPS

© Copyright 1991 BERNSTEIN & ANDRIULLI, INC.

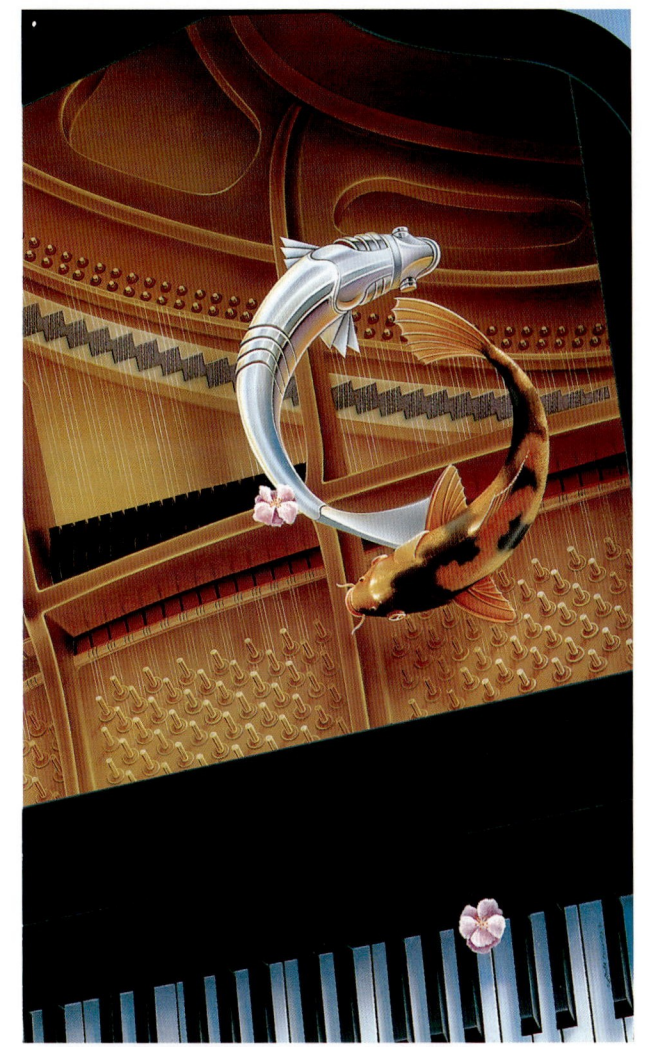

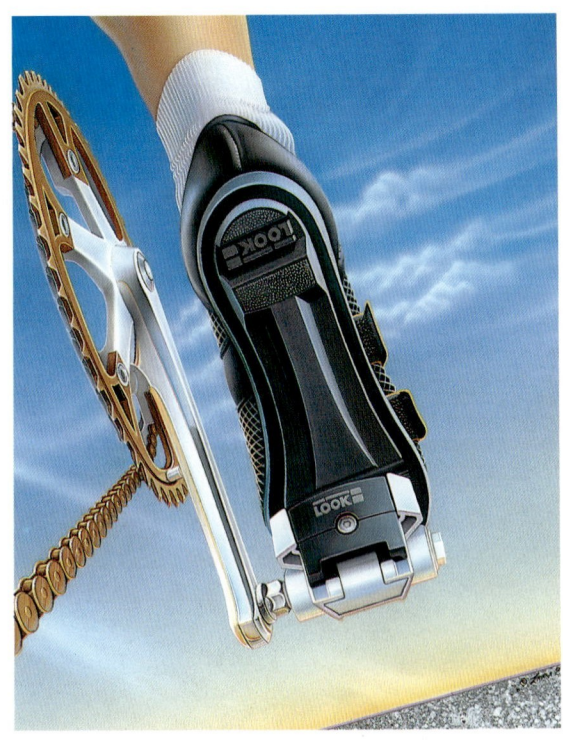

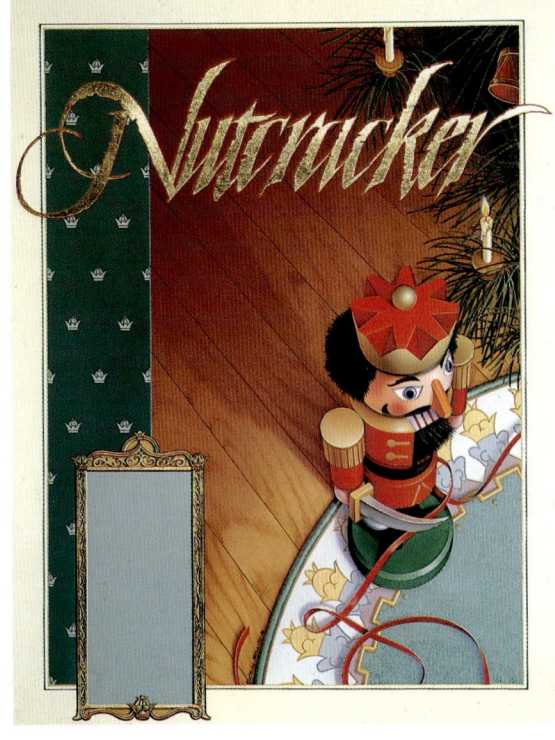

BERNSTEIN & ANDRIULLI INC
REPRESENTATIVES
60 EAST 42ND STREET
NEW YORK NY 10165
FAX [212] 286-1890
TEL [212] 682-1490

JOHN HARWOOD

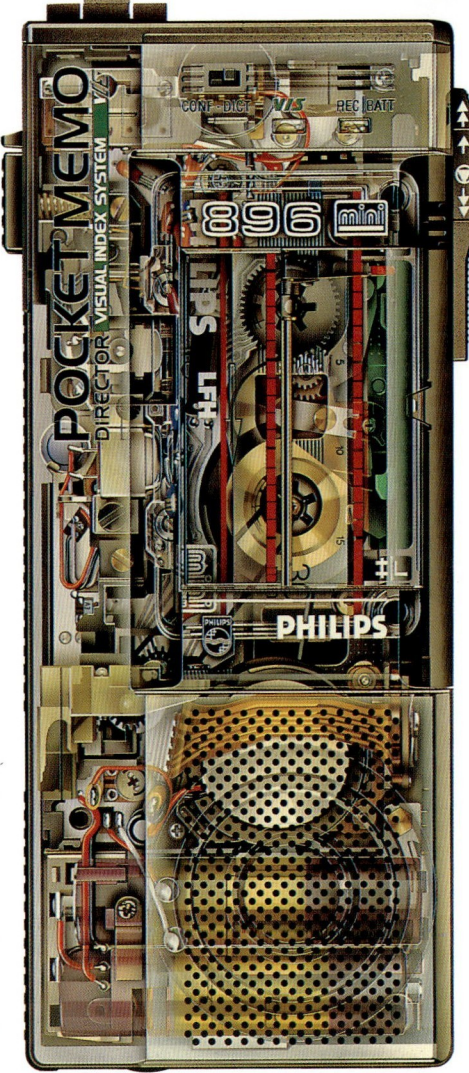

© Copyright 1991 BERNSTEIN & ANDRIULLI, INC.

BERNSTEIN &
ANDRIULLI INC
REPRESENTATIVES
60 EAST 42ND STREET
NEW YORK NY 10165
FAX [212] 286-1890
TEL [212] 682-1490

59

CREATIVE CAPERS

CHARACTER DEVELOPMENT

WORKING WITH ESTABLISHED CHARACTERS

CREATING ORIGINAL CHARACTERS

© Copyright 1991 BERNSTEIN & ANDRIULLI, INC.

BERNSTEIN &
ANDRIULLI INC
REPRESENTATIVES
60 EAST 42ND STREET
NEW YORK NY 10165
FAX [212] 286-1890
TEL [212] 682-1490

RICK BROWN

minnie 'n' me © THE WALT DISNEY COMPANY

© Copyright 1991 BERNSTEIN & ANDRIULLI, INC.

© THE WALT DISNEY COMPANY

BERNSTEIN &
ANDRIULLI INC
REPRESENTATIVES
60 EAST 42ND STREET
NEW YORK NY 10165
FAX (212) 286-1890
TEL (212) 682-1490

PETER STALLARD

BERNSTEIN &
ANDRIULLI INC
REPRESENTATIVES
60 EAST 42ND STREET
NEW YORK NY 10165
FAX [212] 286-1890
TEL [212] 682-1490

© Copyright 1991 BERNSTEIN & ANDRIULLI, INC.

PAM WALL

BERNSTEIN &
ANDRIULLI INC
REPRESENTATIVES
60 EAST 42ND STREET
NEW YORK NY 10165
FAX (212) 286-1890
TEL (212) 682-1490

63

BETTE LEVINE

BERNSTEIN &
ANDRIULLI INC
REPRESENTATIVES
60 EAST 42ND STREET
NEW YORK NY 10165
FAX [212] 286-1890
TEL [212] 682-1490

JON ELLIS

BERNSTEIN &
ANDRIULLI INC
REPRESENTATIVES
60 EAST 42ND STREET
NEW YORK NY 10165
FAX [212] 286-1890
TEL [212] 682-1490

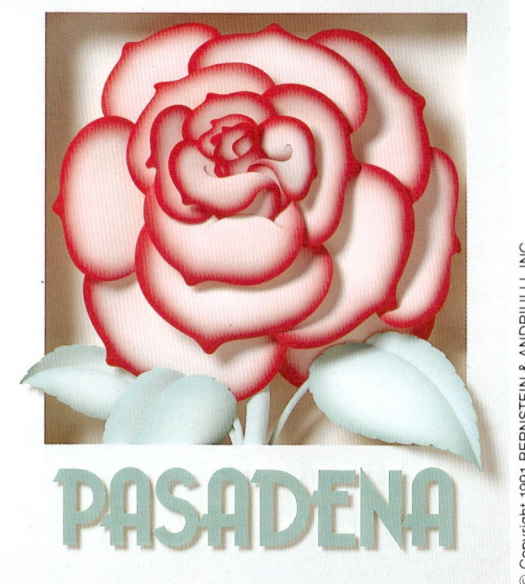

JEFF NISHINAKA

© Copyright 1991 BERNSTEIN & ANDRIULLI, INC.

BERNSTEIN & ANDRIULLI INC
REPRESENTATIVES
60 EAST 42ND STREET
NEW YORK NY 10165
FAX [212] 286-1890
TEL [212] 682-1490

CLAY TURNER

BERNSTEIN &
ANDRIULLI INC
REPRESENTATIVES
60 EAST 42ND STREET
NEW YORK NY 10165
FAX [212] 286-1890
TEL [212] 682-1490

67

RON FLEMING

THE NEXT GENERATION

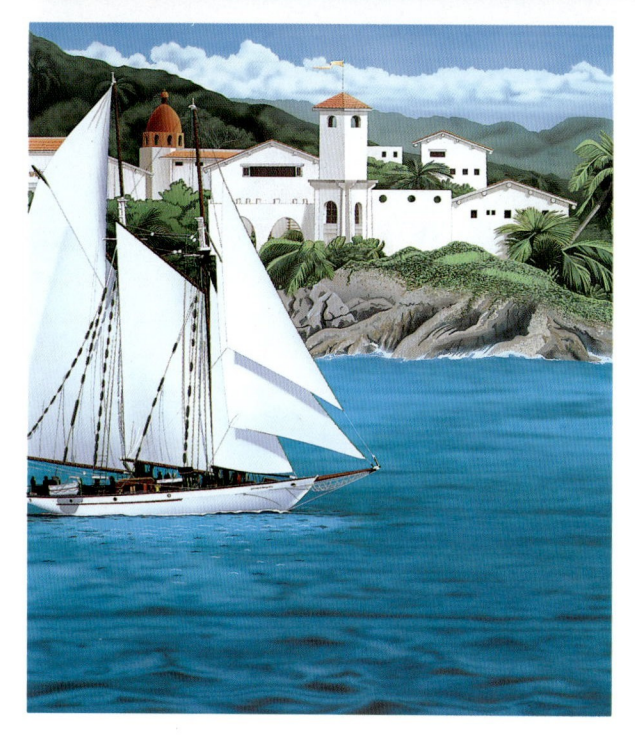

© Copyright 1991 BERNSTEIN & ANDRIULLI, INC.

BERNSTEIN & ANDRIULLI INC
REPRESENTATIVES
60 EAST 42ND STREET
NEW YORK NY 10165
FAX [212] 286-1890
TEL [212] 682-1490

CRAIG NELSON

BERNSTEIN &
ANDRIULLI INC
REPRESENTATIVES
60 EAST 42ND STREET
NEW YORK NY 10165
FAX (212) 286-1890
TEL (212) 682-1490

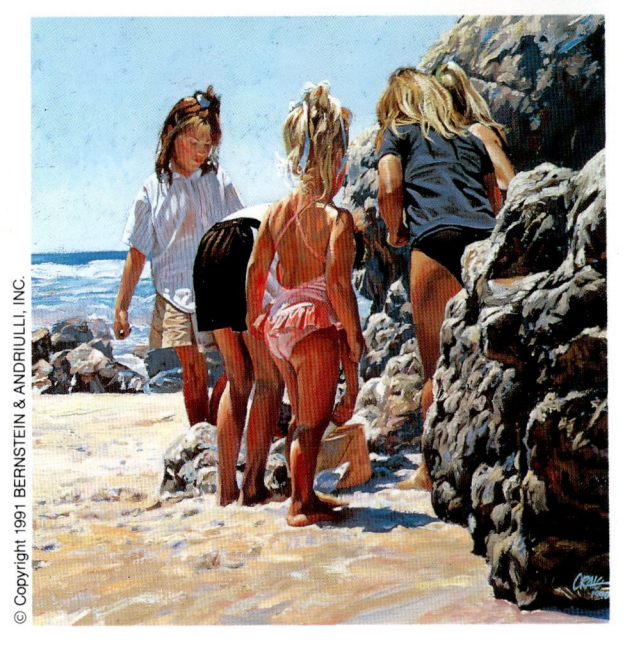

69

PETE MUELLER

BERNSTEIN & ANDRIULLI INC
REPRESENTATIVES
60 EAST 42ND STREET
NEW YORK NY 10165
FAX [212] 286-1890
TEL [212] 682-1490

© Copyright 1991 BERNSTEIN & ANDRIULLI, INC.

PAT BAILEY

BERNSTEIN &
ANDRIULLI INC
REPRESENTATIVES
60 EAST 42ND STREET
NEW YORK NY 10165
FAX [212] 286-1890
TEL [212] 682-1490

© Copyright 1991 EERNSTEIN & ANDRIULLI, INC.

71

GUNAR SKILLINS

© Copyright 1991 BERNSTEIN & ANDRIULLI, INC.

BERNSTEIN &
ANDRIULLI INC
REPRESENTATIVES
60 EAST 42ND STREET
NEW YORK NY 10165
FAX [212] 286-1890
TEL [212] 682-1490

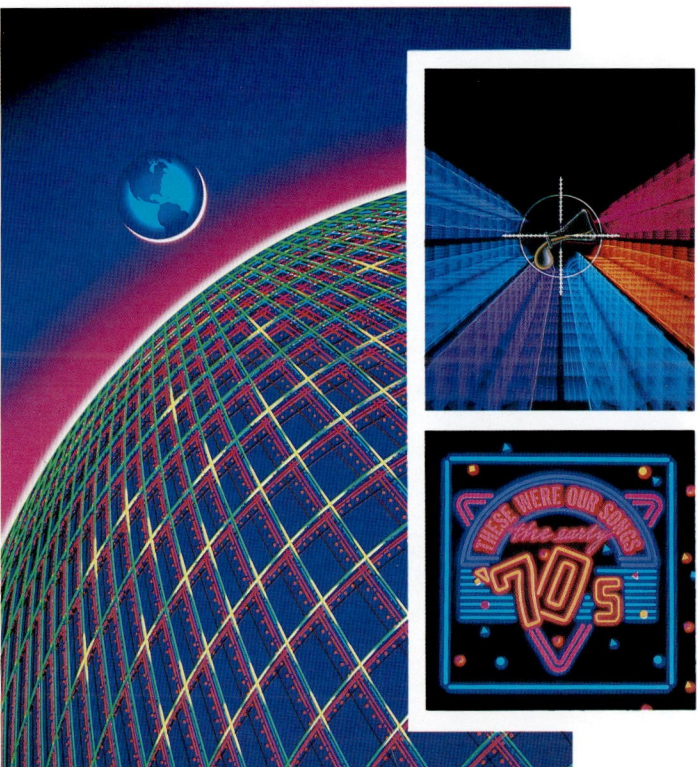

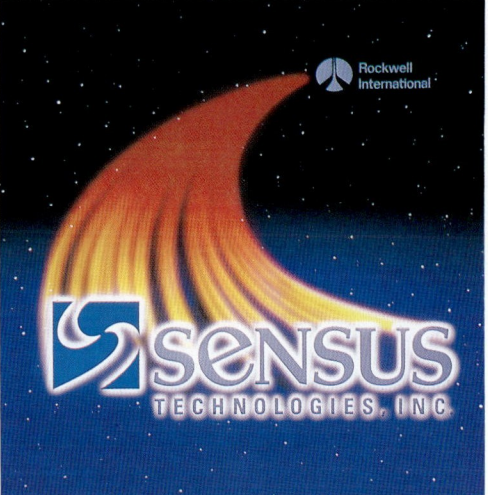

BILL MORSE

BERNSTEIN &
ANDRIULLI INC
REPRESENTATIVES
60 EAST 42ND STREET
NEW YORK NY 10165
FAX [212] 286-1890
TEL [212] 682-1490

73

SPEAR

CHARLES SPEAR
456 NINTH ST.
HOBOKEN, NJ
UNIT. 2 07030
201-798-6466
FAX: 798-9117

HARRY G BATES JR.

570 WESTMINSTER RD. #E10 BKLYN, NY 11230 (718) 693-6304

Zita Asbaghi

104-40 QUEENS BLVD. FOREST HILLS NEW YORK 11375 • (718) 275-1995

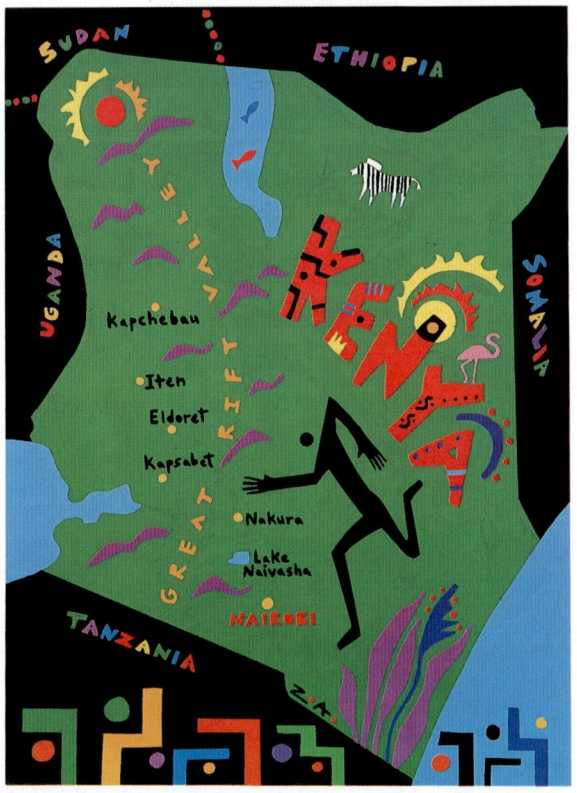

THE NEW AMERICAN CORPORATION

PAINTED BY

JOHN RUSH

123 KEDZIE ST. EVANSTON, IL. 60202

(708) 869-2078

AUTUMN

RICHARD A. OLSON
85 GRAND STREET, NEW YORK, NY • (212) 925-1820

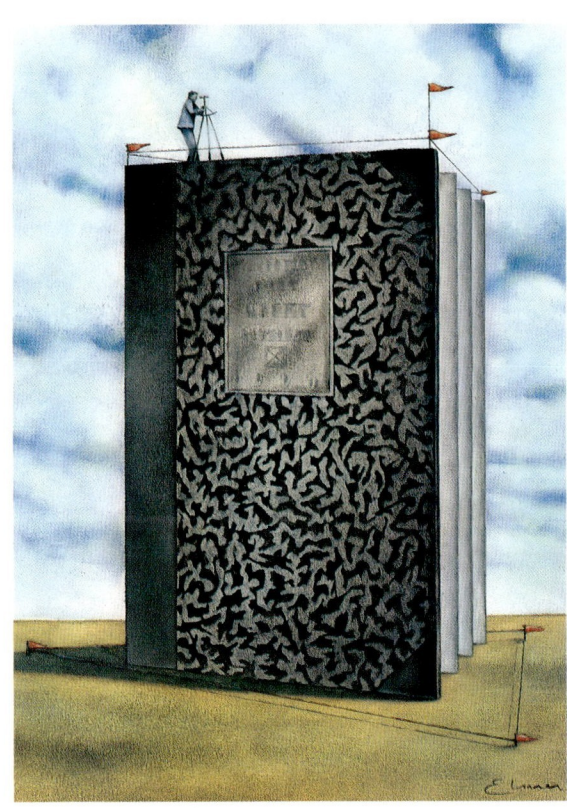

RICHARD ELMER
504 EAST 11th STREET NYC. 10009   (212) 598-4024

MIN JAE HONG 212•674•4320

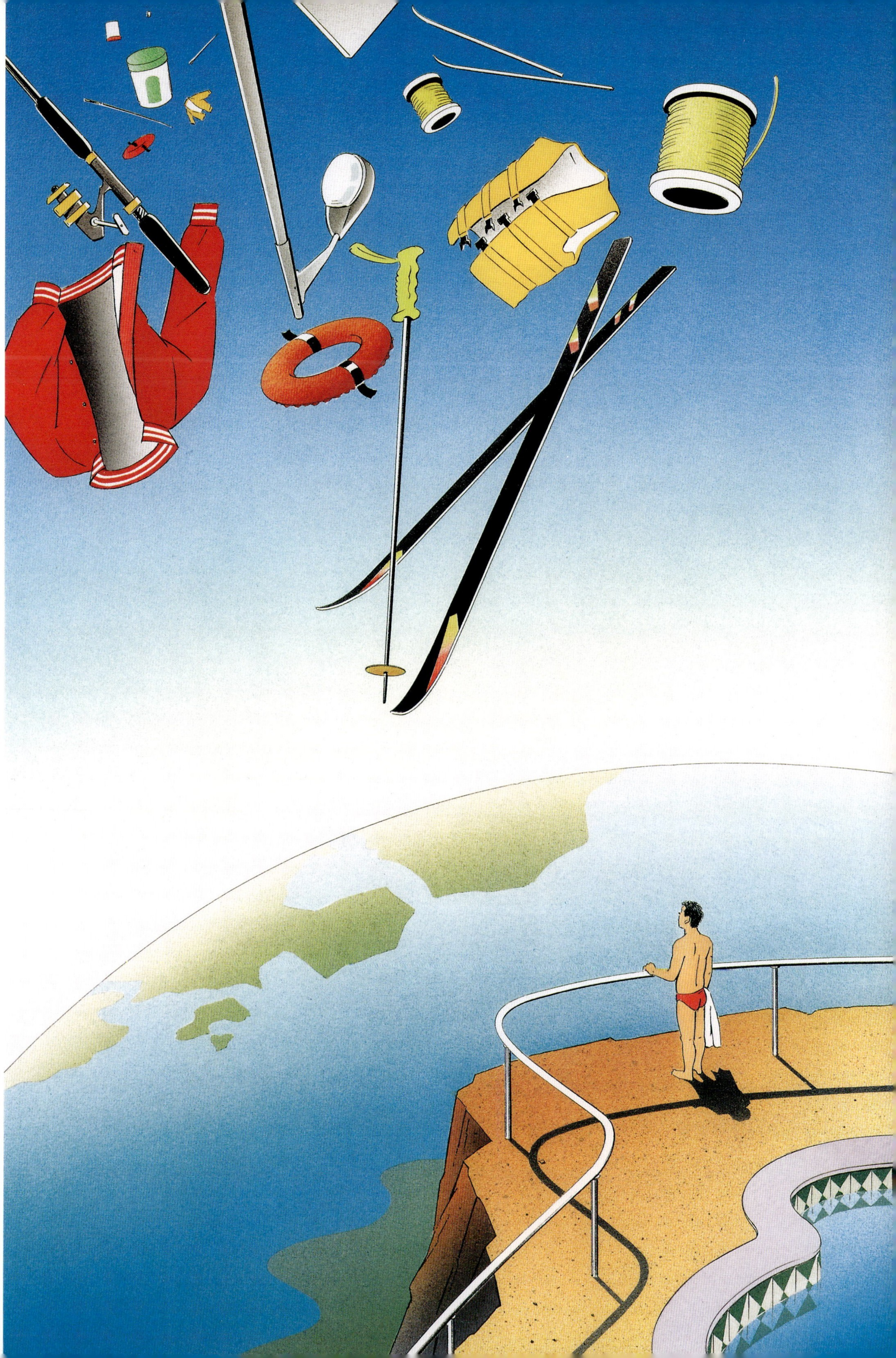

REGGIE HOLLADAY
ILLUSTRATION

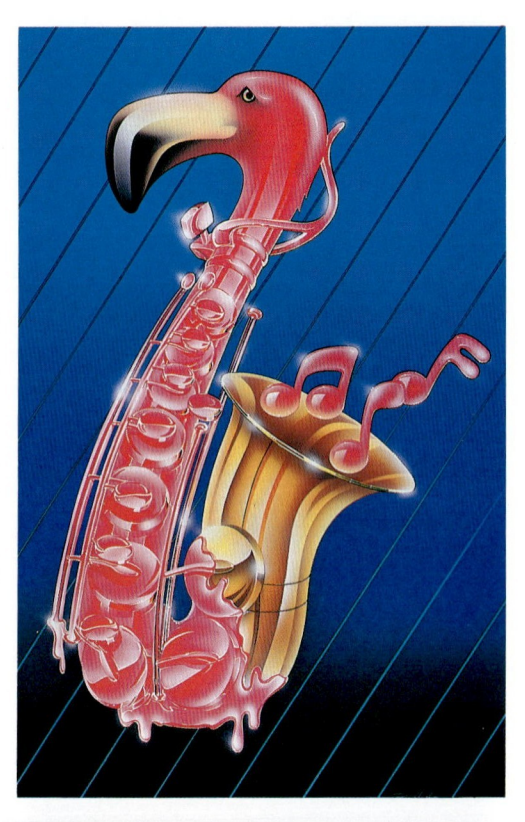

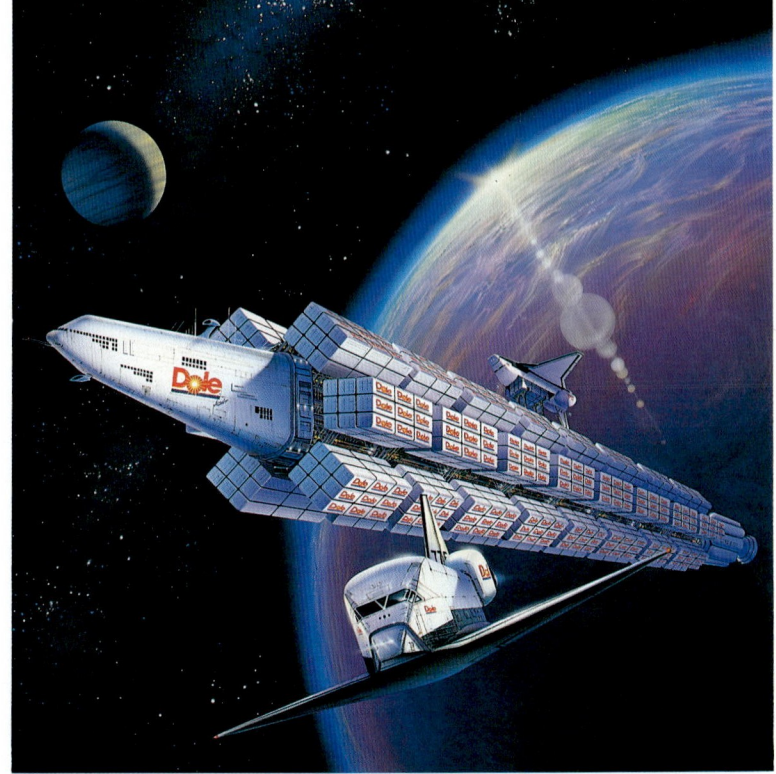

7395 N.W. 51 ST., LAUDERHILL, FL 33319
305 • 749 • 9031

REPRESENTED BY:

ORLANDO • YESAWICH & WELSH 407 • 647 • 3001

CHICAGO • CREATIVE SOURCE 312 • 649 • 9777

LOS ANGELES • ROSENTHAL REPRESENTS 213 • 390 • 9595

SID DANIELS

(212) 673-6520

J.T. illustrations

J.T. Morrow   (415) 355-7899
220 Kavanaugh Way/ Pacifica, Ca. 94044

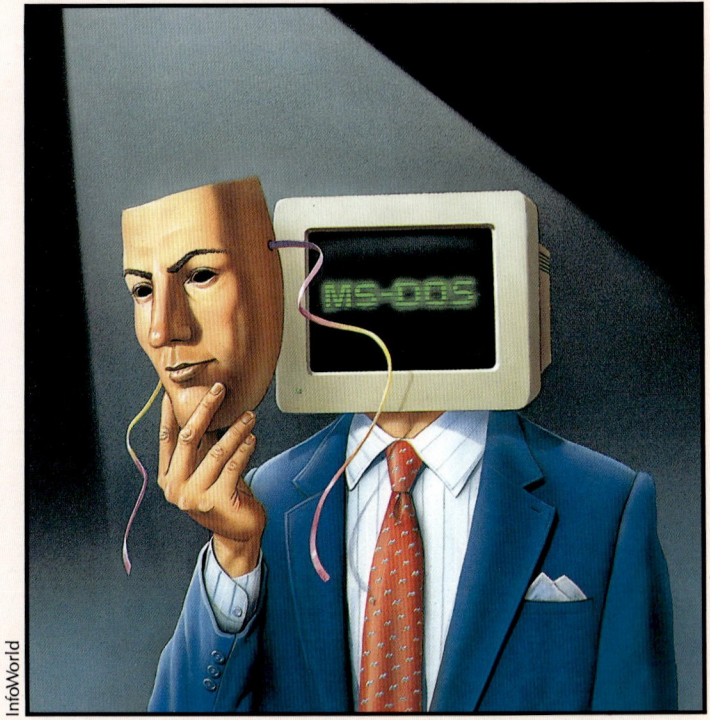

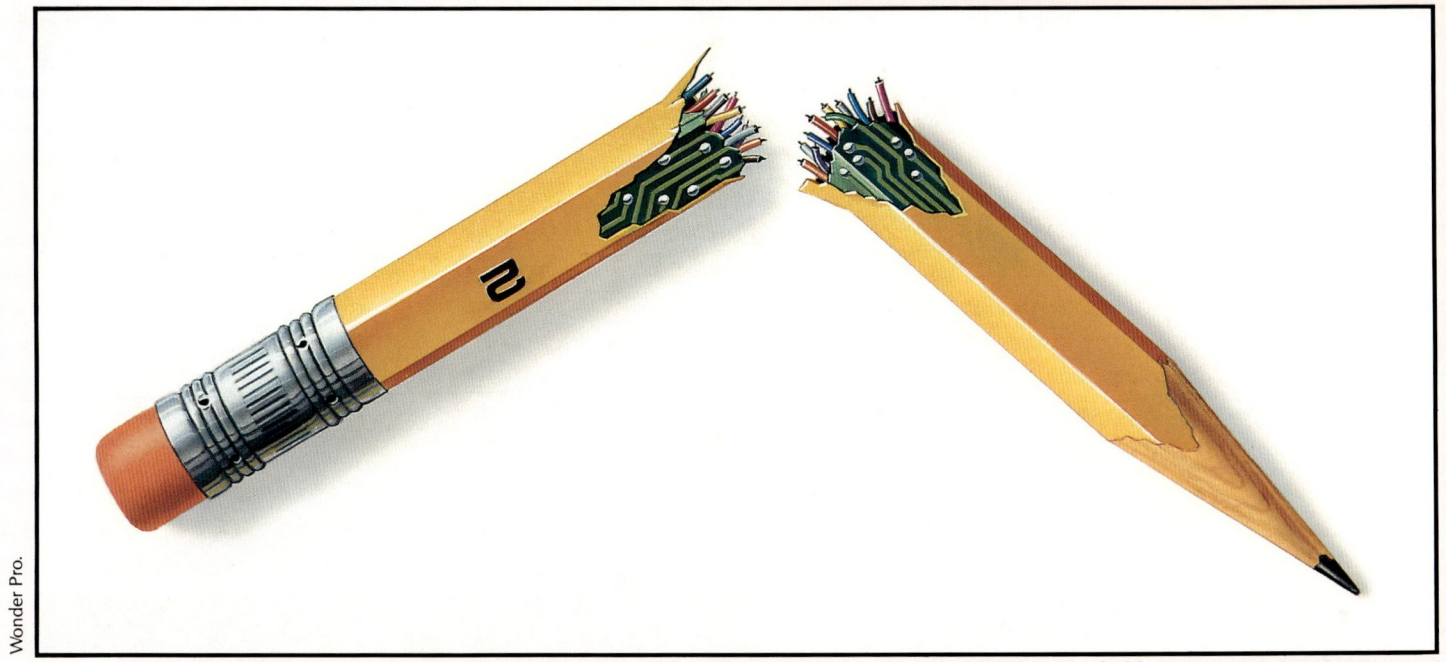

Litton

InfoWorld

Wonder Pro.

Clients include: Pepsi, Chevron, Hewlett-Packard, Memorex, Dole, McKesson, Caesars Tahoe, GTE, Hunts, Shaklee, Transamerica, Sumitomo, Fireman's Fund, Atari, Safeway, Harper & Row, Omni Magazine and more.

EYE LEVEL STUDIOS

TERRY YEE

Humorous Illustration and More . . .

(602) 962-7781
FAX AVAILABLE

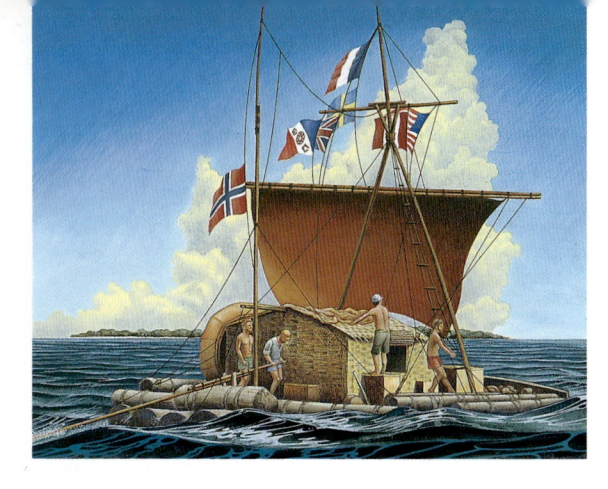

1118 Rosedale Drive #4
Atlanta, Georgia 30306
Phone 404/875-8061
Fax available.

WALT FLOYD

STEVE MACANGA
(201) 403-8967

20 MORGANTINE RD., ROSELAND, NEW JERSEY, 07068

87

the Independent Pencil Company

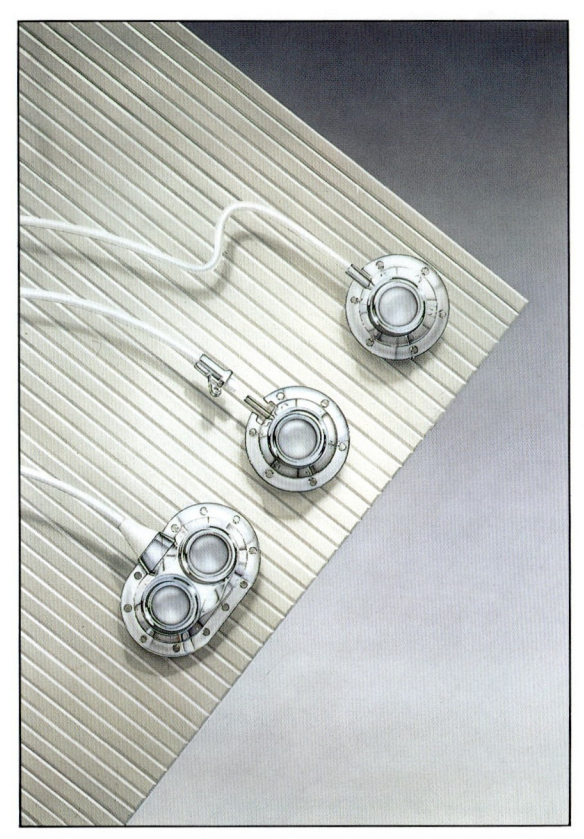

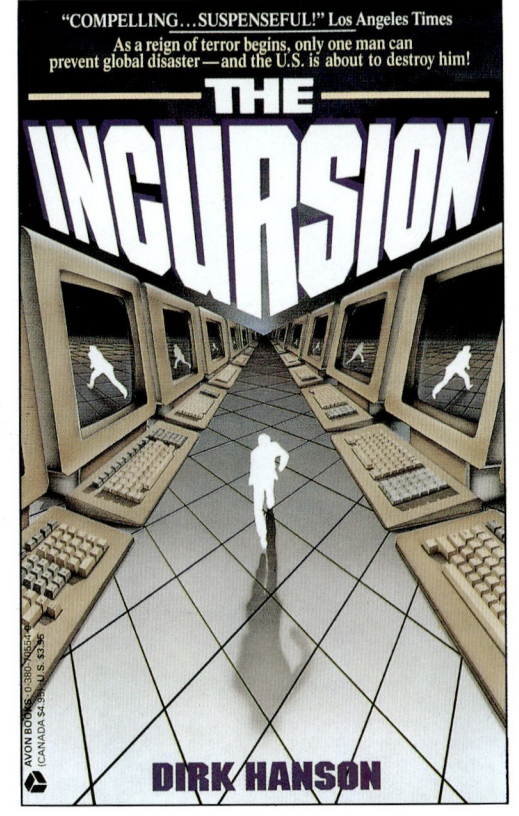

76 State Street
Newburyport, MA 01950
508-462-1948
Fax 508-465-8593

Robert Brun

CLIENTS INCLUDE:
Little Brown & Co.
Avon Books
New England Telephone
Emery Worldwide
Hewlett Packard

Jeanne de la Houssaye
237 Lafayette Street • New Orleans, LA   70130-3213
(504) 581-2167 • FAX (504) 581-1138

INTERNATIONAL · TARPON · RODEO · 84

GRAND ISLE, LA

Call me for food, faces, animals, architecture (spot or 4-color process)- also for the recipe for blackened redfish.

KIM VAN SETERS
29 High St. Wayne, NJ 07470
201-694-5502

Bill Communications ▲ ▼ Private Commission

New York Police Benevolant Association ▲ ▼ Management Review

MARLIES MERK NAJAKA
241 Central Park West, New York, New York 10024   (212) 580-0058

Clients include:
Gerstman + Meyers; Grey Direct; Ogilvy & Mather; Absolut Vodka; Prince Foods; Simon and Schuster; Business Week; Archaeology; Avon; Family Circle; Harcourt Brace Jovanovich; Lally, McFarland & Pantello; Houghton Mifflin Co; Food & Wine; Good Food; Graphic Arts Monthly; Lee Jofa; Graphics Concern; McGraw-Hill; NBC Inc.; Redbook; Scholastic; Homes International; Signature; The Putnam Publishing Group; Young Miss; The Scribner Book Companies; AT&T; Book of the Month Club; Frequent Flyer

To view more work:
Adweek Portfolio 1987, Showcase number 9, GAG Directory number 5, Showcase number 12, Creative Illustration 1

FRANK FRISARI

95-08 112 St.
Richmond Hill, NY 11419

718-441-0919
FAX IN STUDIO

Bob Downs
Humorous Illustration, Cartoons + Stuff...

303-971-0033
11111 Main Range Trail
Littleton, CO 80127

Jonathan Herbert COMPUTER Illustration

324 Pearl Street Suite 2G ▪ New York, NY 10038 ▪ 212 571 4444 Fax 212 571 3881

Jonathan Herbert COMPUTER Illustration

324 Pearl Street Suite 2G ▪ New York, NY 10038 ▪ 212 571 4444 Fax 212 571 3881

· JOHN KANE ·
215-862-0392

© 1991 John Kane

9 WEST BRIDGE ST. NEW HOPE, PA 18938

NEW YORK	CHICAGO	SAN FRANCISCO	SEATTLE
SAM BRODY	KEN FELDMAN	BARB HAUSER	DONNA JORGENSEN
212.758.0640	312.337.0447	415.339.1885	206.284.5080

Fred Hilliard

206.842.6003   206.842.7528 FAX

viviano

Sam Viviano, 25 West 13th Street, New York, NY 10011
Phone (212) 242-1471 / Fax (212) 691-4271

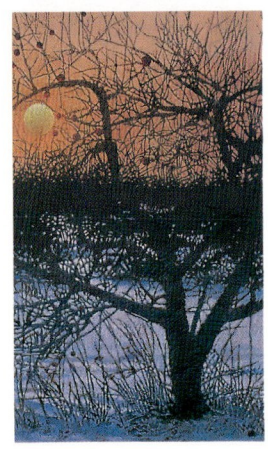

MICHAEL Story
ILLUSTRATION & DESIGN

MICHAEL STORY / 803/256-8813

LES KATZ

Represented by:
Sharon Drexler
110 West 40th St.
Suite 1005
New York, New York 10018
(212) 768-8072
FAX Available

MICHAEL McGURL

718.857.1866

83 EIGHTH AVE. BROOKLYN, N.Y. 11215

Lonni Sue Johnson

New York: Tel 212 873-7749   Fax 212 877-3127   Connecticut: Tel 203 355-9359   Fax 203 355-0676

Rough to finish, clockwise from top: Lotus Development Corporation, Pandick Inc, Corning Inc, Viking Penguin, Peat Marwick

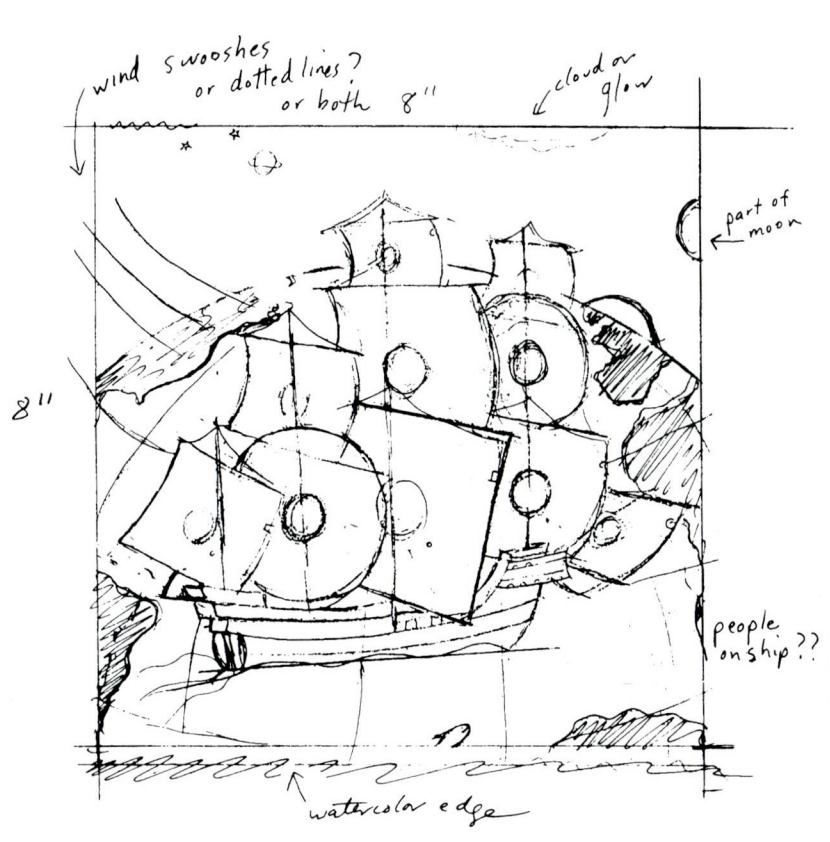

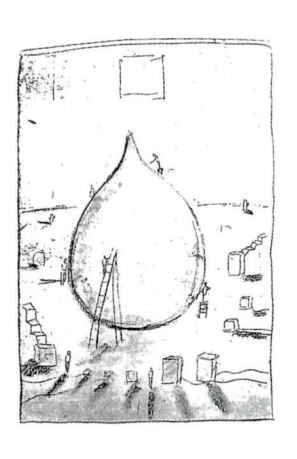

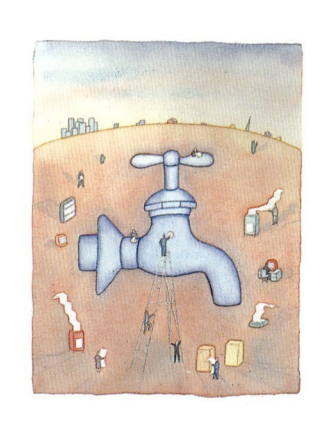

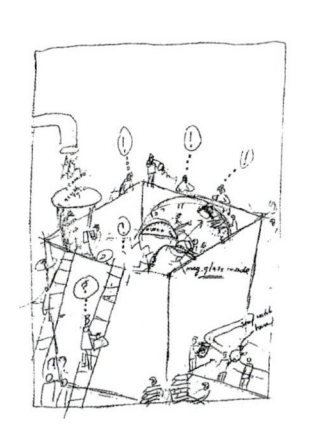

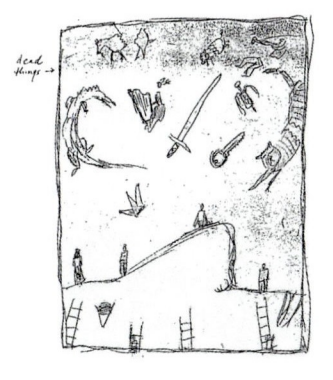

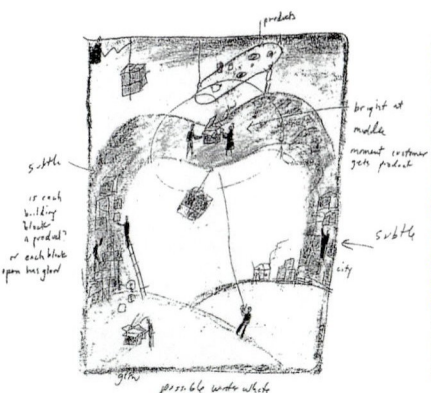

José Ortega

CLIENTS INCLUDE:

WIG WAG
BOSTON GLOBE
GROVE PRESS

MARIE FRANCE
APPLE COMPUTERS
WILLIWEAR

STEREO REVIEW
PROFILE
NEWSWEEK

BLOOMINGDALE'S

☎ 212 772 3329   ⌂ 524 E. 82ND ST. N.Y.C. 10028

Phil Marden

Studio:
28 East 21st St., #2B
New York, NY 10010
(212) 260-7646
FAX: (212) 260-7701

Represented By:
David Starr
(212) 254-0321

Clients: Adweek, American Baby, The Atlantic, Barron's, Boston Globe, Broadcast Arts, Business Week, Detroit Free Press, Food & Wine, HBO, Musician, New York Magazine, New York Times, Ogilvy & Mather, Premiere, Redbook, Self, Spy, Woman's Day, Working Woman, WBMG, Whittle Communications.

From *LAN Times*

COCO MASUDA

Illustration & Design In Style

Business Week

Bloomingdale's

Business Week

Bloomingdale's

COCO MASUDA DESIGN, 541 HUDSON STREET NEW YORK NY 10014   212.727.1599   Fax: 212.727.2650

Original

Lear's

105

GUSTAFSON

GLENN GUSTAFSON
ILLUSTRATION
1300 IVY COURT
WESTMONT, IL 60559
708.810.9527
708.810.9526 FAX

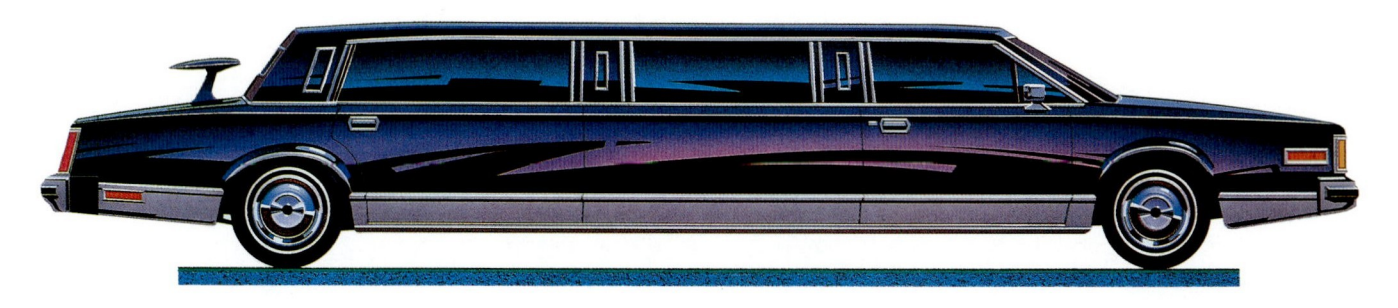

REPRESENTED IN THE SOUTHWEST BY REPERTOIRE 214.369.6990

REPRESENTED IN MINNEAPOLIS BY MARIETTA MASON 612.729.1774

P O R A Z I N S K I

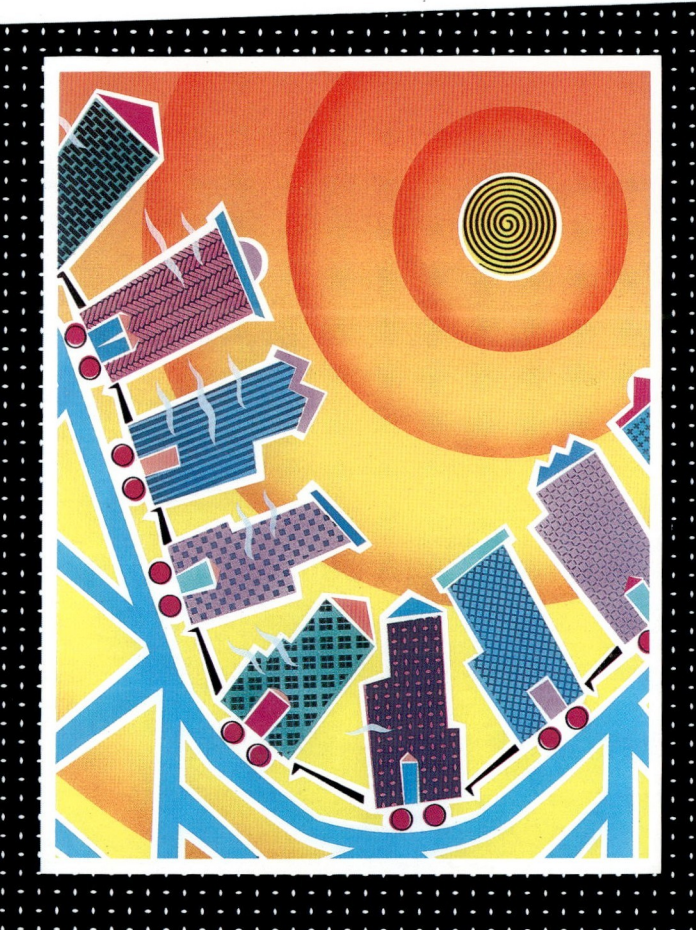

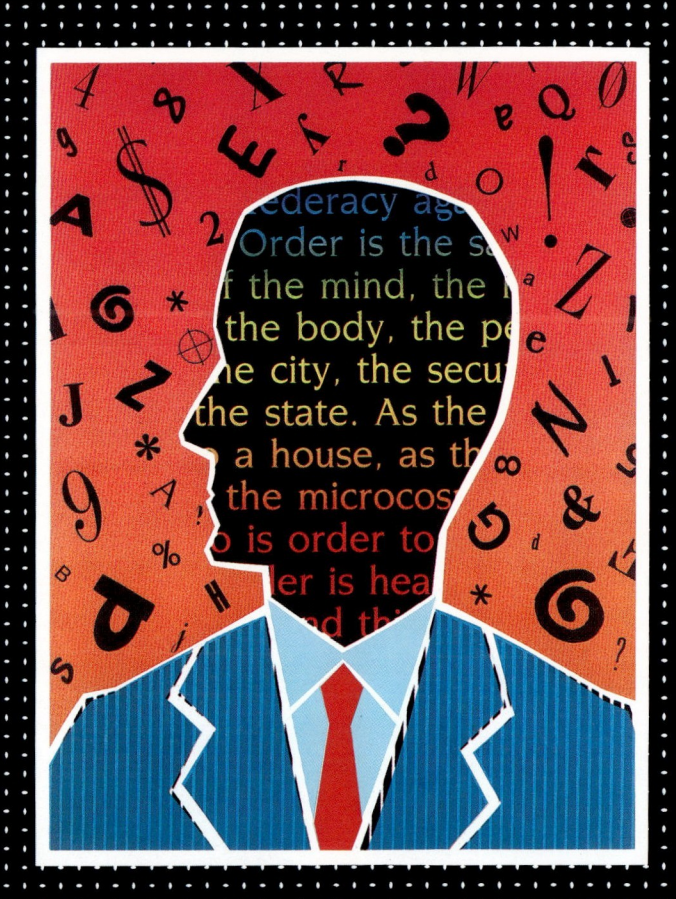

Jim Hanson and Talent   Chicago 312-337-7770   FAX 312-337-7112   Studio 312-745-9005

CAN DRAW THINGS BESIDES FISH

BILL MAYER INC. 240 FORKNER DR., DECATUR, GA 30030 404-378-0686 FAX 404-373-1759

©BILL MAYER 1991

Jacqui Morgan
STUDIO: 692 GREENWICH STREET • NYC 10014 • 212•463•8488

Clients include: American Express, Architectural Digest, AT&T, Black Enterprise, Booz-Allen & Hamilton, Champion Papers, Citibank, Colgate Palmolive, Family Circle, General Foods, Hilton International, Holland America, IBM, ITC, Johnson Wax, Kellogg's, Kinney Shoes, Kmart, Lear's, Mother Earth News, New Woman, New York Hospital for Special Surgery, New York Magazine, Oxford University Press, Pfizer, Proctor & Gamble, Scott Paper co., Self Magazine, Southern Bell, Stolichnaya, TransAtlantic Magazine.

C. Winston Taylor
818-363-5761 • FAX 818-363-2589

111

Harrison Houle

Interval House/The Ritz-Carlton, Laguna Niguel

Hoffman Printing Company

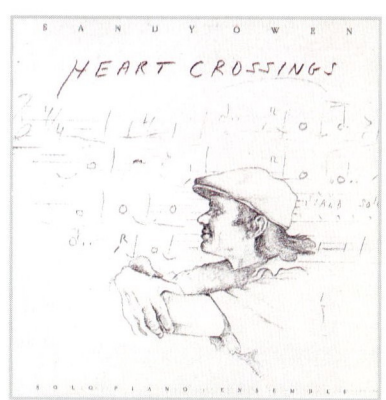

Ivory Records

Neenah Paper Company

HARRISON HOULE ILLUSTRATION/DESIGN
3543 Woodcliff Rd. / Sherman Oaks, CA 91403 / **LA:** (818) 783-6563 **SF:** (415) 871-9163 **FAX:** (818) 783-8110

BASEMAN

CLIENTS INCLUDE: AT&T, TIME, APPLE COMPUTERS, BOSTON GLOBE, ATLANTIC, MANUFACTURER'S HANOVER, SPORTS ILLUSTRATED, WARNER BROS. RECORDS

IN THE EAST
WORLD FAMOUS STUDIOS
718.499.9358

OUTSIDE THE EAST
JAN COLLIER
415.552.4252

BOSTON UNIVERSITY SCHOOL OF THEATRE ARTS

THE MAN WHO CAME TO DINNER
BY GEORGES KAUFMAN
MOSS HART
DIRECTED BY RICHARD SEER

November 8 - 11 at 8.00 pm. Matinees November 11 & 12 at 2.00 pm
Tickets: $8, $6, $3 Students & Senior Citizens. For tickets call 266 3913

Boston University Theatre, 264 Huntington Avenue, Boston, Massachusetts

JUDY FILIPPO
120 BROOK ST.
BROOKLINE
MA. 02146

617·731·4277

114

CHRIS CONSANI

REPRESENTED BY

AMERICAN ARTISTS

(212) 682-2462
(212) 582-0023

MICHAEL KOZMIUK

MAGNET MARKETING

REPRESENTED BY
AMERICAN ARTISTS
(212) 682-2462
(212) 582-0023

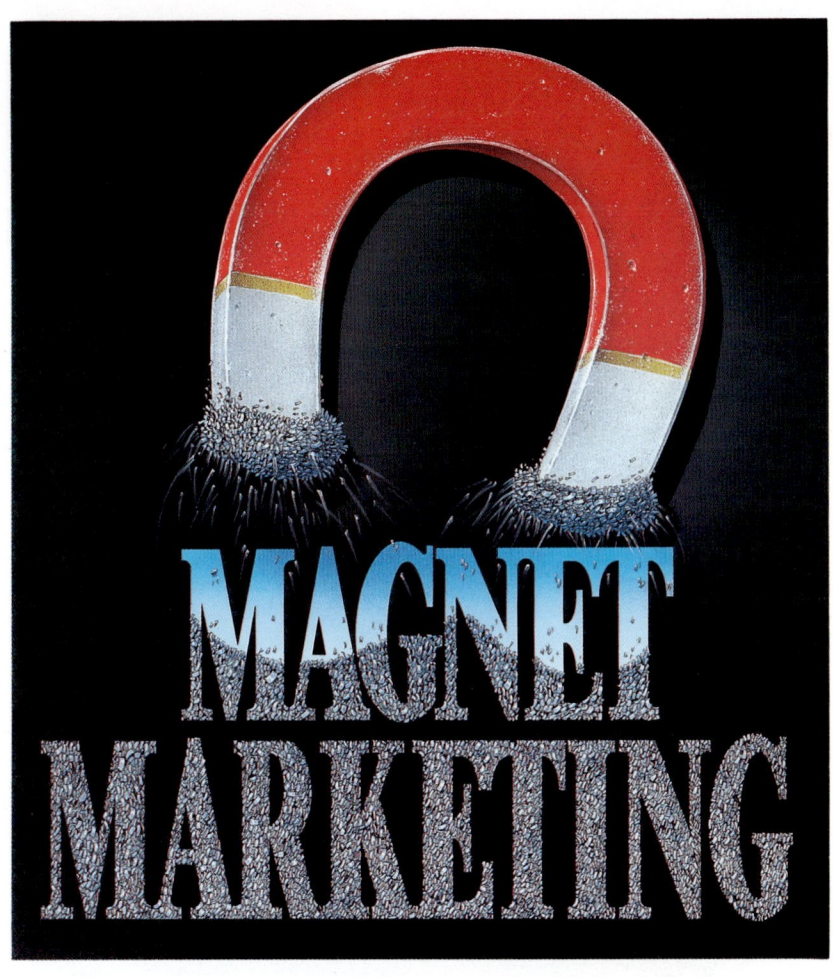

GEORGE GAADT

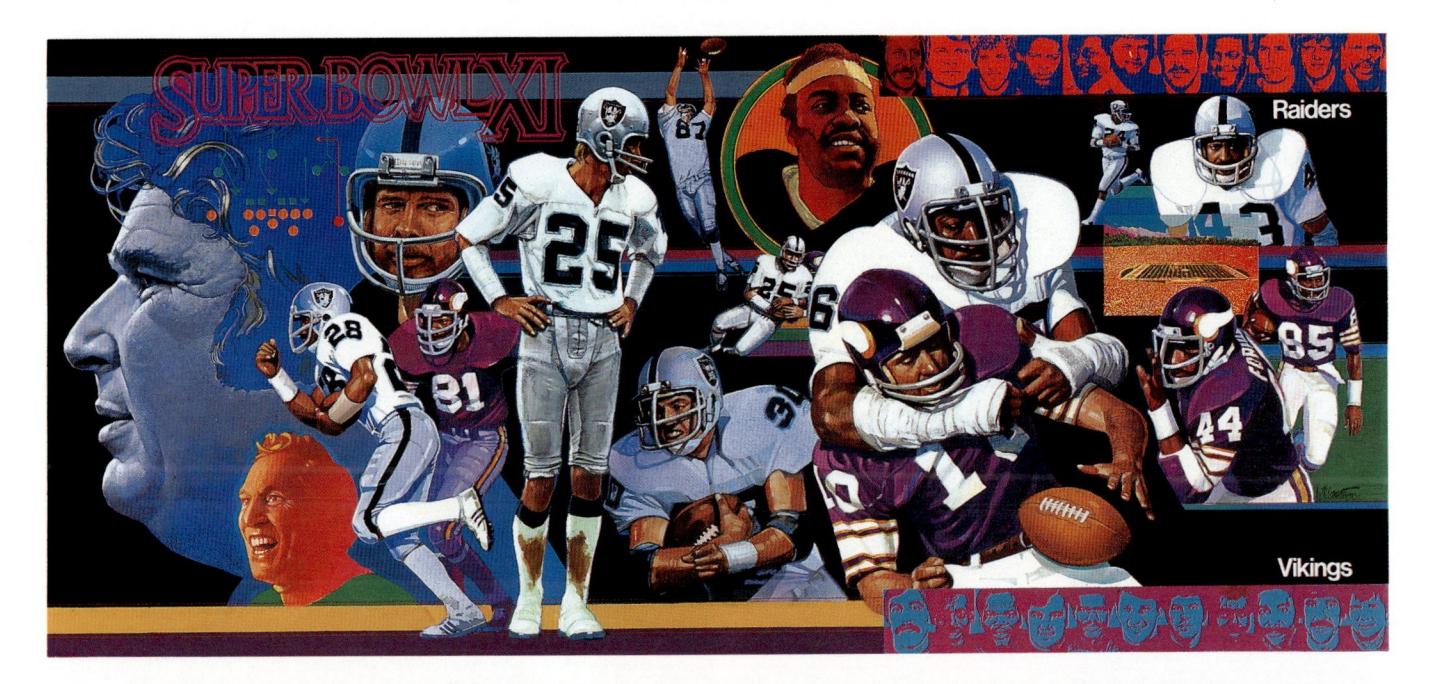

1. NFL Properties 25th Super Bowl Anniversary Book.
2. Monongahela Valley Project Council
3. Ben Franklin Lever Brothers
4. Lionel Toy Co.

REPRESENTED BY
AMERICAN ARTISTS
(212) 682-2462
(212) 582-0023

117

DAVE MILLER
A.I.R. STUDIO

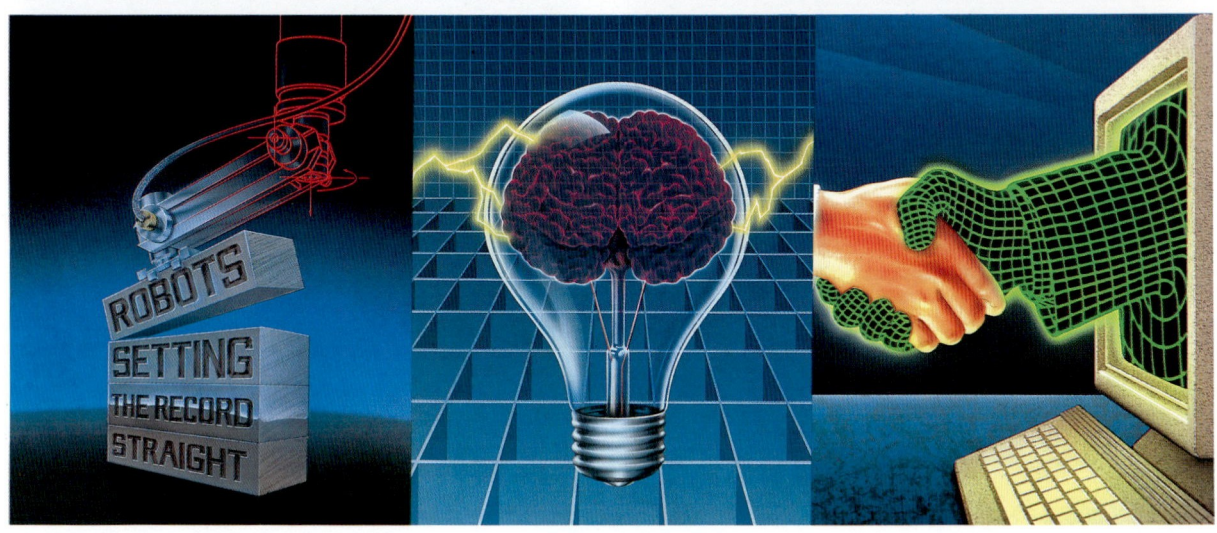

REPRESENTED BY

AMERICAN ARTISTS

(212) 682-2462
(212) 582-0023

JIM EFFLER
A.I.R. STUDIO

REPRESENTED BY
AMERICAN ARTISTS
(212) 682-2462
(212) 582-0023

119

KEITH BATCHELLER

REPRESENTED BY
AMERICAN ARTISTS
(212) 682-2462
(212) 582-0023

RON MAHONEY

REPRESENTED BY
AMERICAN ARTISTS
(212) 682-2462
(212) 582-0023

RICHARD PEMBROKE

ENTER THE CONTEST CREATED ESPECIALLY FOR SMOKERS WITH EXPENSIVE TASTES AND A
RICH IMAGINATION

Read Benson & Hedges' BUSINESS AND BEYOND for a wealth of ideas that could make you a winner.

JUST TELL US HOW YOU'D SPEND $10,000 IN 12 HOURS... from 6:00 in the evening until 6:00 the next morning... in New York, Los Angeles, Chicago, New Orleans, or any one of America's top 20 cities or top 10 resorts, as described in our new gift book, BUSINESS AND BEYOND. If you win, we'll give you $10,000 to live out your fantasy.

As you'll see, BUSINESS AND BEYOND is packed cover to cover with the best of the best of America. Exclusive hotels, fine restaurants, sophisticated nightlife, and superb shopping. Certainly it is a wonderful springboard from which to let your imagination soar.

The contest is fun, the rules are easy, and anyone over 21 may enter. Here's a chance to explore your dreams to the limit, and beyond. Points will be awarded for creativity, flamboyance, your own sense of style and individual tastes.

So start dreaming your wildest fantasies. Extravagance is the name of the game. And happy dreams.

REPRESENTED BY
AMERICAN ARTISTS
(212) 682-2462
(212) 582-0023

ROGER BERGENDORFF

REPRESENTED BY
American Artists
(212) 682-2462
(212) 582-0023

123

ALAN LEINER

SEE ADDITIONAL WORK IN:
CREATIVE ILLUSTRATION BOOK #1
AMERICAN SHOWCASE #13, 14

BLUE MARINE ENGINES

REPRESENTED BY
AMERICAN ARTISTS
(212) 682-2462
(212) 582-0023

RUSS FARRELL

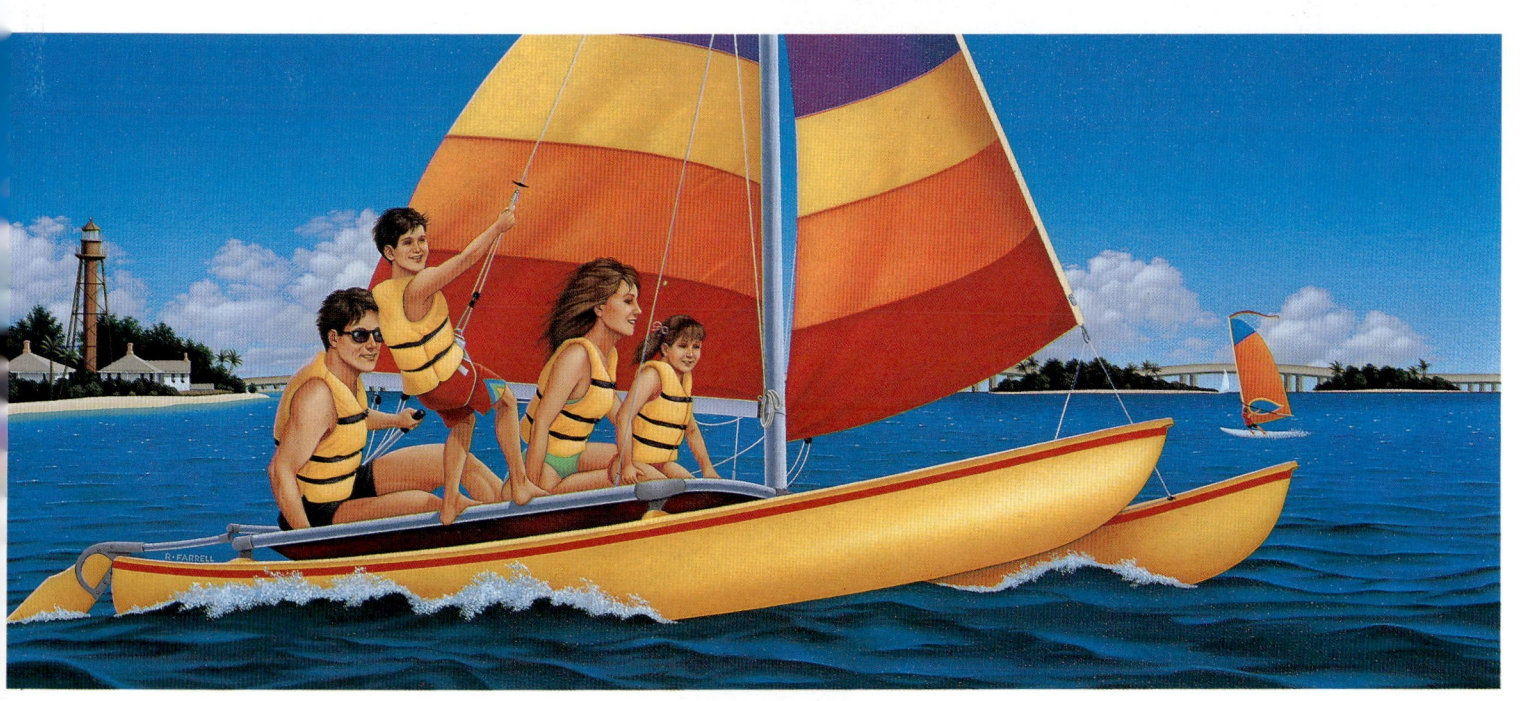

REPRESENTED BY
AMERICAN ARTISTS
(212) 682-2462
(212) 582-0023

125

JOHN HAMAGAMI

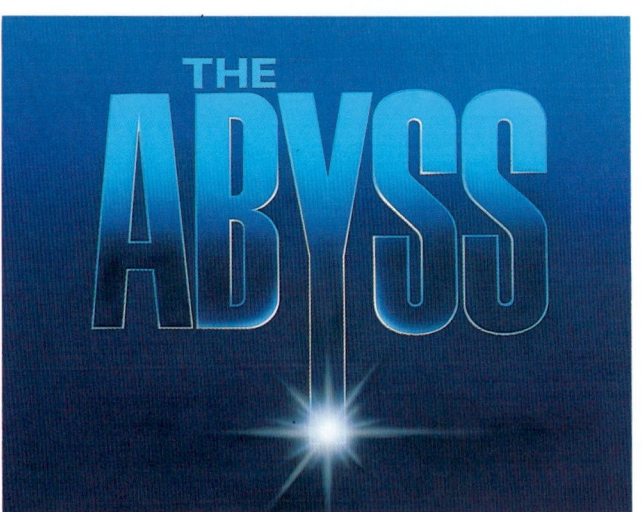

REPRESENTED BY
AMERICAN ARTISTS

(212) 682-2462
(212) 582-0023

LANE DuPONT

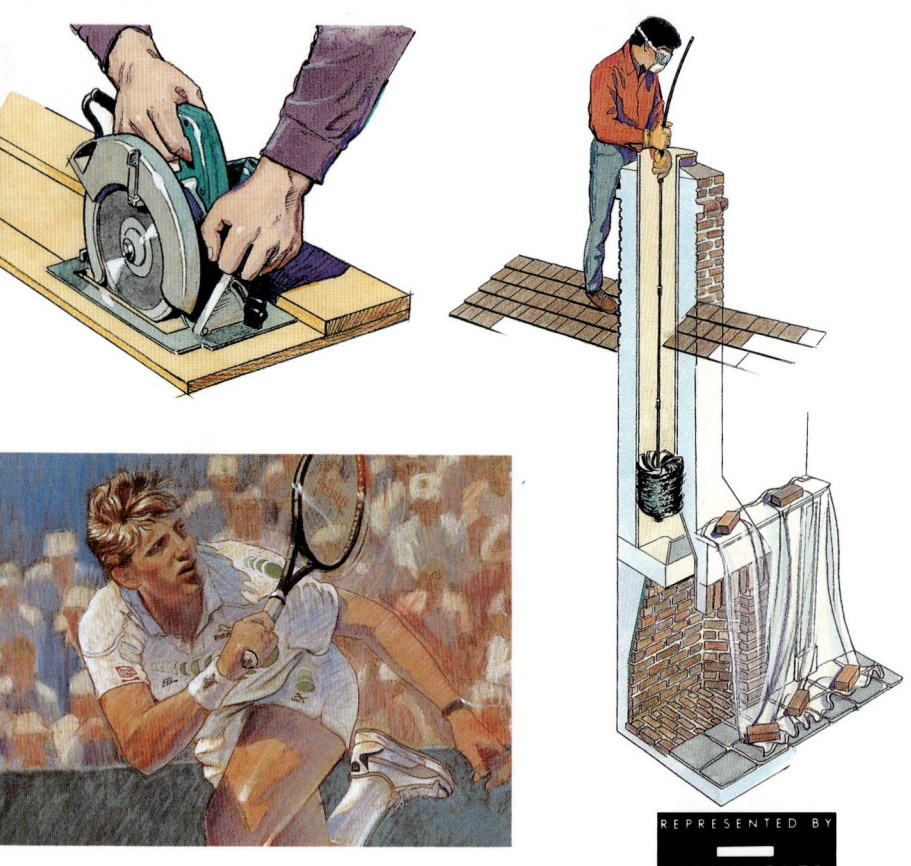

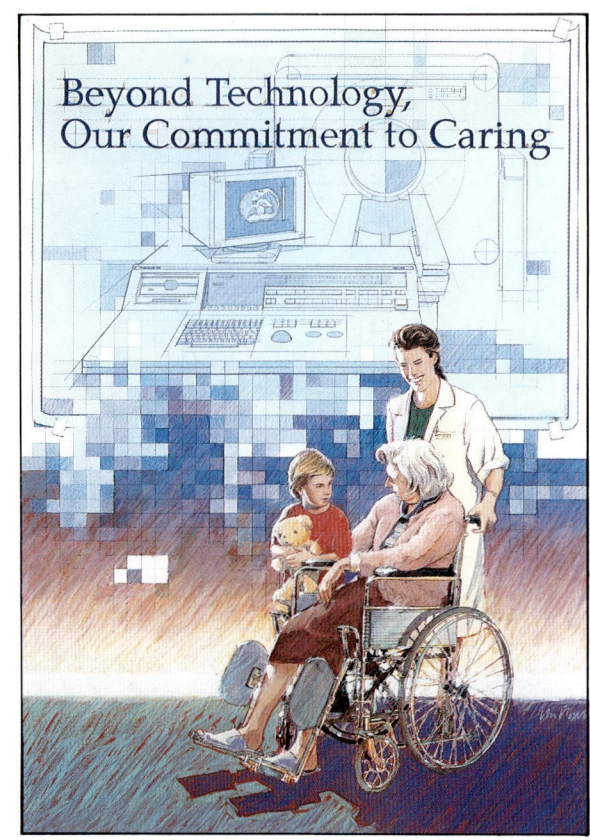

Beyond Technology, Our Commitment to Caring

REPRESENTED BY
AMERICAN ARTISTS
(212) 682-2462
(212) 582-0023

127

DICK THORN

CLIENT: FRANKEL & CO.

REPRESENTED BY
AMERICAN ARTISTS
(212) 682-2462
(212) 582-0023

CHRIS BUTLER

PEN & INK — PAPER SCULPTURE

Only You Can Prevent Forest Fires

REPRESENTED BY
AMERICAN ARTISTS
(212) 682-2462
(212) 582-0023

129

KAREL HAVLICEK

black raspberries
red raspberries
blueberries
strawberries
gooseberries
boysenberries
blackberries

REPRESENTED BY
AMERICAN ARTISTS
(212) 682-2462
(212) 582-0023

JOHN HULL

REPRESENTED BY
American Artists
(212) 682-2462
(212) 582-0023

STAN WATTS

REPRESENTED BY

AMERICAN ARTISTS

(212) 682-2462
(212) 582-0023

ILLUSTRATION

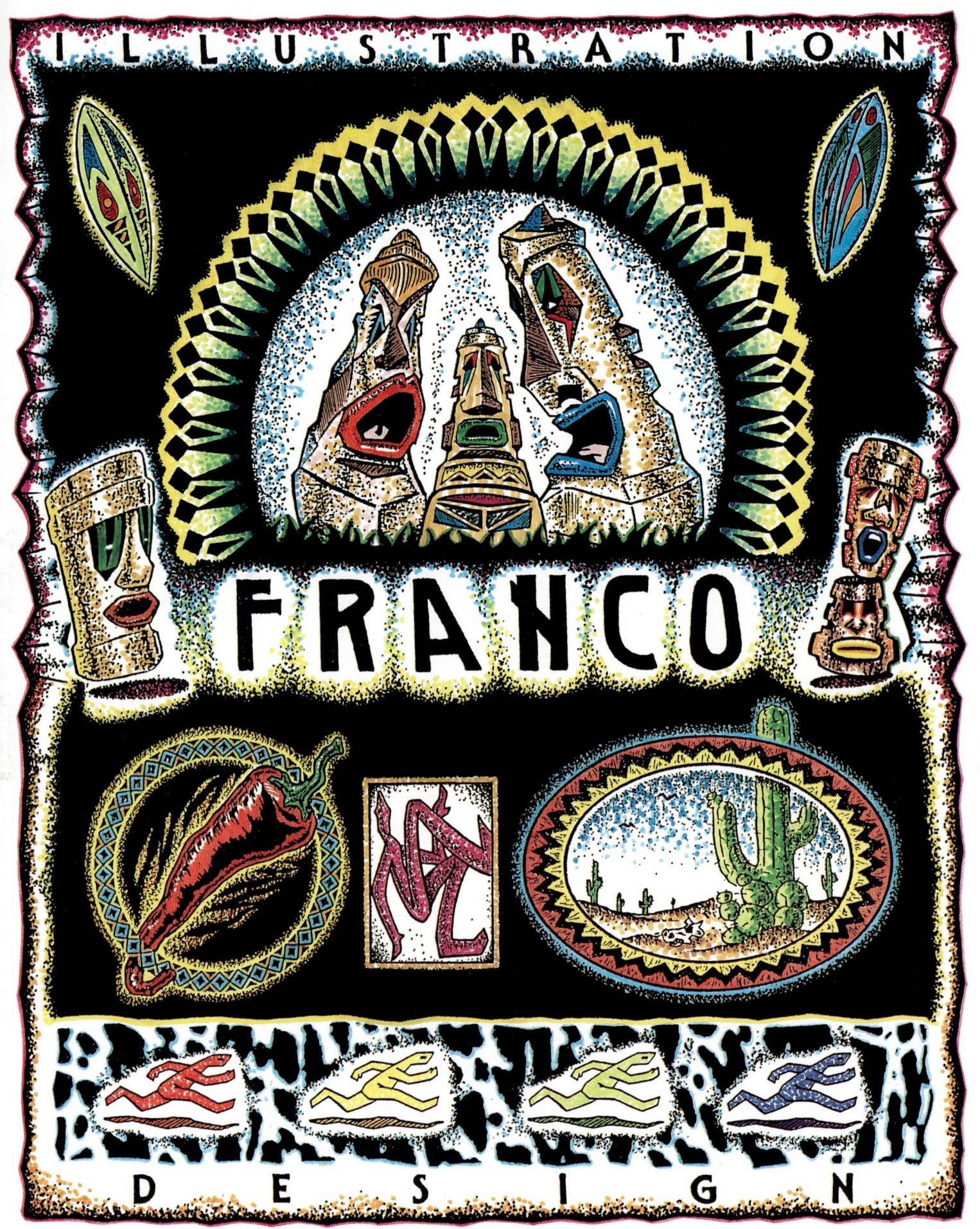

FRANCO

DESIGN

95-08 112 St.   Richmond Hill, NY 11419
718-441-0919   FAX IN STUDIO

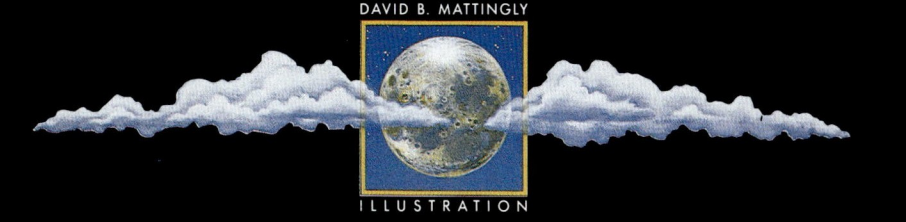

DAVID B. MATTINGLY

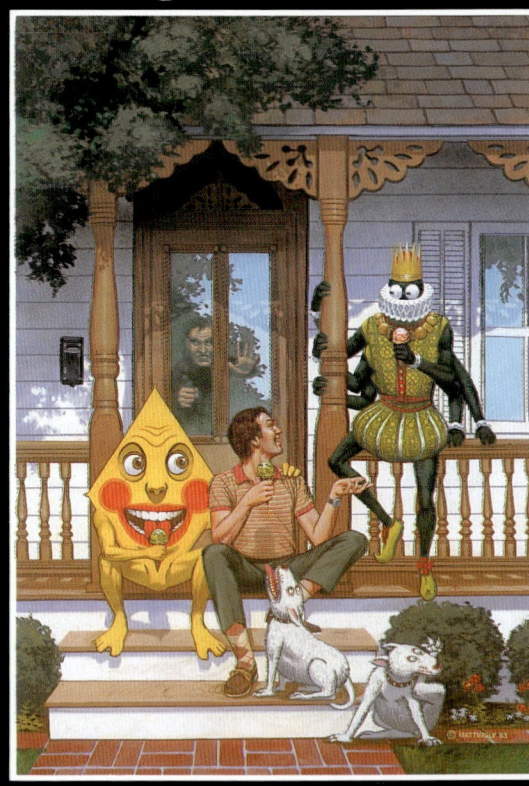

THE FINEST IN SCIENCE FICTION AND FANTASY ILLUSTRATION
201-659-7404

MARGARET CHODOS-IRVINE

311 FIRST AVENUE SOUTH   ROOM 314
SEATTLE, WASHINGTON   98104
206-624-2480

REPRESENTED BY JAZ & JAZ
206-783-5373
FAX 206-784-8528

135

Carol Schweigert

**Carol Schweigert
Illustrator
791 Tremont Street
Boston, MA   02118
617.262.8909**

Call for fax.

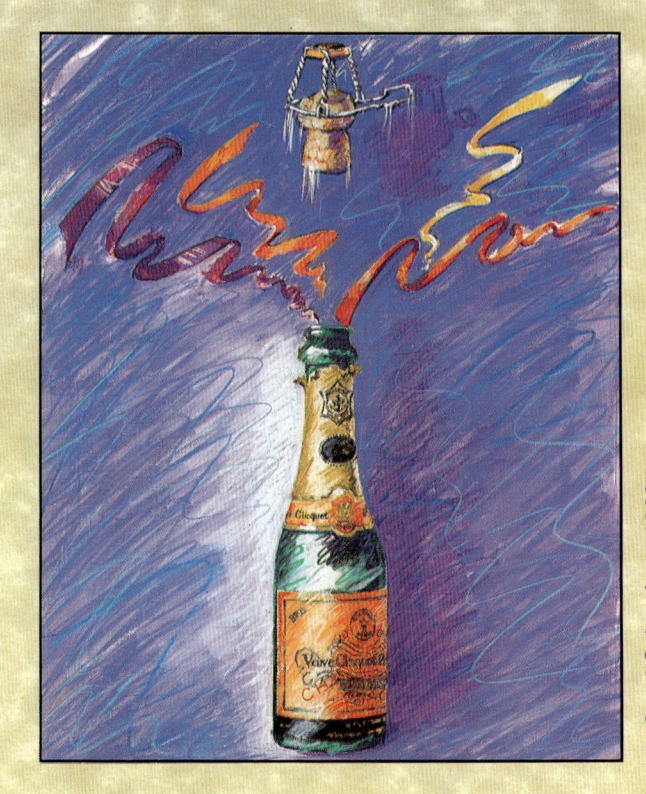

© Carol Schweigert 1990

Doug Oudekerk

Jan Knutsen
REPRESENTING
612-884-8083

Steve Mark

PACHYDERMATOLOGIST

Jan Knutsen
REPRESENTING
612-884-8083

BILL REYNOLDS

JONATHAN · McINTOSH · FIRESIDE

ATLANTIC SALMON

Atlantic Salmon are the aristocrats of fish ~ powerful, elegant, stylish. Although they do not feed when in fresh water, they will strike a fly. The White Wulff is a showy, high riding dry, invented by Lee Wulff, America's dean of fly fishing and the pioneer of dry fly angling for Atlantic Salmon.

JAN KNUTSEN
REPRESENTING
612-884-8083

139

Russell E. Pratt
Studio 212-685-7955

Russell E. Pratt
150 East 35th Street #440
New York, NY 10016

212-685-7955

Fax available

Specializing in Pen and Ink; Graphically Rendered Illustration, Technical Fine Line Drawing, Charts, Diagrams, Graphic Design, and Finished Lettering.

Member Graphic Arts Guild

Clients Include: Elizabeth Arden, R.H. Macy*s, Avon Products, Estee Lauder, Cosmair, Colgate-Palmolive, PCA Apparel, Du Pont, Telemundo, N.W. Ayer, Citibank, Widmann & Co., American Cyanamid.

© Russell Pratt 1990

Kenn Richards

3 Elwin Place, East Northport, NY 11731
Phone (516) 499-7575 • Fax (516) 499-0749

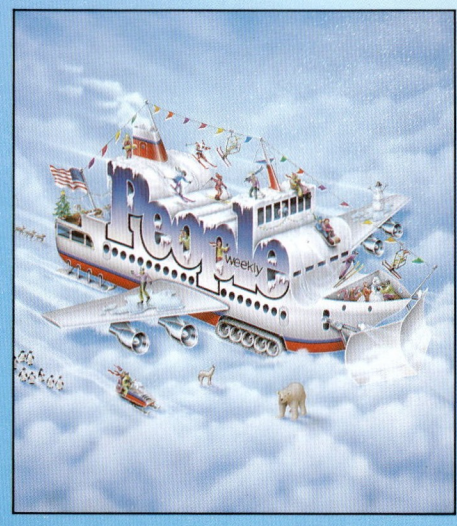

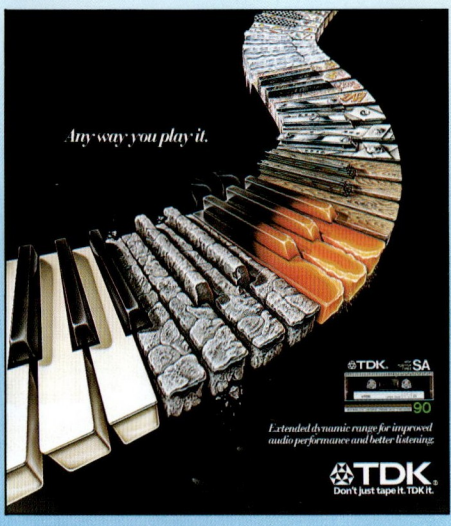

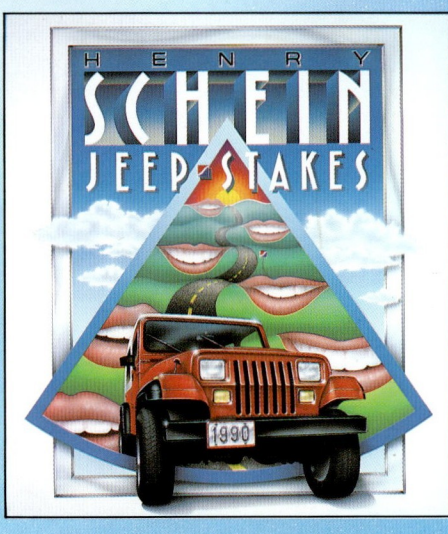

SULLIVAN

Suzánne Hughes Sullivan
212•581•6112

STEVE SMALLWOOD

STUDIO 201 585·7923 FAX AVAILABLE

Jim DeLapine · 516·225-1247
398 31st. Street · Lindenhurst · New York · 11757

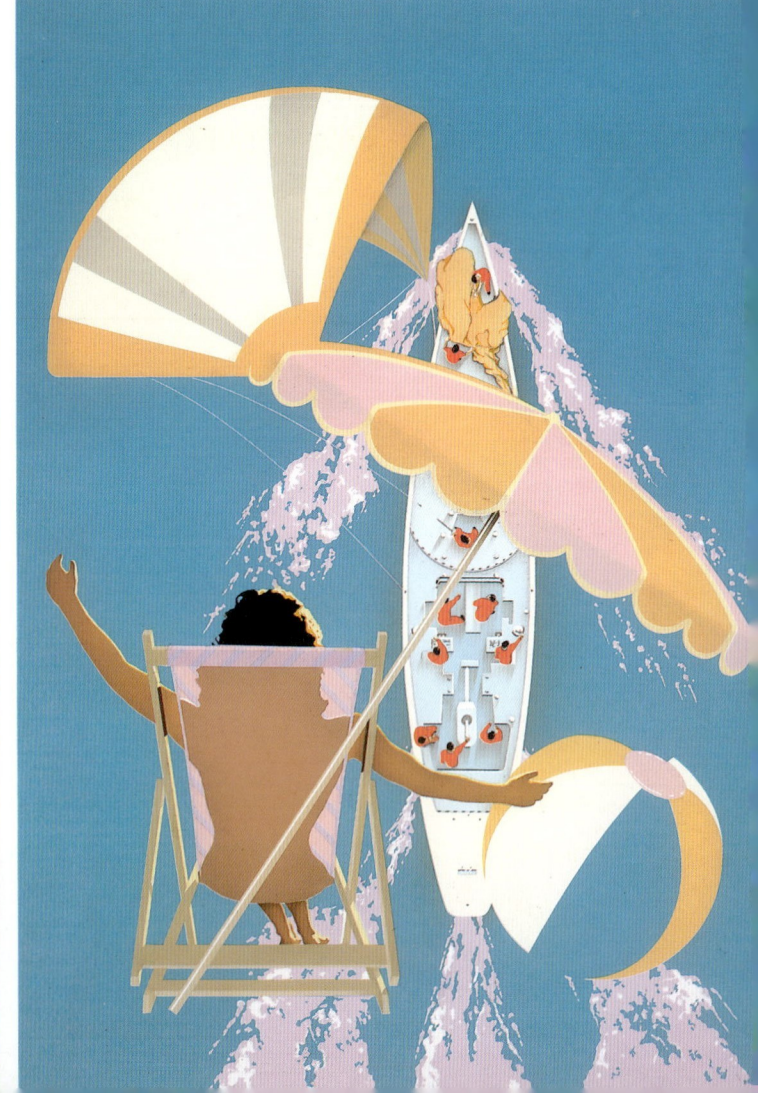

Joe Saffold

719 Martina Drive, N.E.
Atlanta, Georgia 30305
404·231·2168
FAX 404·364·9014

KIMMERLE
MILNAZIK
ILLUSTRATION
73-2 DREXELBROOK DRIVE
DREXEL HILL, PENNA. 19026
TELEPHONE (215) 259-1565

FLOOD

represented by Sell Inc.
312·565·2701
FAX 312·565·2811

PATRICIA DOKTOR
ILLUSTRATION

© PATRICIA DOKTOR 1990

95 HORATIO ST. 9A N.Y.C. N.Y. 10014 (212)645-4452

BARRY JACKSON
ILLUSTRATION

95 HORATIO ST. 9A N.Y.C. N.Y. 10014 (212)645-4452

CATY BARTHOLOMEW

721 CARROLL ST, APT 3, BROOKLYN, NY 11215
718.636.1252

LOTUS MAGAZINE

SAN FRANCISCO FOCUS

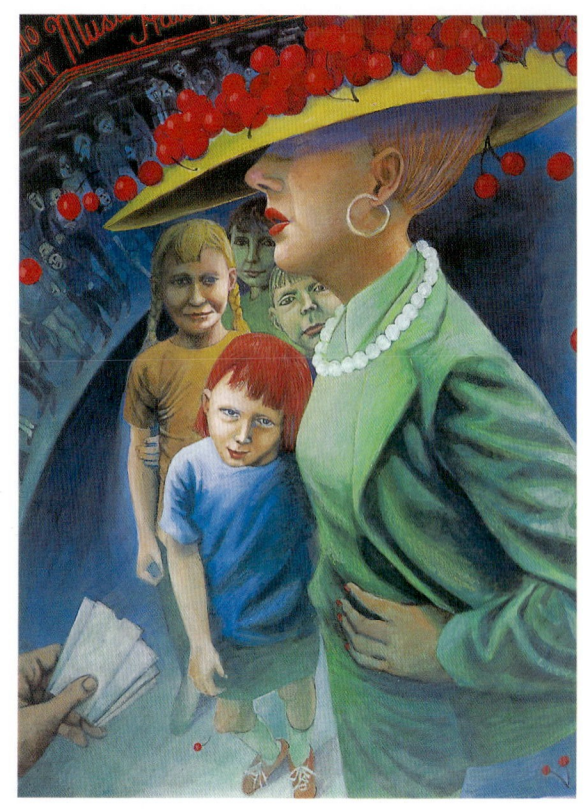

NEW YORK WOMAN

NEW ENGLAND MONTHLY

Marc Rosenthal
#8 Route 66
Malden Bridge, New York 12115
(518) 766-4191
FAX: (518) 766-4191

Clients include:
Altman & Manley Advertising,
Book of the Month Club, Fortune,
Time, Newsweek, New Woman, Savvy,
New York Magazine, Compugraphic
Corp., Simon & Schuster, Whittle
Communications, The Boston Globe,
The Washington Post, The New York
Times, The Philadelphia Inquirer

The Smoker Oil on board

JAMES KACZMAN

Illustration   7 Chester Street   Watertown   Massachusetts   02172   (617) 923-4605

CATHY LUNDEEN

Represented by ▲ JoAnne Schuna (612) 343-0432 ▲ Frank Schuna (612) 343-0104

CINDY BERGLUND

Represented by ▲ JoAnne Schuna (612) 343-0432 ▲ Frank Schuna (612) 343-0104

JIM ▶RY▶EN

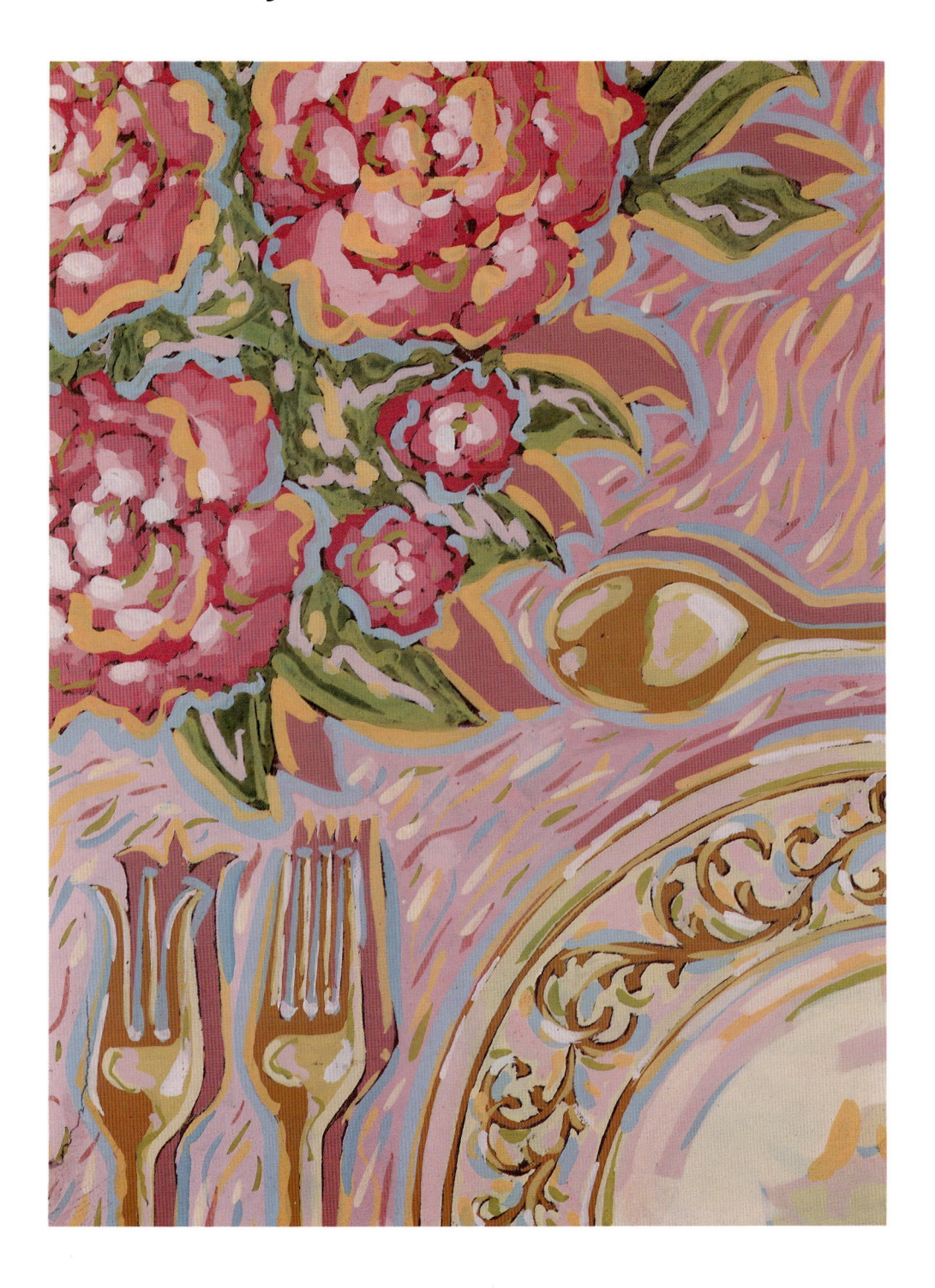

Represented by ▲ JoAnne Schuna (612) 343-0432 ▲ Frank Schuna (612) 343-0104

ALEX BOIES

Represented by ▲ JoAnne Schuna (612) 343-0432 ▲ Frank Schuna (612) 343-0104

NEVERNE COVINGTON

Represented by ▲ JoAnne Schuna (612) 343-0432 ▲ Frank Schuna (612) 343-0104

SI Member

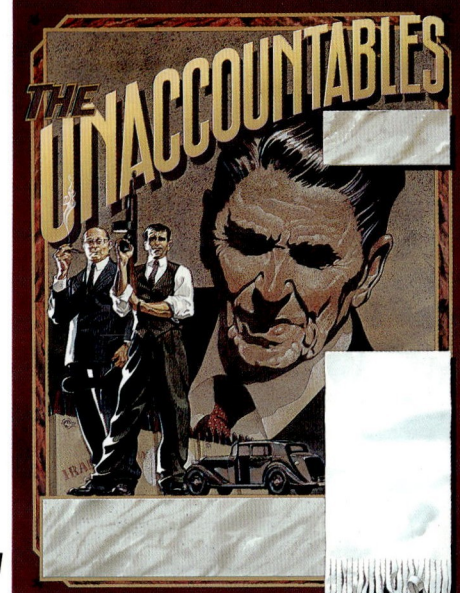

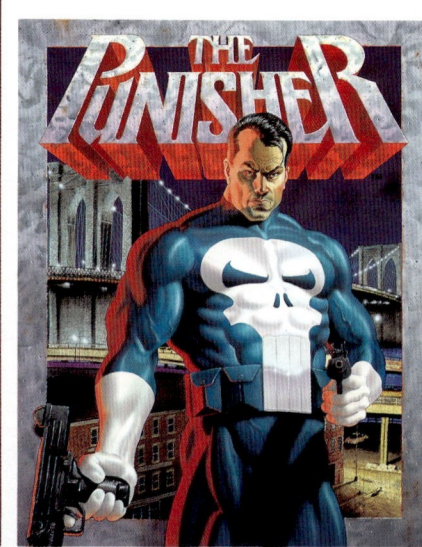

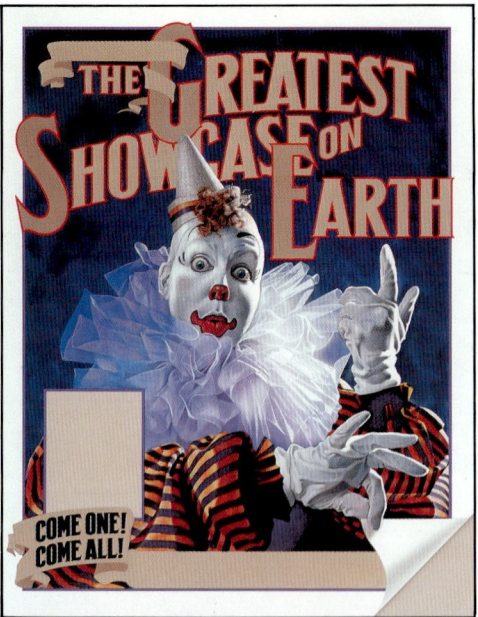

Advertising
Editorial
Institutional
and Collateral
Illustration

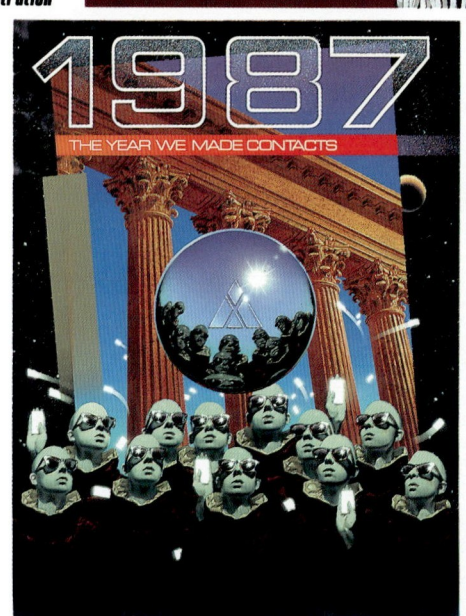

Selected for SI Annual 33

Eloqui

Mark Stutzman
100 G Street
Mt. Lake Park, MD 21550

301 334 4086
FAX 334 4186

Eloqui is a studio devoted exclusively to illustration. A complete portfolio is available upon request.

Stewart McKissick
250 Piedmont Road
Columbus, Ohio 43214
(614) 262-3262

DAVID GROVE   382 Union Street San Francisco California 94133   415 • 433 • 2100

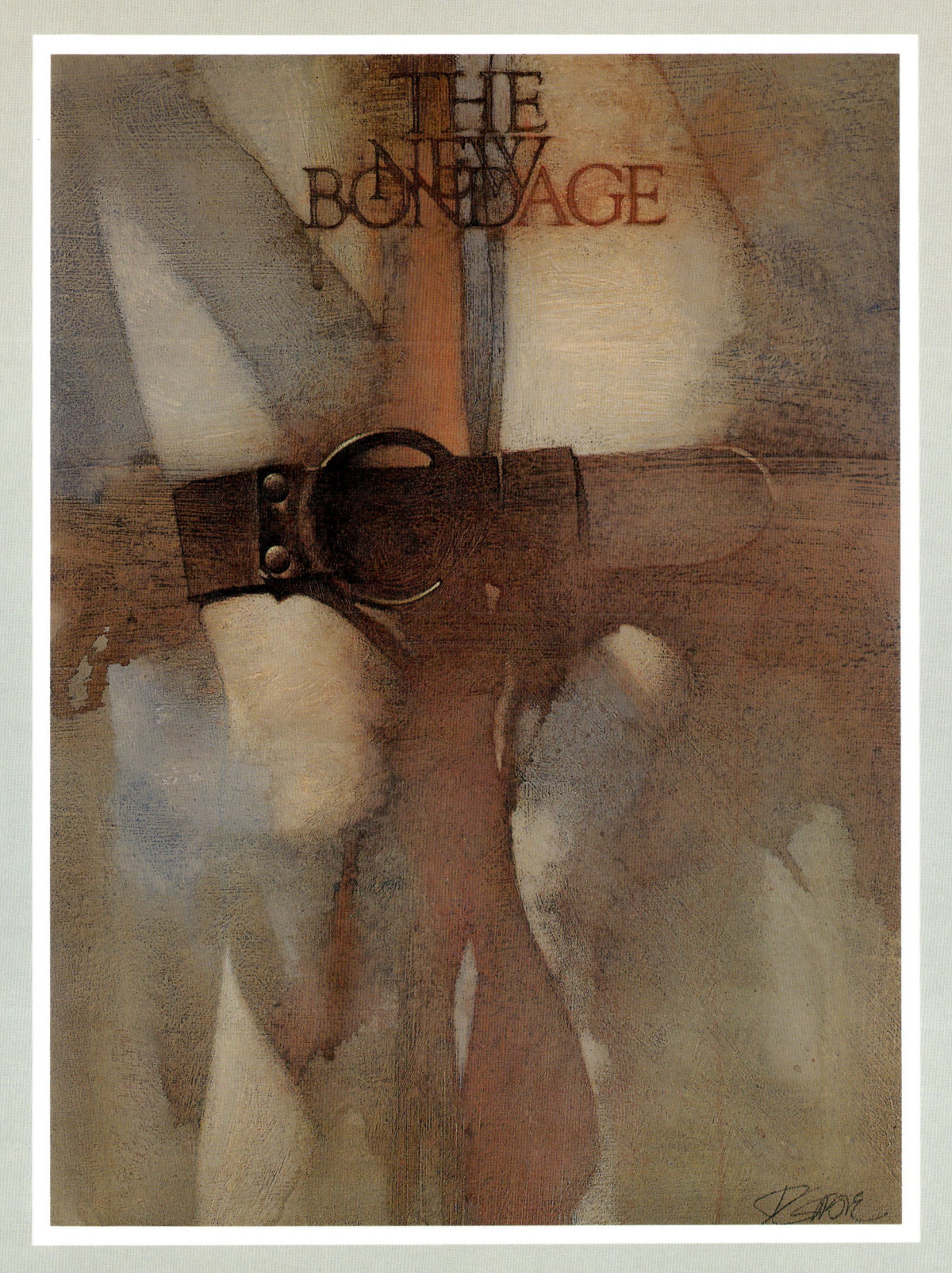

DAVID GROVE

382 Union Street
San Francisco California 94133
415 • 433 • 2100
Fax in Studio

TIM WILLIAMS
ILLUSTRATOR

520 Country Glen Court
Alpharetta, Georgia 30201   (404) 475-3146   Fax In Studio

John Gampert

(718) 441-2321

P.O. BOX 219, KEW GARDENS, N.Y. 11415

Illustration and design from comp to finish for major publishers and advertising agencies.
Private Collections
Member: Graphic Artists Guild

163

CHRIS GRANDSTAFF

12704 HARBORVIEW COURT • WOODBRIDGE, VA 22192

703.494.0422

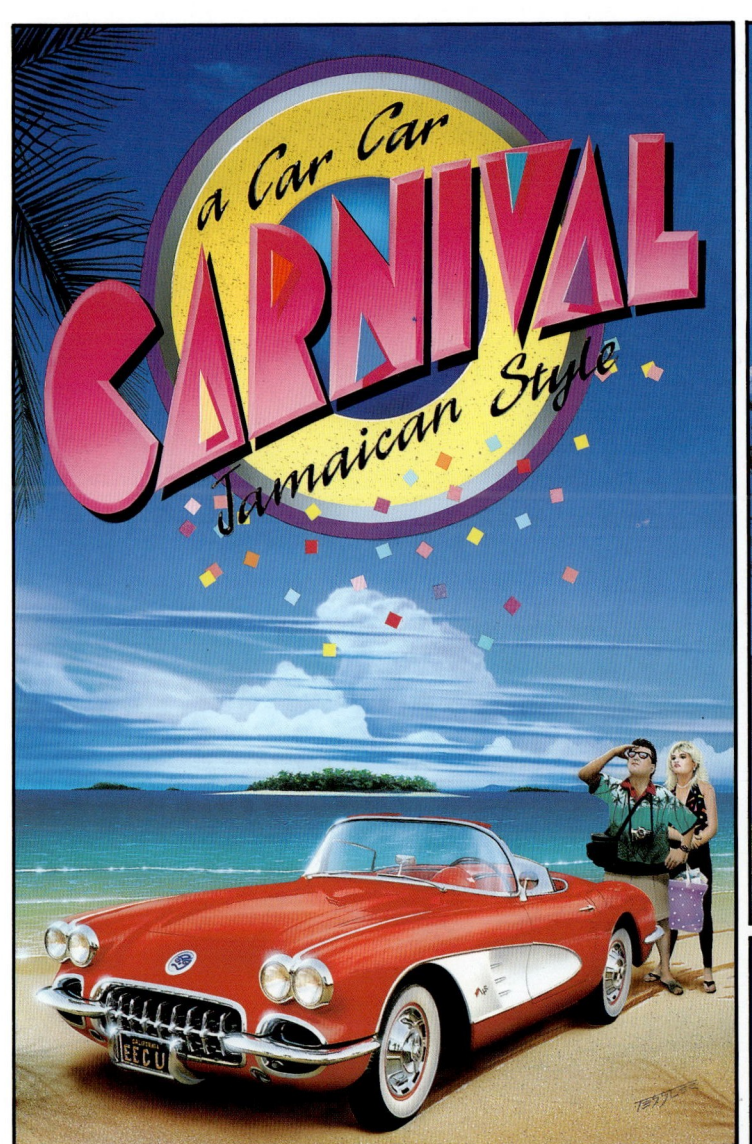

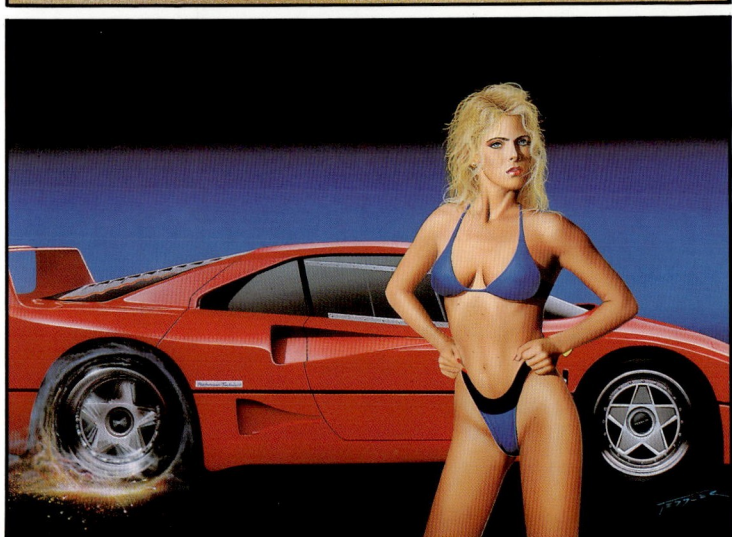

JOHN TESSLER

REPRESENTED BY LUNIA BLUE GRAPHICS • 4625 RAVENWOOD AVENUE • SACRAMENTO, CA • 95821

(916) 488-3425

Member of the Sacramento Illustrators Guild

ILLUSTRATION **Nikolai Punin** DESIGN

Book Jackets • Editorial Illustrations
Posters • Brochures • Annual Reports
Advertising Art • Black/White Drawings

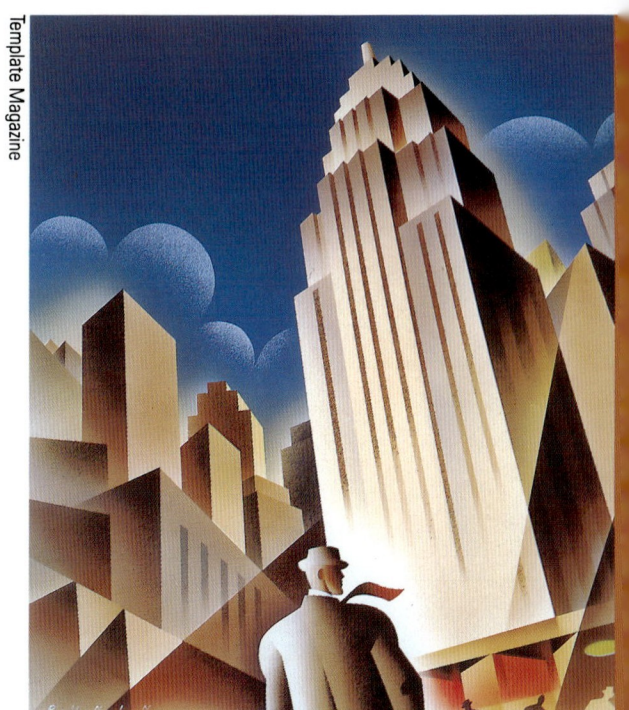

Template Magazine

161 West 16th Street #18E

New York, New York 10011

Tel/Fax (212) 727·7237

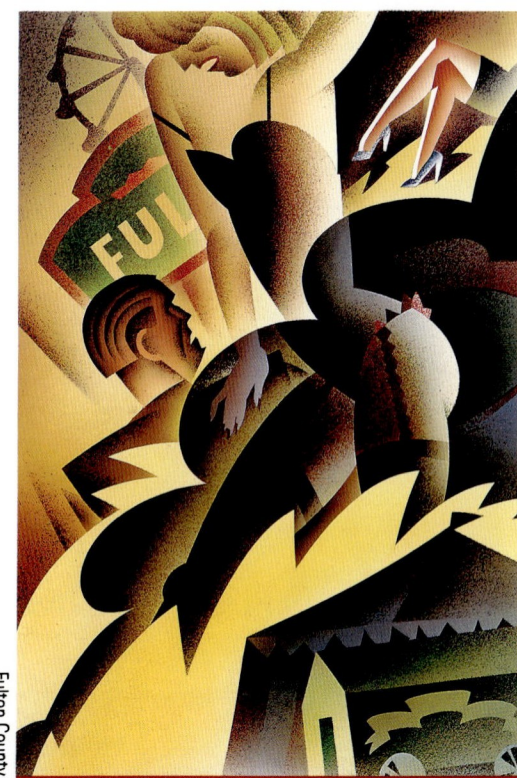

Garcia Lorca

Fulton County

166

TIME

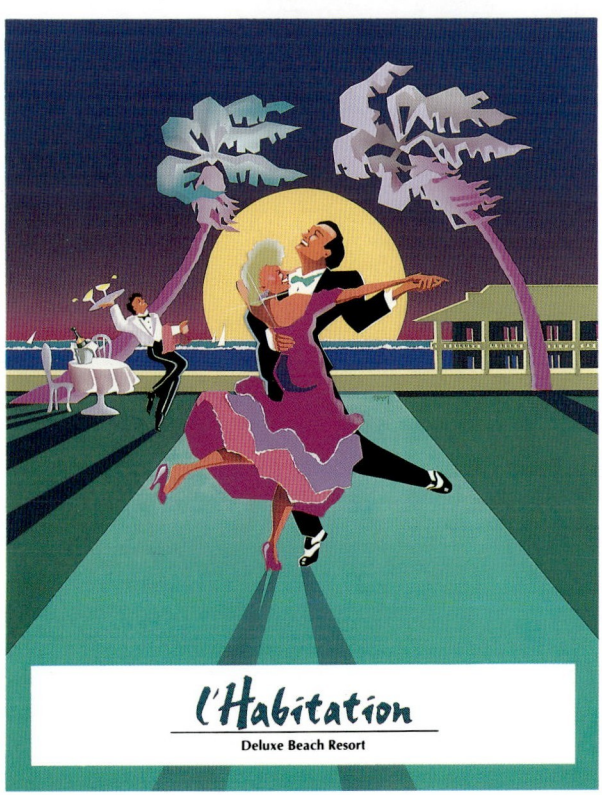

l'Habitation
Deluxe Beach Resort

PETER GERGELY
cut paper art
914•446•2367

167

SHARON WATTS
REPRESENTED BY CAROLYN BRINDLE & PARTNER
203 E. 89th STREET, NEW YORK, NY 10128 • (212) 534-4177

DONNA MEHALKO

REPRESENTED BY CAROLYN BRINDLE & PARTNER, INC.
203 E. 89th STREET, NEW YORK, NY 10128 • (212) 534-4177

NEDSHAW

Contemporary Airbrush Illustration
812·333·2181

Clients include:
Forbes, Business Week, Travel and Leisure, New York Times, Video Magazine, Chief Executive, Washington Post, Random House, Macmillan Computer Publishing, Citibank, Mayflower, Children's Television Workshop

Awards include:
Silver Funnybone Award, Society of Illustrators; Silver Award, Florida Magazine Association; Silver Award, Art Directors Club of Indiana

Member Graphic Artists Guild

2770 North Smith Pike • Bloomington • Indiana • 47404 • (812) 333-2181 • FAX (812) 331-0420

David JARVIS

THE 1989 RIGHT GUARD Halfway Challenge CHAMPIONS

FLORIDA TOMATOES
Ripen Naturally
NEVER REFRIGERATE

STUDIO:
200 S. Banana River Blvd.
Cocoa Beach, FL 32931
(407) 784·6263
FAX (407) 799·3052

Representation in the Northeast:
KANE & BUCK
566 Seventh Avenue
New York City, NY 10018
(212) 221·8090
FAX (212) 221·8092

EDDIE CORKERY

REPRESENTED IN CHICAGO

BY

SHARON LANGLEY

(312) 527-2128 FAX (312) 822-9607

DAVE ROTOLONI

REPRESENTED IN CHICAGO

BY

SHARON LANGLEY

(312) 527-2128   FAX (312) 822-9607

New Work

Wallop Manyum **Represented by Michèle Manasse**

16 West 75th Street, 2nd Floor
New York, New York, 10023
Telephone: (212) 873-3797

Prevention Magazine

Global Finance Magazine

Visa/Chemical Bank

1991 © Wallop Manyum

New Work

Terry Widener

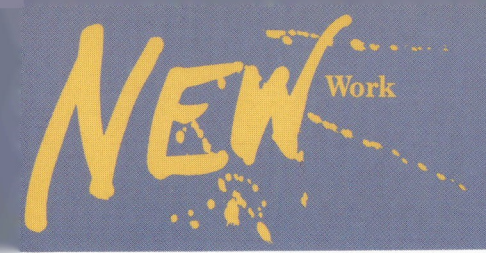

Represented by Michèle Manasse

16 West 75th Street, 2nd Floor
New York, New York, 10023
Telephone: (212) 873-3797

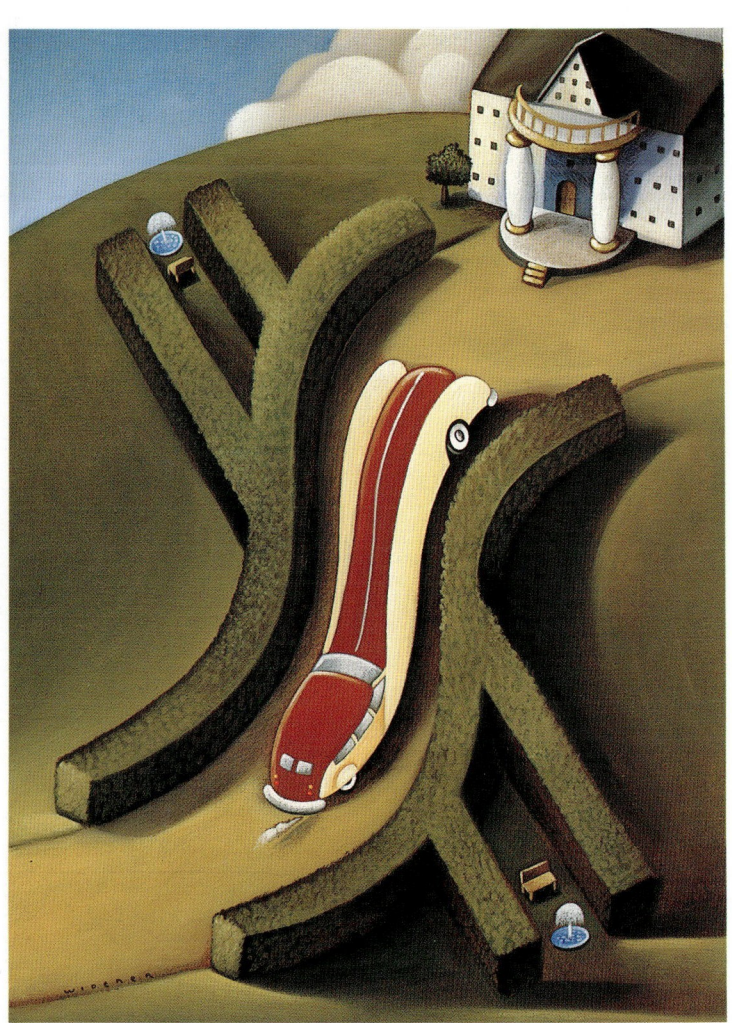

New York Magazine

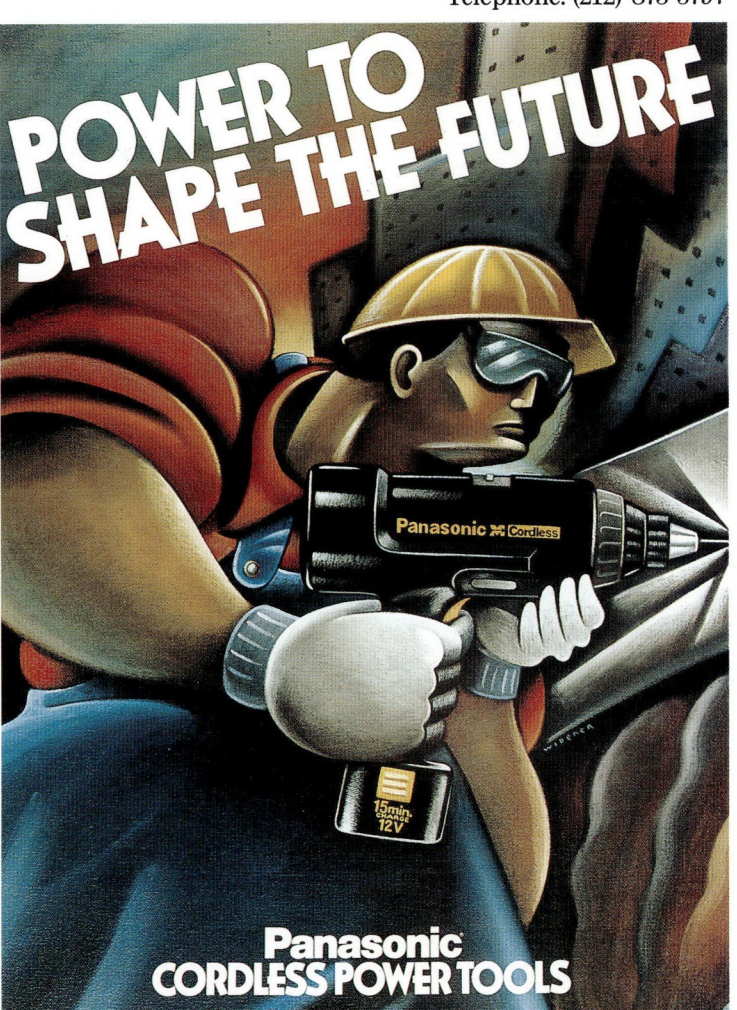

Martin, Marshall, Jaccoma & Mitchell

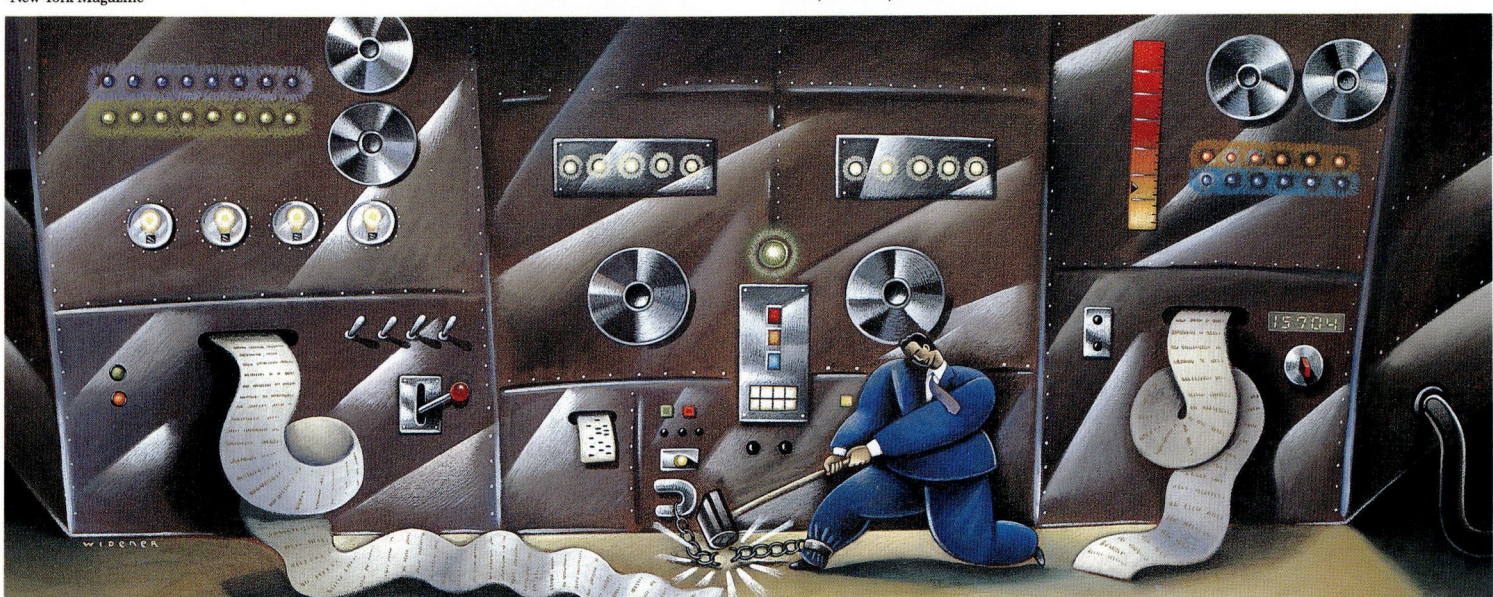

NCR Corporation

1991 © Terry Widener

175

New Work

Roger Roth

Represented by Michèle Manasse
16 West 75th Street, 2nd Floor
New York, New York, 10023
Telephone: (212) 873-3797

California Lawyer Magazine

1991 © Roger Roth

New Work

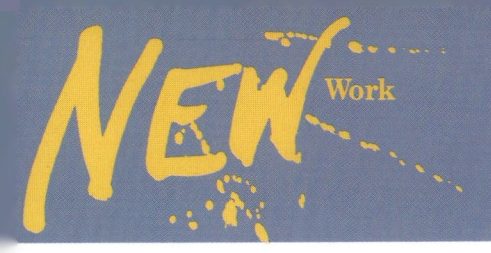

Roger Roth

Represented by Michèle Manasse

16 West 75th Street, 2nd Floor
New York, New York, 10023
Telephone: (212) 873-3797

National Geographic Traveler Magazine

The Wall Street Journal

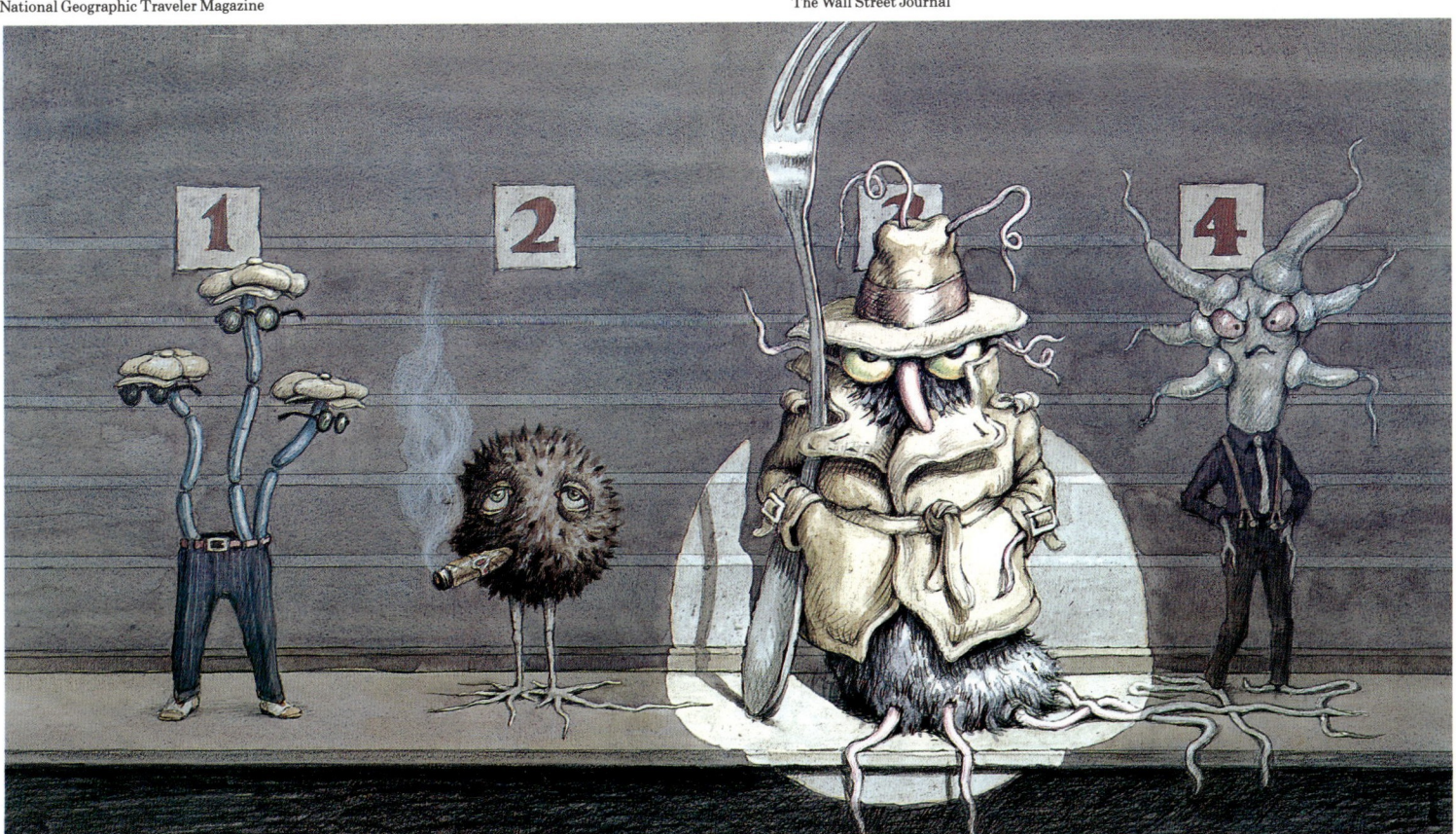

Time-Life Discover Magazine/Geo Magazine

1991 © Roger Roth

177

New Work

Maxine Boll

Represented by Michèle Manasse

16 West 75th Street, 2nd Floor
New York, New York, 10023
Telephone: (212) 873-3797

New Woman Magazine

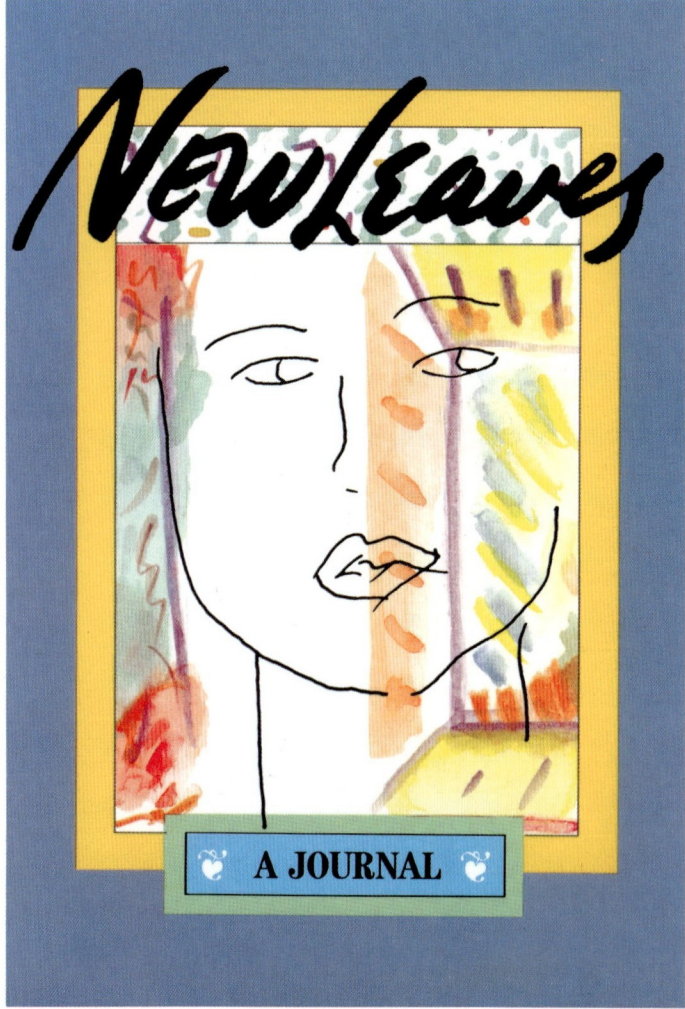

New Leaves — A JOURNAL
New Chapter Press Inc.

MUSIC FESTIVAL 1989
Leisure Technology Inc.

CHARDONNAY
THE WINE SOCIETY OF AMERICA
1987 Produced and bottled by Heldsberg Winery
Heldsburg California
24 fluid ounces
Alcoholic Content 10%

The Wine Society of America Inc.

1991 © Maxine Boll

New Work

Traian Alexandru Filip

Represented by Michèle Manasse
16 West 75th Street, 2nd Floor
New York, New York, 10023
Telephone: (212) 873-3797

Nagard Publishers (Italy)

Book-of-the-Month Club

The New York Times

Nagard Publishers (Italy)

1991 © T.A. Filip

New Work

Sheldon Greenberg

Represented by Michèle Manasse

16 West 75th Street, 2nd Floor
New York, New York, 10023
Telephone: (212) 873-3797

New York Morning

Amsterdam Scene

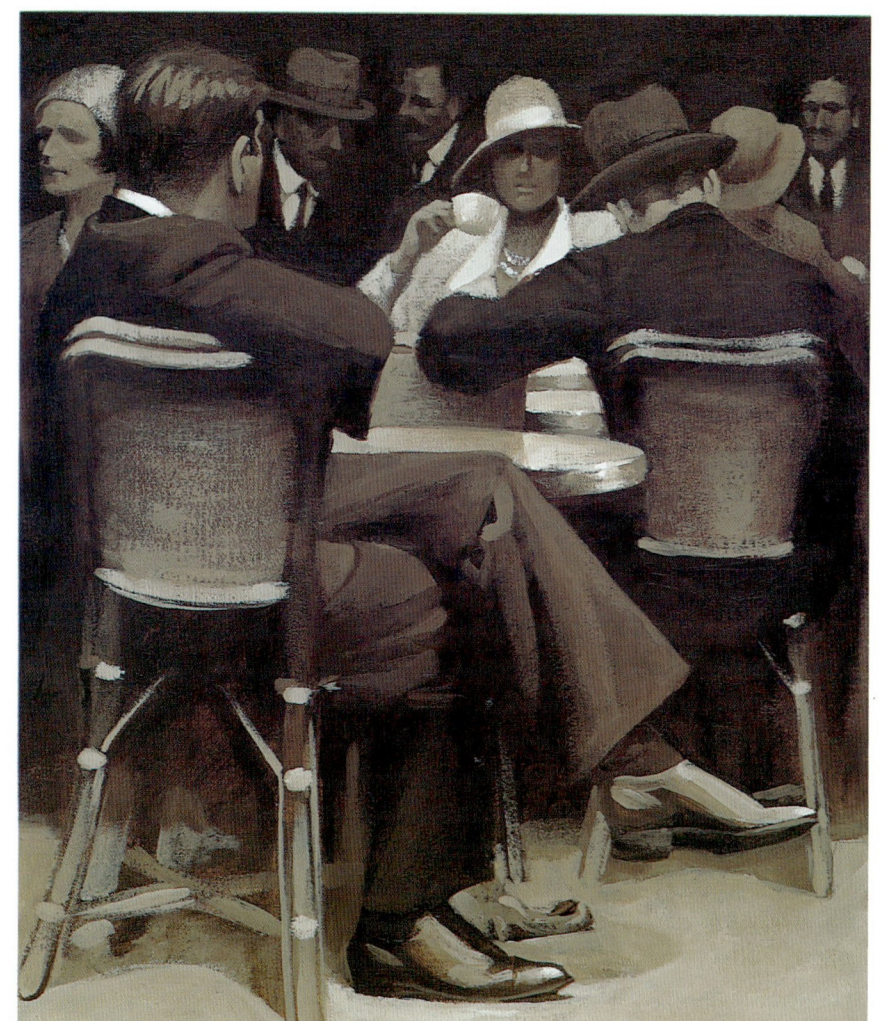

Warner Communications

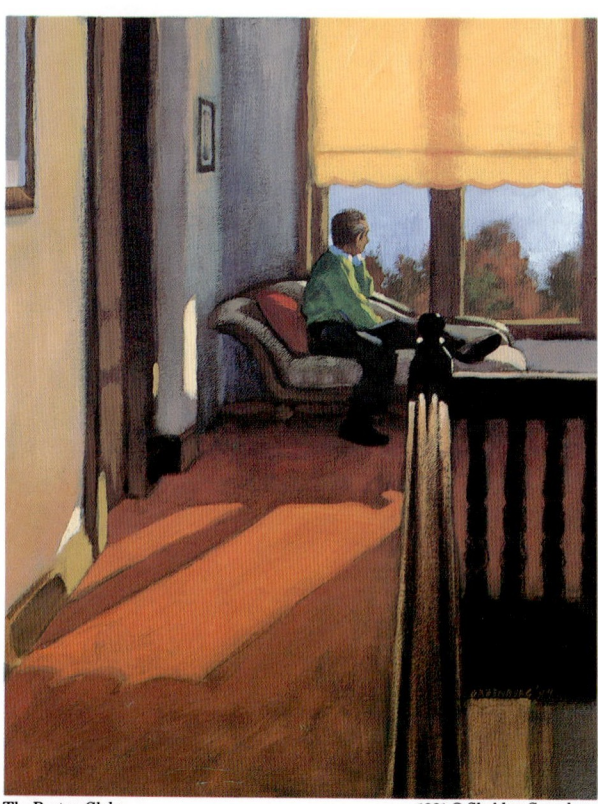

The Boston Globe

1991 © Sheldon Greenberg

New Work

Cathy Christy O'Connor

Represented by Michèle Manasse

16 West 75th Street, 2nd Floor
New York, New York, 10023
Telephone: (212) 873-3797

Saint Michèle

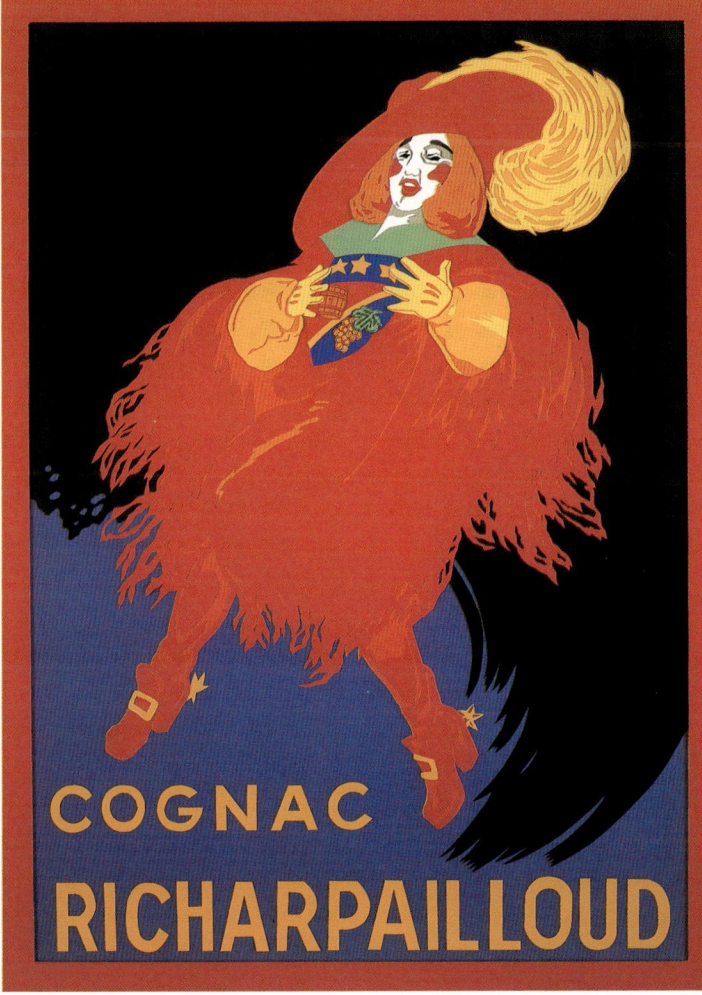

Cognac Richarpailloud (unpublished)

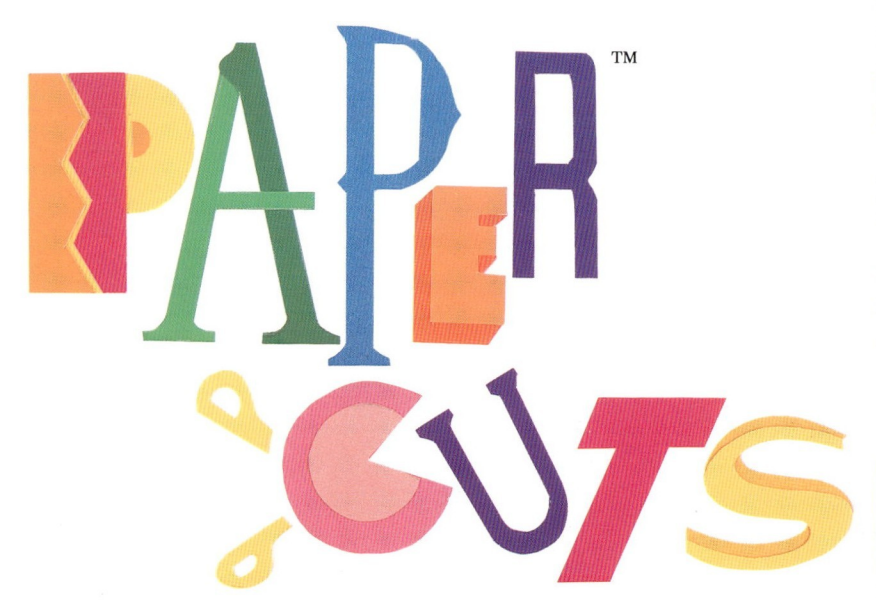

Green Market Poster (unpublished)

Coca-Cola (unpublished)

1991 © Cathy Christy O'Connor

New Work

Narda Lebo

Represented by Michèle Manasse

16 West 75th Street, 2nd Floor
New York, New York, 10023
Telephone: (212) 873-3797

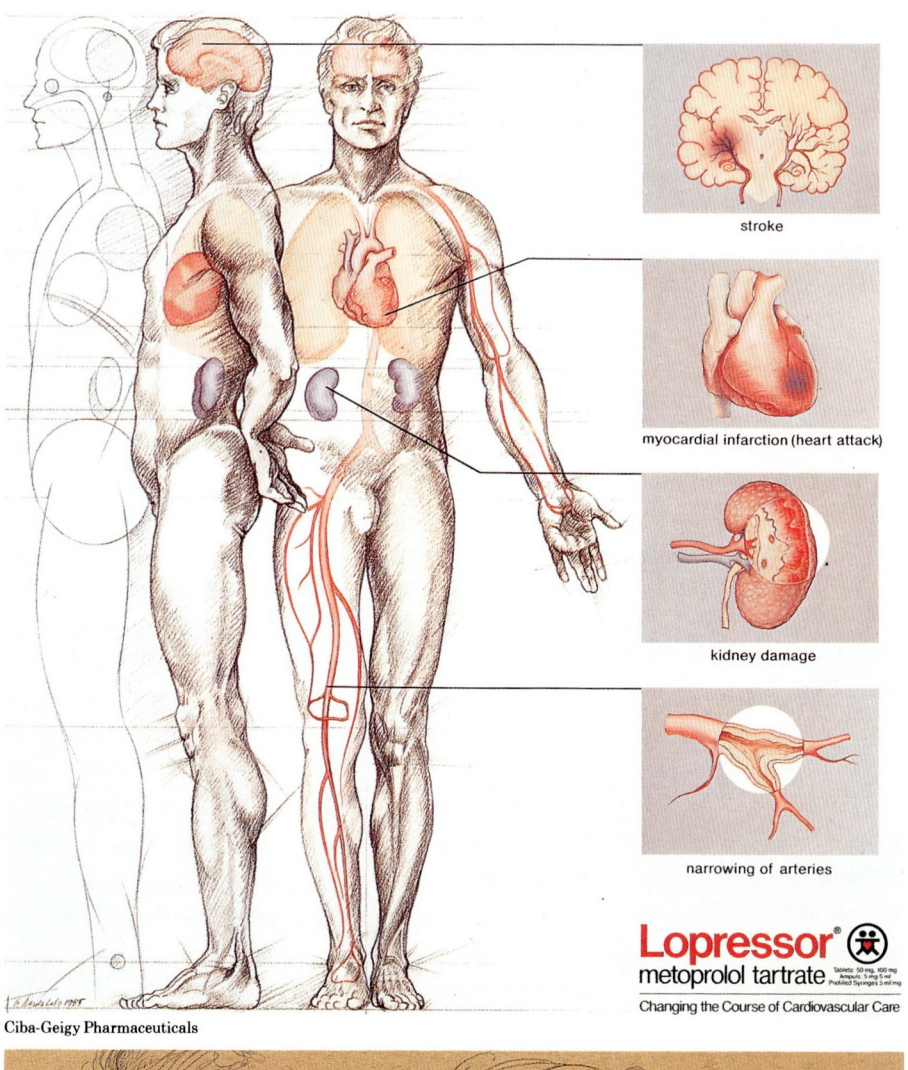

Ciba-Geigy Pharmaceuticals

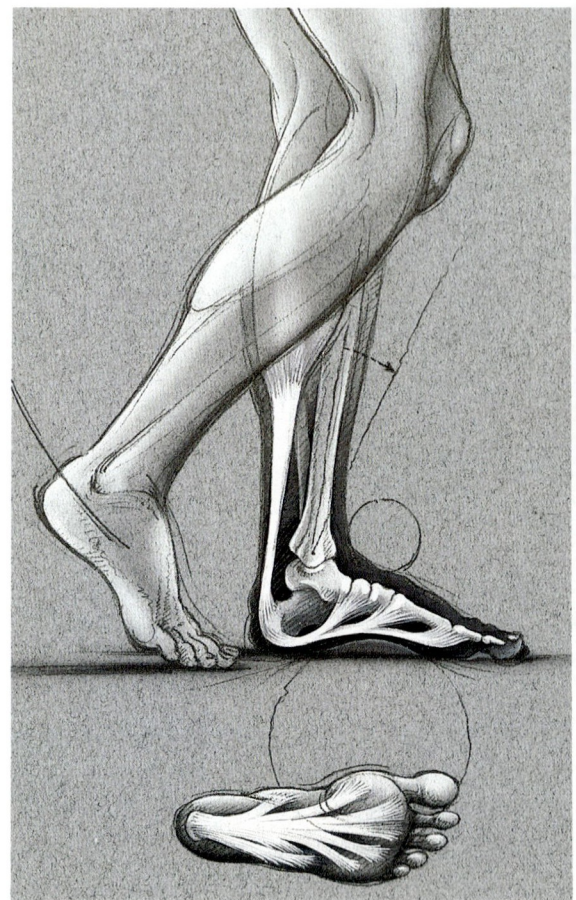

Prevention Magazine

Prevention Magazine

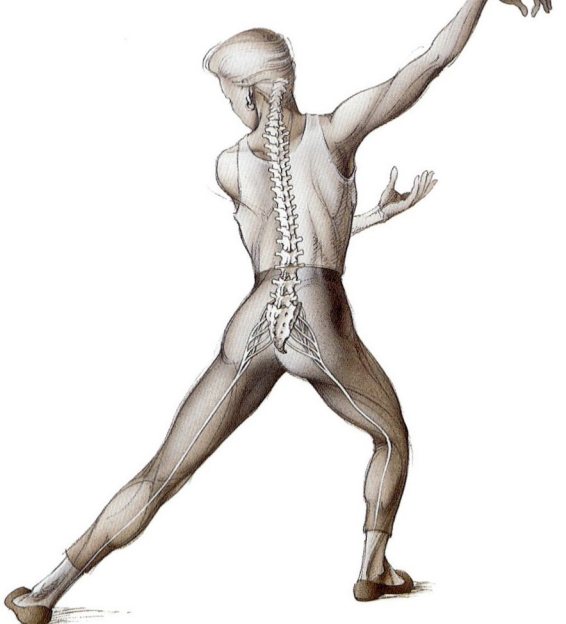

Rodale Press

1991 © Narda Lebo

New Work

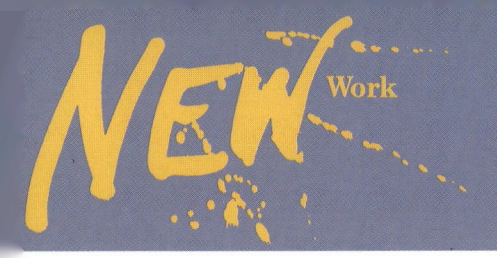

Narda Lebo

Represented by Michèle Manasse
16 West 75th Street, 2nd Floor
New York, New York, 10023
Telephone: (212) 873-3797

Harvard Business Review

American Heritage Magazine

The New York Times

1991 © Narda Lebo

183

New Work

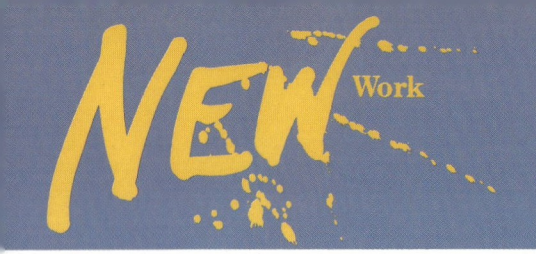

Carol Inouye

Represented by Michèle Manasse

16 West 75th Street, 2nd Floor
New York, New York, 10023
Telephone: (212) 873-3797

Greens with Red Pepper

Still Life

McMillan & Company

McMillan & Company

1991 © Carol Inouye

WANDA MAIORESCO DECA
(212) 838-2509

PHOTOGRAPHED BY PETER BUZOIANU

JEANETTE ADAMS
212·732·3878

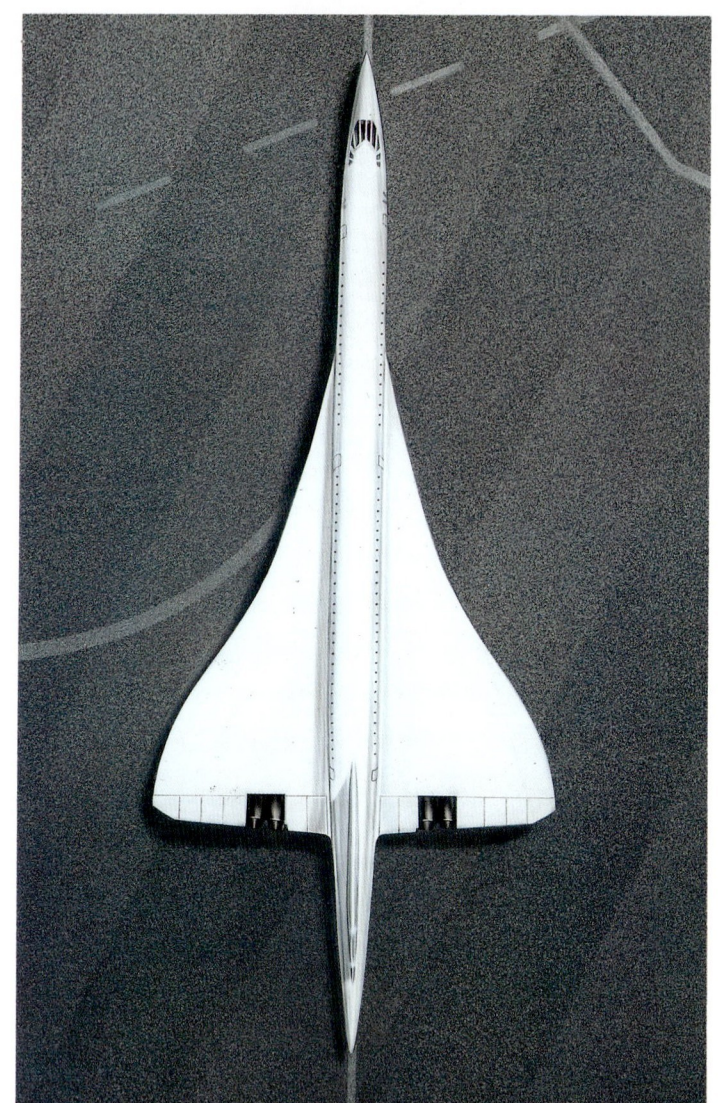

NAN BROOKS

Clients:
J.W. Thompson/Oscar Mayer
OshKosh Inc.
McDonalds
Inside Chicago
Scott Foresman Inc.
WorldBook Inc.
McGraw Hill
NEC/Turbografx
Arthur E. Wilk/Colgate-Palmolive

Studio: 708-256-2304
Fax in Studio
Representative:
Holly Hahn
Phone: 312-973-0410

Mike Lester

Contact: Mike Lester at (404) 447-5332 Fax (404) 447-9559

Mike Lester

Contact: Mike Lester at (404) 447-5332 Fax (404) 447-9559

Hans Angermueller – Vice Chairman, Citicorp

ED LITTLE
112 Wewaka Brook Road, Bridgewater, CT 06752
Telephone (203) 350 6523

ED LITTLE

112 Wewaka Brook Road, Bridgewater, CT 06752
Telephone (203) 350 6523

West Coast Representative: Carole Newman & Assocs.
Telephone (213) 394 5031   Fax (213) 394 7590

©1990 Unicover Corporation

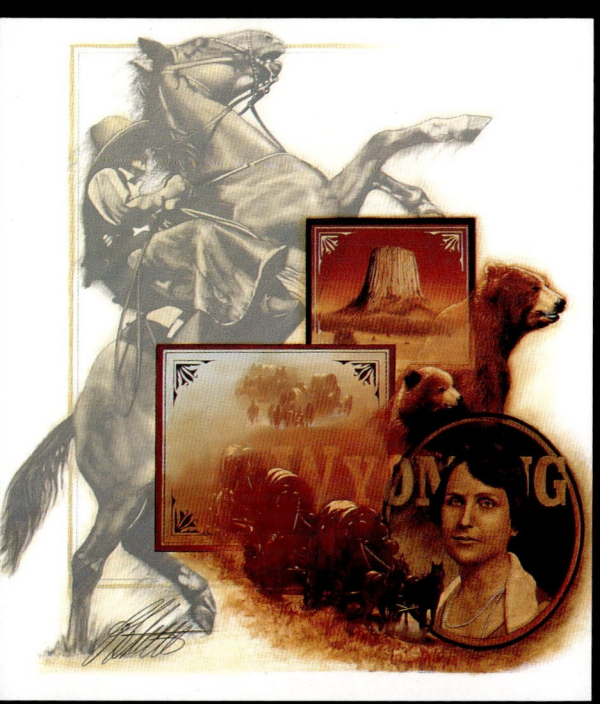

©1990 Unicover Corporation

eddie young

**Character design
Illustration**

CAROLE NEWMAN & ASSOCIATES
CREATIVE AGENCY   (213) 394-5031

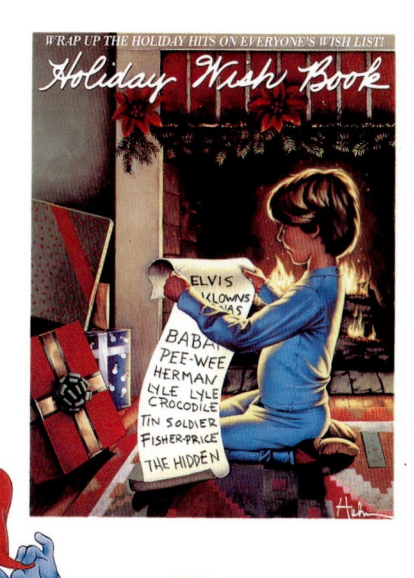

© 1989 Landmark Entertainment Group

tim huhn

fiona stokes

Illustration
Giftware/Ceramics
Greeting Cards
Textiles/Home Furnishings

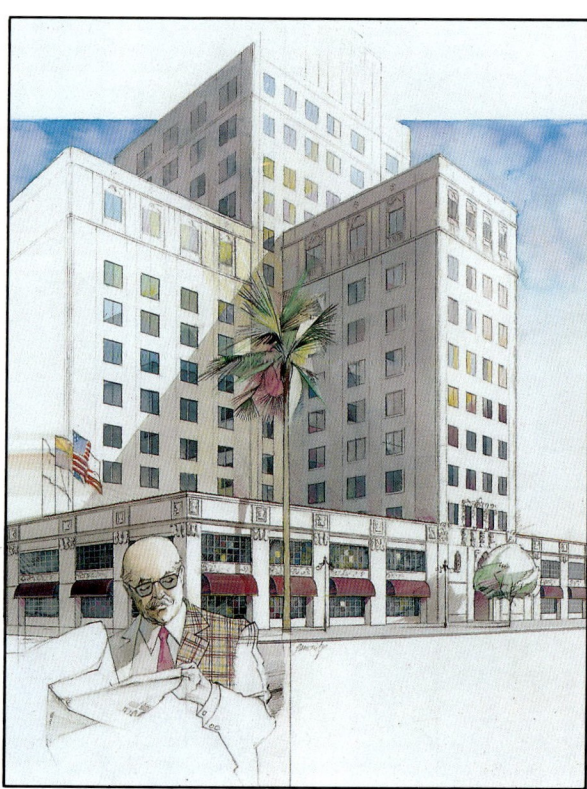

CAROLE NEWMAN & ASSOCIATES
CREATIVE AGENCY (213) 394-5031

paul janovsky

193

vladimir paperny

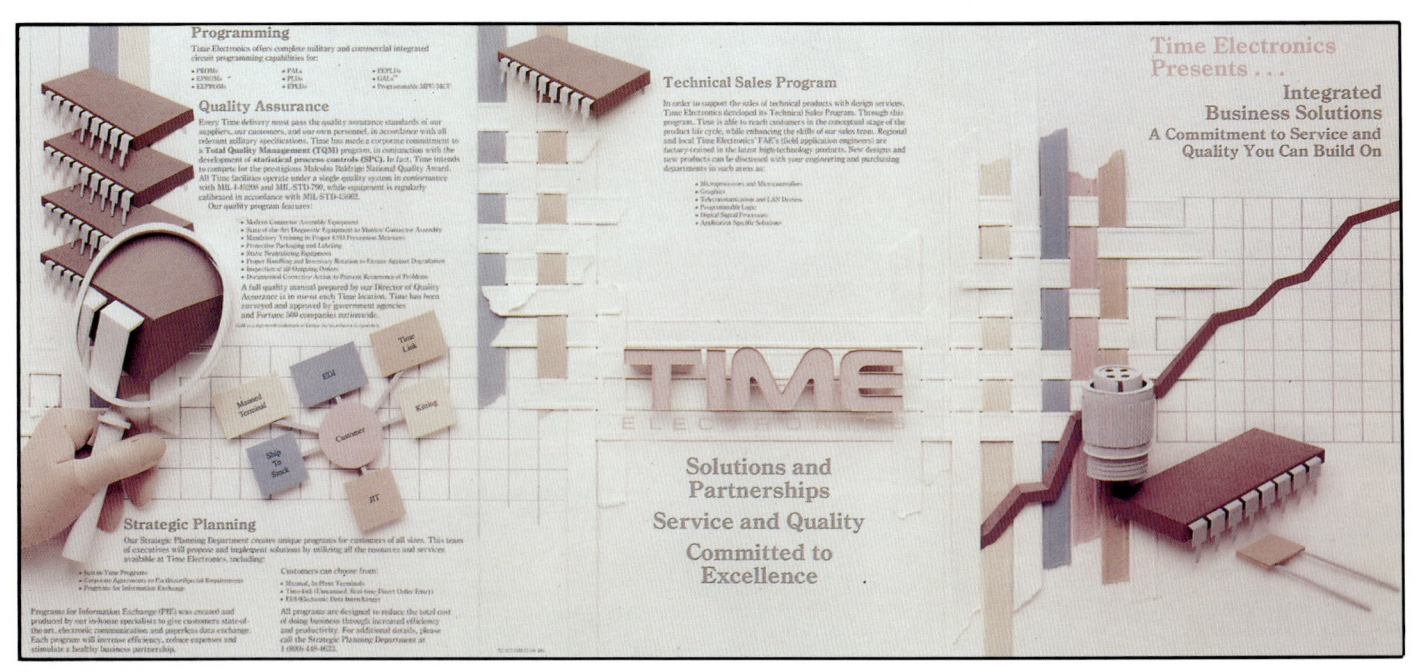

Paper Sculpture
Photography
Design

CAROLE NEWMAN & ASSOCIATES
CREATIVE AGENCY   (213) 394-5031

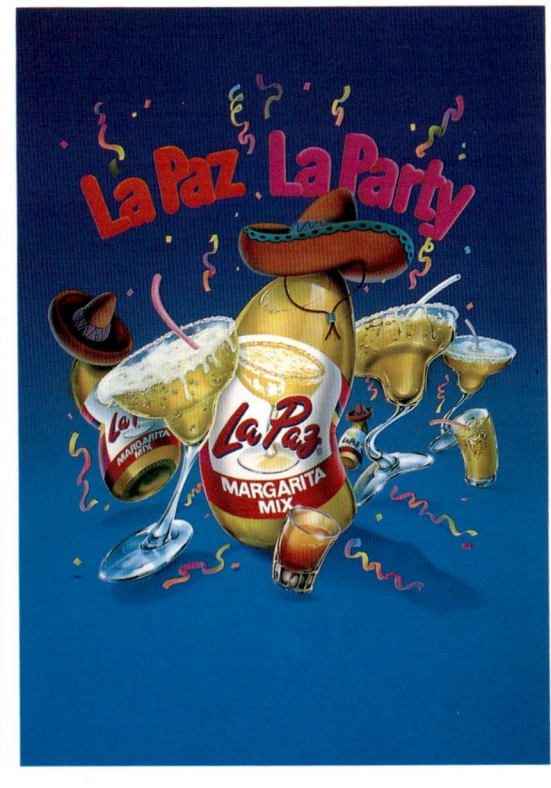

© DISNEY

michael humphries

ROBERT MARGULIES
MARGULIES MEDICAL ART

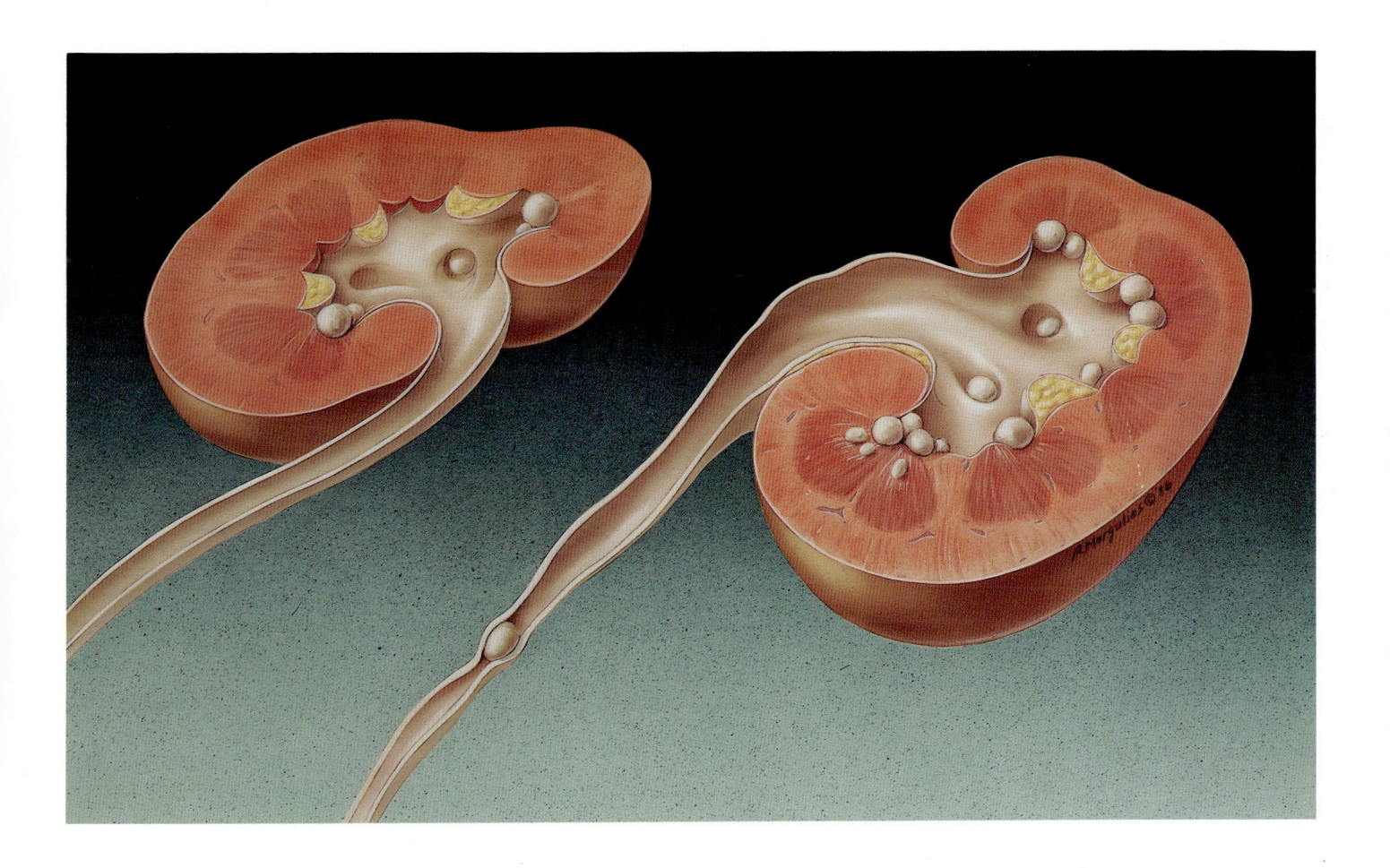

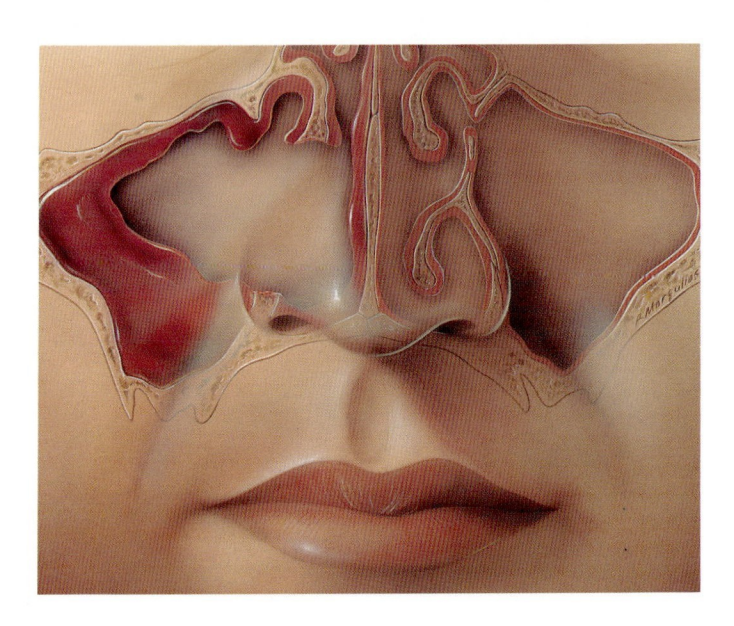

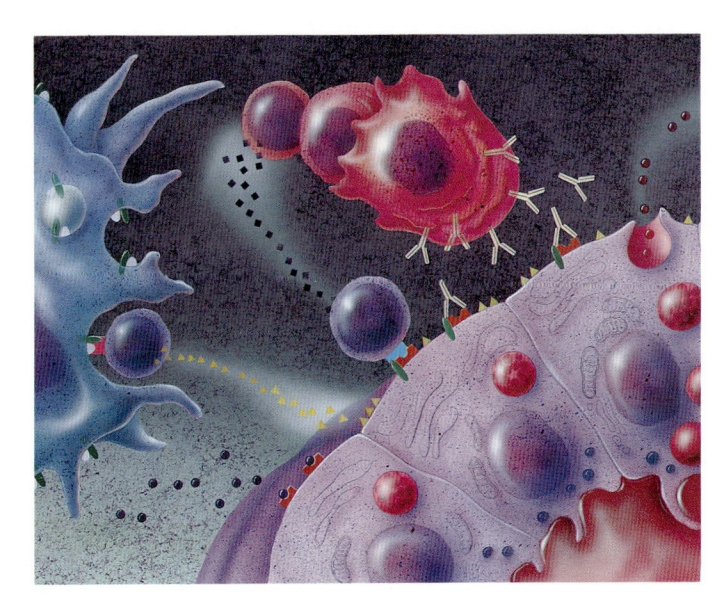

561 BROADWAY ROOM 10B • NEW YORK, N.Y. 10012
TEL: (212) 219-9621   FAX: (212) 334-8459

195

Maud Geng
Represents Artists
25 Gray Street
Boston, Massachusetts 02116
(617) 236-1920
Fax (617) 482-5940

MART / UD (MAUD ART logo)

Robert Kasper

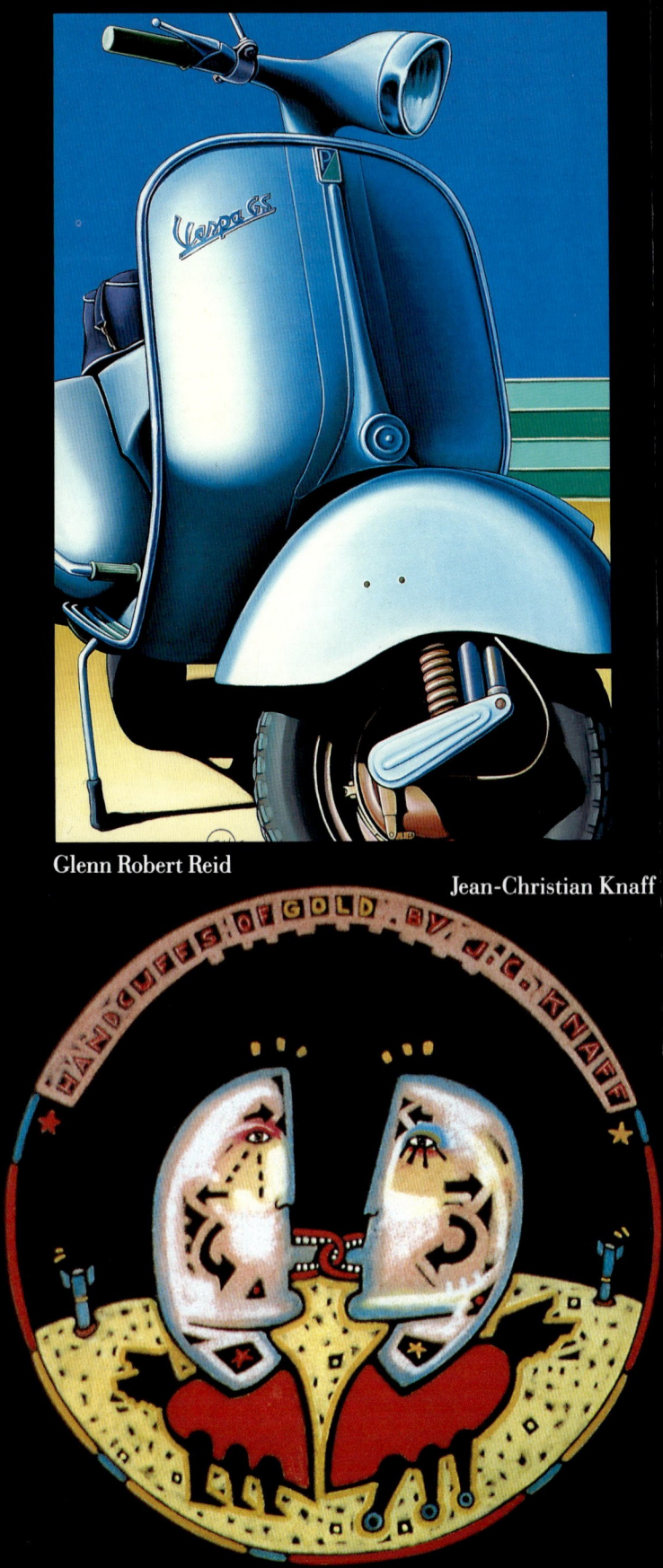

Suzanne Barnes

Glenn Robert Reid

Jean-Christian Knaff

Maud Geng
Represents Artists
5 Gray Street
Boston, Massachusetts 02116
(617) 236-1920
Fax (617) 482-5940

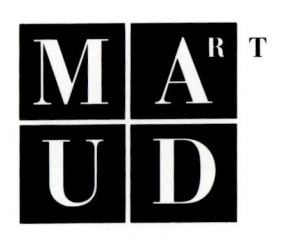

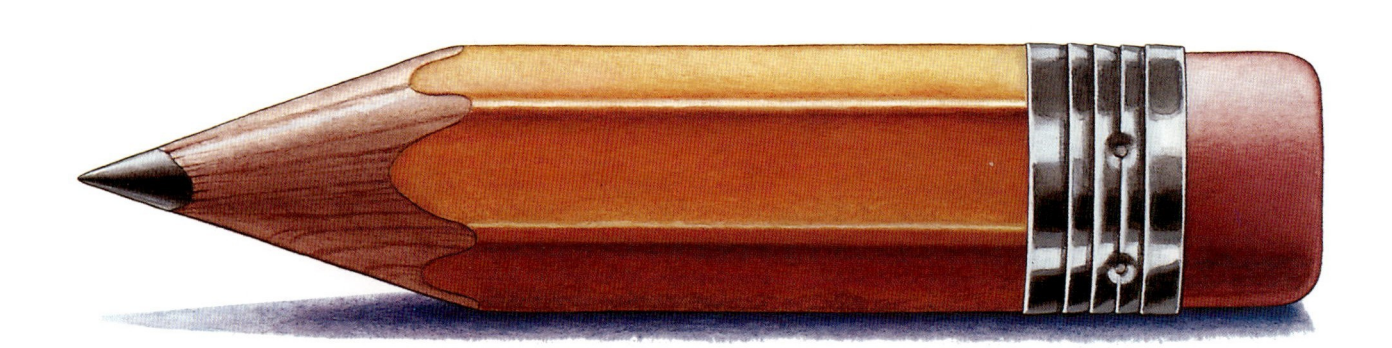

MART
UD

Caroline Alterio   Jon McIntosh   Vicki Smith

C. ALTERIO ©90

ELSA WARNICK

(503) 228-2659 • FAX: (503) 223-5727 • 812 S.W. ST. CLAIR #2 • PORTLAND, OR 97205
REPRESENTED BY SAM BRODY • TEL: (212) 758-0640 • FAX: (212) 697-4518

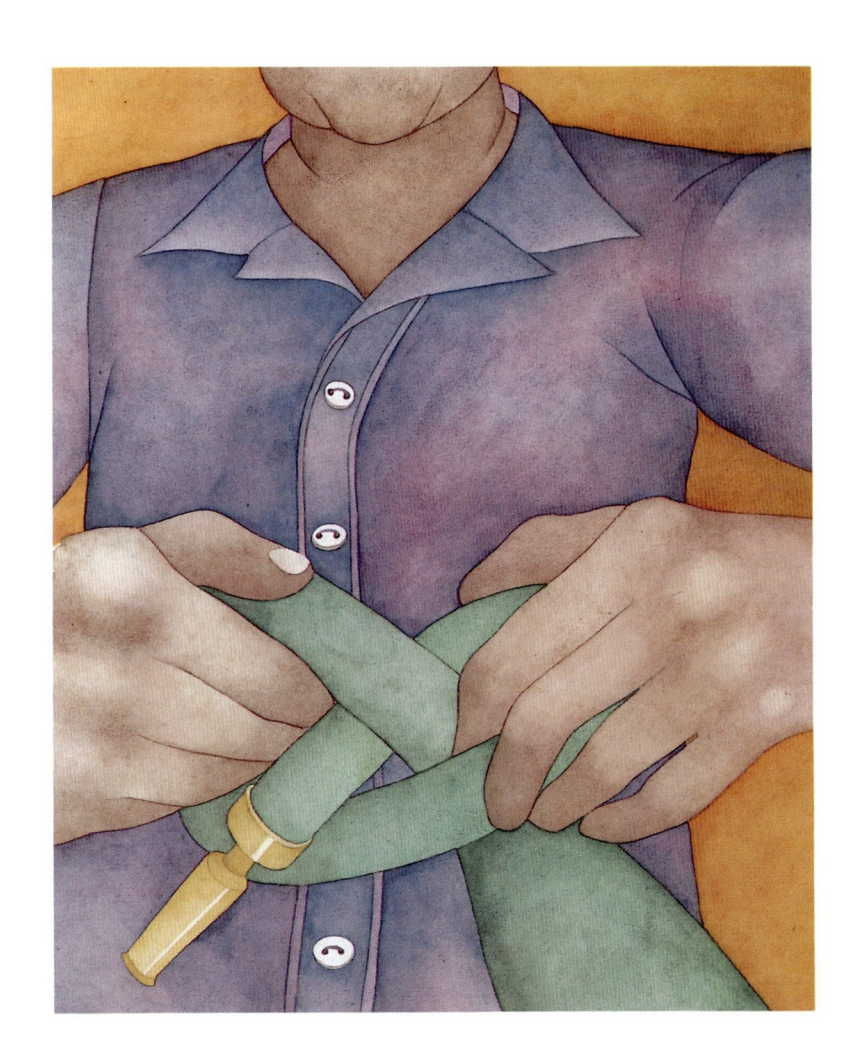

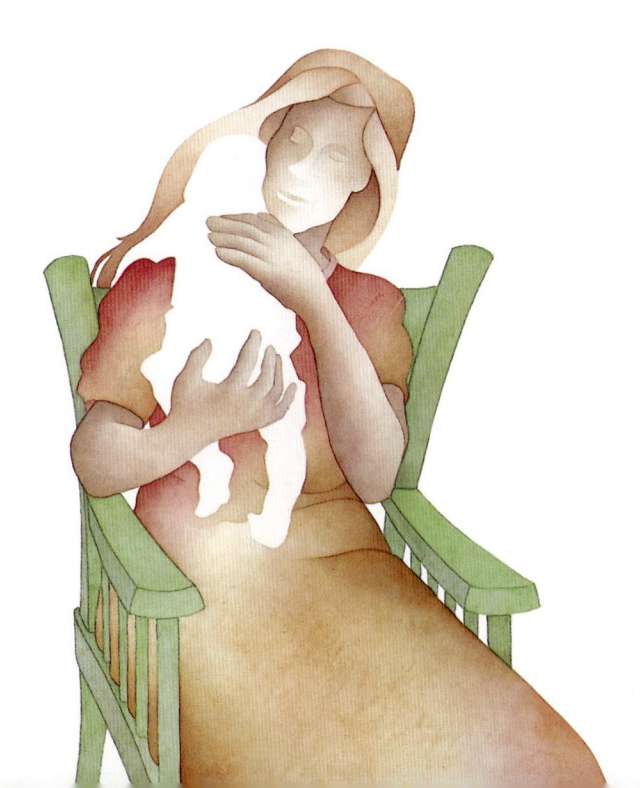

SOME DOGS
DON'T GO TO HEAVEN

... AND THIS LITTLE PIGGY
WASN'T FEELING SO WELL.

NATIONAL SAFETY COUNCIL

T. SIRRELL
708·213·9003
FAX IN STUDIO

© TERRY SIRRELL

199

TOM FOTY

3836 SHADY OAK RD
MINNETONKA, MN 55343
612•933•5570
FAX 612•933•5570

CALL TO VIEW
COMPLETE PORTFOLIO

JOEL SPECTOR • 130 EAST 16TH STREET • NEW YORK, NY 10003 • (212) 254-3527

Also represented by Irmeli Holmberg • (212) 545-9155 • FAX (212) 545-9462

IRMELI HOLMBERG
280 MADISON AVE / NEW YORK, NY 10016

TEL: 212-545-9155
FAX: 212-545-9462

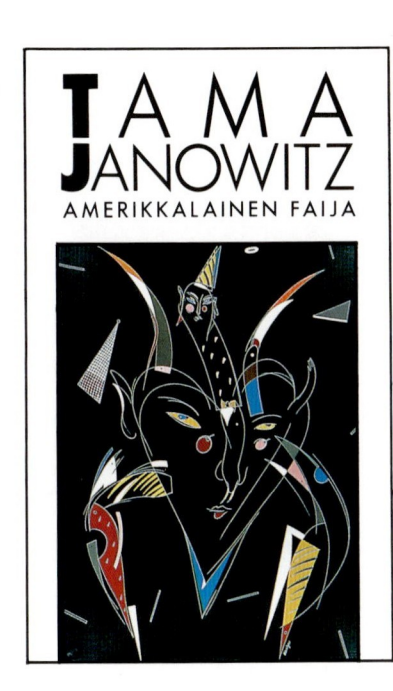

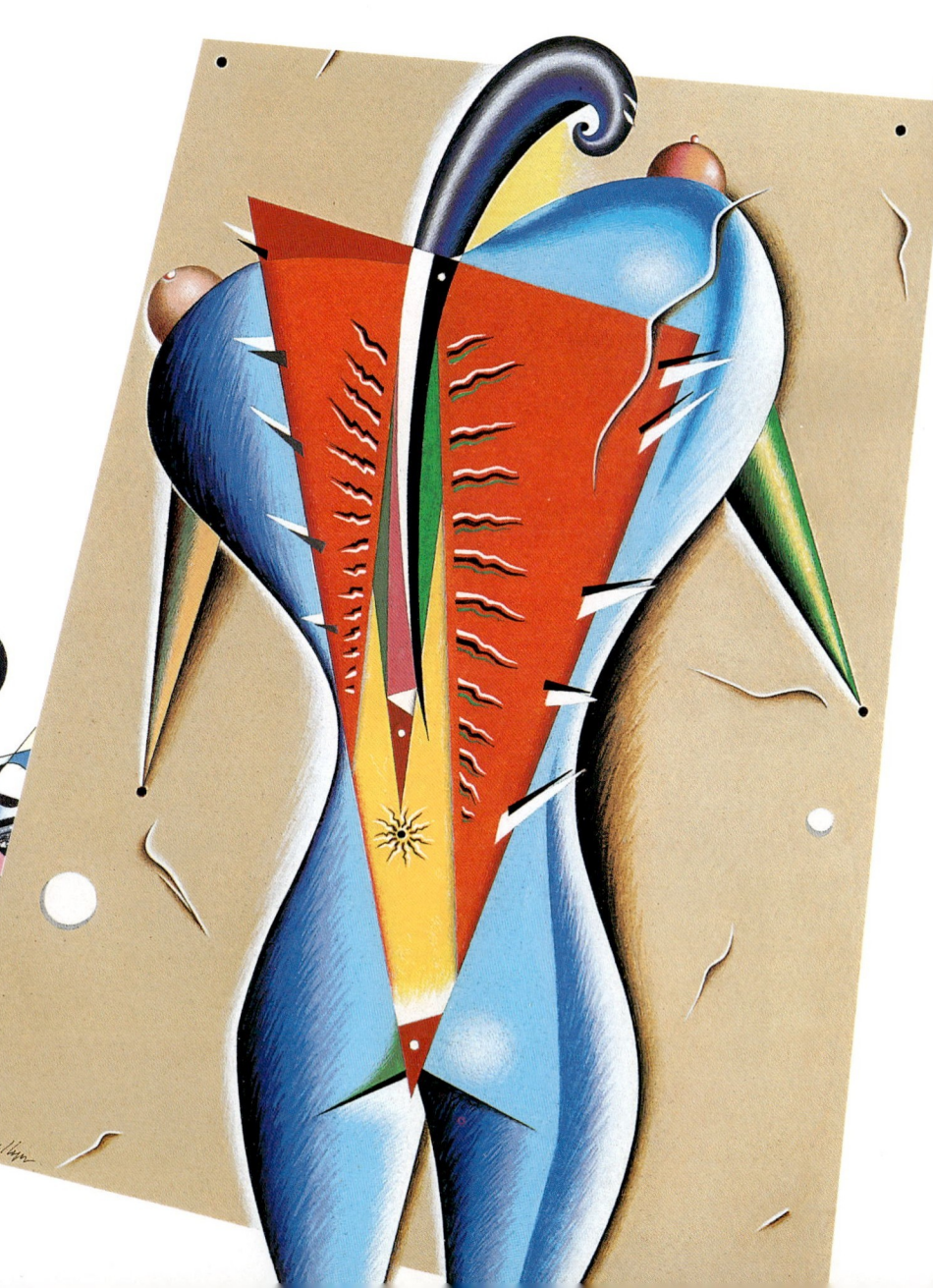

SUE LLEWELLYN

IRMELI HOLMBERG
280 MADISON AVE / NEW YORK, NY 10016

TEL: 212-545-9155
FAX: 212-545-9462

DAN BRIDY

IRMELI HOLMBERG
280 MADISON AVE / NEW YORK, NY 10016

TEL: 212-545-9155
FAX: 212-545-9462

DEBORAH PINKNEY

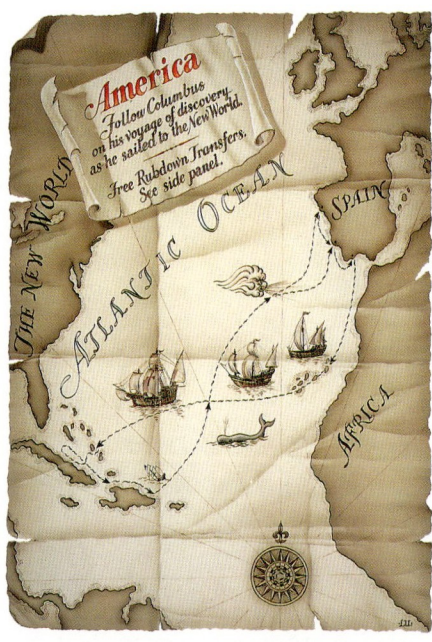

IRMELI HOLMBERG
280 MADISON AVE / NEW YORK, NY 10016

TEL: 212-545-9155
FAX: 212-545-9462

LU MATTHEWS

IRMELI HOLMBERG
280 MADISON AVE / NEW YORK, NY 10016

TEL: 212-545-9155
FAX: 212-545-9462

RANDIE WASSERMAN

IRMELI HOLMBERG
280 MADISON AVE / NEW YORK, NY 10016

TEL: 212-545-9155
FAX: 212-545-9462

I Loved You, Logan McGee! by Irene Bennett Brown

KAREN PRITCHETT

207

LADEN WITH HUMOR

NINA LADEN
ILLUSTRATION & IDEAS · 1517 McLENDON AVE NE · ATLANTA GA 30307 · (404) 371-0052 · FAX IN STUDIO

LADEN WITH CHARACTER

NINA LADEN

ILLUSTRATION & IDEAS · 1517 McLENDON AVE NE · ATLANTA GA 30307 · (404) 371-0052 · FAX IN STUDIO

TISH TENUD
3427 FOLSOM BLVD
SACRAMENTO · CA
9 · 5 · 8 · 1 · 6
916 · 455 · 0569
FAX IN STUDIO

Life is not mysterious,
it's really no charade.

Nothing is so serious,
it's only life's parade.

Member of the Sacramento Illustrators Guild

GARY PENCA
ILLUSTRATION

8335 N.W. 20th St., Coral Springs, FL 33071
(305) 752-4699
Fax in Studio
REPRESENTED IN NEW YORK BY: BILL & MAURINE KLIMT
(212) 799-2231

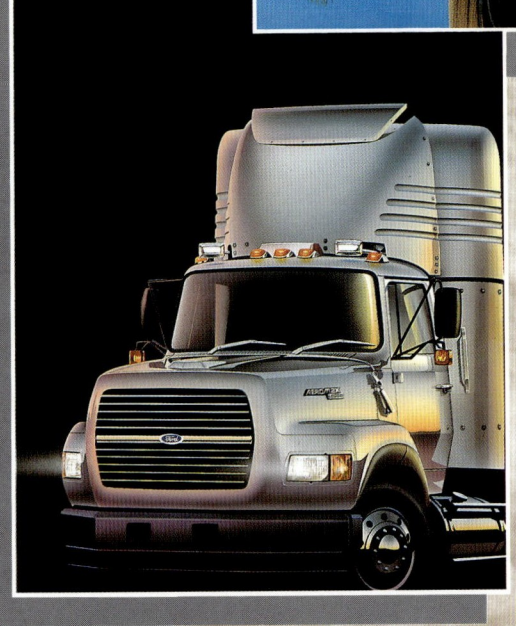

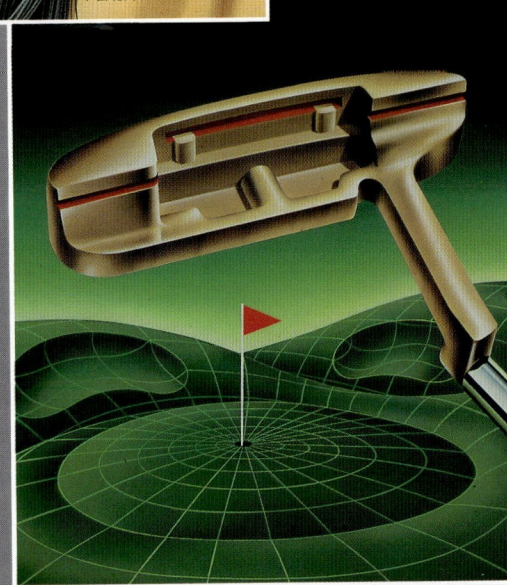

ED LINDLOF

Studio:
Ed Lindlof
(512) 472-0195

In New York:
American Artists
(212) 682-2462

In San Francisco:
Barb Hauser
(415) 339-1885

A. J. ALPER

New York

212 935 0039

Los Angeles

213 666 6036

GEO SIPP

PHONE: 404/876-0312 FAX: 404/876-2010
380 GARDEN LANE, NW ATLANTA, GA 30309

ATLANTA 1990
SUMMER GAMES 1996

Clients include:
ABC Sports, Atlanta Ballet, Atlanta Convention & Visitors Bureau, Atlanta Journal & Constitution, Beefeater Gin, Blue Cross & Blue Shield, Boston Globe, Chicago Tribune, Coca-Cola, 1988 Democratic Nat'l Convention, Major League Baseball, Sea & Ski, Sports Illustrated, Virginia Slims Tennis Tour

PAUL COZZOLINO

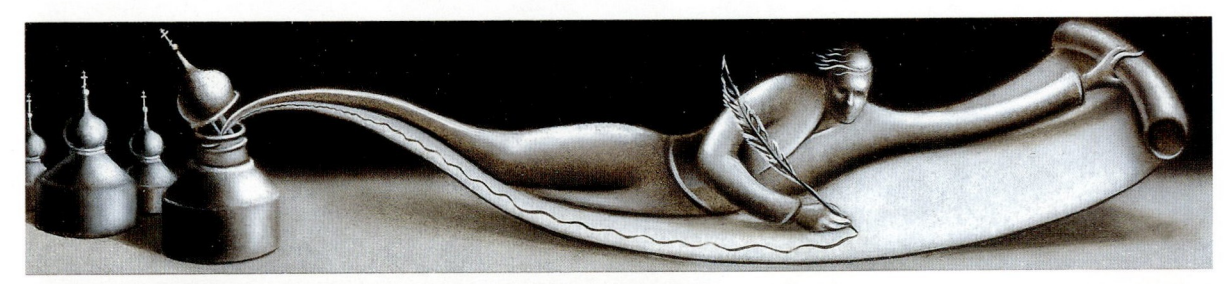

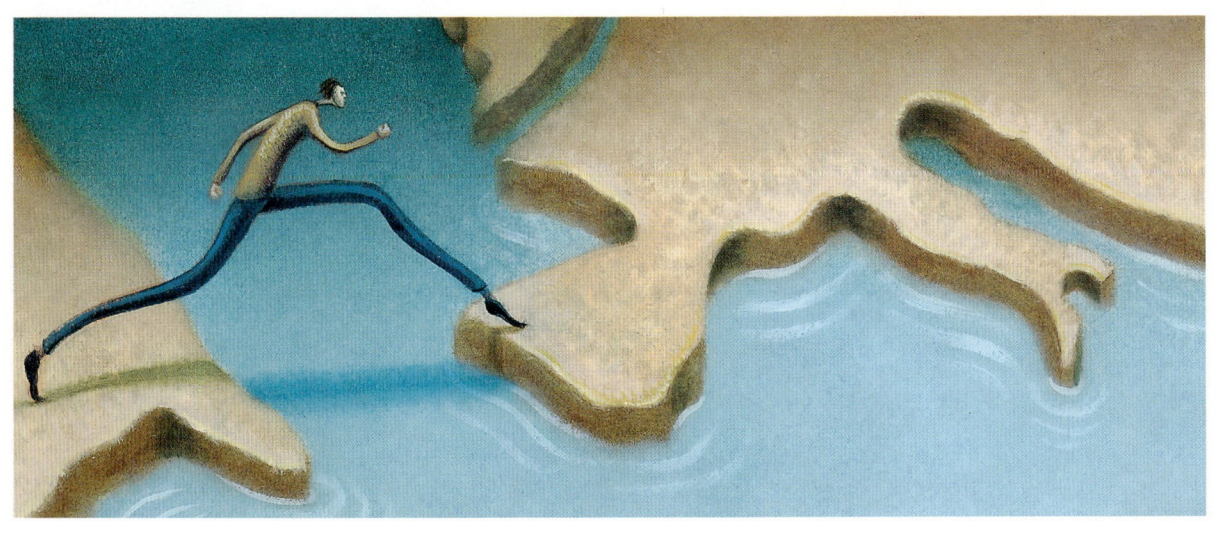

(212) 969-8680

ROBERT G. ROTH

AT&T
American Airlines
RCA Records
Philips Laboratories
Gulf & Western
Simon & Schuster
Felton Worldwide
Marvel Corporation
McGraw-Hill
Random House
Reader's Digest
Ginn & Co.
Houghton Mifflin
Bergelt Litchfield
Knopf Zimmerman Schultheis
AJN Corporation
Hospital Publications
Medical Economics Co.
The New York Times
The Boston Globe
Whitney Smith
Haymarket Group
The Grammy Awards
World Yacht

Marvel / Annual Report

AJN Corporation

West Hills Associates

516 544 4232   148 Lakebridge Drive, Kings Park, NY 11754   FAX 516 544 4225

ROBERT G. ROTH

Ron Rob Corporation

Haymarket Group

RCA Records

516 544 4232   148 Lakebridge Drive, Kings Park, NY 11754   FAX 516 544 4225

lyn martin
ILLUSTRATION
P.O. Box 51972 • Knoxville, TN 37950-1972 • 615/588-1760

Nature teaches beasts to know their friends.
—Shakespeare

©1990 Storm & Greeley, Inc.

We are so fond of one another because our ailments are the same.
—Jonathon Swift

Clients include: The Abbey Press; Addison-Wesley; Harper/Hazelden; Humpty Dumpty's Magazine; Child Life Magazine; Children's Playmate Magazine; Storm & Greeley, Inc.; Sunrise Publications; The United Methodist Publishing House; Baptist Sunday School Board; Great American Chocolate Chip Cookie Company.

Fred Warter
ILLUSTRATION
818 995 1935

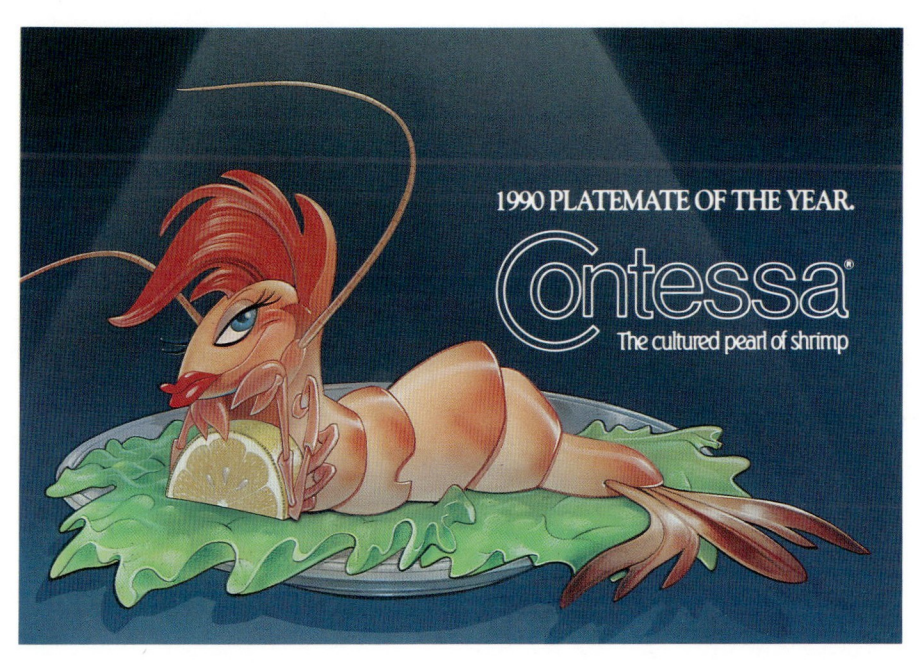

1990 PLATEMATE OF THE YEAR.

Contessa®
The cultured pearl of shrimp

Member of the Sacramento Illustrators Guild

Buz Walker Teach
ILLUSTRATION STUDIO □ 916/454-3556

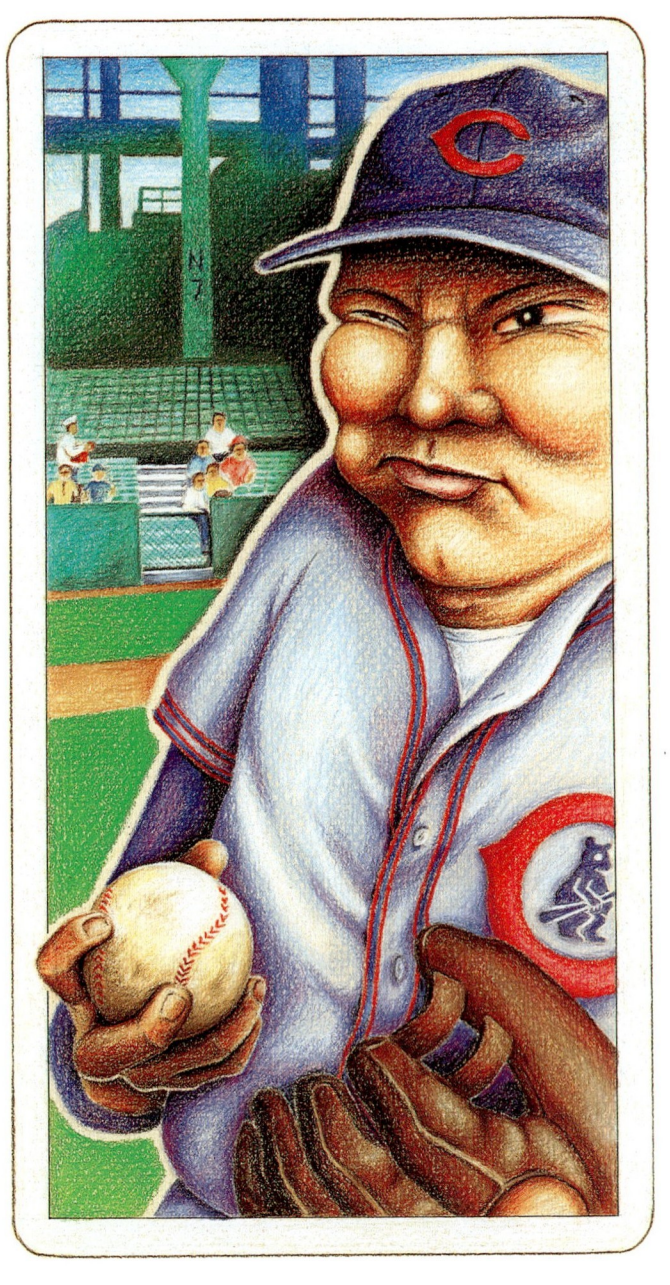

HARDIMAN

MILES W. HARDIMAN
30 Village Drive
Littleton, Colorado 80123
(303) 798-9143
FAX: (303) 795-8559
Mobil Phone: (303) 880-9143

221

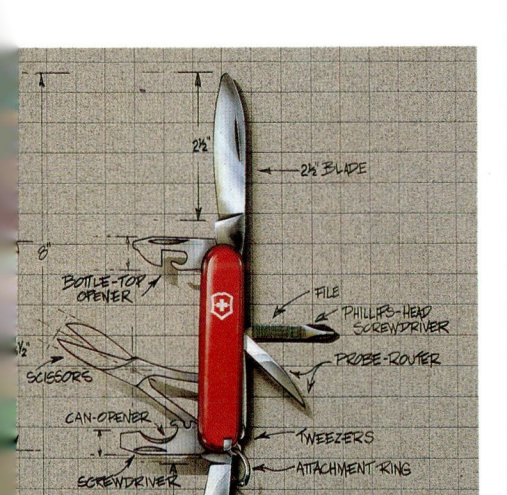

SCRATCHY STUDIO

Fran O'Neill

617.267.9215

P.O. Box 716 . Prudential Station . Boston . MA . 02199

© F.J.O. 1990

SUSAN MELRATH

ILLUSTRATION

1211 Reading Terrace
W. Palm Beach, FL 33414
(407) 790-1561
FAX (407) 790-4915

Represented in the N.E. by
Creative Freelancers, Inc.
62 W. 45th Street
New York, N.Y. 10036
(212) 398-9540

223

CARL NAKAMURA

213 936 2620
FAX 213 931 3091

135 South La Brea • Los Angeles, California • 90036

MIKE QUON DESIGN OFFICE • NYC 212•226•6024
568 BROADWAY SUITE 703 NEW YORK, NY 10012 FAX 212•219•0331
A FULL SERVICE DESIGN STUDIO SPECIALIZING IN ADVERTISING ART

THE NEW SCHOOL FOR SOCIAL RESEARCH

AT&T

U.S. ARMY

AT&T

© MIKE QUON DESIGN OFFICE, INC. 1990

225

DANIEL ABRAHAM

Box 2528 Rockefeller Center Station · N.Y.C. 10185
718 · 499 · 4006 · FAX IN STUDIO

©1990 Daniel Abraham

EVAN POLENGHI · ILLUSTRATION

718 · 499 · 3214

LARRY SALK
5455 Wilshire Blvd., Suite 1212
Los Angeles, California 91356
(213) 934-1975

INTERNATIONAL CAPITAL ACCESS GROUP "Find the 150 Companies Contest"

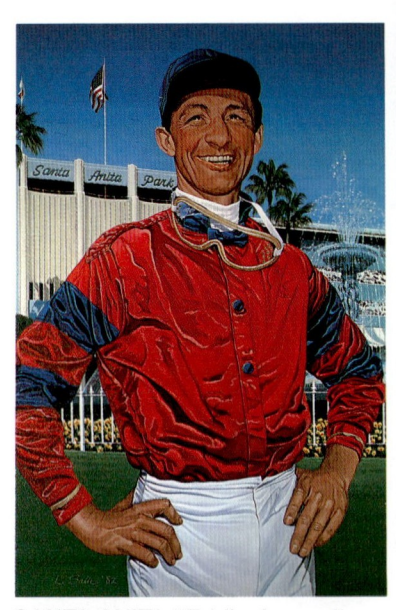

SANTA ANITA "Eddie Arcaro"

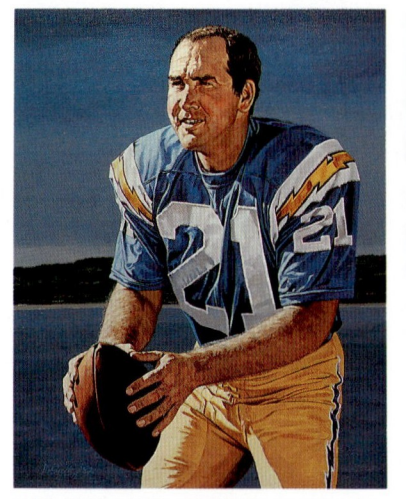

NFL HALL OF FAME "John Hadl"

USAF "C-130 Loadmaster"

In Los Angeles call Rosenthal Represents (213) 390-9595

Illustration
DAVID G KLEIN
408-7TH-ST
BROOKLYN-NY
11215
(718) 788-1818

New York Times, Forbes, Bulletin of the Atomic Scientists, Franklin Library, Inx., Society of Illustrators.

FAX services available.

229

Creative Freelancers

REPRESENTING

STEVE DININNO

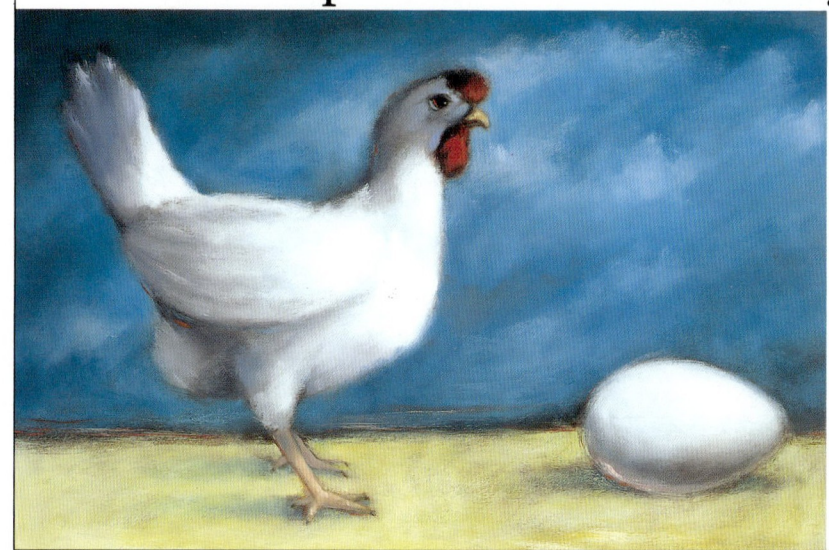

First We Solved The Age-Old Problem Of Hardware Vendor Dependence. Now For The Easy One.

It seemed an impossible puzzle. A company's strategic needs or the needs imposed by its application software: which should come first?

Although the answer may seem obvious, until now, most companies were caught in the cycle of using hardware which dictated software which then limited their future hardware, software and strategic options.

But not anymore. Enter Liant Software Corporation with system software which gives you portable applications which can run on virtually any system, regardless of manufacturer or operating environment.

It's a big claim. And it took more than 500 man-years to develop the software which could make it a reality. Plus three powerful Liant companies to cover the full spectrum of applications: Language Processors, Inc. (scientific and engineering programming systems), Template Graphics Software, Inc. (graphical programming systems), and Ryan McFarland Corporation (commercial programming systems). It's a combination that has finally broken the cycle of hardware dependence.

Ryan McFarland's RM/COBOL-85® for commercial applications is a good example. Its Proprietary Object Portability System—POPS™—allows you to rehost your company's software to any platform and database without recompilation. With POPS, your total investment is protected no matter what system you have today or what system is popular tomorrow. But it's only the beginning.

Call us at **1-800-662-9866.** You'll find that Liant really does have all the answers. Well, almost all of them.

LIANT
LIANT SOFTWARE CORPORATION
959 CONCORD STREET, FRAMINGHAM, MA 01701-4613
(508) 626-0006 FAX (508) 626-2221

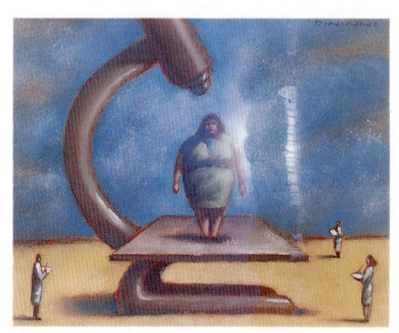

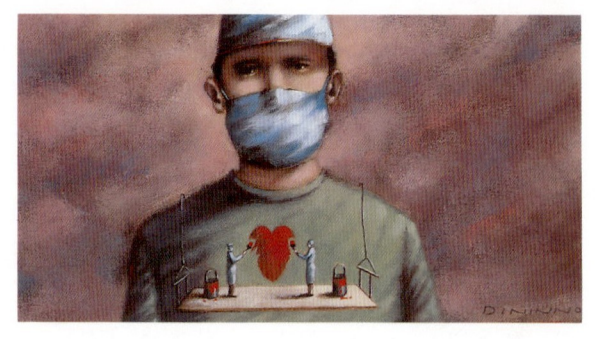

62 WEST 45TH STREET, NEW YORK, N.Y. 10036   (212) 398-9540   FAX (212) 398-9547

Creative Freelancers

REPRESENTING

MICHAEL NG

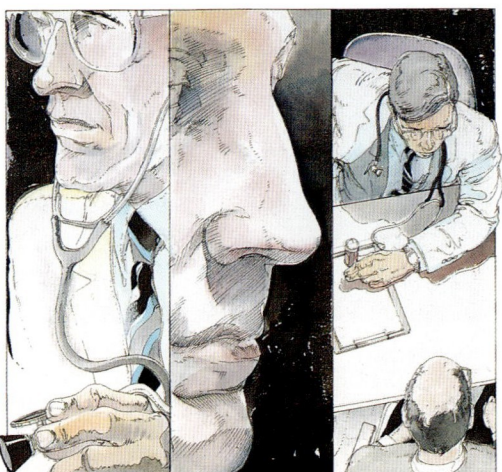

62 WEST 45TH STREET, NEW YORK, N.Y. 10036   (212) 398-9540   FAX (212) 398-9547

CREATIVE FREELANCERS

REPRESENTING

LIONEL TALARO

62 WEST 45TH STREET, NEW YORK, N.Y. 10036   (212) 398-9540   FAX (212) 398-9547

Creative Freelancers

REPRESENTING

WENDE CAPORALE

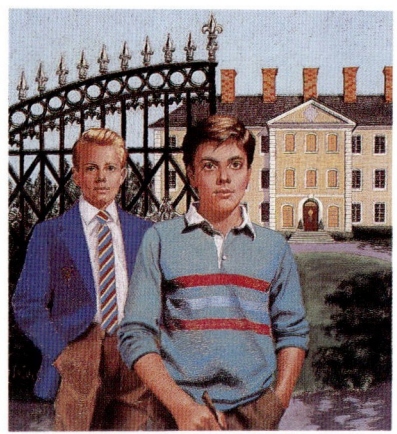

62 WEST 45TH STREET, NEW YORK, N.Y. 10036   (212) 398-9540   FAX (212) 398-9547

Creative Freelancers

REPRESENTING

MERYL ROSNER

62 WEST 45TH STREET, NEW YORK, N.Y. 10036   (212) 398-9540   FAX (212) 398-9547

Creative Freelancers

REPRESENTING

JOHN DZEDZY

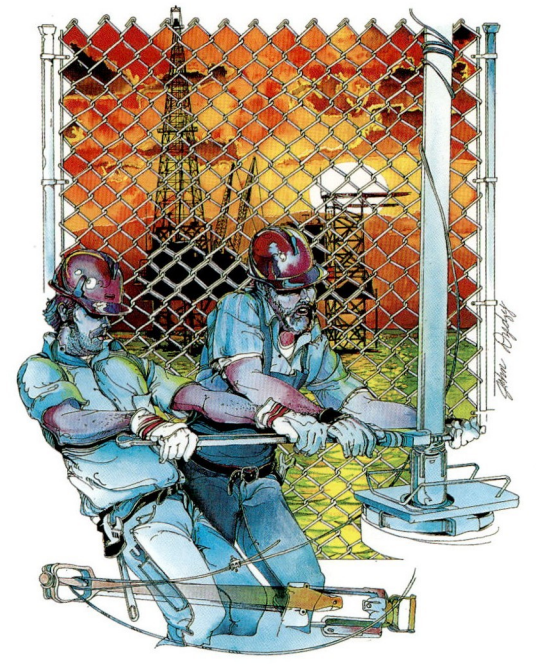

62 WEST 45TH STREET, NEW YORK, N.Y. 10036   (212) 398-9540   FAX (212) 398-9547

235

Creative Freelancers

REPRESENTING

JOE DE CERCHIO

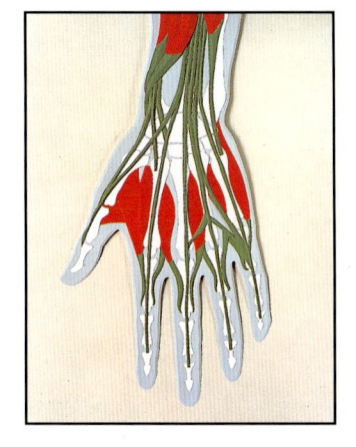

62 WEST 45TH STREET, NEW YORK, N.Y. 10036 (212) 398-9540 FAX (212) 398-9547

LOU CARBONE

LOU CARBONE

NAIAD EINSEL — *Fabric Collage*

MYRON GROSSMAN

ROGER T. DE MUTH

ROGER T. DE MUTH

MENA DOLOBOWSKY

MENA DOLOBOWSKY

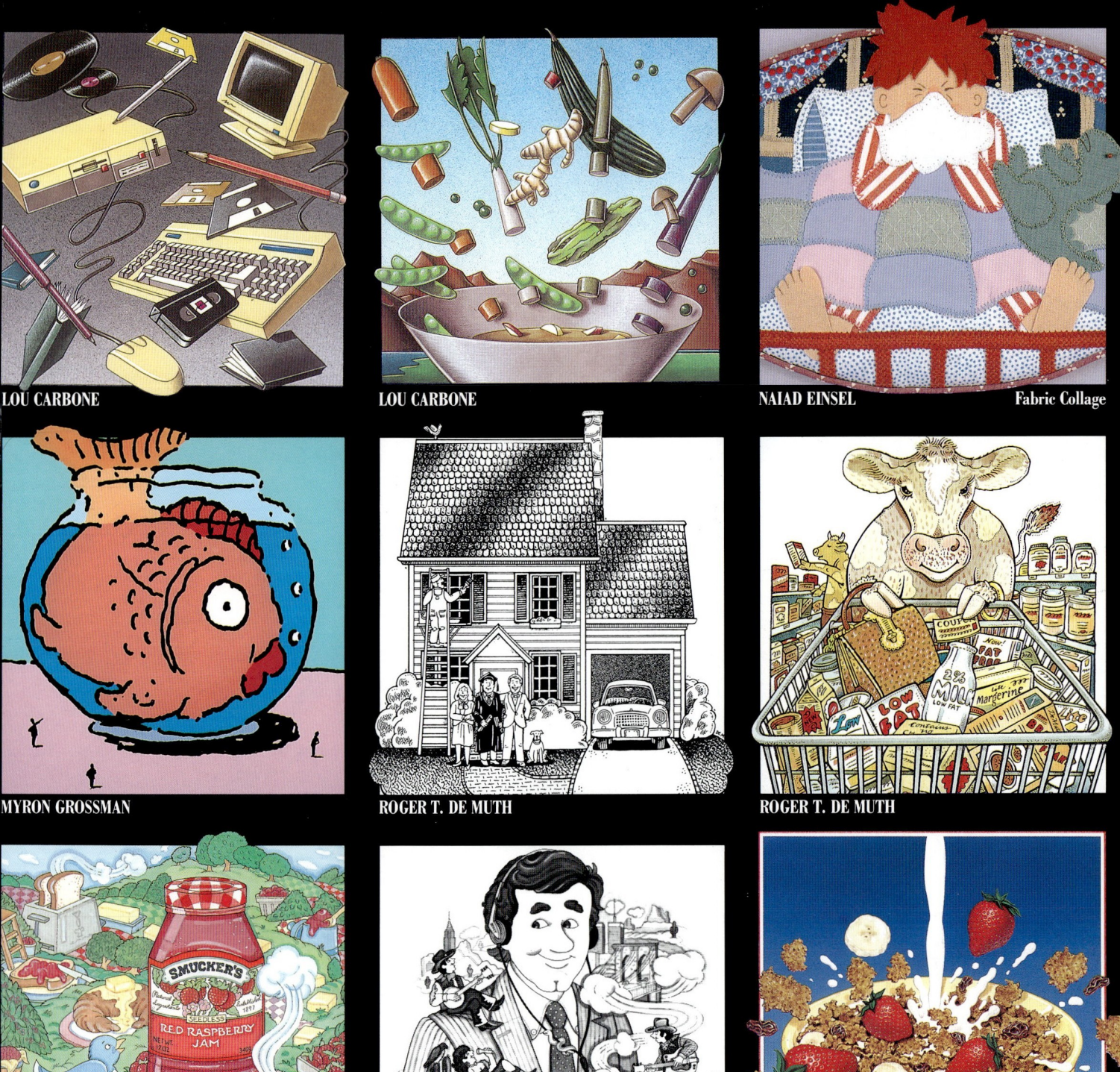

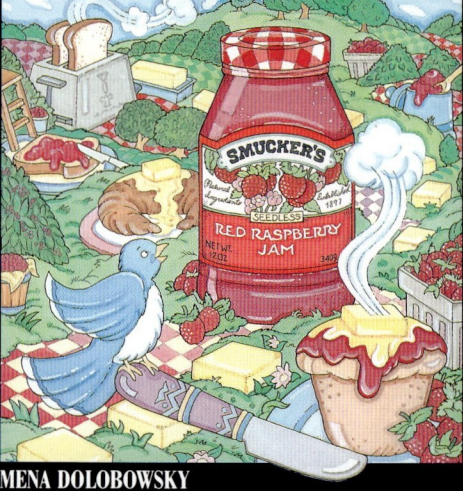

JEFF LLOYD

HELEN ROMAN ASSOCIATES, INC

Representing: Lou Carbone, Roger T. De Muth, Mena Dolobowsky, Naiad Einsel, Walter Einsel; *sculpture*, Myron Grossman, Jeff Lloyd, Sandra Marziali; *super-realistic airbrush*, Andrea Mistretta; *soft and hard edge airbrush*, Anna Rich; *painterly & humor.* Call for a sample portfolio for your files.

212-874-7074

Fax Available

TUKO FUJISAKI ▼ ILLUSTRATION ▼ 619.484.2211

JOHN F SCHMIDT

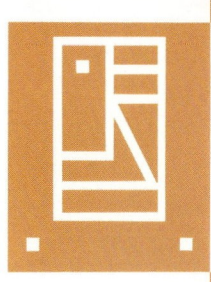

7 3 0 8
LEESVILLE BLVD.
SPRINGFIELD VA
2 2 1 5 1

7 0 3   7 5 0   0 9 2 7

MAURICE LEWIS

STUDIO:
3704 HARPER STREET
HOUSTON, TX. 77005
(713) 664-1807

REPRESENTED BY:
AMERICAN ARTISTS REP., INC.
353 WEST 53rd STREET
NEW YORK, N.Y. 10019
(212) 682-2462

People, Places, Personality.

Client: First Fidelity   Agency: E.B. Wilson

AD: David Leedy

Tom Graham   (718) 680-2975

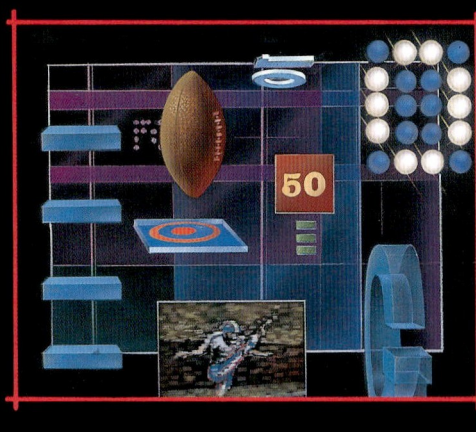

ERIC VON SCHMIDT
8 1 8 · 2 4 6 · 7 8 9 3
D E S I G N
I L L U S T R A T I O N

// m. Garé

Contact: Gary Hallgren   212.947.1054   516.399.5531   Fax on premises

Clients include: A & E Network/McCaffrey and McCall • Ammirati and Puris • Mademoiselle • New York

N.Y. Health and Racquet Club • Philadelphia • Premiere • Seventeen

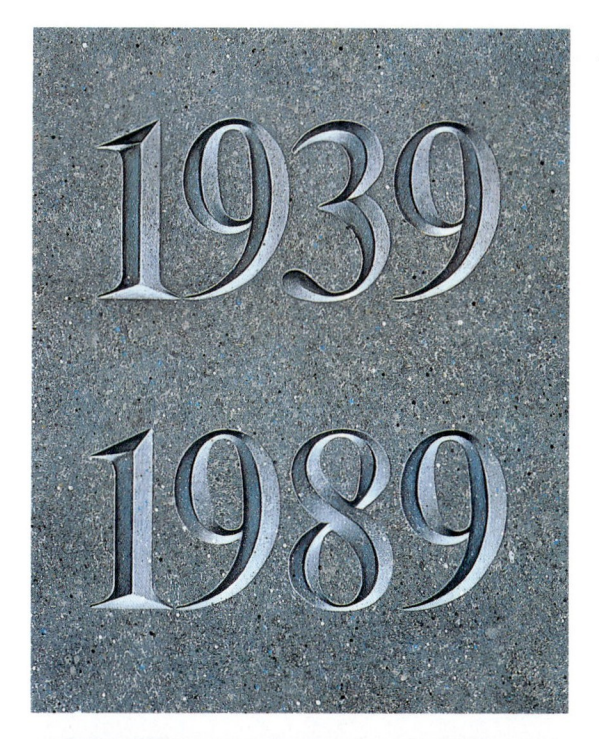

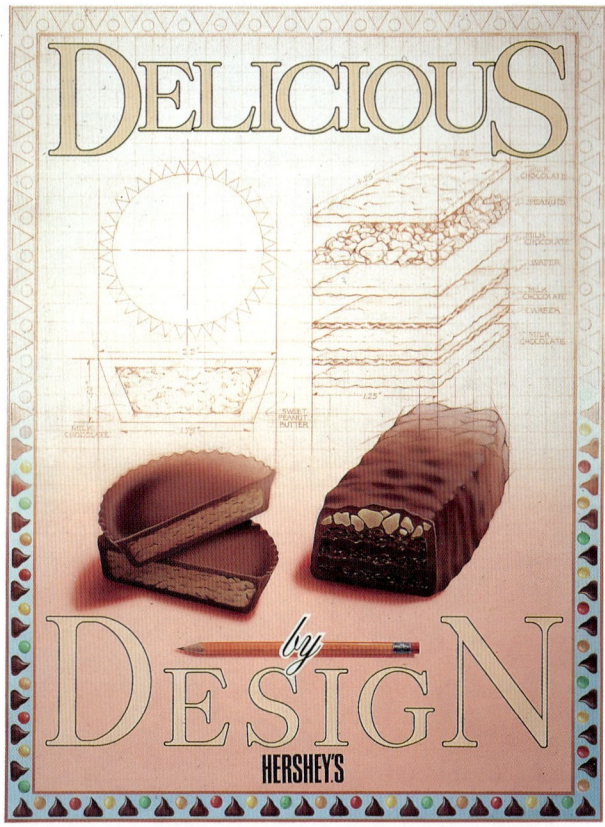

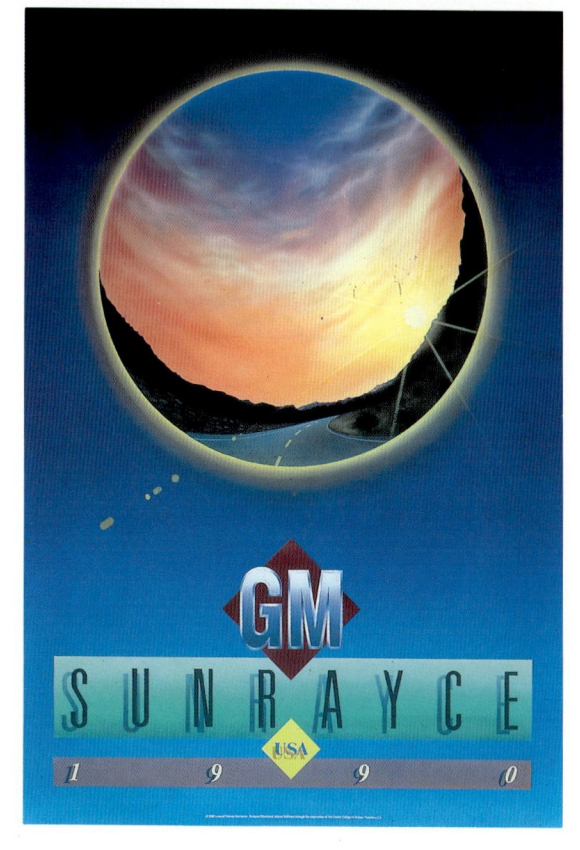

ALLISON
BELLIVEAU
illustration

8 1 8 · 5 7 7 · 2 7 6 9

D·I·E·R·K·S·E·N

JANE BRUNKAN DIERKSEN ▲ ILLUSTRATION & DESIGN

3332 Shadylawn Dr., Duarte, CA. 91010   (818) 359-7745

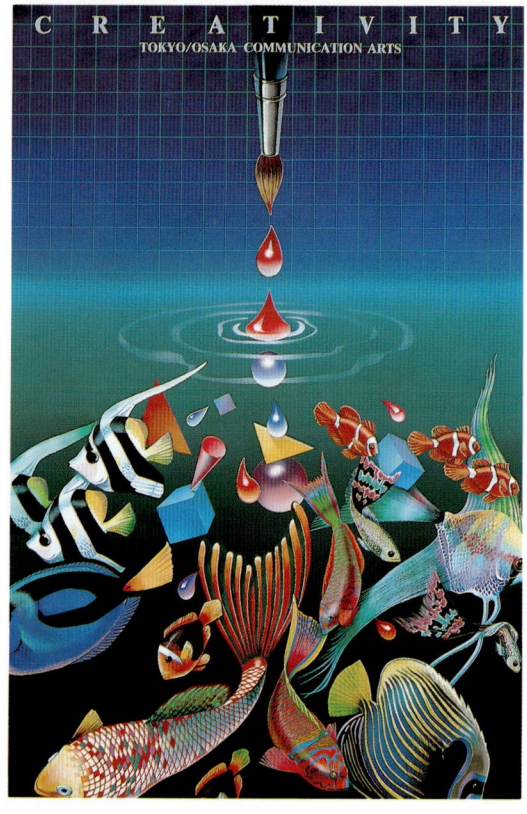

245

RILEY ILLUSTRATION

Metropolitan
Doomed. Bourgeois. In love.

Paul Degen

Pierre Le-Tan

Jeffrey Fisher

J.J. Sempé

Also representing: Elaine Clayton, Paul Hogarth, Paul Meisel, Jim Parkinson Lettering, Cheryl Peterson & Other Artists

Whit & Iréné Stillman   (212) 925-3053   RILEY ILLUSTRATION   81 Greene St. (Box 51)   New York, NY 10012

RILEY ILLUSTRATION

William Bramhall

David Small

Benoît

BY USING A PIECE OF PLEXIGLASS ALBERT WAS ABLE TO PREVENT HIS TIE FROM FLUTTERING IN THE WIND.

Chris Demarest

Also representing: Elaine Clayton, Paul Hogarth, Paul Meisel, Jim Parkinson Lettering, Cheryl Peterson & Other Artists

Whit & Iréne Stillman   (212) 925-3053   RILEY ILLUSTRATION   81 Greene St. (Box 51)   New York, NY 10012

S.I. International

Sergio Martinez

Contact: Herbert Spiers/Donald Bruckstein
Phone: 212 254.4996/fax 212 995.0911

S.I. International

Art Ruiz

Contact: Herbert Spiers/Donald Bruckstein
Phone: 212 254.4996/fax 212 995.0911

Dennis Davidson

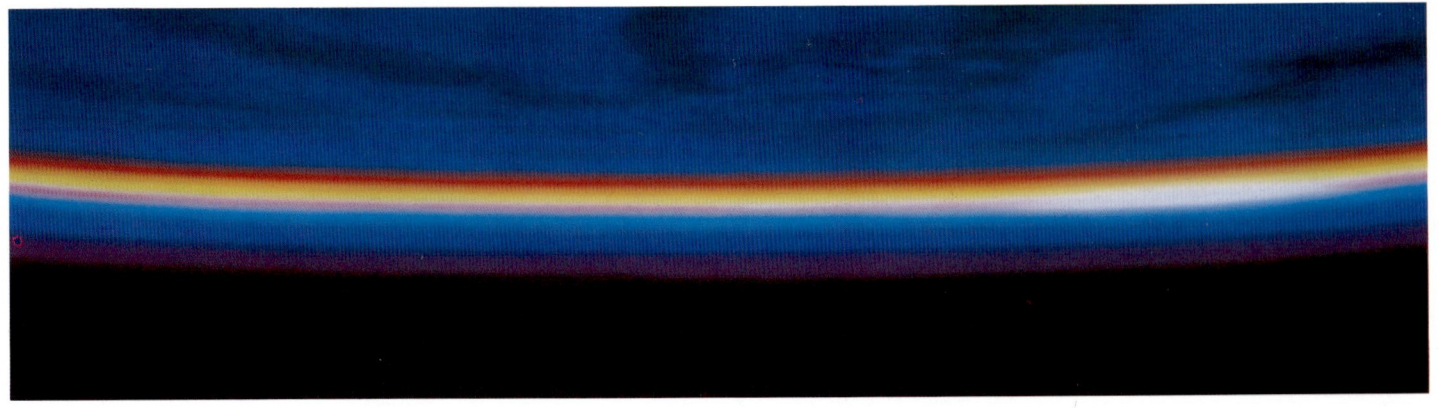

As seen from space, earth is a single entity - part of the solar system's complex living environment . . .

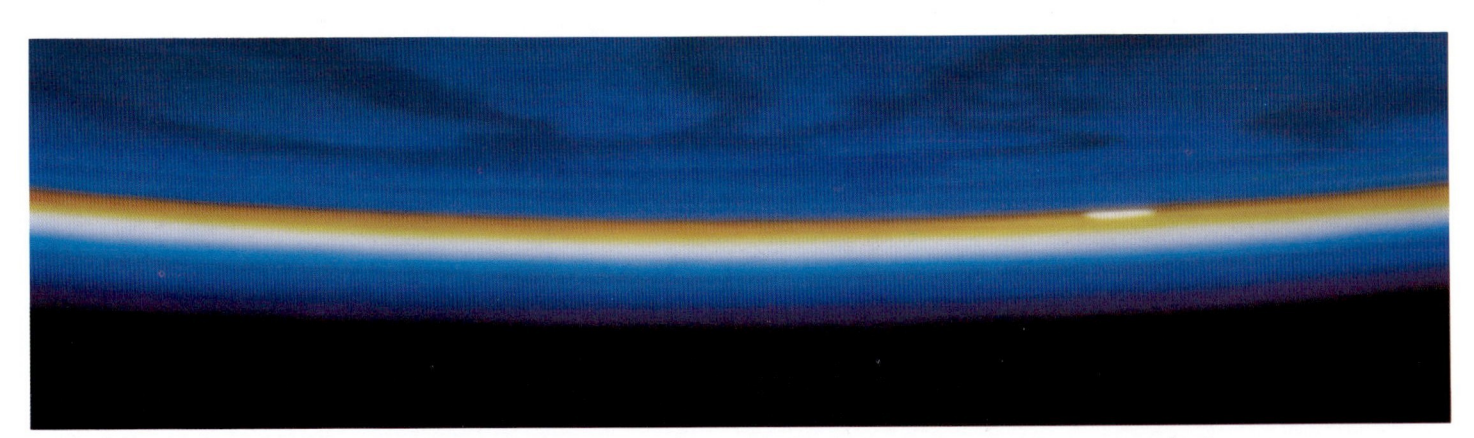

astronauts who have orbited the planet on several occasions over the past twenty years have remarked with alarm that earth has qualitatively degraded . . .

a planetary ethic must be developed to meet the needs of a mature global culture.

S.I. International

Contact: Herbert Spiers/Donald Bruckstein
Phone: 212 254.4996/fax 212 995.0911

Jack Brusca

S.I.
International

Contact: Herbert Spiers/Donald Bruckstein
Phone: 212 254.4996/fax 212 995.0911

S.I. International

Mel Grant

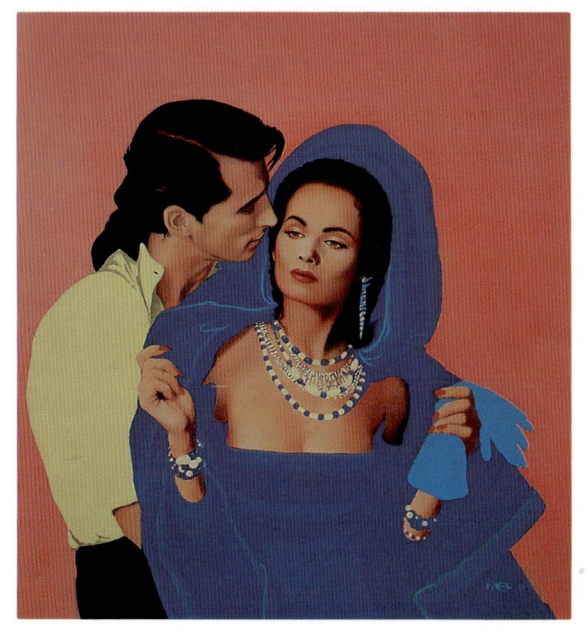

Contact: Herbert Spiers/Donald Bruckstein
Phone: 212 254.4996/fax 212 995.0911

Karen Baumann

S.I. *International*

Contact: Herbert Spiers/Donald Bruckstein
Phone: 212 254.4996/fax 212 995.0911

Richard Leonard

S.I.
International

Linoleum and wood cuts

Contact: Herbert Spiers/Donald Bruckstein
Phone: 212 254.4996/fax 212 995.0911

Allen Davis

S.I. International

Contact: Herbert Spiers/Donald Bruckstein
Phone: 212 254.4996/fax 212 995.0911

Melodye Rosales

S.I. International

Contact: Herbert Spiers/Donald Bruckstein
Phone: 212 254.4996/fax 212 995.0911

Franc Mateu

S.I. International

Contact: Herbert Spiers/Donald Bruckstein
Phone: 212 254.4996/fax 212 995.0911

S.I. International

Sherry Hoover

Contact: Herbert Spiers/Donald Bruckstein
Phone: 212 254.4996/fax 212 995.0911

Paul Wenzel

S.I.
International

Contact: Herbert Spiers/Donald Bruckstein
Phone: 212 254.4996/fax 212 995.0911

Steve Haefele

S.I. International

The Beverly HILLBILLIES THE NEXT GENERATION

Contact: Herbert Spiers/Donald Bruckstein
Phone: 212.254.4996/fax 212.995.0911

Ted Enik

S.I. International

MRS. CLAUS

Contact: Herbert Spiers/Donald Bruckstein
Phone: 212 254.4996/fax 212 995.0911

Steve Parton

S.I. International

Contact: Herbert Spiers/Donald Bruckste[in]
Phone: 212 254.4996/fax 212 995.0911

S.I. International

Oscar Chichoni

Contact: Herbert Spiers/Donald Bruckstein
Phone: 212 254.4996/fax 212 995.0911

A. Martins de Barros

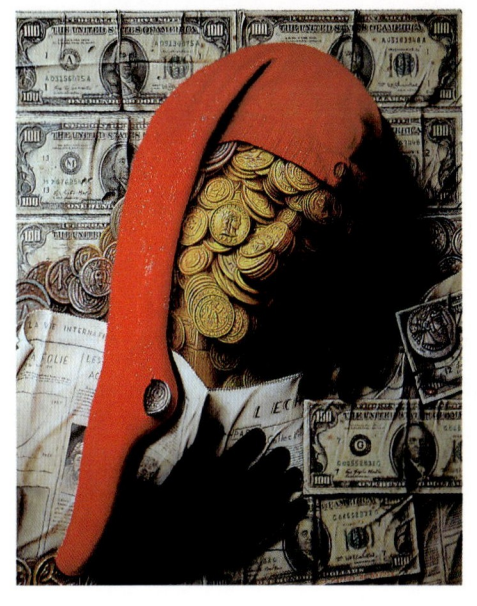

S.I. International

Contact: Herbert Spiers/Donald Bruckstein
Phone: 212 254.4996/fax 212 995.0911

264

Daniela Codarcea

S.I. *International*

Contact: Herbert Spiers/Donald Bruckstein
Phone: 212 254.4996/fax 212 995.0911

S.I. International

Courtney Studios

Contact: Herbert Spiers/Donald Bruckstein
Phone: 212 254.4996/fax 212 995.0911

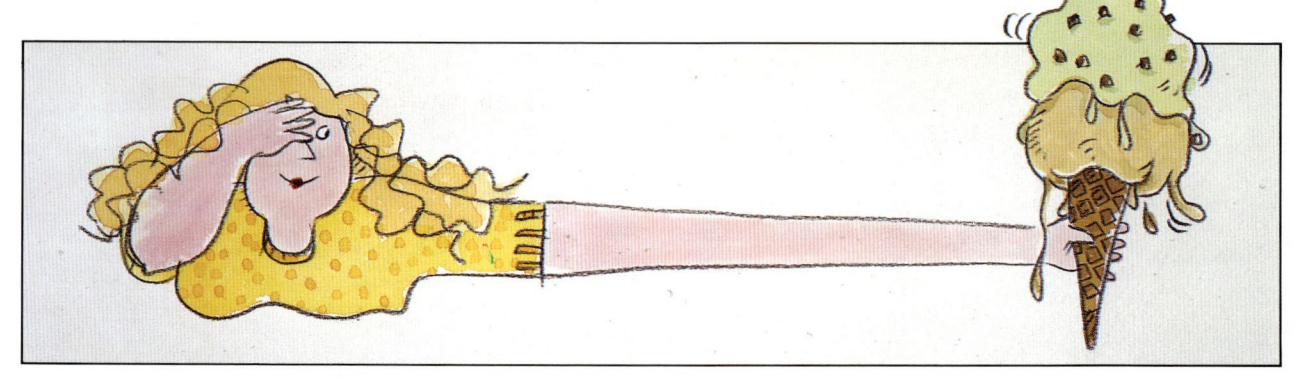

IVOR PARRY
280 MADISON AVE.
NEW YORK, NY 10016
TEL 212-779 1554
TEL 914-961 7338
FAX 212-447 7848

267

DAVE CLEGG

ILLUSTRATION

(404) 887-6306

FAX IN STUDIO

268

BENNETT

Gary Bennett, 3304 Startan Court, Louisville, KY 40220

Gary Bennett illustrations (502) 458-0338

GARY MEYER
21725 Ybarra Road
Woodland Hills, California 91364
(818) 992-6974
FAX (818) 992-4538

Best of show, Illustration West
First Place, Key Arts Awards
First Place, TIMA
First Place, TIMA
Best of Category, Illustration West

Best of Category, Illustration West
Certificate of Excellence, CA Magazine
Certificate of Excellence, CA Magazine
8 Special Judges Awards, Illustration West
Over 100 Certificates of Distinction and Merit

Artist Fellow in the American Society of Aviation Artists, Society of Illustrators, Society of Illustrators of Los Angeles

Copyright, 1989, Author Services, Inc. Prints available through L. Ron Hubbard Gallery

Constance McLennan

9 1 6 . 6 2 4 . 1 9 5 7

3 9 0 8 B A L T I C C I R C L E , R O C K L I N , C A L I F O R N I A 9 5 6 7 7

ROBERT EVANS ♦ 1045 Sansome #306 ♦ San Francisco CA 94111 ♦ (415) 397-5322

Clients include: Del Monte, United Airlines, Wells Fargo, Harrah's, Safeway, Capri-Sun, University of California, Hills Brothers, Dreyer's Ice Cream, Sunset Magazine, Wente Brothers, Carnation, Treesweet, MacWorld Magazine, Dole, Vittel, Amdahl, Levi Strauss…

Marc Ericksen ♦ 1045 Sansome #306 ♦ San Francisco CA 94111 ♦ (415) 362-1214

©PC Games Magazine

©IDG Inc.

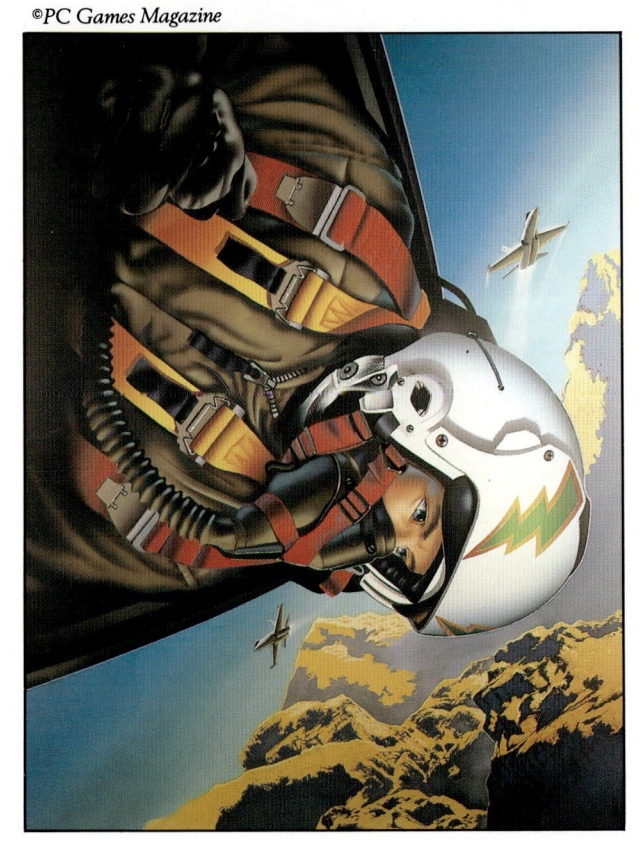

©PC Games Magazine

Property of Laguna Seca Raceway

Clients include: Airborne Inc., Amdahl, Activision, Atari, Broderbund Inc., Bank of America, Crossman Inc., Crown Zellerbach, Del Monte, East West Network, Electronic Arts, Hewlett Packard, Hesware, Hexcel, Intel, Jacuzzi, Kaiser Aluminum, Kelsey Hayes, Levi Strauss, Liquid Air Corp., Litton, Masport America, McKesson Corp., Oceanspray, Pacific Bell, Prolog Computers, San Francisco Magazine, Searle Inc., Siemiens Inc., Trans International Airlines, TransWorld Airlines, United Airlines, Viacom, Zehntel Inc.

STEPHEN HARRINGTON
ILLUSTRATOR
71 AIKEN STREET · UNIT B · 10 · NORWALK · CT · 06851
(203) 847·6430

SERGIO BARADAT

210 WEST 70 ST. #1606 N.Y. N.Y. 10023 (212) 721-2588

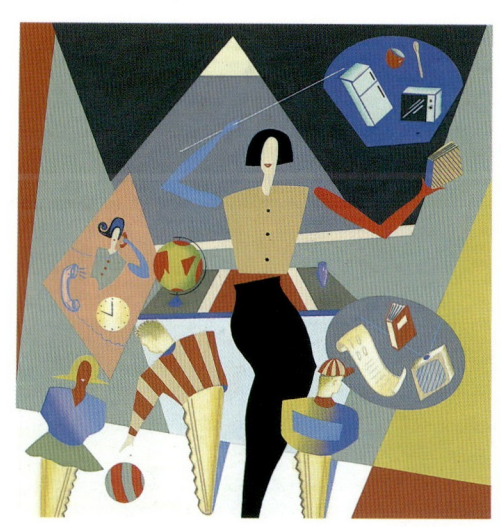

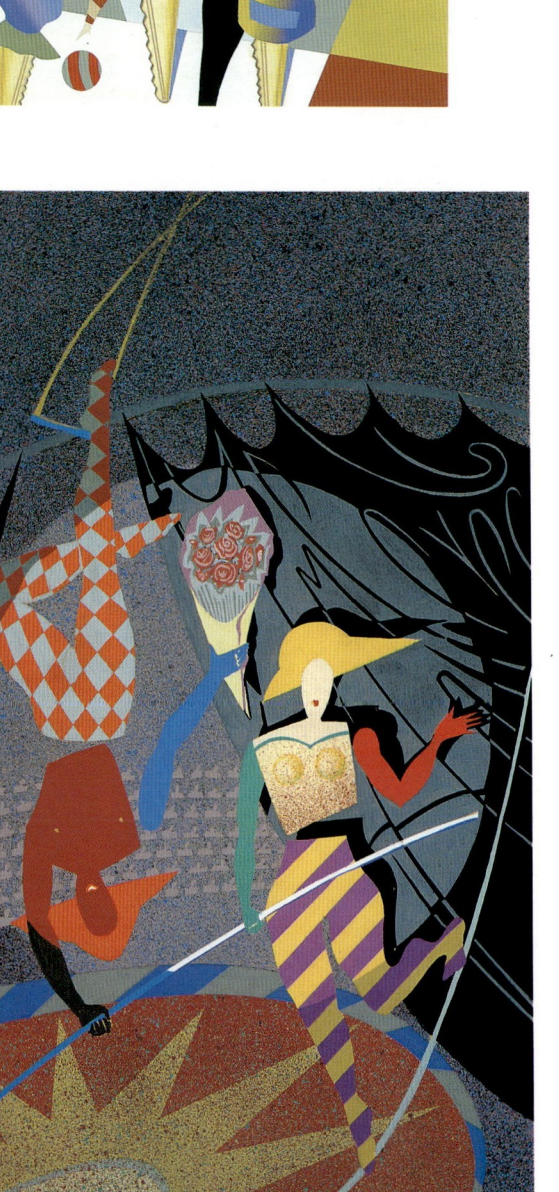

Clients:
AT&T
Berlitz
Bloomingdale's
BusinessWeek
Condé Nast
Fairchild
FP (Japan)
Int'l Design Grp.
L.A. Times
Macy's
N.Y. Times
Parsons
Polygram Records
Psychology Today
Scholastic
Time Inc.
Travel & Leisure
U.S. News
View (Japan)

American Illustration 9
Creative Illustration 1
American Showcase 12

275

GLASGOW & ASSOCIATES INFORMATION GRAPHICS

GLASGOW & ASSOCIATES
4493
Andy Court
Woodbridge
Virginia
22193
Business
(703) 590-1702
FAX
(703) 590-8855

Design: Maurice Davis
Photograph: Katherine Lambert
Illustration: Dale Glasgow

Dale Glasgow

Philosophy/Approach:
The marriage of information and graphics. When we approach a project we consider what is the most important information and how it can be shown creatively.

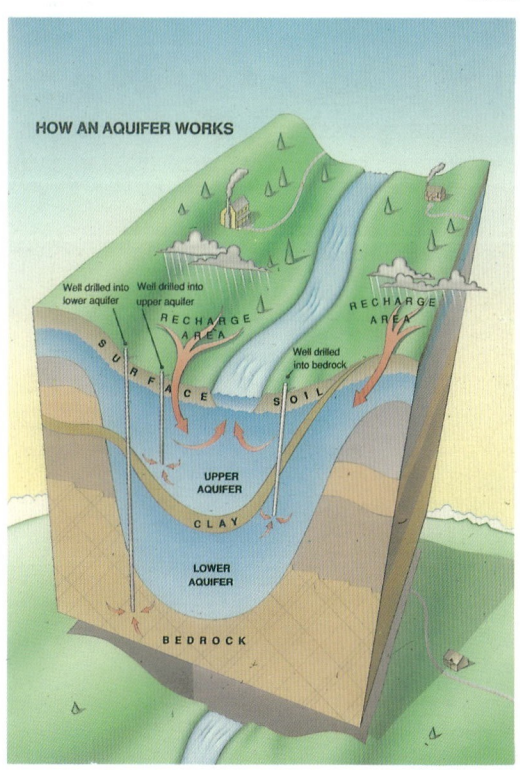

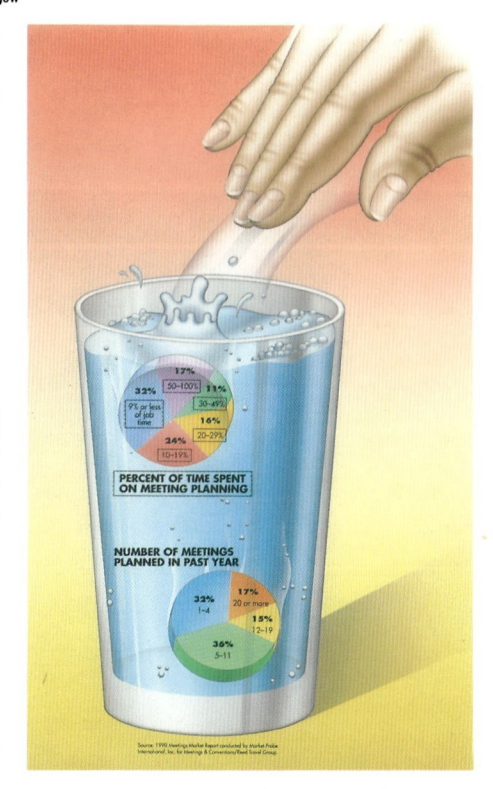

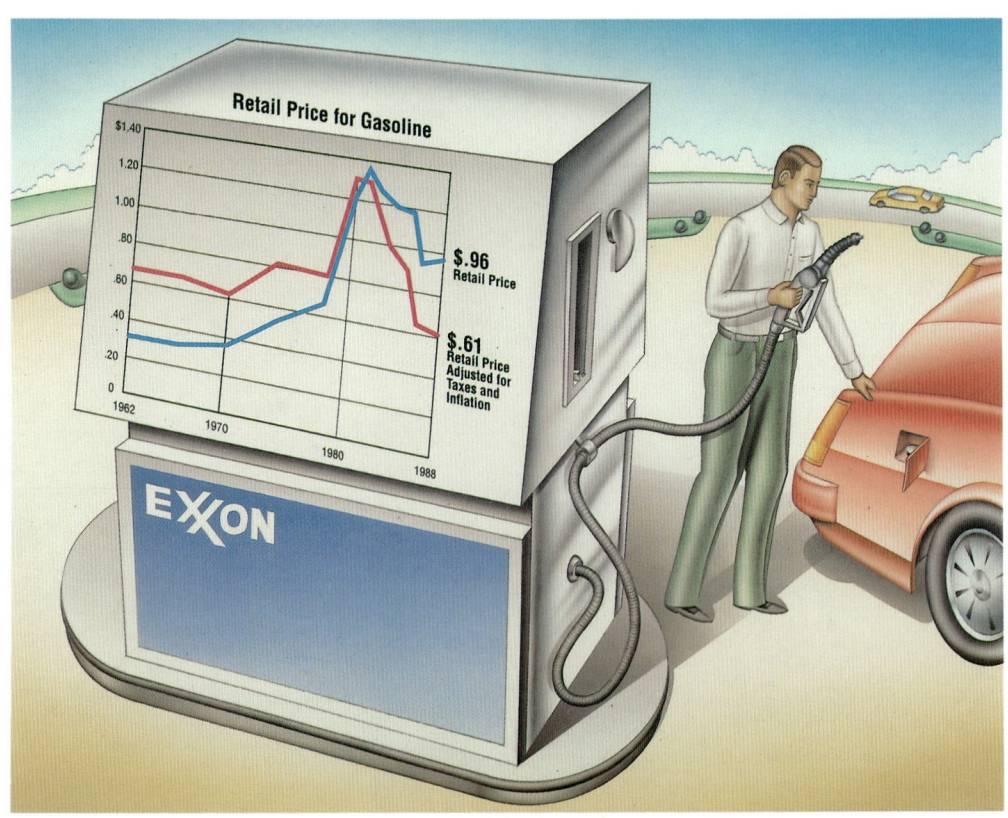

Client list:
Air&Space, Aldus, AMS, Bell Atlantic, *Business Month*, Champion, *Changing Times*, Exxon Corporation, Gannett, General Motors, *Good Housekeeping*, GOVERNING, INC., Johns Hopkins, Ligature, Mortgage Bankers Association, *National Geographic*, *Nation's Business*, Ogilvey & Mather, *Personal Computing*, *Prevention*, *Psychology Today*, *SAIL*, Scott Forsman, Sallie Mae, *USA TODAY*, USG, *U.S. News & World Report*, *Washington Post*, Whittle Communications.

Area of Expertise:
From illustrations—to annual reports—to posters, we specialize in illustrating & designing information in an intelligent, creative way.

Awards:
AIGA 1988, Print's Regional Design Annual 1986-88, Art Directors Club of Metropolitan Washington 1986-88, DESI 1987, Publication Designers 1988

To view more work:
Adweek Porfolios, 1988,1989,1990
The Creative Illustration Book 1990,1991
American Showcase 1991

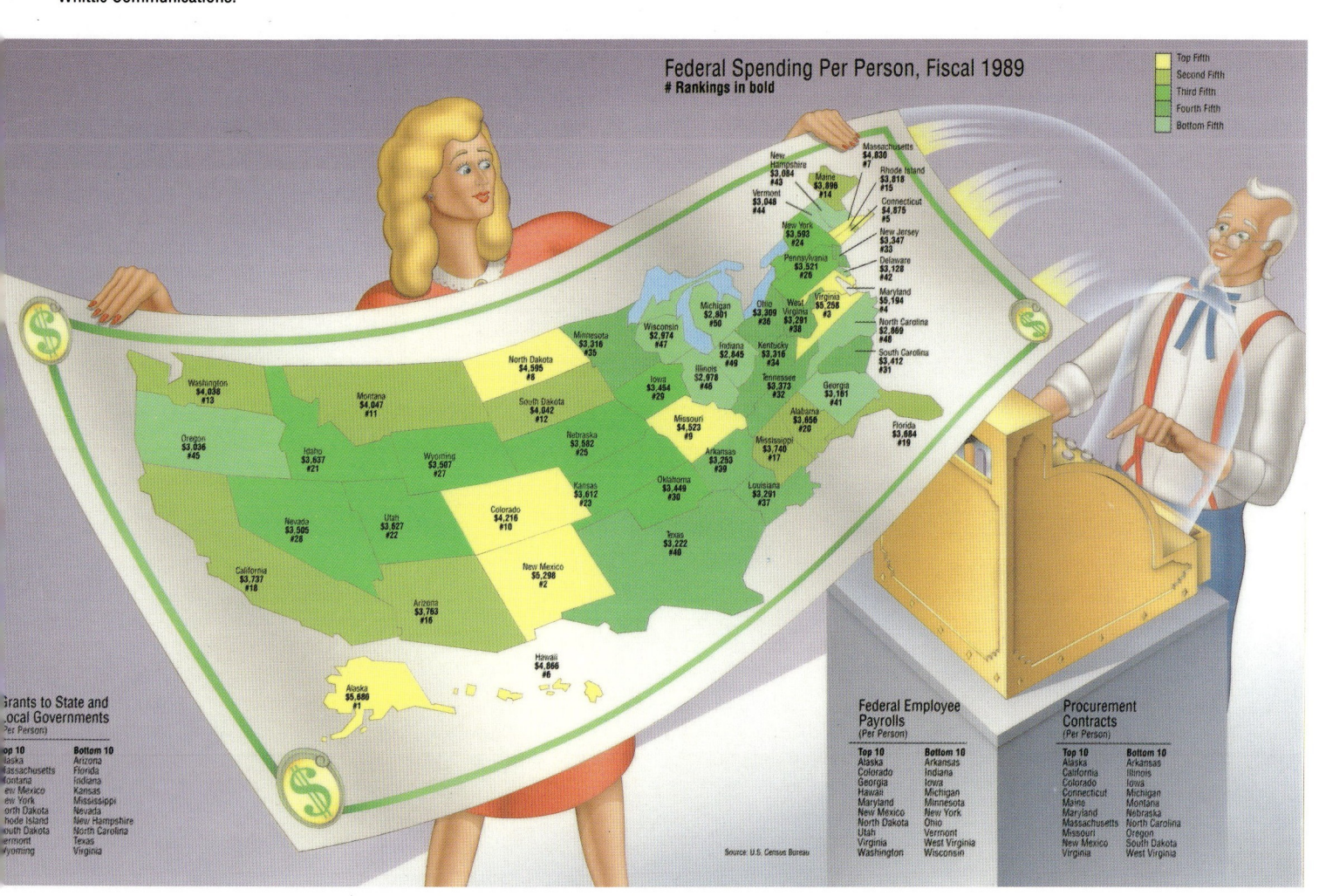

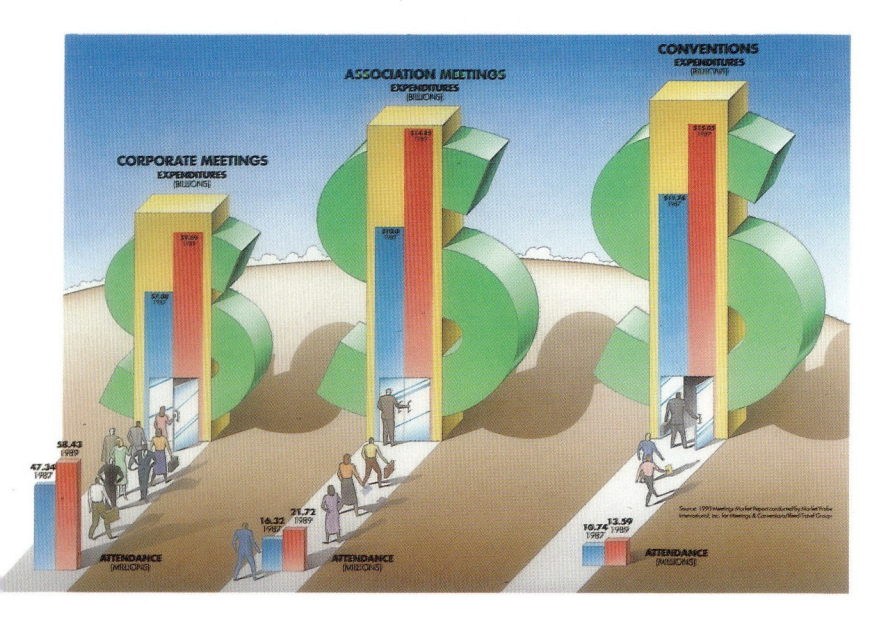

277

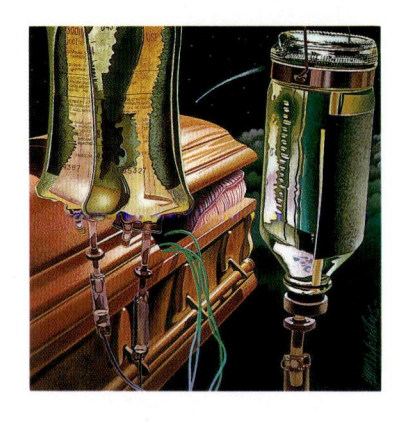

BRITT TAYLOR COLLINS

Represented by:

Will Sumpter & Associates
1728 North Rock Springs Road
Atlanta, Georgia 30324
404-874-2014
Studio FAX available

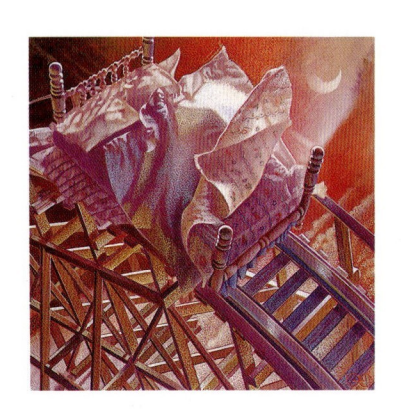

© 1990

BRENDA LOSEY

Represented by:

Will Sumpter & Associates
1728 North Rock Springs Road
Atlanta, Georgia 30324
404-874-2014
Studio FAX available

© 1990

CHARLES CASHWELL

Represented by:

Will Sumpter & Associates
1728 North Rock Springs Road
Atlanta, Georgia 30324
404-874-2014
Studio FAX available

© 1990

DREW ROSE

Represented by:

Will Sumpter & Associates
1728 North Rock Springs Road
Atlanta, Georgia 30324
404-874-2014
Studio FAX available

BARON
LEATHERS

© 1990

BOB COOPER

Represented by:

Will Sumpter & Associates

1728 North Rock Springs Road

Atlanta, Georgia 30324

404-874-2014

Studio FAX available

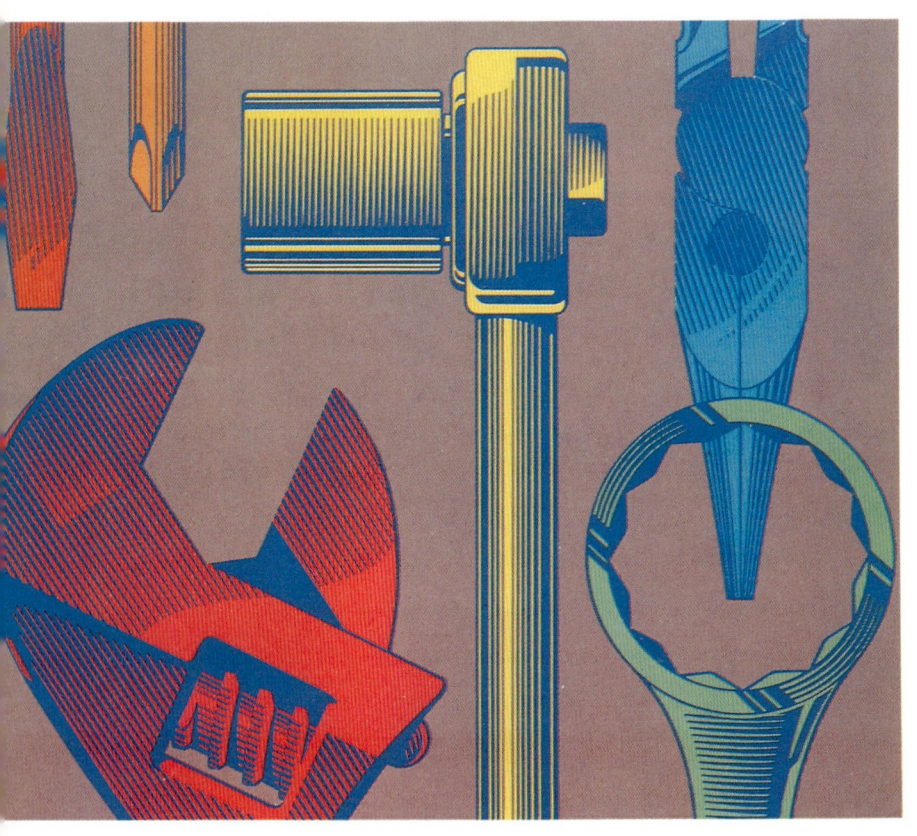

© 1990

DAVID MOSES

Represented by:

Will Sumpter & Associates
1728 North Rock Springs Road
Atlanta, Georgia 30324
404-874-2014
Studio FAX available

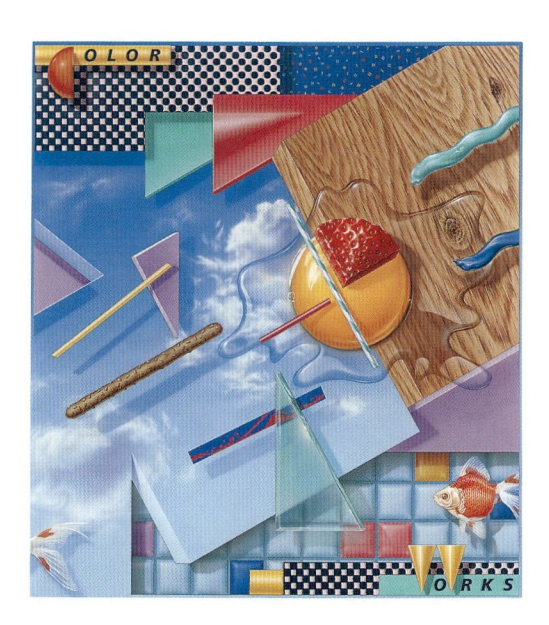

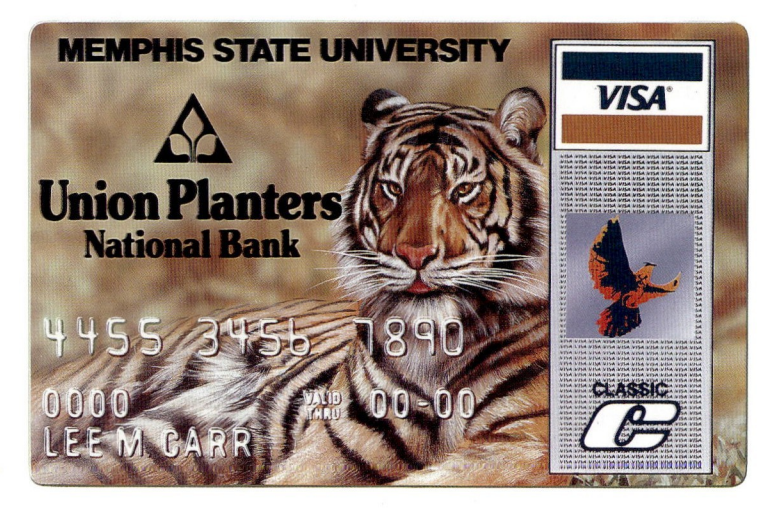

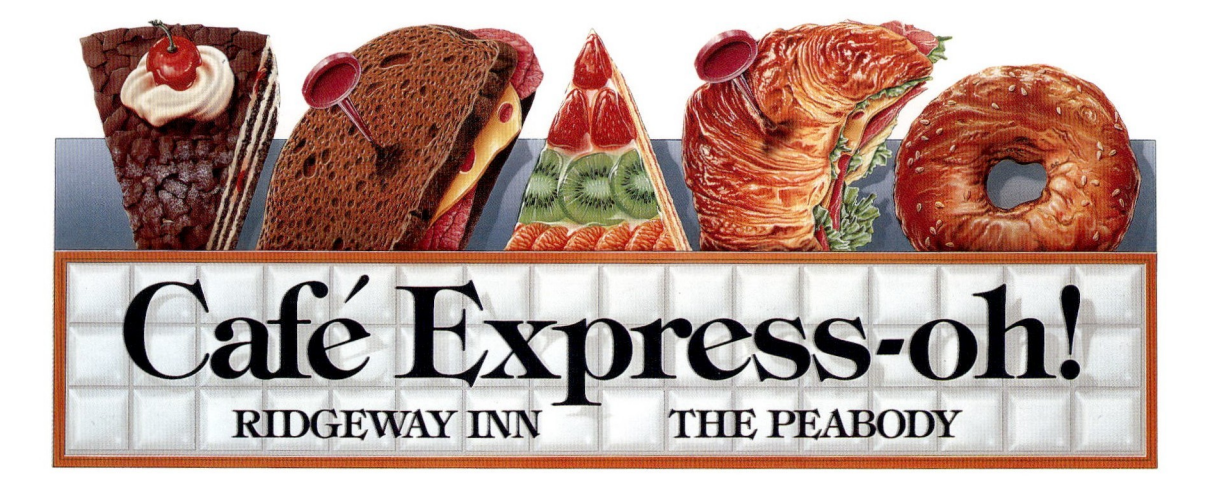

© 1990

JACKIE PITTMAN

Represented by:

Will Sumpter & Associates
1728 North Rock Springs Road
Atlanta, Georgia 30324
404-874-2014
Studio FAX available

© 1990

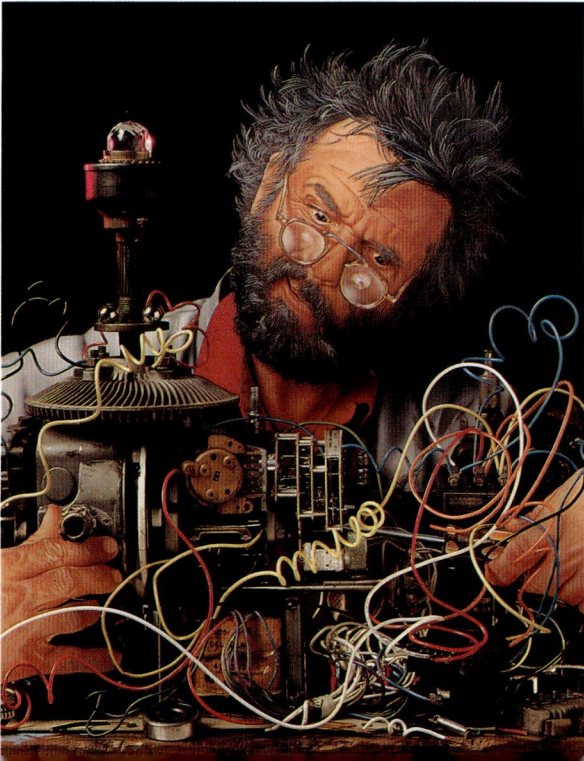

DAVID GAADT

Represented by:

Will Sumpter & Associates
1728 North Rock Springs Road
Atlanta, Georgia 30324
404-874-2014
Studio FAX available

PHILIP WENDE

Represented by:

Will Sumpter & Associates

1728 North Rock Springs Road

Atlanta, Georgia 30324

404-874-2014

Studio FAX available

How We Keep Produce From Going Bad.

HAVE BREAKFAST, WILL TRAVEL.

Kellogg's

Omni International Hotel Catering

© 1990

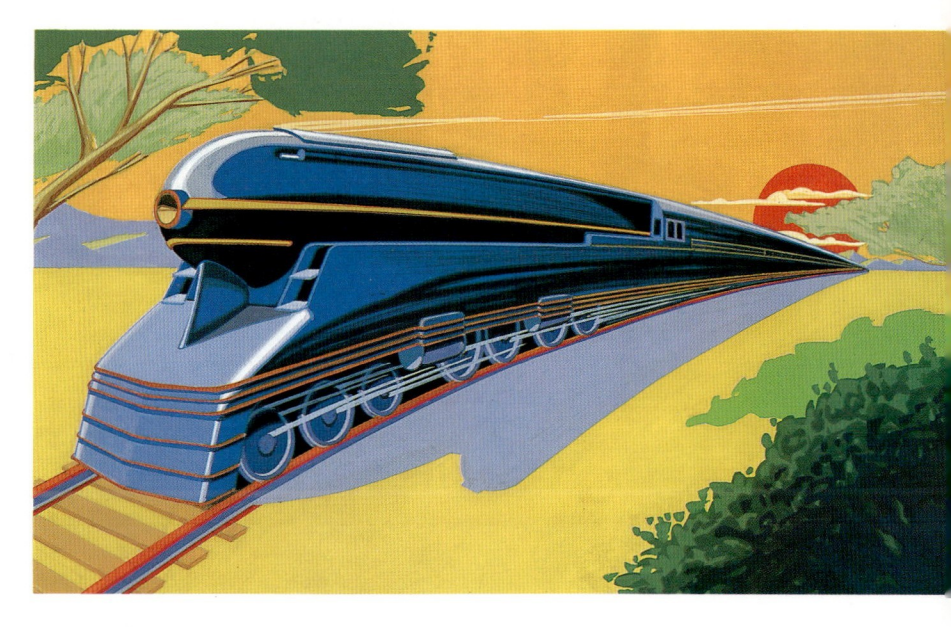

CLARKE TATE

Represented by:

Will Sumpter & Associates
1728 North Rock Springs Road
Atlanta, Georgia 30324
404-874-2014
Studio FAX available

© 1990

287

TONY DE LUZ

**49 MELCHER STREET
BOSTON, MA. 02210
(617)   695-0006**

SEE ALSO: 1990 CREATIVE ILL.BK AND 1991 AMERICAN SHOWCASE

SUSAN DETRICH • 718-237-9174

SUSAN DETRICH • 253 Baltic Street • Brooklyn New York 11201 • 718-237-9174

Additional work may be seen in the Graphic Artists Guild's Directory of Illustration 5, 6 & RSVP 16 • Fax service available

KEN CALL ILLUSTRATION
1836 North Winchester
Chicago, IL 60622
312.489.2323
FAX: 312.489.0939

In New York City and the East
Sid Buck & Barney Kane
212.221.8090

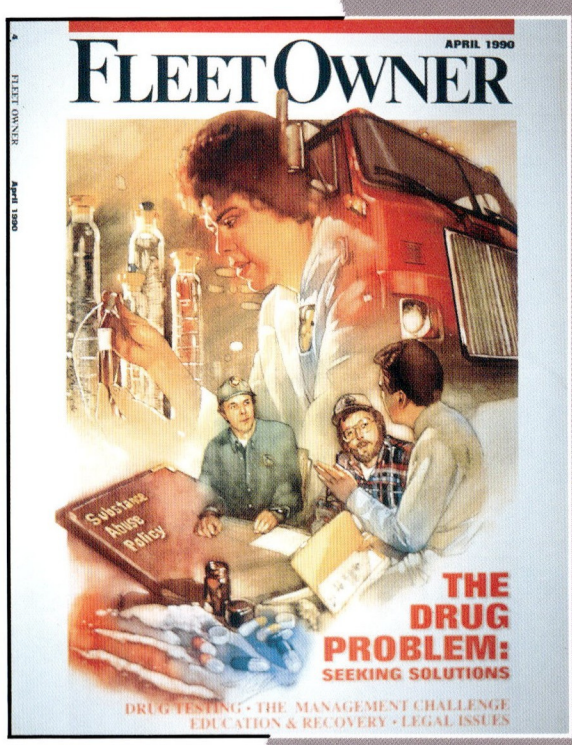

Fleet Owner Publications

McCann Healthcare Advertising

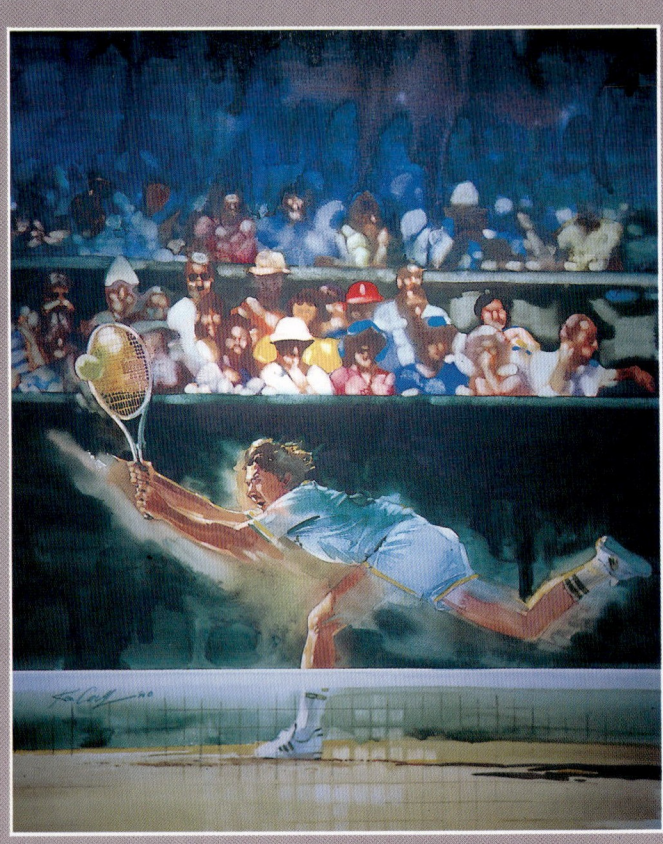

Scafa Tornabene, Inc.

Scafa Tornabene, Inc.

S T E V E

A R M E S

2 1 4

7 2 1 0 1 6 4

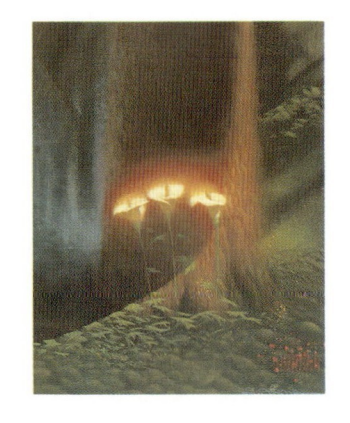

DAVID TAYLOR

STUDIO (317) 634-2728   FAX (317) 685-1550

Curiosity is the path that leads to discovery. Call!

SCOTT
MOWRY

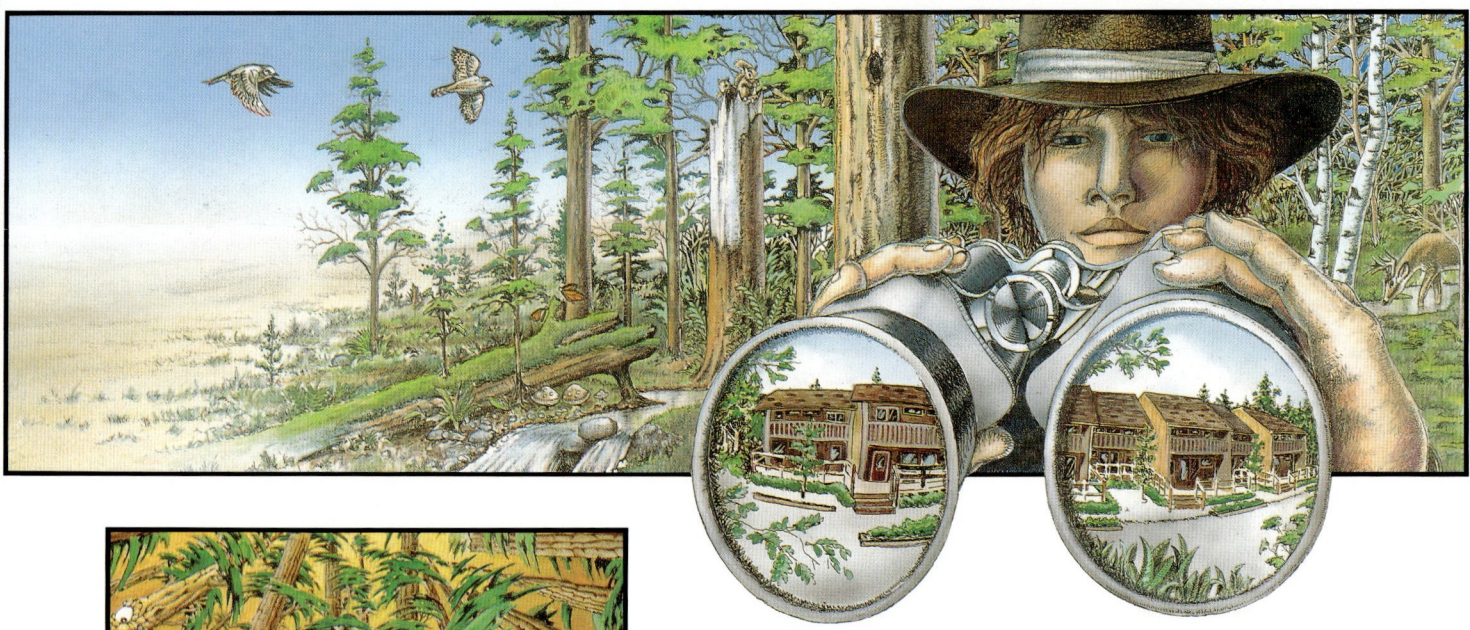

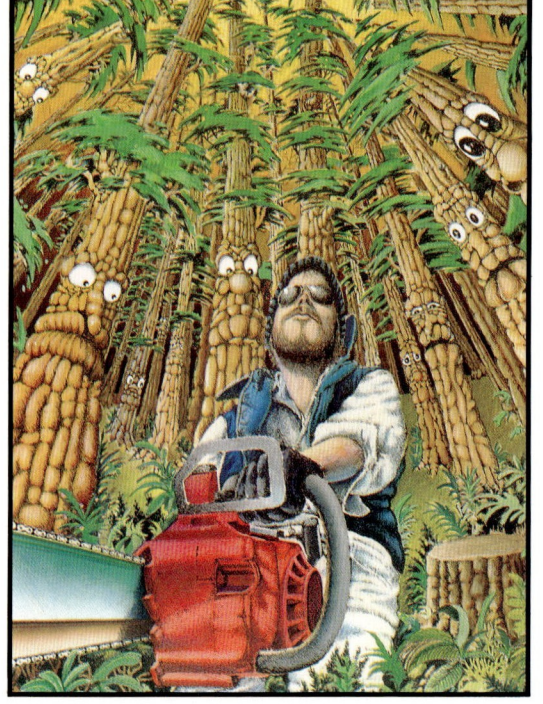

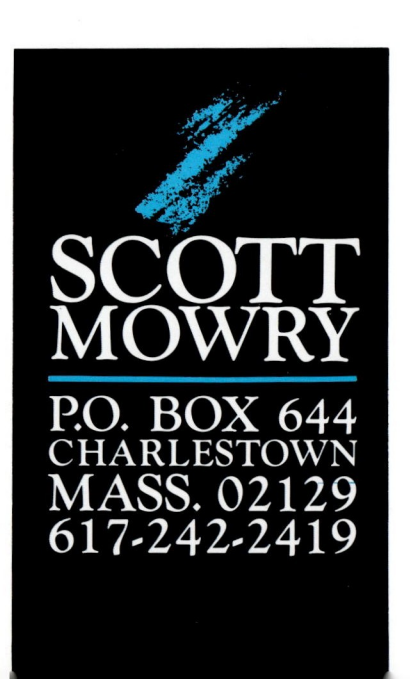

P.O. BOX 644
CHARLESTOWN
MASS. 02129
617-242-2419

Mona Conner

One Montgomery Place
Brooklyn, New York 11215
718-636-1527

Partial client list: Lenox • Mobil Chemical Company • Letraset • FCB Leber/Katz • Ted Bates • Harper & Row • McGraw-Hill • Alfred A. Knopf • Random House • Macmillan • Viking Penguin • G.P. Putnam's Sons • Gruner & Jahr • St. Martin's Press • Ms. Magazine • The Daily News • American Druggist • High-Tech Marketing • Promised Land Productions

To view more work: GAG Directory 5, 6 • RSVP 9, 11, 13 • CA Annual '84

©1990 Mona Conner

Kenny Yamada Illustrations

(415) 841-4415
2330 Haste Street, Suite 306 Berkeley, California

Rosenthal Represents
Call Elise Rosenthal or Neil Sandler (213) 390-9595

295

MICHAEL TEDESCO
120 Boerum Place, #1E
Brooklyn, N.Y. 11201
718-237-9164
For additional work, see American Showcase vols. 11, 12 and 13.

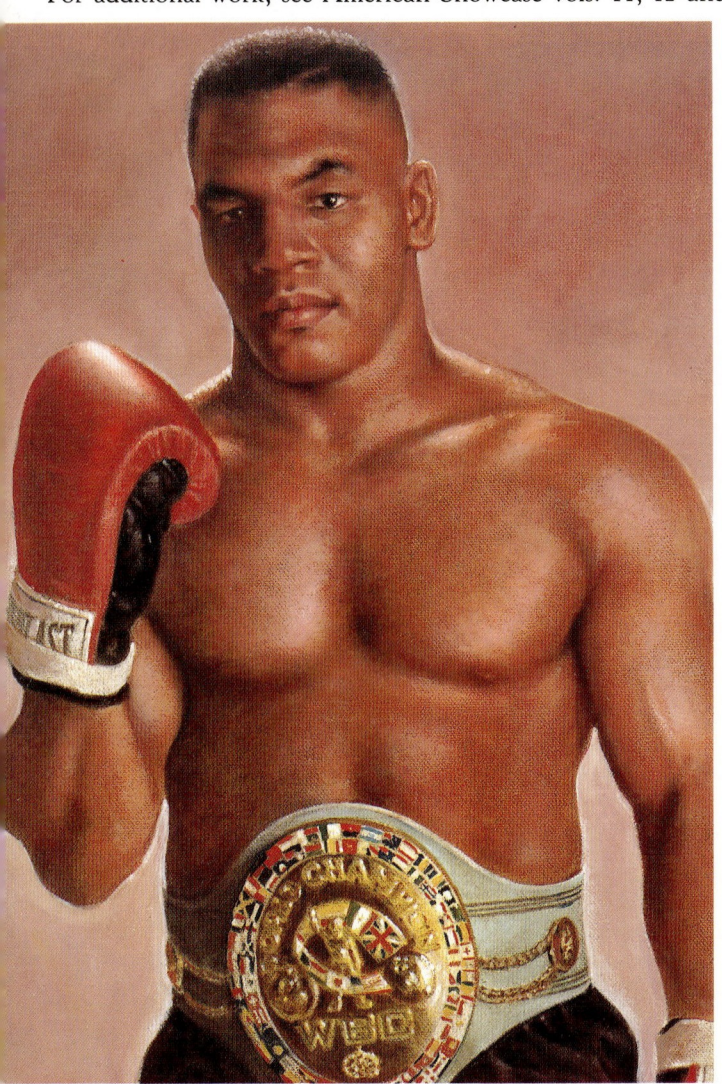

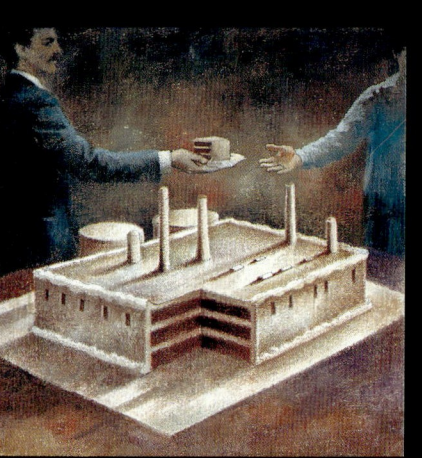

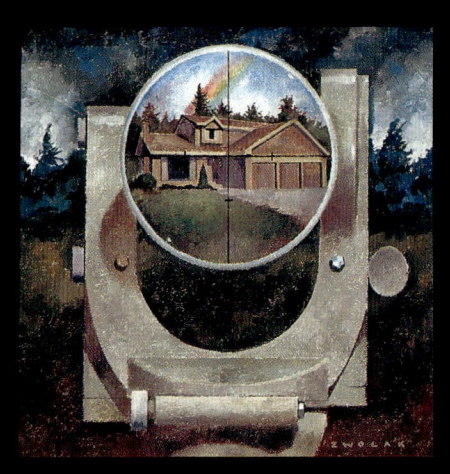

Paul Zwolak

11 Prince Rupert Avenue, Toronto Ontario M6P 2A8 (416) 531-6253

ROBERTO

LIGRESTI

Illustrations Comps Animatics

6 9 7 0 6 5 0

NEW YORK

ROBERTO LIGRESTI

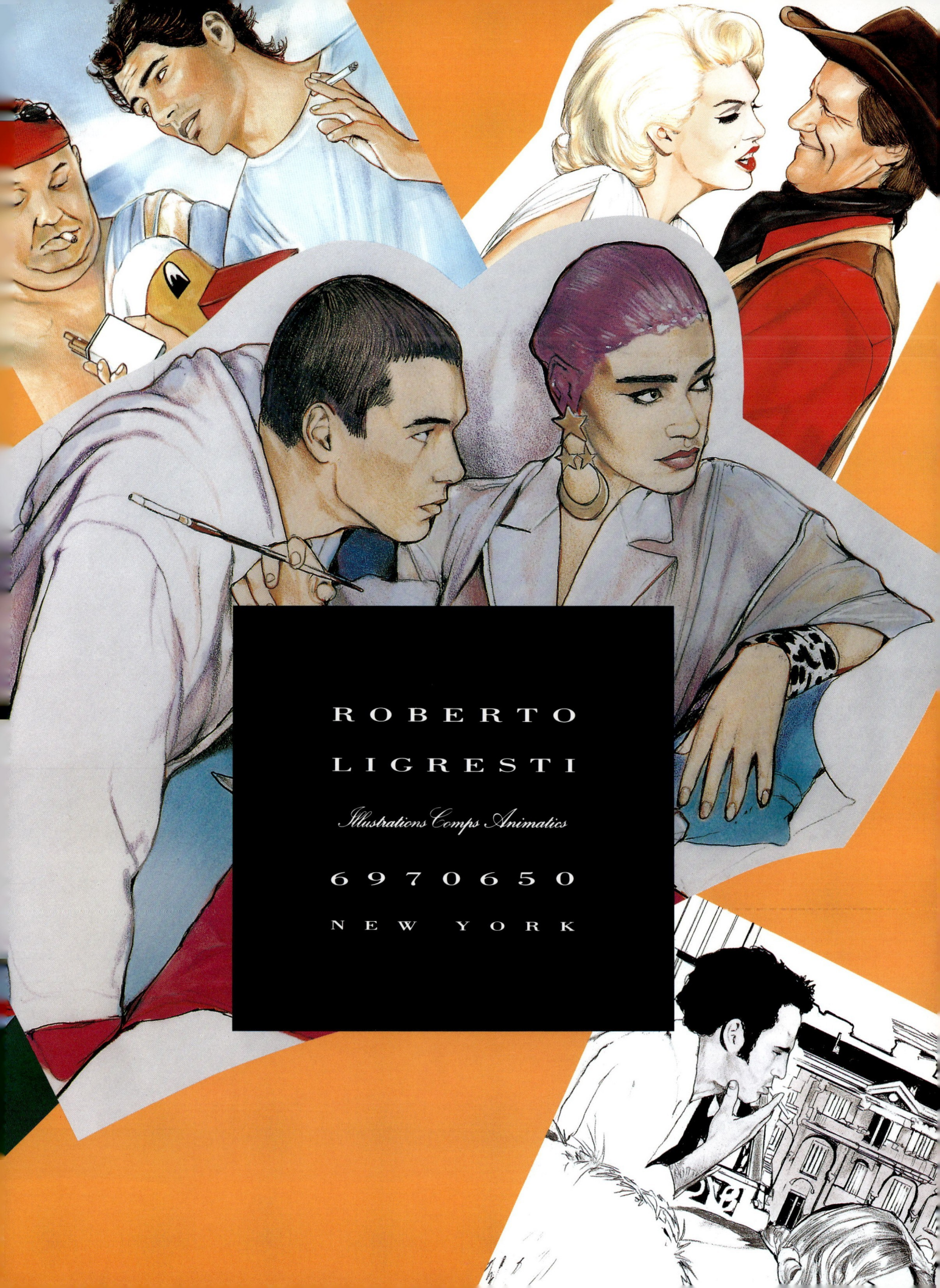

Illustrations Comps Animatics

6 9 7 0 6 5 0

NEW YORK

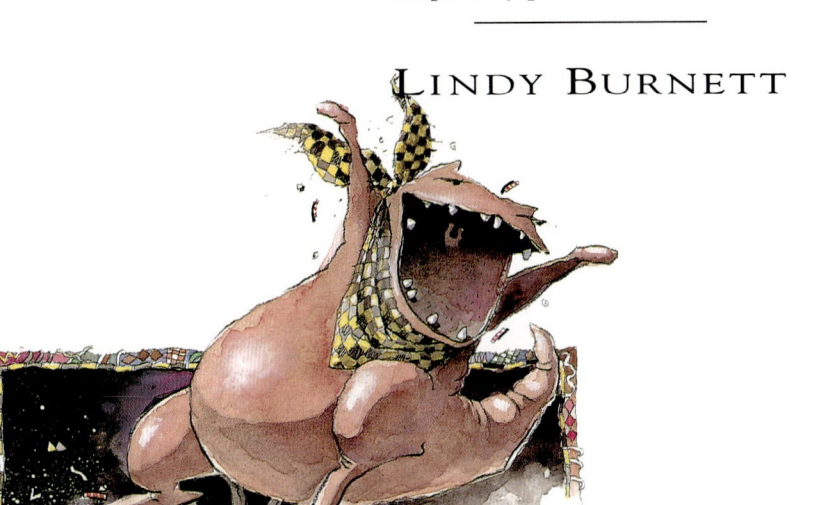

Represented by
Alexander/Pollard
Atlanta phone: 404-875-1363
FAX: 404-875-9733
Tampa Bay phone: 813-725-4438

Lindy Burnett

Represented by
Alexander/Pollard
Atlanta phone: 404-875-1363
FAX: 404-875-9733
Tampa Bay phone: 813-725-4438

LINDY BURNETT

Represented by
Alexander/Pollard
Atlanta phone: 404-875-1363
FAX: 404-875-9733
Tampa Bay phone: 813-725-4438

Elizabeth Traynor

Represented by
Alexander/Pollard
Atlanta phone: 404-875-1363
FAX: 404-875-9733
Tampa Bay phone: 813-725-4438

CHERYL COOPER

Represented by
Alexander/Pollard
Atlanta phone: 404-875-1363
FAX: 404-875-9733
Tampa Bay phone: 813-725-4438

KATHY LENGYEL

OPTIONAL GREEN HOUSE
DO THE ORCHIDS COME WITH IT?
I LOVE THE SUNKEN TUB!
WHERE WILL WE PUT THE PIANO?
HOW 'BOUT NEXT TO THE POOLTABLE
WE COULD RENT THE SPARE ROOM
WE'LL TAKE IT! WHO DO WE SEE?
REAR VIEW MONITOR
COMBINATION SAUNA/BARBEQUE MODULE
THEN WE HAVE THE 6 BEDROOM, 4 BATH MODEL ..UH.. WITHOUT THE GREENHOUSE
EMERGENCY VEHICLE DROP
WHAT BASEMENT?
GOOD STUFF STORAGE
UP
DOWN
RETRACTABLE ESCALATOR
AAAAOOGA
NEW
GO ANYWHERE DO ANYTHING IN THE SWIFT CHALET
INCREASE SMILEAGE
Call me for very friendly illustration and design that sells. And sells. And sells.
David Scott Goodwin
GOODWIN & FRIENDS INC.
(503)488-2355
FAX (503)482-4729
◄ ONE OF A SERIES OF DISPLAY PANELS- FIRST INTERSTATE BANK
CLEARLY, THE USE OF HELMETS POSE A SERIOUS HAZARD UNDER CERTAIN CIRCUMSTANCES...
UHMR NUFF NEPH?
MOTOR CYCLE SAFETY BILL
▲ POLITICAL/EDITORIAL- CALIFORNIA TAXPAYER'S ASSOCIATION
▲ PACKAGING ILLUSTRATION GREAT AMERICAN UGHS
◄ EDITORIAL ▼
WE TAKE OUR HUMOR SERIOUSLY!
▼ SELF PROMOTIONAL (MYSELF & FRIENDS)
PRUDENCE DELIGHTS IN THE KNOWLEDGE THAT HER POTTED LAWN CONSERVES WATER.
COMMUNICA SERVICES DEPAR
YA KNOW, I THINK IT'S TIME WE LOOK INTO THIS FAX THING...
URGENT
• OREGON STATE LOTTERY
• FEDERAL RESERVE BANK
• PACIFICORP
• ARCO
• OREGON TOURISM
• MacFRIENDS
• OLYMPIA BEER
and others...

Mike Reed
illustrator

1314 Summit Avenue

Minneapolis,

Minnesota 55403

612 374-3164

Represented by
Jo Anne Schuna
612 343-0432
Frank Schuna
612 343-0104

Ted Fuka

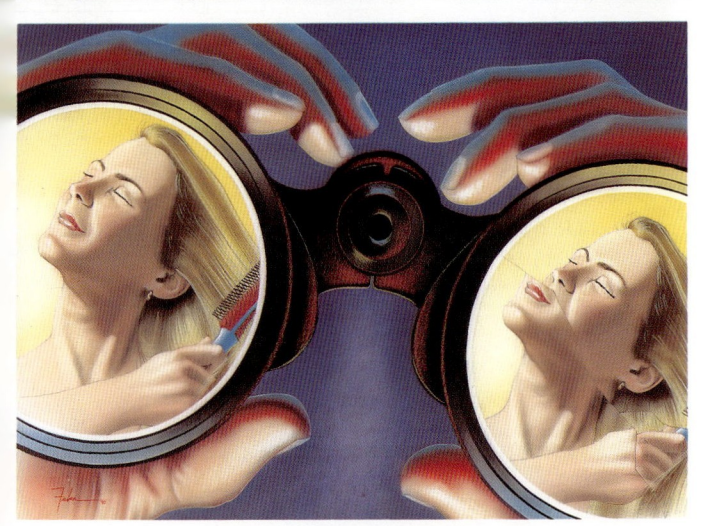

Gary Krejca

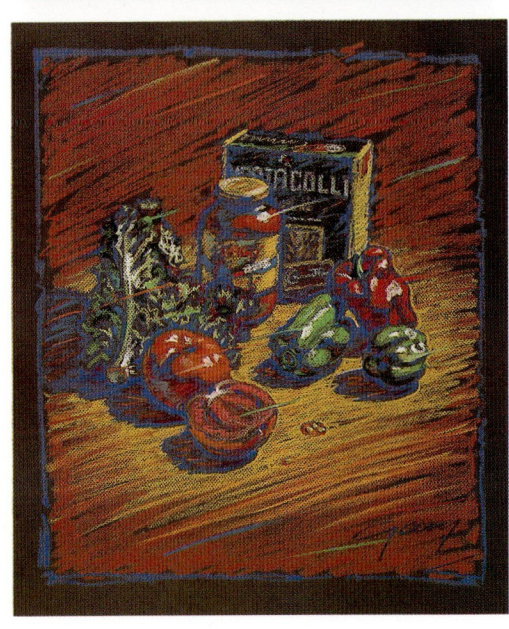

312·585·2314

602·829·0946

307

KARL EDWARDS

(916) 265-5666
FAX (916) 265-8118

Represented By:
Wendy Morgan
Network Studios
5 Logan Hill Road
Northport, NY 11768

NETWORK

(516) 757-5609
FAX (516) 261-6584
Member Graphic Artists Guild

See additional work in The Creative Illustration Book #1 Page 156

"THE PEN IS MIGHTIER THAN THE SWORD..."

EDWARDS

© Karl Edwards 1990

F·R·E·D S·C·H·R·i·E·R

Crowd Noise - Beacon Magazine

Coffee Mug - American Greetings

NOTHING MAKES SENSE BEFORE NOON.

NETWORK

Represented by Wendy Morgan, Network Studios, Tele.(516) 757-5609, FAX (516) 261-6584
(Fax in artist's Studio) Member of Graphic Arts Guild

Work also appears in: Corporate Showcase #3 - page 38, American Showcase #10 - page 305, The Creative Illustration Book #1 - page 157, Humor I and Humor II
Clients: B.P. America, Pepsi, General Electric, Cleveland Browns, American Greetings, TNT Skypak, Federal Reserve Bank, New England Business, Penton Publishing, CMP Publications

grace de vito
140 hoyt street • #4e • stamford, ct 06905 • (203)967-2198

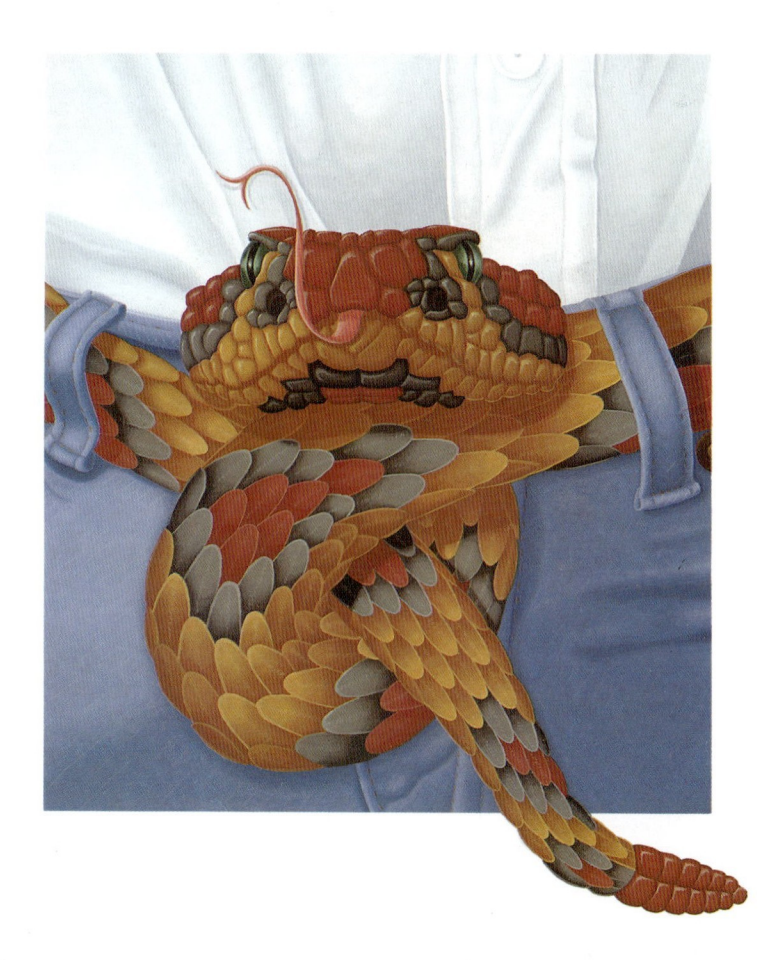

MARTIN FRENCH

PRESENTED BY IVY GLICK & ASSOCIATES   **415-543-6056**   REPRESENTED IN SEATTLE BY PAT HACKETT   **206-447-1600**   STUDIO   **206-867-3939**

Matthew Holmes

REPRESENTED IN
THE EAST BY
RENARD REPRESENTS
TEL 212-490-2450
FAX 212-697-6828

REPRESENTED IN
THE WEST, MIDWEST
AND SOUTH BY
IVY GLICK
& ASSOCIATES
TEL 415-543-6056

STUDIO
TEL 916-944-7270

DEREK GRINNELL

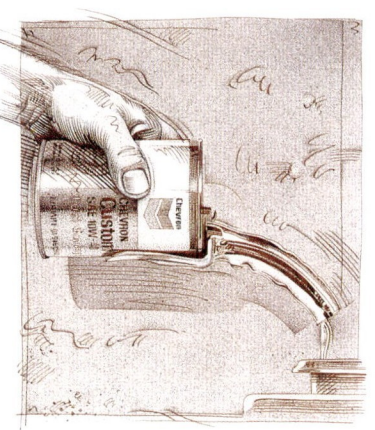

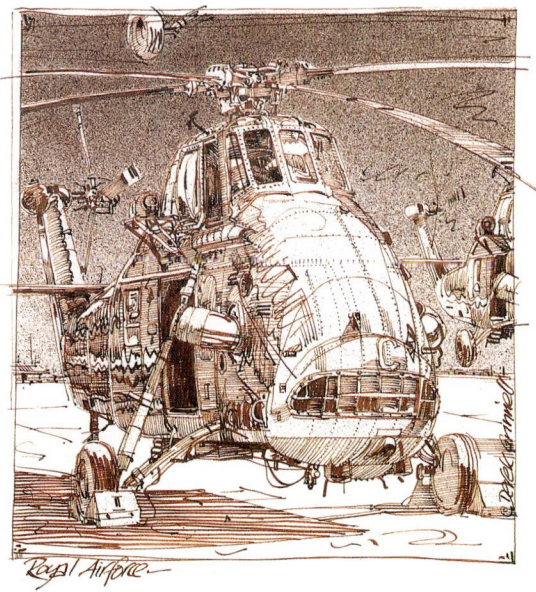

IvyGlick
& ASSOCIATES

415 · 543 · 6056
350 TOWNSEND · SAN FRANCISCO, CA 94107

STUDIO PHONE: (415) 221-2820

MEMBER SAN FRANCISCO SOCIETY OF ILLUSTRATORS

313

AMY BRYANT
STUDIO 214-902-0163

REPERTOIRE

LARRY & ANDREA LYNCH

5521 GREENVILLE

DALLAS, TEXAS 75206

214-369-6990

FAX 214-369-6938

DENISE CHAPMAN CRAWFORD
STUDIO 713-529-3634

REPERTOIRE

LARRY & ANDREA LYNCH

5521 GREENVILLE

DALLAS, TEXAS 75206

214-369-6990

FAX 214-369-6938

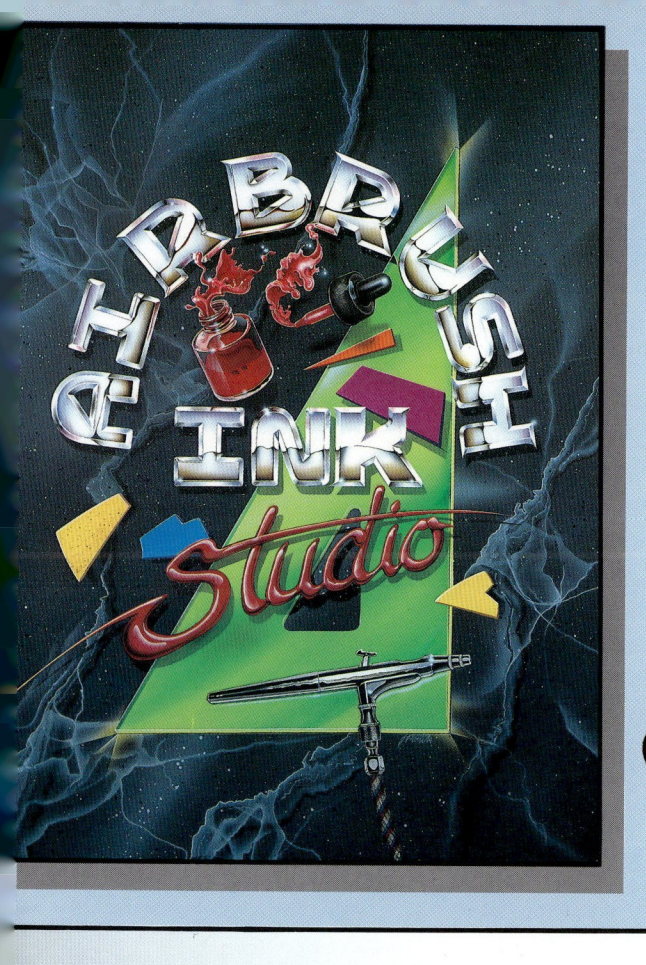

AIRBRUSH INK STUDIO
Joseph Pomilla
58 Forest Avenue
Ronkonkoma, N.Y. 11779
(516) 471-2728

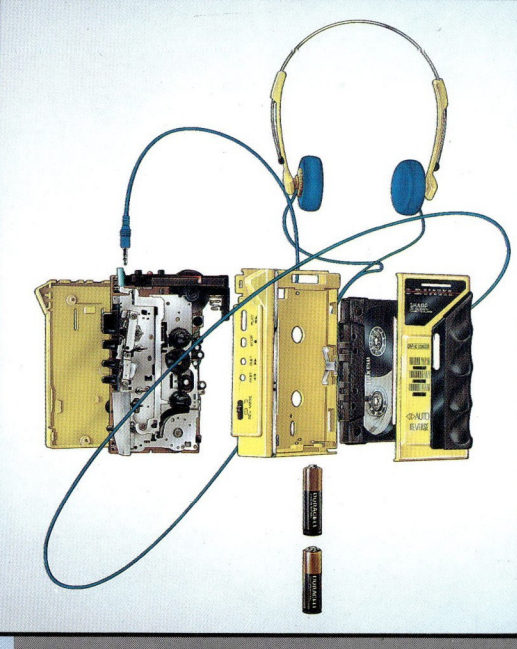

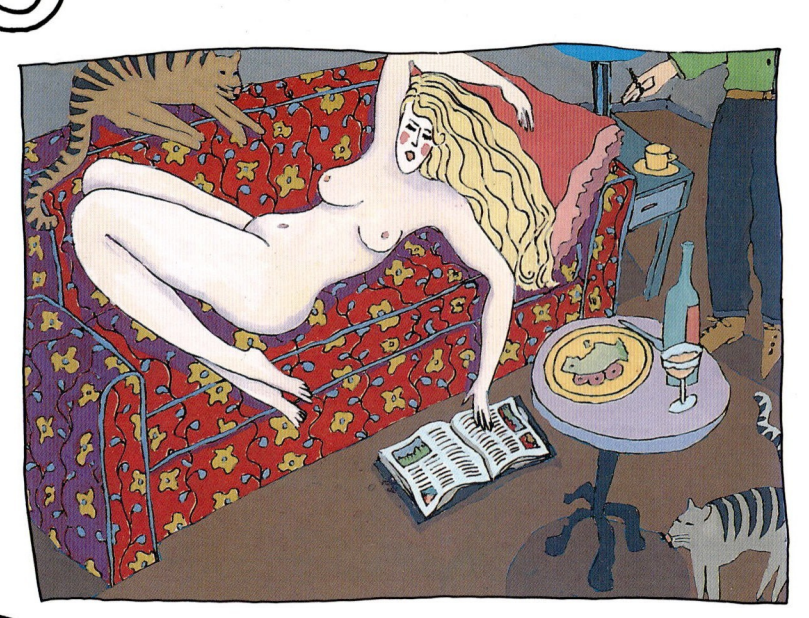

Caroline Burton

330 8th Street, Jersey City, NJ 07302 (201) 656-6502 Fax (201) 963-0332

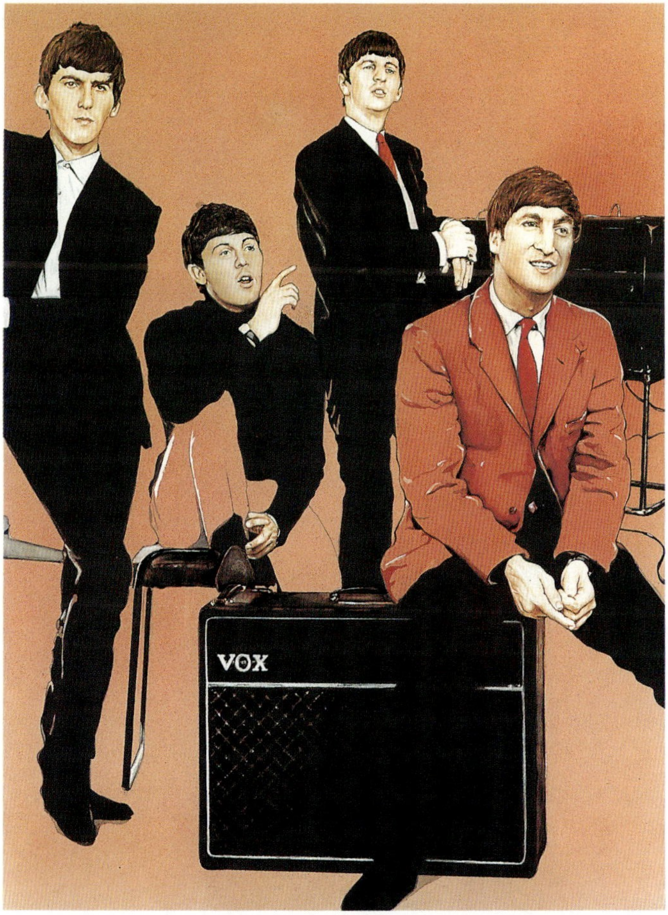
VOX

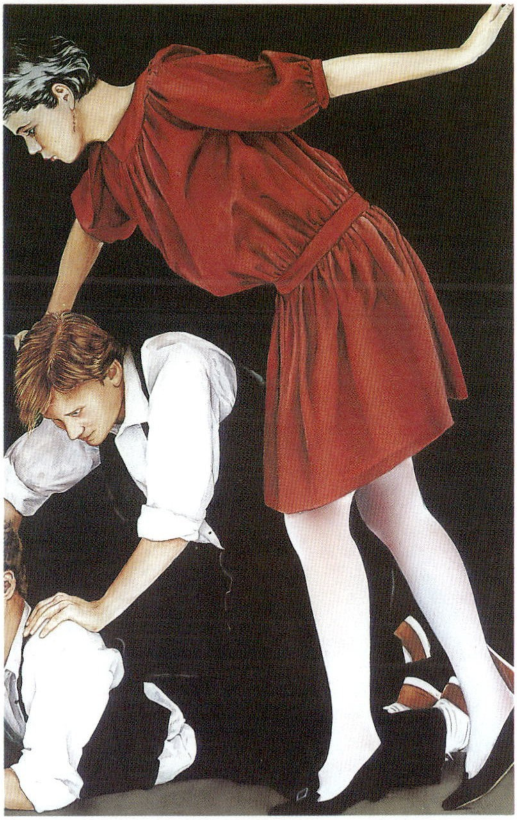

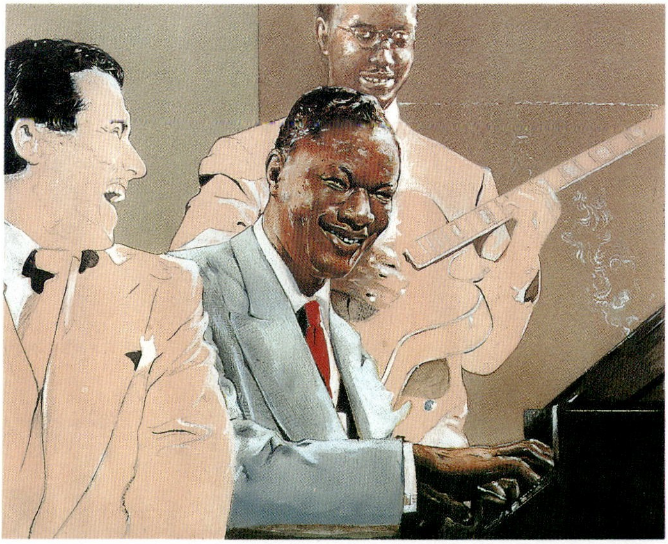

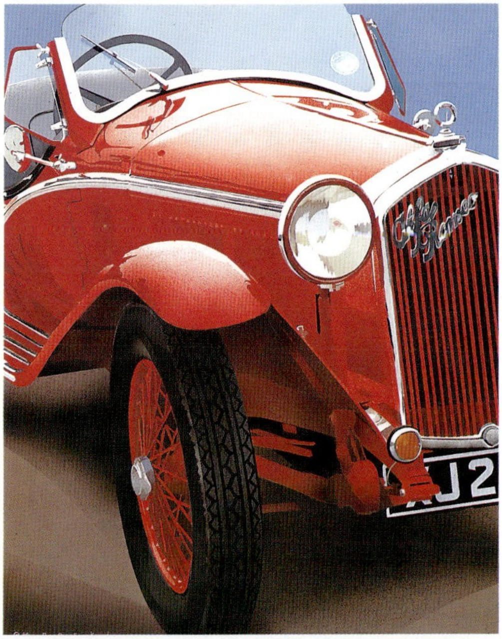

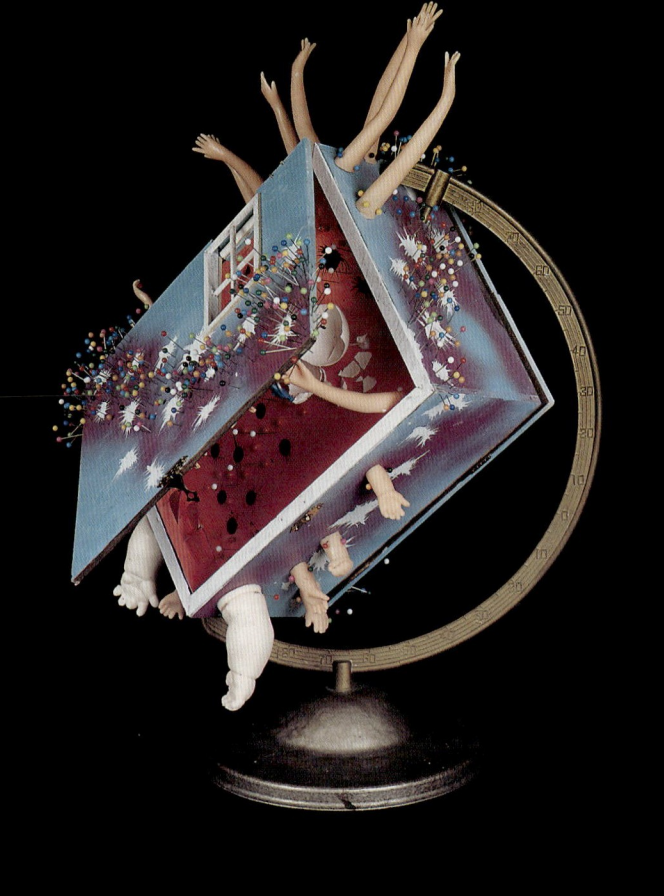

PRESTON McGOVERN

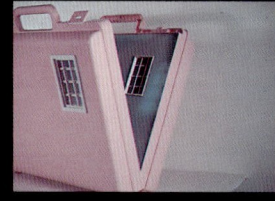

CONSTRUCTION AND COLLAGE ILLUSTRATION
157 EAST 3RD STREET   NEW YORK, NEW YORK 10009
TEL (212) 982-8595

Dorothy Gulick

(213) 695-3490
Fax Available

ART·SCIENCE

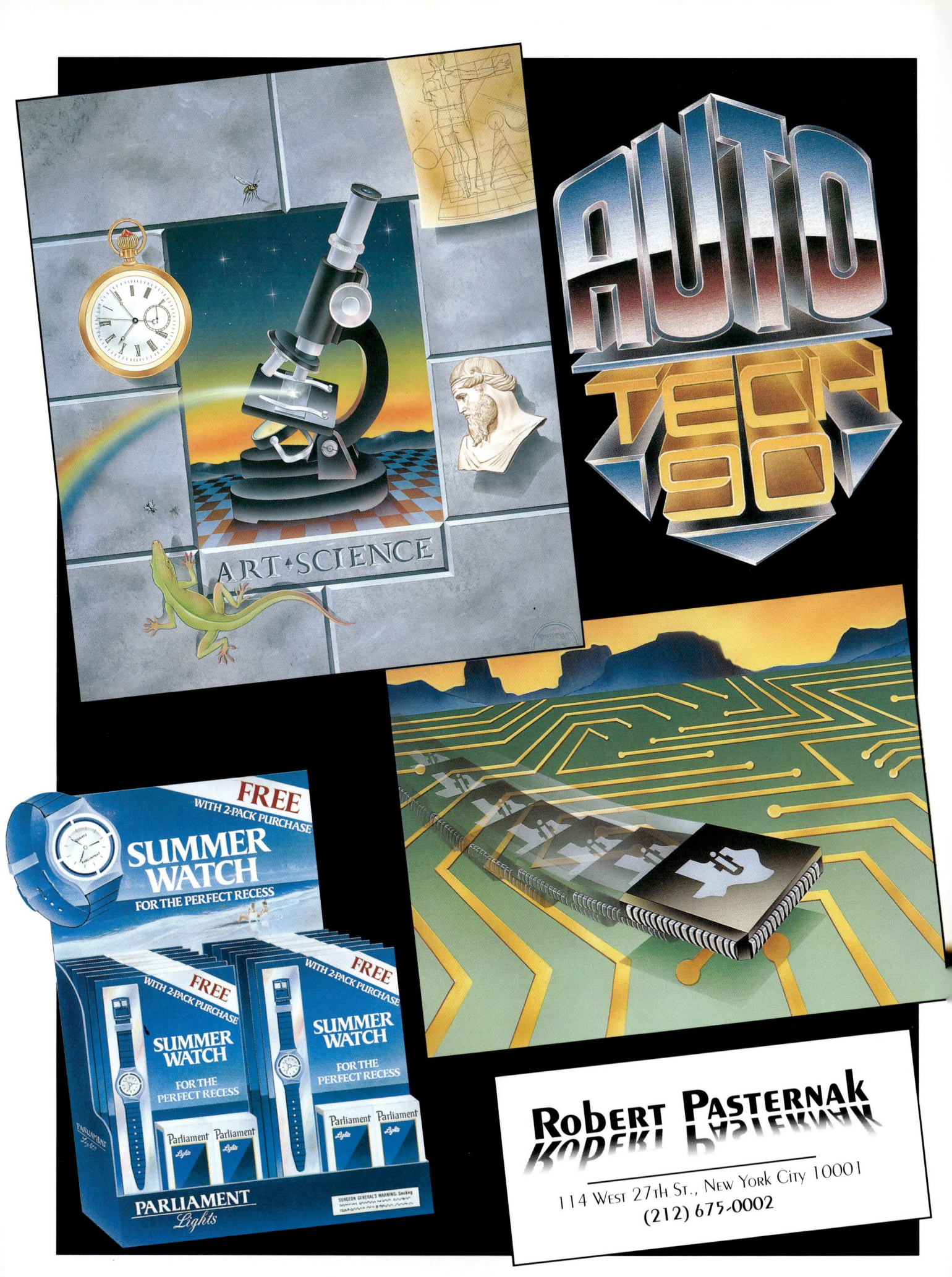

AUTO TECH 90

FREE WITH 2-PACK PURCHASE
SUMMER WATCH
FOR THE PERFECT RECESS
Parliament Lights

Robert Pasternak
114 West 27th St., New York City 10001
(212) 675-0002

WILLIAM
HARRISON

Renard Represents
Tel: (212) 490·2450
Fax: (212) 697·6828

© 1991 WILLIAM HARRISON

STEVE BJÖRKMAN
Available for Print and Film

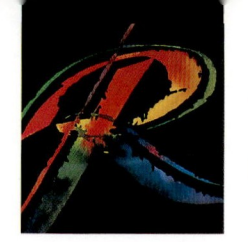

Renard Represents
Tel: (212) 490·2450
Fax: (212) 697·6828

© 1991 STEVE BJÖRKMAN

JUD GUITTEAU

Renard Represents
Tel: (212) 490·2450
Fax: (212) 697·6828

© 1991 JUD GUITTEAU

323

THEO RUDNAK

Renard Represents
Tel: (212) 490·2450
Fax: (212) 697·6828

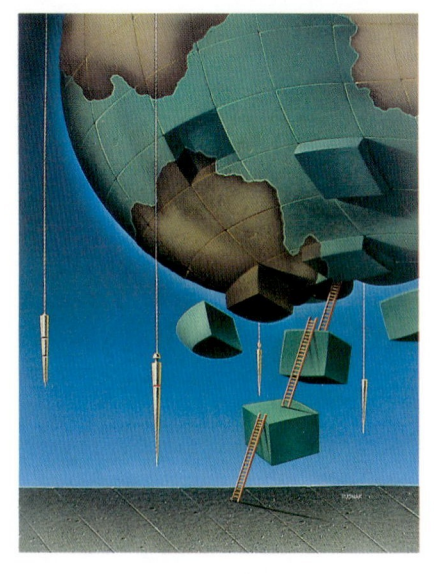

© 1991 THEO RUDNAK

WAYNE McLOUGHLIN

Renard Represents
Tel: (212) 490·2450
Fax: (212) 697·6828

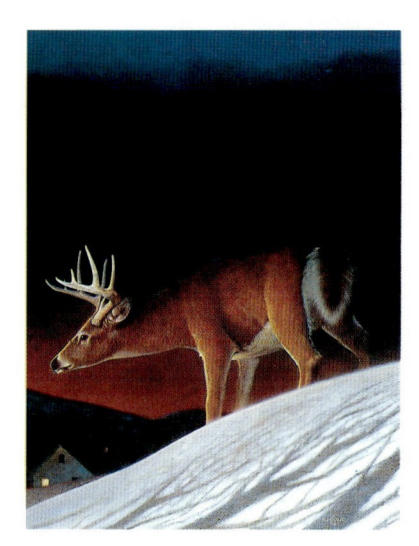

© 1991 WAYNE McLOUGHLIN

DAN GARROW

Renard Represents
Tel: (212) 490·2450
Fax: (212) 697·6828

CHANGING CAREERS

CORPORATE TAKEOVER

GLENN DEAN

Renard Represents
Tel: (212) 490·2450
Fax: (212) 697·6828

© 1991 GLENN DEAN

327

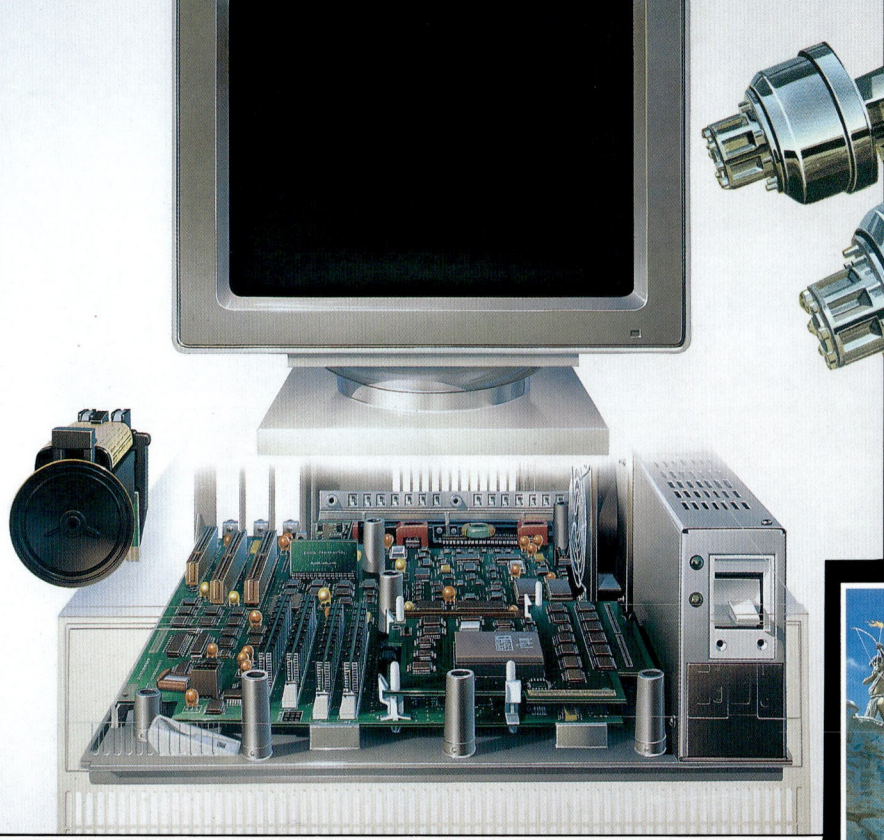

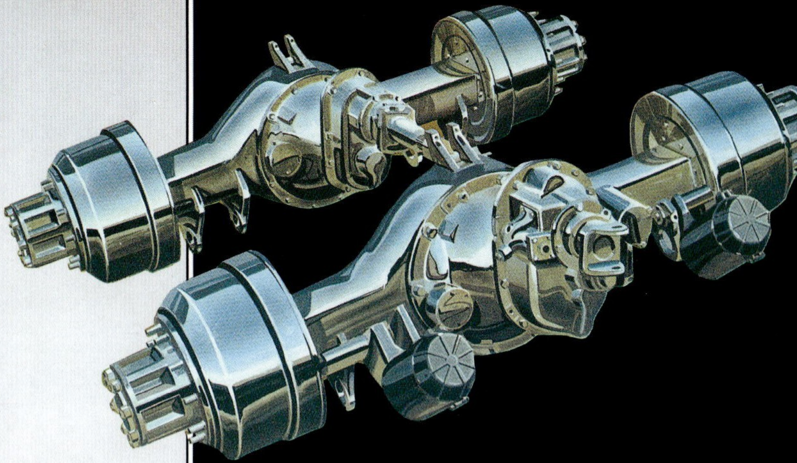

TERRY RYAN

REPRESENTED BY **TOM PRITCHETT** • **(212) 688-1080**
330 WEST FOURTH STREET • NEW YORK, NY 10014

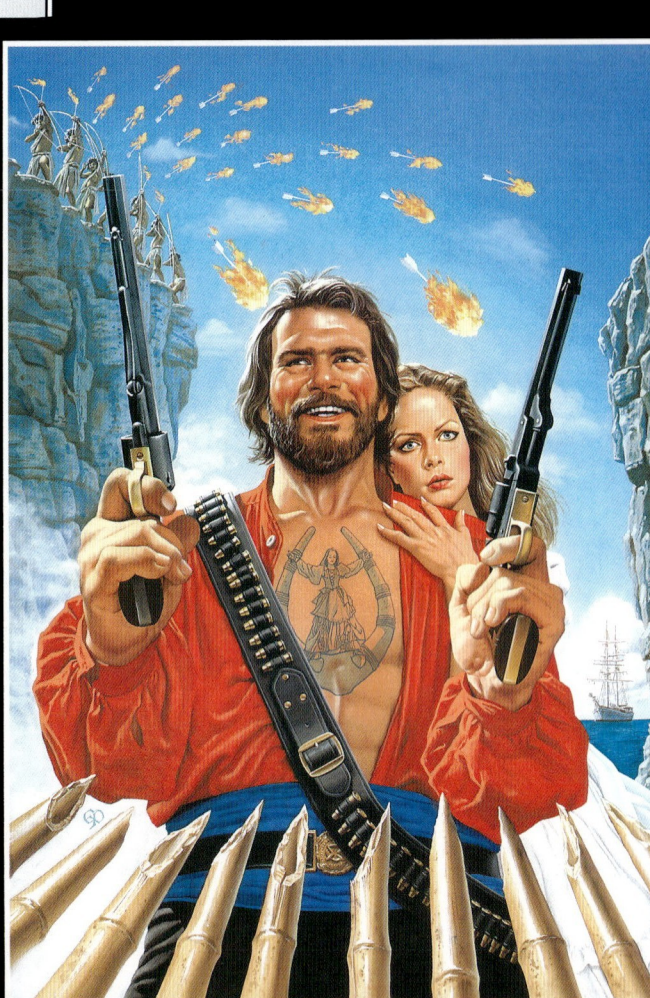

GEORGE I. PARRISH, JR

GEORGE KANELOUS

JIM GILBERT ILLUSTRATOR

136 N. SUMMIT
TOLEDO, OH
43604

PHONE
419-243-7600

FAX
419-243-8815

CLIENT LIST

Proctor & Gamble
Discover Card
Owens-Corning
Smith & Wesson
Armstrong Ceilings
The Toledo Symphony
The Toledo Zoo
Weyerhaeuser
Goodyear

Call Jim

LESLIE HARRIS

(404) 872-7163 FAX IN STUDIO

DON WELLER

Studio
(801) 649-9859
Fax (801) 649-4196
P.O. Box 726
Park City
Utah 84060

In Los Angeles
Jae Wagoner
(213) 392-4877
Fax (213) 396-6828

In New York
Daniele Collignon
(212) 243-4209
Fax (212) 463-0634

In Chicago
Jim Hanson
(312) 337-7770
Fax (312) 337-7112

In Northern California
Jan Collier
(415)552-4252

JON HUL

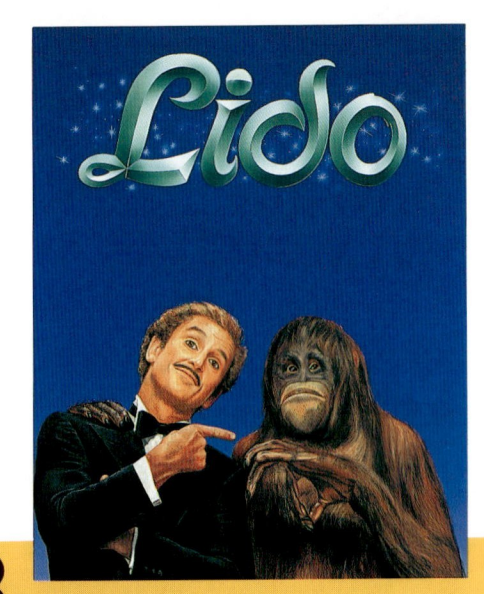

(818) 508 8228

· · FAX IN STUDIO · ·

· PLATO · TALEPOROS ·

If necessity is the mother of invention, then Minolta just gave birth.

If retrieving information in your office has become a tall order, Minolta has innovations that put it in the proper perspective.

With Minolta's MI³MS 1000 you can retrieve your documents in seconds from optical disks holding up to 40,000 each. And thanks to MI³MS functions at up to four keyboard/display workstations. All this from a single personal computer without the use of a network.

And Minolta will support your document management needs for years to come. No other system can add workstations or expand

ISIS COMBINES FLEXIBILITY & EASE WITH SPEED & POWER

(212) 689-3138
333 EAST 23RD ST
NY CITY, 10010

333

Tina Rosenbaum

Trudy Sands
ARTIST REPRESENTATIVE

214-748-8663 • FAX 214-748-4965
233 YORKTOWN, DALLAS, TX 75208

Michael Sours

Trudy Sands
ARTIST REPRESENTATIVE

214-748-8663 • FAX 214-748-4965
233 YORKTOWN, DALLAS, TX 75208

3-D POP UP

335

Tim McClure

Trudy Sands
ARTIST REPRESENTATIVE

214-748-8663 • FAX 214-748-4965

233 YORKTOWN, DALLAS, TX 75208

John Cook

Trudy Sands
ARTIST REPRESENTATIVE

214-748-8663 • FAX 214-748-4965
233 YORKTOWN, DALLAS, TX 75208

COOL FRONT

TAMARA INCORPORATED

**Tamara Linden
Artists' Representative**
3565 Piedmont Road
Two Piedmont Center, Suite 300
Atlanta, Georgia 30305
(404) 262-1209

Representing: Gail Chirko, Tom Fleck, Joseph M. Ovies, Charles A. Passerelli

THOMAS GONZALEZ
Represented by ALDRIDGE REPS, INC.
755 Virginia Avenue, Atlanta, Georgia 30306
404-872-7980
FAX (404) 874-9681

Aldridge

Jeff FARIA

© 1991 by Jeff Faria, 937 Garden Street, Hoboken, New Jersey 07030

*J*oin the crowd that gets my mailings regularly. New additions to my mailing list will receive a 3-D version of this semi-handsome Attack of the Chinese Waiters poster, complete with genuine 3-D glasses. Available while supplies last (or possibly longer).

Mash Notes from my Clients:

"It was certainly a pleasure working with (him)... not only (was he) pleasant and accommodating (especially on a hectic account), but the work was very well executed, upbeat, fun, to the point and zany."

Joanne DeCarlo
Art Buyer
Saatchi & Saatchi
New York City

"A great original approach"

Kathryn Kurgas
Art Director
Boston, Mass.

"Fun, fast, and flexible, and smart too"

Miriam Smith
Art Director
New York Newsday

"I loved Jeff's work from the moment I saw it. It was fresh, and gave my ad the sense of humor and sophistication I was after. And on top of that, he was even nice."

Lisa Rettig-Falcone
Vice President,
Art Director
Scali, McCabe, Sloves, Inc.

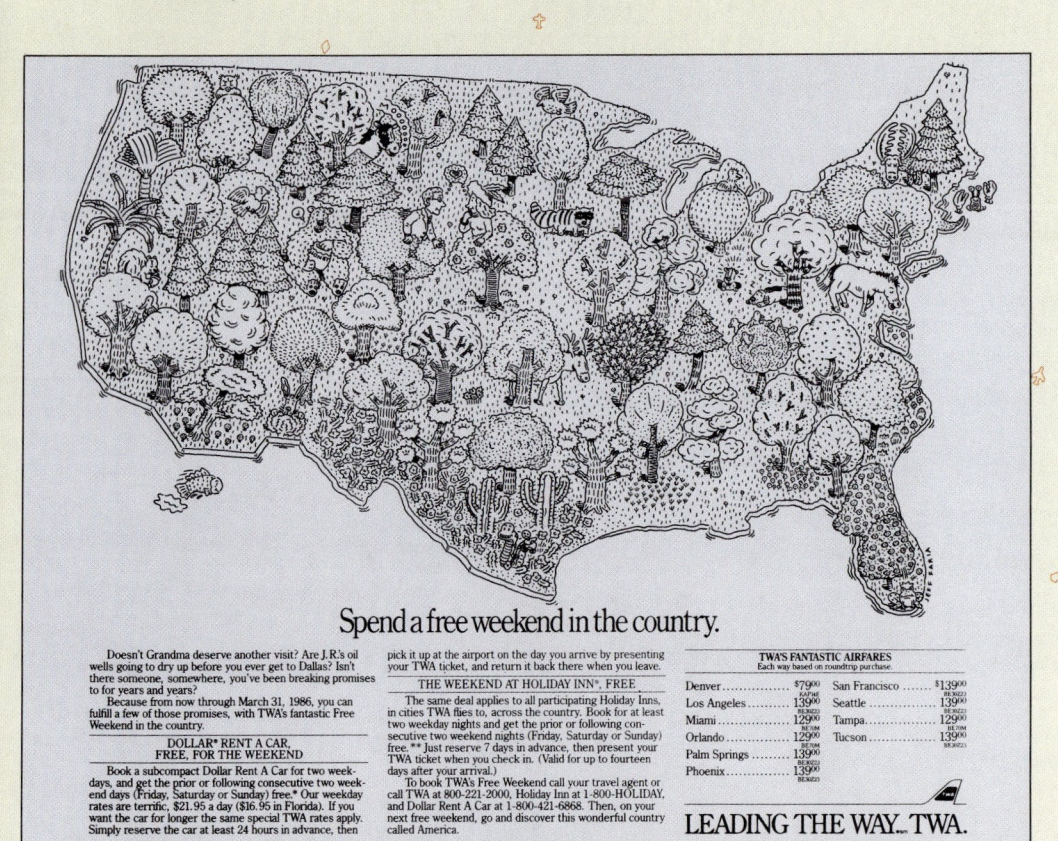

Voice: 201-656-3063

WHAT DO YOU WANT FROM LIFE?

Well, if you're like most people you want Italian shoes, French wines, German cars, Indian mysticism, Japanese gadgets and American cartoons. That's why all *my* cartoons are drawn 100% right here in America's humor capital: beautiful Hoboken (even the name is funny) New Jersey. So remember: Buy only genuine U.S.-made cartoons. Don't let America lose its sense of humor.

Photo: Marion Goldman
Coloring: Susan Bloch

Fax: 201-659-8032

Spend a free weekend in the country.

Doesn't Grandma deserve another visit? Are J.R.'s oil wells going to dry up before you ever get to Dallas? Isn't there someone, somewhere, you've been breaking promises to for years and years?

Because from now through March 31, 1986, you can fulfill a few of those promises, with TWA's fantastic Free Weekend in the country.

DOLLAR® RENT A CAR, FREE, FOR THE WEEKEND

Book a subcompact Dollar Rent A Car for two weekdays, and get the prior or following consecutive two weekend days (Friday, Saturday or Sunday) free.* Our weekend rates are terrific, $21.95 a day ($16.95 in Florida). If you want the car for longer the same special TWA rates apply. Simply reserve the car at least 24 hours in advance, then pick it up at the airport on the day you arrive by presenting your TWA ticket, and return it back there when you leave.

THE WEEKEND AT HOLIDAY INN®, FREE

The same deal applies to all participating Holiday Inns, in cities TWA flies to, across the country. Book for at least two weekday nights and get the prior or following consecutive two weekend nights (Friday, Saturday or Sunday) free.** Just reserve 7 days in advance, then present your TWA ticket when you check in. (Valid for up to fourteen days after your arrival.)

To book TWA's Free Weekend call your travel agent or call TWA at 800-221-2000, Holiday Inn at 1-800-HOLIDAY, and Dollar Rent A Car at 1-800-421-6868. Then, on your next free weekend, go and discover this wonderful country called America.

TWA'S FANTASTIC AIRFARES			
Denver	$79.00	San Francisco	$139.00
Los Angeles	139.00	Seattle	139.00
Miami	129.00	Tampa	129.00
Orlando	129.00	Tucson	139.00
Palm Springs	139.00		
Phoenix	139.00		

LEADING THE WAY...TWA.

FARE CONDITIONS: Seats are limited. Fares are subject to change, advance purchase, cancellation penalty, and minimum stay requirements. May require travel on specific days of the week. For exact travel and holiday period restrictions, call today. *Dollar Rent A Car standard age, credit and driver qualifications apply. Rates are non-discountable. Gas, tax and optional items are not included. Offer limited to one free weekend per rental, subject to availability. Not available in Harrisburg. **Hotel offer not available in New York City, Las Vegas, San Diego, West Palm Beach and Wichita. Offer subject to availability. Applies to corporate and regular weekday rates. Fares service from New York and airports.

Here's what the well-dressed Art Director will be wearing this season. All jobs of $600 or more will be accompanied by this shirt with my popular Yuppies in Shoe Cars drawing silkscreened thereon. (I'll also give a free shirt to anyone who can rewrite that last sentence for me.)

341

Paul Blakey

Yankee Magazine

Geer DuBois

Charles Willis Design

Represented by Susan Wells
(404) 255-1430 FAX 255-3449

Paul Blakey (404) 977-7669

Susan Wells
ARTISTS' REPRESENTATIVE
5134 Timber Trail, N.E. / Atlanta, Georgia 30342 / (404) 255-1430

Jack Unruh

Triton Energy Corp.

The Sportsman's Guide To Texas

Sports Afield

SUSAN WELLS
ARTISTS' REPRESENTATIVE
5134 Timber Trail, N.E. / Atlanta, Georgia 30342 / (404) 255-1430

Represented by Susan Wells
(404) 255-1430 FAX 255-3449

Represented on the west coast by Ron Sweet

343

Barb Hogan

Represented by Susan Wells
(404) 255-1430 FAX 255-3449

SUSAN WELLS
ARTISTS' REPRESENTATIVE

5134 Timber Trail, N.E. / Atlanta, Georgia 30342 / (404) 255-1430

Christy Mull

Represented by Susan Wells
(404) 255-1430 FAX 255-3449

Don Loehle

Represented by Susan Wells
(404) 255-1430 FAX 255-34

Also by: CAROLYN POTTS & ASSOC, Chic
(312) 944-1130, Fax (312) 988-4236.

Susan Wells
ARTISTS' REPRESENTATIVE
5134 Timber Trail, N.E. / Atlanta, Georgia 30342 / (404) 255-1430

Ted Burn

Represented by Susan Wells, (404) 255-1430, fax 255-3449 • Studio, (404) 977-9246, fax 971-3882.

Tommy Stubbs

Represented by Susan Wells
(404) 255-1430 FAX 255-3449

SUSAN WELLS
ARTISTS REPRESENTATIVE
5134 Timber Trail, NE / Atlanta, Georgia 30342 / (404) 255-1430

Bob Radigan

Represented by Susan Wells (404) 255-1430 FAX 255-3449

Represented in New York by Irmeli Holmberg   Tel. (212) 545-9155
Represented in L.A. by Rosenthal Represents   Tel. (213) 390-9595

Susan Wells
ARTISTS' REPRESENTATIVE
5134 Timber Trail, N.E. / Atlanta, Georgia 30342 / (404) 255-1430

CLOWNBANK STUDIO
ILLUSTRATION · LETTERING · DESIGN
FAX IN STUDIO

CONTACT: PETER BARTCZAK • (408) 426-4247 • P.O. BOX 7709 • SANTA CRUZ, CA 95061
CLIENTS: ATARI, BUCCI SUNGLASSES, SYBEX COMPUTER BOOKS, THE CROSSING PRESS, ANTIC MAGAZINE, DIDONATO ASSOC. INC., RECYCLED PAPER PROD., BORLAND INTERNATIONAL, & WAVEFORM CORP.
Additional work in Volume 12 **American Showcase Illustration** and **Idea** Magazine #207.

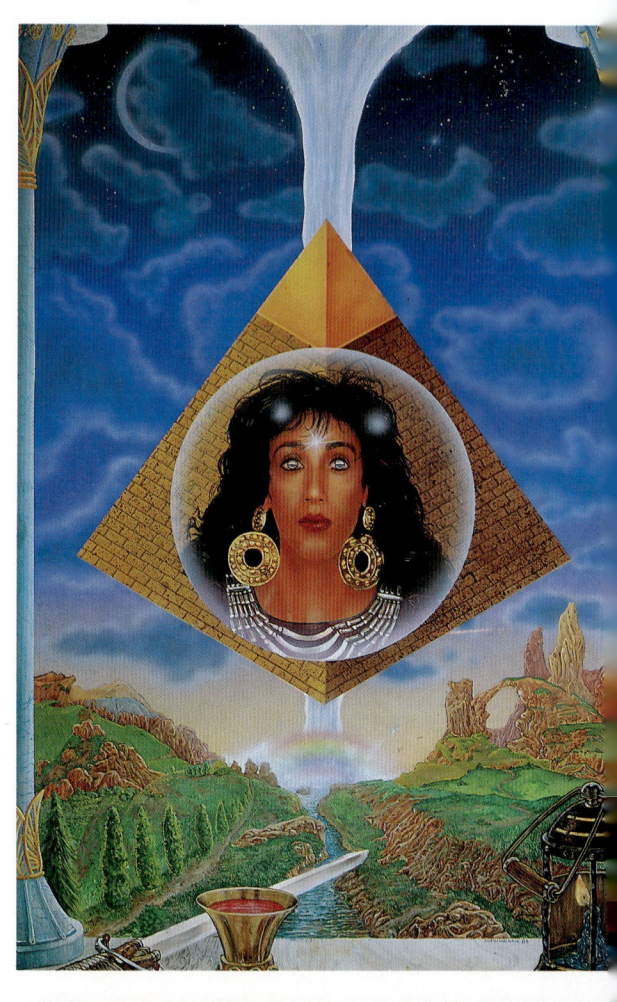

MIKE BENNY
ILLUSTRATION
916 ▪ 447 ▪ 8629

1 2 2 8 N S T.

S U I T E 9

S A C R A M E N T O

C A 9 5 8 1 4

Member of the Sacramento Illustrators Guild

351

MICHAEL DAVID BIEGEL
Illustration
(201) 825-0084

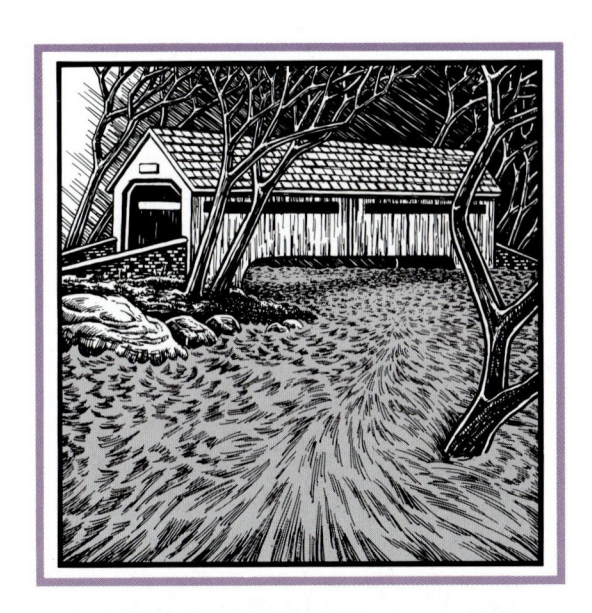

CONTEST

HOME IS WHERE THE ART IS

Aren't you a little tired of turning so many directory pages, only to find an artist who can meet a deadline?

Well, here's your opportunity to have a little fun, play our game, and WIN A TRIP!

All you have to do is identify the locations illustrated by our artists on the following thirteen pages. Each painting has been created as a special clue to help you. In addition, we've included other clues "just in case."

On November 1, 1991, a drawing of correct responses will be held and the winner may select a trip for two to any of the locations illustrated in North America.

Mail to Susan Gomberg
Artist Representative, Inc.;
145 East 22 Street; New York NY 10010

Susan, I think I know where all your artists are from!

Neil Brennan: _____

Steve Carver: _____

Robert Dale: _____

Laura Fernandez: _____

Allen Garns: _____

Ralph Giguere: _____

Rick Jacobson: _____

Jeff Leedy: _____

Dan McGowan: _____

Enzo Messi & Urs Schmidt: _____

Marti Shohet: _____

James Tughan: _____

Mark Weakley _____

My name is _____

Company _____

Address _____

_____

Phone _____

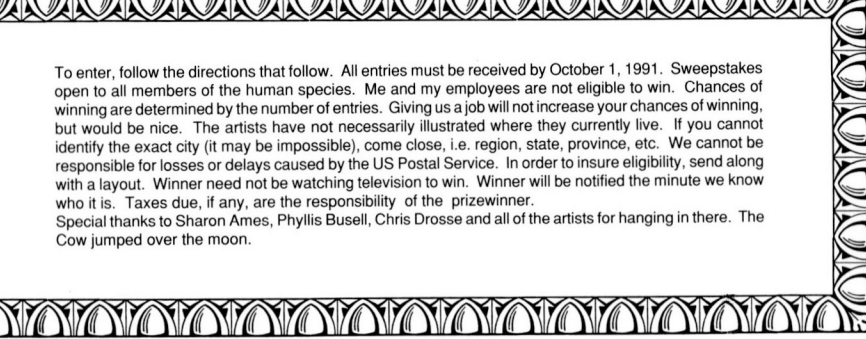

To enter, follow the directions that follow. All entries must be received by October 1, 1991. Sweepstakes open to all members of the human species. Me and my employees are not eligible to win. Chances of winning are determined by the number of entries. Giving us a job will not increase your chances of winning, but would be nice. The artists have not necessarily illustrated where they currently live. If you cannot identify the exact city (it may be impossible), come close, i.e. region, state, province, etc. We cannot be responsible for losses or delays caused by the US Postal Service. In order to insure eligibility, send along with a layout. Winner need not be watching television to win. Winner will be notified the minute we know who it is. Taxes due, if any, are the responsibility of the prizewinner.

Special thanks to Sharon Ames, Phyllis Busell, Chris Drosse and all of the artists for hanging in there. The Cow jumped over the moon.

Neil Brennan

"So this young fella come up to me totin' a camera. Says he's some kinda artist... wants to take my picture so he can make a drawin' of me..."

Caleb "Buck" Barnett

05 PHF

We shared a few stories about the past season. Then I thanked Mr. Barnett for his time. As I turned to leave, Buck stopped me to ask..."By the way son, what d'ya do for real work?"

ELLA FITZGERALD and PEARL BAILEY
were both born here in 1918

212•206•0066
FAX•206•0136

SUSAN GOMBERG

ARTISTS
REPRESENTATIVE
INCORPORATED

41 UNION SQUARE
NEW YORK NY 10003

Rick Jacobson

Birthplace of Art Linkletter

Tiger Lily

"The Lord said 'let there be wheat' and
_____ was born."

Stephen Leacock, *My Discovery of America*

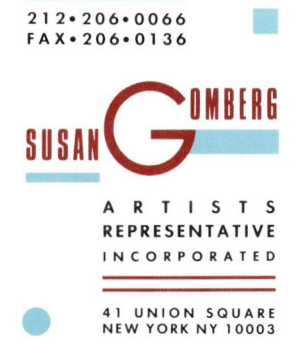

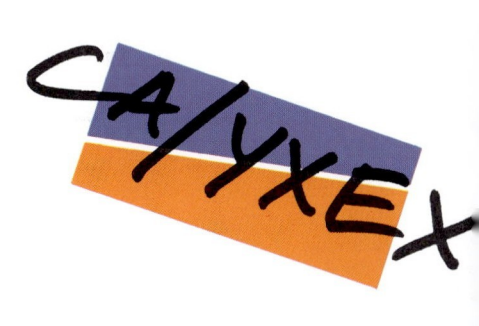

212•206•0066
FAX•206•0136

SUSAN GOMBERG
ARTISTS REPRESENTATIVE INCORPORATED

41 UNION SQUARE
NEW YORK NY 10003

CALYXEX

Laura Fernandez

K.D. LAING was country born and bred in this part of Canada.

"They say of _ _ _ _ _ _ that it's going to look really great when it finally gets uncrated."

—Robert Fox, BBC Radio

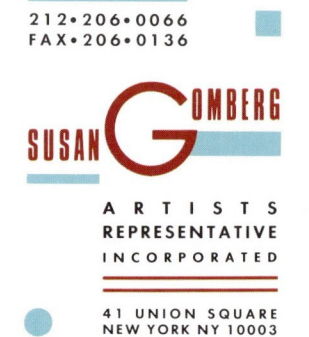

212•206•0066
FAX•206•0136

SUSAN GOMBERG
ARTISTS REPRESENTATIVE INCORPORATED

41 UNION SQUARE
NEW YORK NY 10003

Enzo Messi & Urs Schmidt

15,941 sq. mi.; pop. 6,036,000; cap. Bern

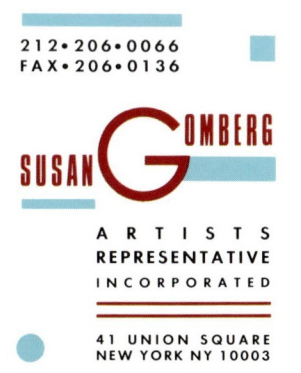

Culture Park

212•206•0066
FAX•206•0136

SUSAN GOMBERG

ARTISTS
REPRESENTATIVE
INCORPORATED

41 UNION SQUARE
NEW YORK NY 10003

"Exquisite postal service. No bothersome demonstrations, no spiteful strikes. Alpine butterflies. Fabulous sunsets—just west of my window, spangling the lake, splitting the crimson sun! Also, the pleasant surprise of a metaphorical sunset in charming surroundings."

—*Vladimir Nabokov, Interview, October, 1971*

Mark Weakley

"Remember the Alamo!"
—*Sidney Sherman*

14RNV

212•206•0066
FAX•206•0136

SUSAN GOMBERG

ARTISTS
REPRESENTATIVE
INCORPORATED

41 UNION SQUARE
NEW YORK NY 10003

CAROL BURNETT
was born here on April 26, 1936

Allen Garns

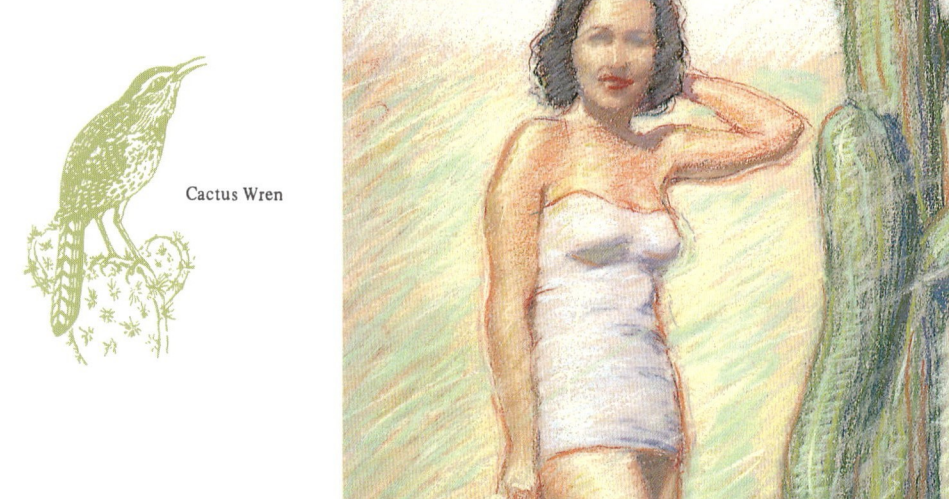

Cactus Wren

Cubs and Angels
Spring Training hom

18MSC

212•206•0066
FAX•206•0136

SUSAN GOMBERG
ARTISTS REPRESENTATIVE INCORPORATED

41 UNION SQUARE
NEW YORK NY 10003

n. flat tableland with steep sides.

James Tughan

"America's Sweetheart,"
Mary Pickford
born here in 1893!

"The houses and stores at _ _ _ _ _ _ _ are not to be compared with those American towns opposite. But the Englishman has built according to his means—the American according to his expectations."

—*Capt. Frederick Marryat*

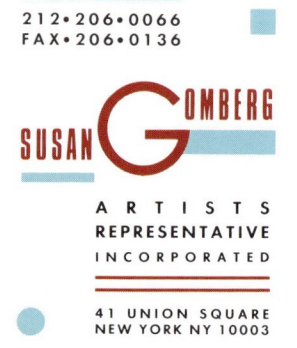

212•206•0066
FAX•206•0136

SUSAN GOMBERG

ARTISTS
REPRESENTATIVE
INCORPORATED

41 UNION SQUARE
NEW YORK NY 10003

CAYYZ

Ralph Giguere

"On the whole, I'd rather be in..."
—*W.C. Fields Epitaph*

Birthplace of
American Bandstand, Fabian, Frankie
Avalon, Chubby Checker
and the
Streetcorner Symphony.

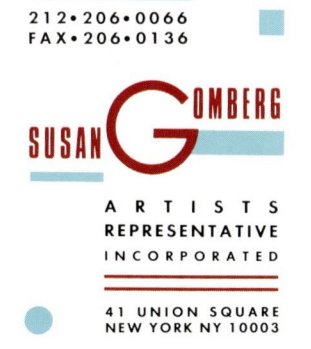

84 PSQ

212•206•0066
FAX•206•0136

Susan Gomberg

ARTISTS REPRESENTATIVE INCORPORATED

41 UNION SQUARE
NEW YORK NY 10003

Steve Carver

The dramatic heights in this county brought Rod Serling to the edge of the Twilight Zone.

"...is on top of a steep hill, with a long thin ice-cold lake below it, into which run streams through spectacular—or, as the Americans say, scenic—gorges; these gorges are used by the students for suicide."

—Louis MacNeice

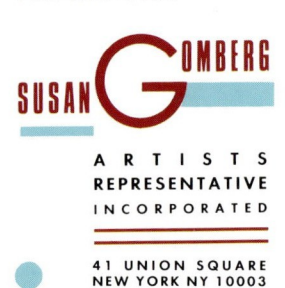

791TH

212•206•0066
FAX•206•0136

SUSAN GOMBERG

ARTISTS
REPRESENTATIVE
INCORPORATED

41 UNION SQUARE
NEW YORK NY 10003

Dan McGowan

GYPSY ROSE LEE
was born here in 1914

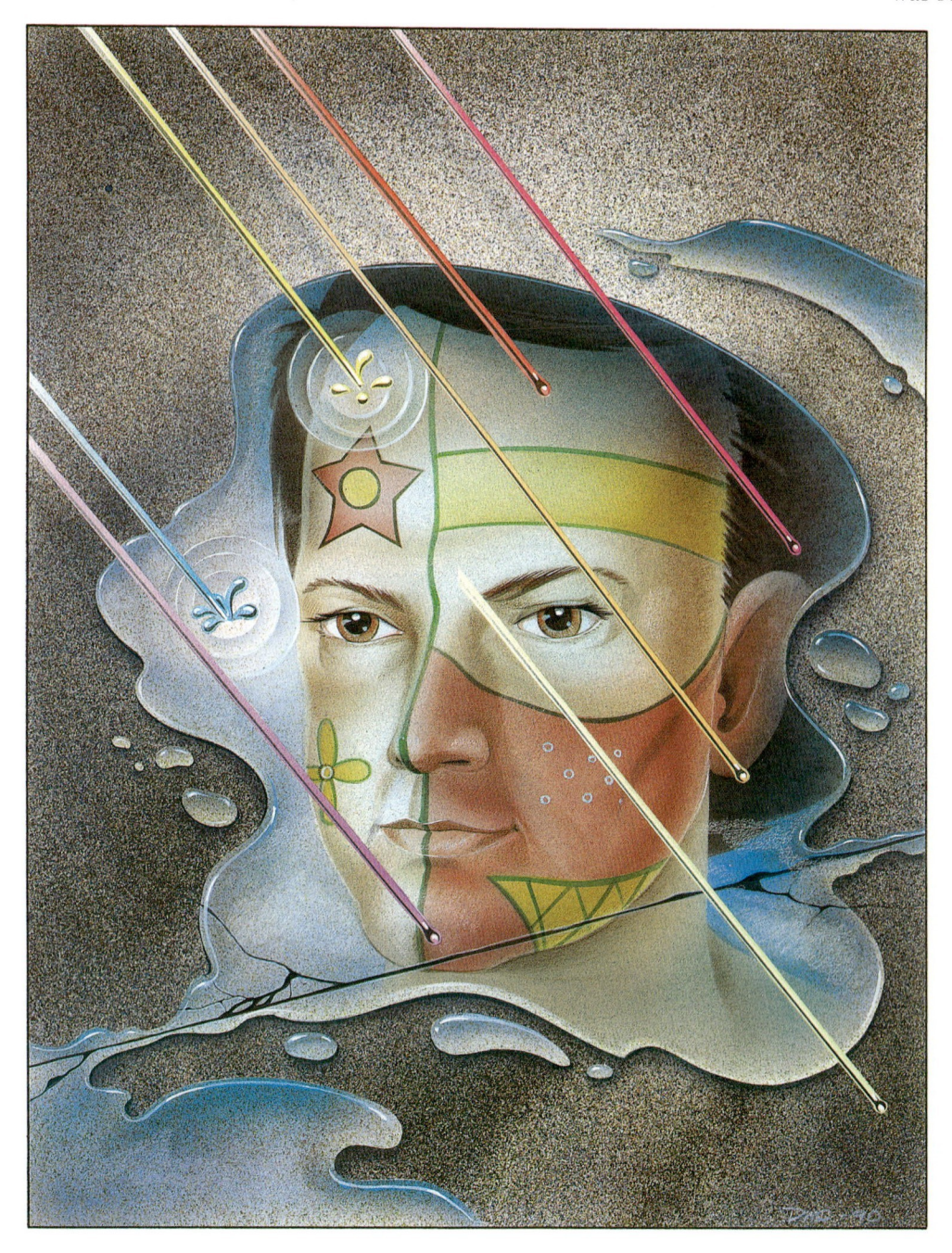

"It's streets are so steep, like those of San Francisco, that you practically need spikes in your shoes, and it's politics are almost as spectacular as the scenery."
—*John Gunther*

212•206•0066
FAX•206•0136

SUSAN GOMBERG

ARTISTS
REPRESENTATIVE
INCORPORATED

41 UNION SQUARE
NEW YORK NY 10003

USA Today's Best Place to Live in America in 1990.

Site of the first Skid Row.

Robert Dale

If I win, I'm going to stay home and order in!!

OH! OH!

212·206·0066
FAX·206·0136

SUSAN GOMBERG

ARTISTS REPRESENTATIVE INCORPORATED

41 UNION SQUARE
NEW YORK NY 10003

77WTC

Marti Shohet

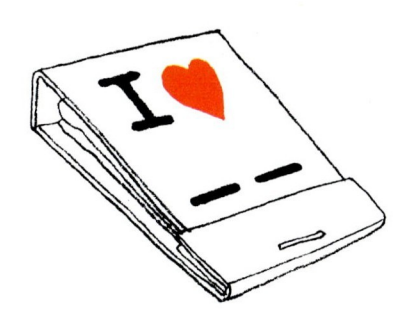

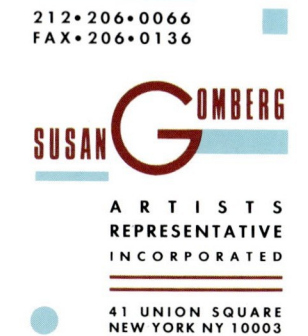

212•206•0066
FAX•206•0136

SUSAN **G**OMBERG

ARTISTS
REPRESENTATIVE
INCORPORATED

41 UNION SQUARE
NEW YORK NY 10003

Jeff Leedy

ony Bennett left something here.
1 on the Richter Scale!

"When you get tired of walking around
___ _____, you can always lean against it."

—TransWorld Getaway Guide

19SRF

212•206•0066
FAX•206•0136

SUSAN GOMBERG

ARTISTS
REPRESENTATIVE
INCORPORATED

41 UNION SQUARE
NEW YORK NY 10003

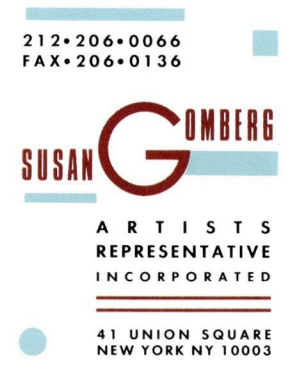

BENTON MAHAN

Phone or Fax 419•768•2204•6301 Twp. Rd. 179 • P.O. Box 66 • Chesterville, Ohio 43317

Partial Client List: Psychology Today; Golf Magazine; Current Cards; Raintree Publishing; Eveready Batteries; Columbus Dispatch; Muscle and Fitness Magazine; Curriculum Concepts Inc.; Dun's Business Month; Harrowsmith Magazine; Grosset and Dunlap; Scott-Foresman; H.B.J. Publishing; Akron Beacon Journal; Macmillan Publishing; Yankee Magazine; Scribner; Holt Publishing; I.T.T.; McGraw-Hill; Doubleday; Children's Television Workshop; Silver Burdett; Lord, Sullivan, and Yoder; Fahlgren and Swink; and many others. Give me a call or fax me a layout, I'm easy to work with.

314 361 4484

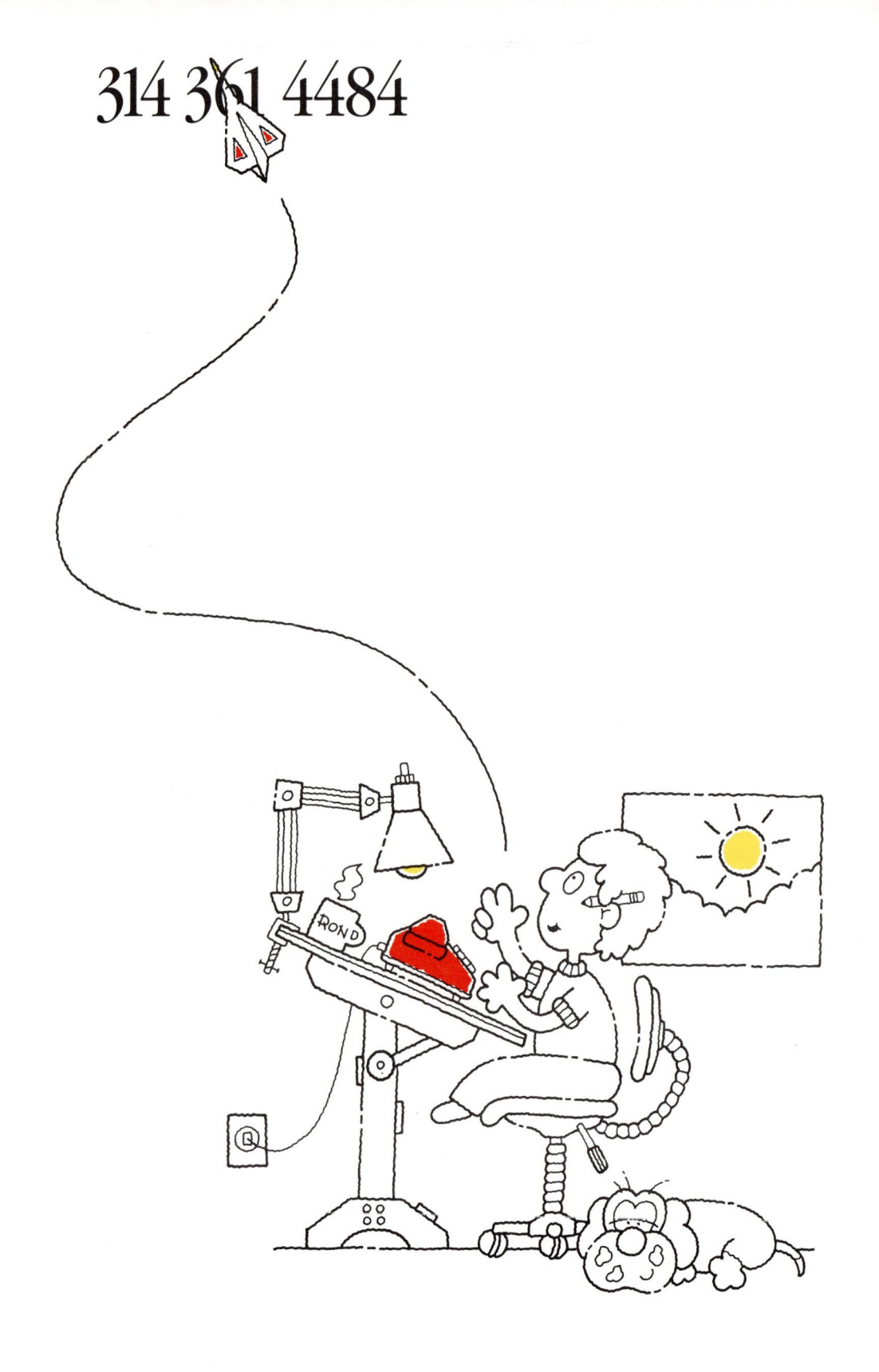

Ron Laney

Illustration

Saint Louis

FRANCIS LIVINGSTON

(415) 456-7103

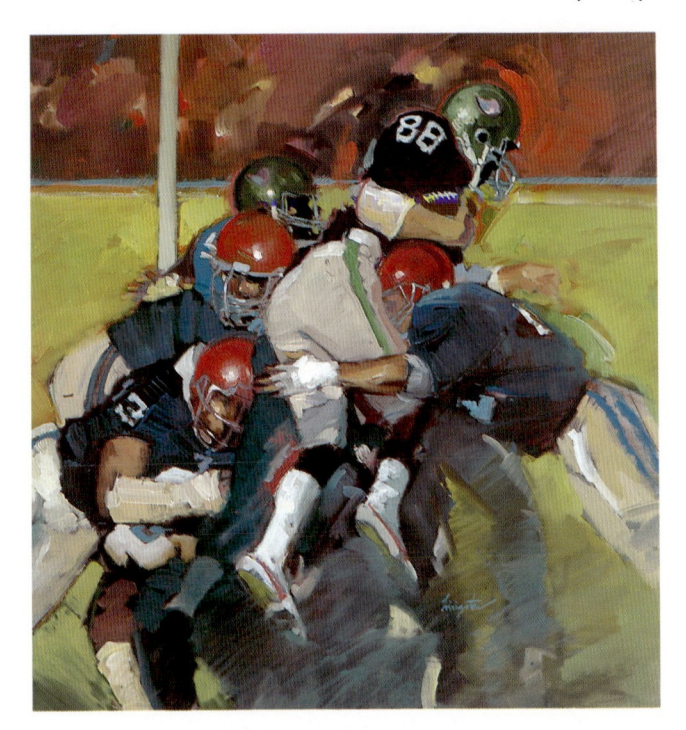

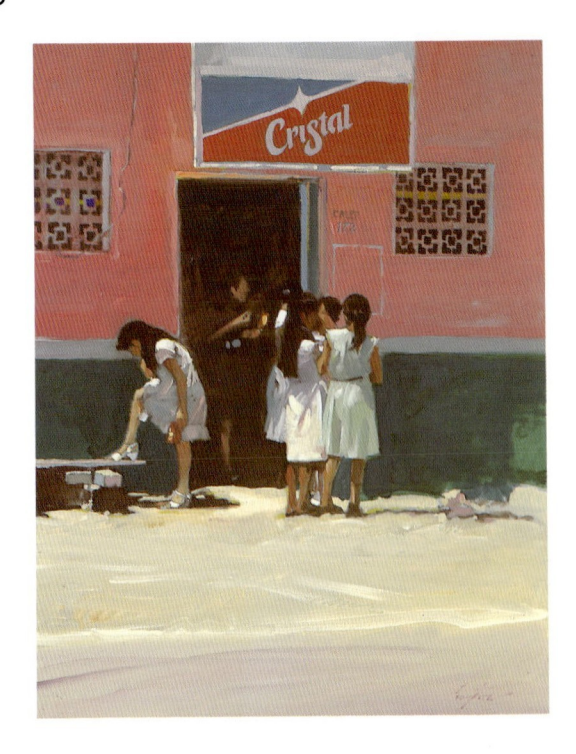

Jerry Leff Associates, Inc., New York
TEL: (212) 697-8525   FAX: (212) 949-1843

Freda Scott, San Francisco
TEL: (415) 621-2992   FAX: (415) 621-5202

I Do Art
MIKE WIMMER
900 N.W. 36TH, SUITE 105, NORMAN, OK 73072, 405-329-0478

Mike specializes in painting the warm and natural relationships between people, and their environments. His understanding of light captures the viewer and makes them become part of the scene. Whether working with editorial, advertising, or corporate clients, his first goal is to strike that harmonizing chord of truth, with the appropriate character, directed to the specific needs of the client. Some of these clients include: American Airlines, Doubleday, Harper & Row, McGraw-Hill, Milton Bradley, Putnam & Grossett, Readers Digest, Southwestern Bell, Texas Instruments, Zebco.

Represented in New York by:

MENDOLA LTD.
GRAY BAR BLDG., 420 LEXINGTON AVE., PENTHOUSE, NEW YORK, N.Y. 10170, (212) 986-5680

NORMAN HINES

555 Douglas #100
W. Sacramento, CA 95605
(916)373-0466 / FAX(916)446-1130

CALIFORNIA BUILDER

AUTOMOTIVE ECONOMICS, Dr. P. Berg, South Bend

(916)373-0466

CLIENTS: TIME, INC.; CATERPILLAR; WABCO
READER'S DIGEST; AEROJET

ARTISTIC LICENSE, INC.: "Learning Curve", Sacramento

J. HOLS: INTERNATIONAL COMMUNICATIONS, Spokane

NORMAN HINES
MEMBER: Sacramento Illustrator's Guild

372

TRACY
duCharme
illustration

213•396•6316

© Larry Moore 1990

LARRY MOORE
ILLUSTRATION · DESIGN
407 · 648 · 0832

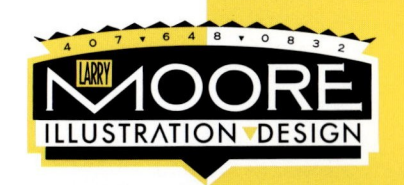

LARRY MOORE

ILLUSTRATION DESIGN

1635 DELANEY AVENUE

ORLANDO FL 32806

407 648 0832

Barry Littmann

57 Overlook Drive, Hackettstown, N.J. 07840

(201) 850-4405
Fax: (201) 850-4672

Things to do on vacation

Three weeks in the Israeli army

Rafting down the Amazon

Small game hunting

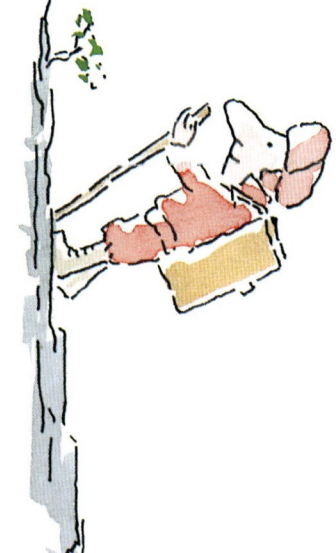

Trekking the Himalayas

Co-operative camping

Standing around doing nothing

David Lesh
5693 N. Meridian Street
Indianapolis, IN 46208

317.253.3141

Joanne Palulian
Representative
18 McKinley Street
Rowayton, CT 06853

203.866.3734
212.581.8338

Dickran Palulian

Joanne Palulian
Representative

212 · 581 · 8338
203 · 866 · 3734
Fax# 203 · 857 · 0842

Bonnie Timmons

Joanne Palulian
Representative

212 • 581 • 8338
203 • 866 • 3734
Fax # 203 • 857 • 0842
Studio: 215 • 247 • 3556

Gayle Kabaker

Joanne Palulian
Representative

212 · 581 · 8338
203 · 866 · 3734
Fax # 203 · 857 · 0842

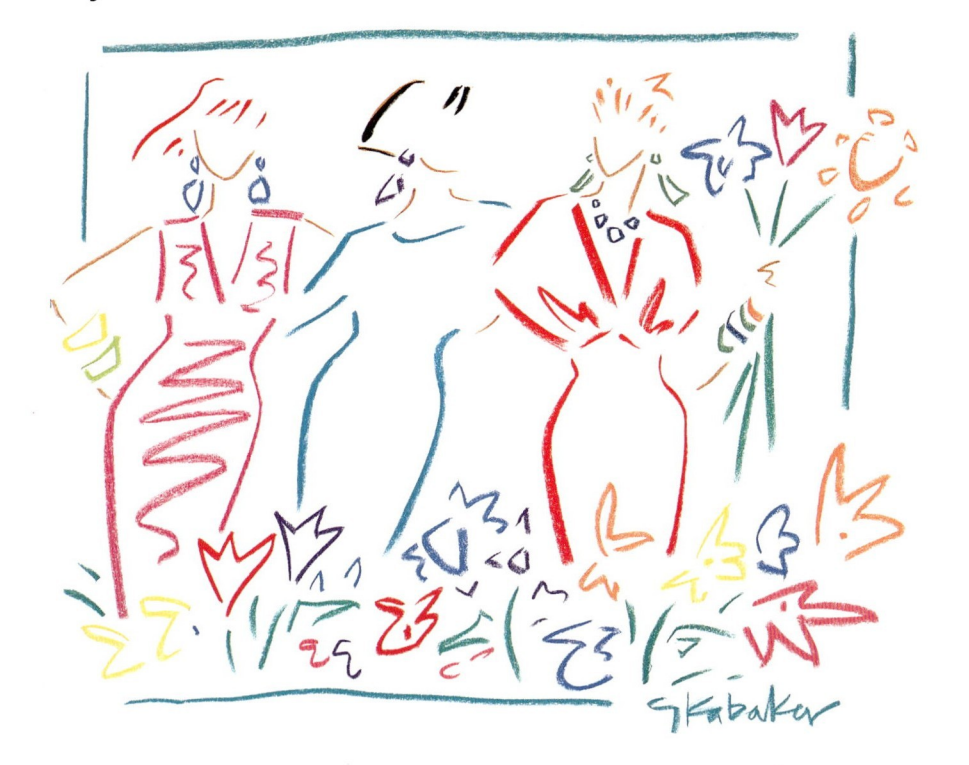

PUT YOUR COMPANY'S IMAGE ON THE LINE.

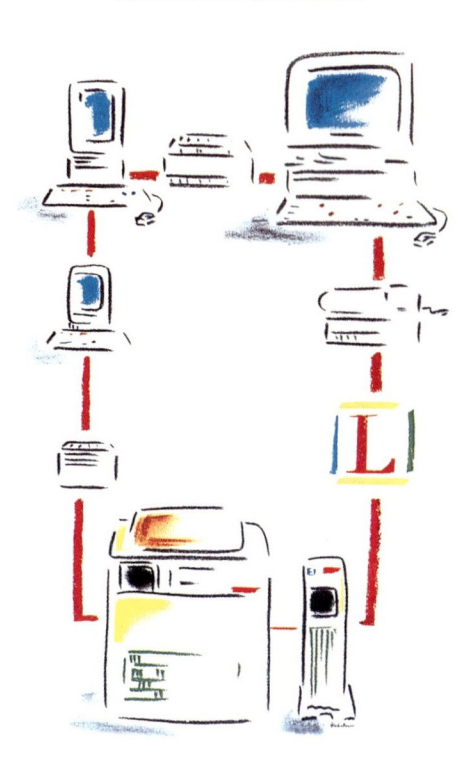

Linotype

This is the second-fastest way to the best shopping in Europe.

You're just a short hop from non-stop shopping and 150 of the world's finest shops and boutiques. View the latest arrivals from Europe at the *Runway to Spring* Fashion Show on March 18 at 2 PM.

THE MALL AT SHORT HILLS
The ultimate shopping trip.

michael
fleishman
illustration
247 whitehall drive
yellow springs
ohio 45387
phone: (513) 767-7955
fax: (513) 767-9167

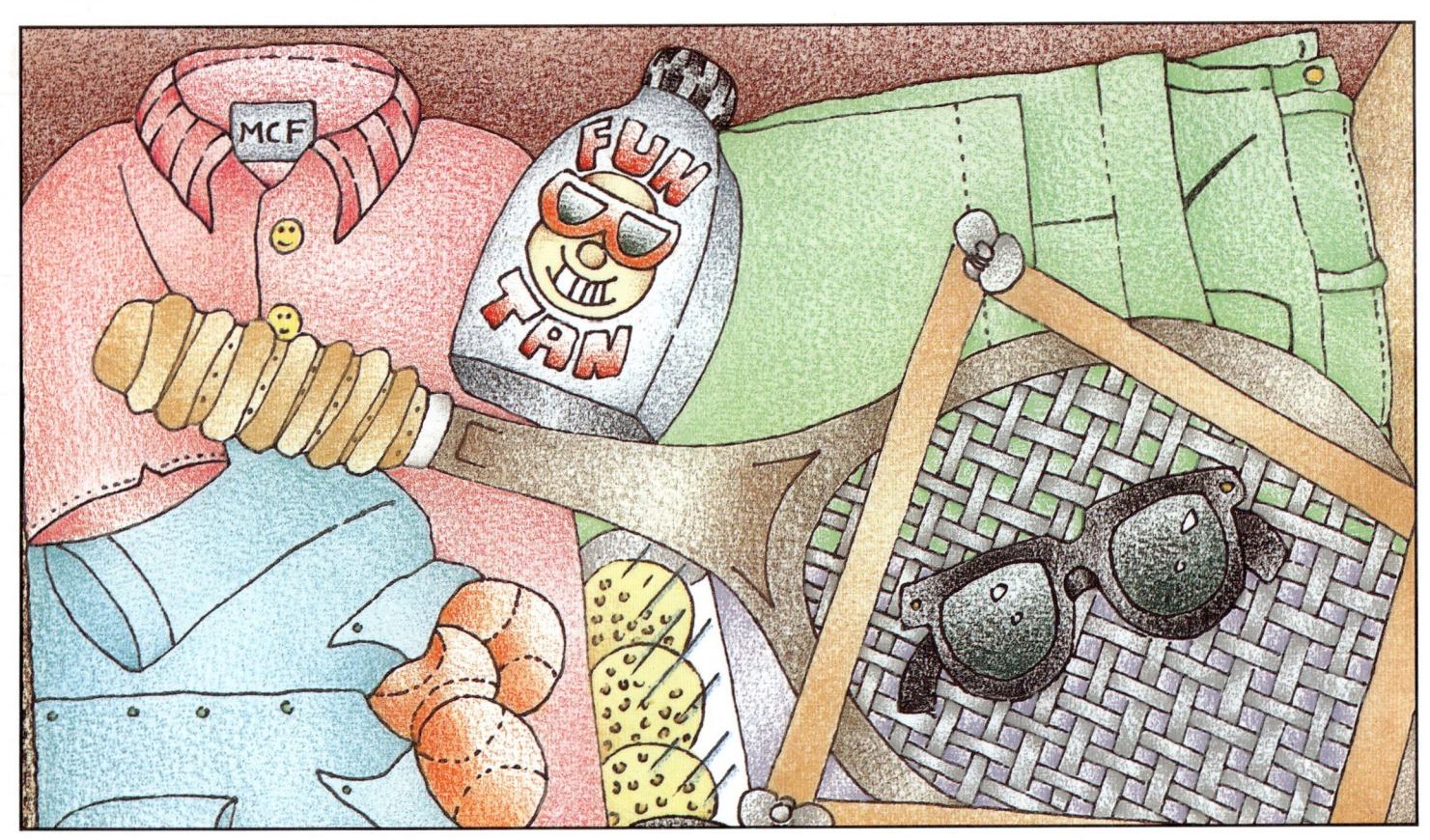

AMANDA SCHAFFER
ILLUSTRATION

619 • 788 • 0388

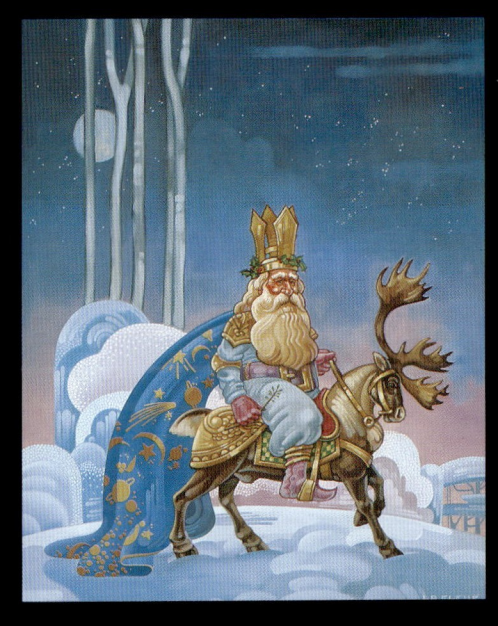

Client List:
Activision,
American Bar Association,
American Products, Atari,
Campus Life, Cessna,
Coast to Coast Hardware,
Coca Cola, Coleman,
Colorado Lottery, Coors,
Denver Post,
Ft. Lauderdale News,
Godfathers Pizza,
Hewlett-Packard,
Hotel Intercontinental, Intel,
Jovan, Kansas Lottery,
Learjet, Los Angeles Examiner,
Lotto America, New Age,
Pizza Hut,
Price Stern Sloan Publishing,
Questron, Sacramento Bee,
San Jose Mercury News,
Seven-Up, Shaklee,
Silver Burdett & Gin Publishing,
Spa Hotels, Swanson Foods,
Taco Tico

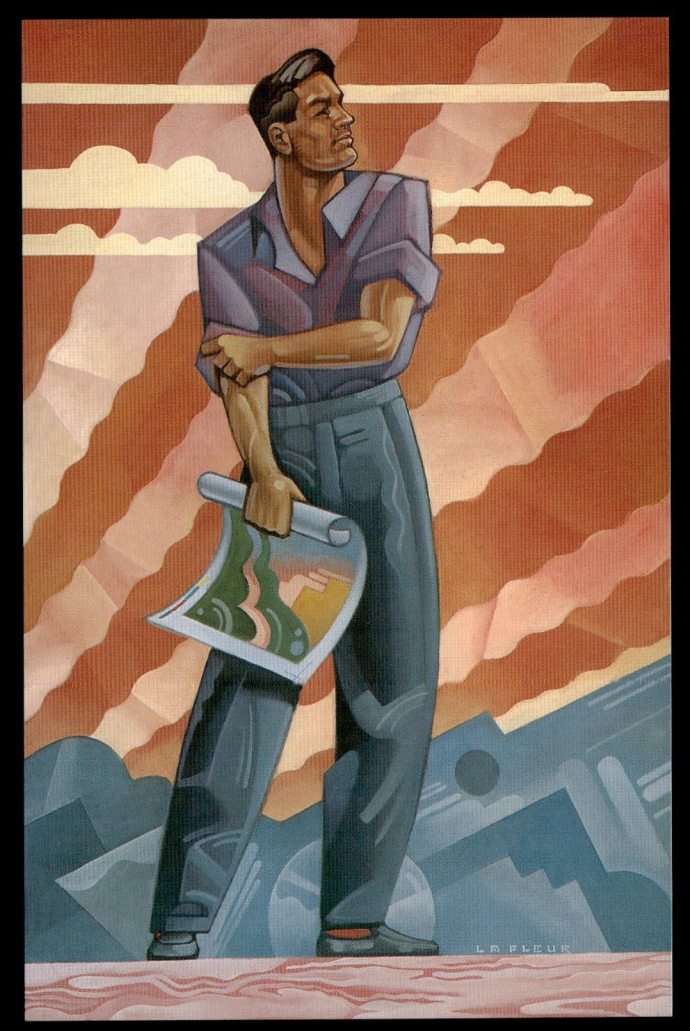

LA FLEUR

Dave LaFleur

610 North Woodlawn

Derby, Kansas 67037

Phone 316.788.0253

Fax in studio

RICHARD BERNAL

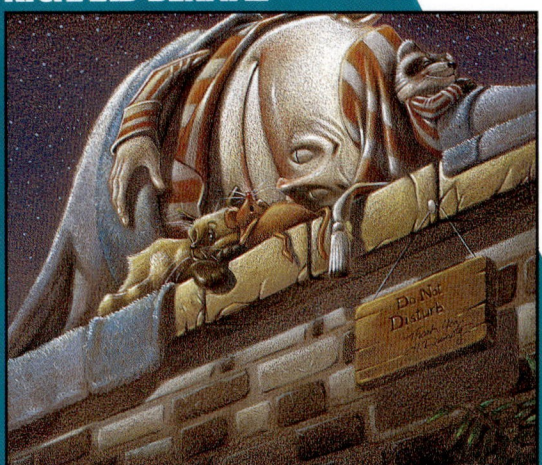

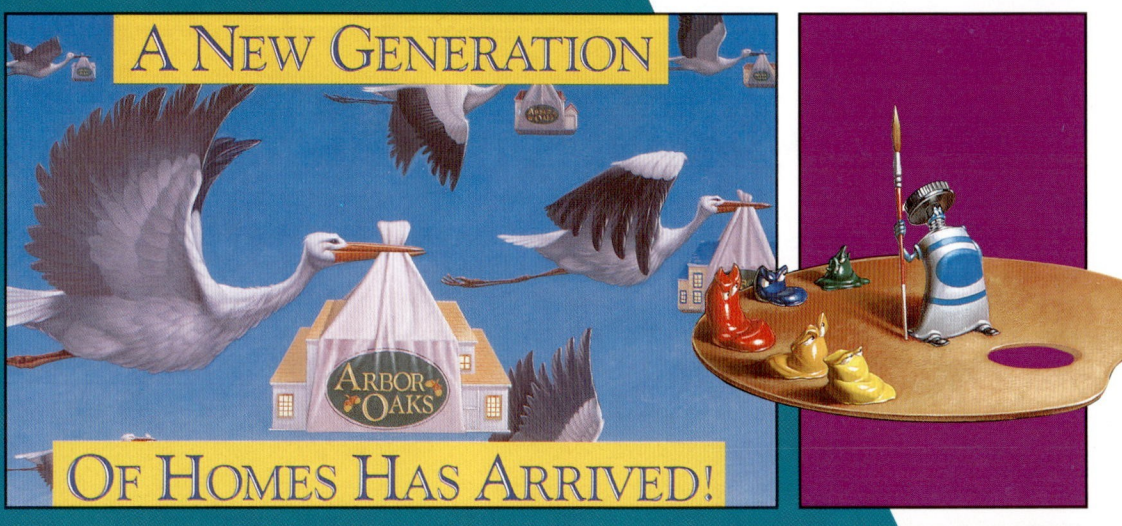

A NEW GENERATION OF HOMES HAS ARRIVED!

ARBOR OAKS

Additional work
'Night, Zoo
'Night, Mother Goose
Both Calico Books
Published by
Contemporary Books, Inc.
Chicago • New York

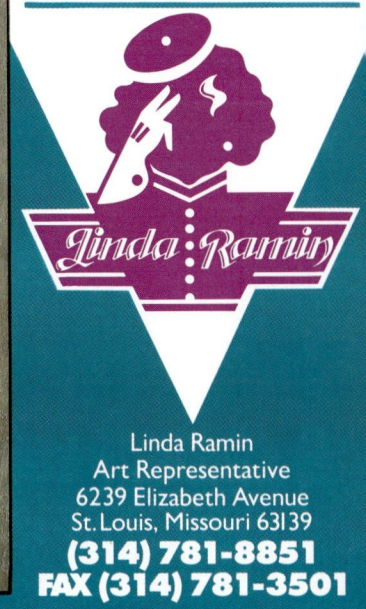

Service Beyond The Call of Duty

Linda Ramin

Linda Ramin
Art Representative
6239 Elizabeth Avenue
St. Louis, Missouri 63139
(314) 781-8851
FAX (314) 781-3501

BILLY O'DONNELL

Additional work
Cover and Feature artist
JCA Annual 9
N.Y. Society of Illustrators

Service Beyond The Call of Duty

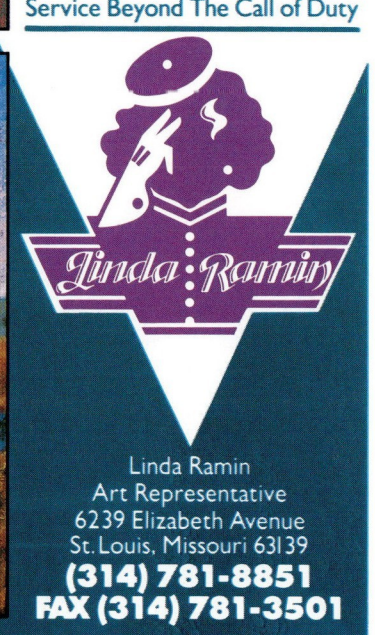

Linda Ramin
Art Representative
6239 Elizabeth Avenue
St. Louis, Missouri 63139
(314) 781-8851
FAX (314) 781-3501

DON CURRAN

ROY SMITH

JACK WHITNEY

MIKE WHITNEY

Additional work appears in a variety of publications. Portfolio samples upon request.

Service Beyond The Call of Duty

Linda Ramin
Art Representative
6239 Elizabeth Avenue
St. Louis, Missouri 63139
(314) 781-8851
FAX (314) 781-3501

JOHN S. DYKES

17 MORNINGSIDE DR. S.   WESTPORT CT 06880
203-222-8150   FAX-222-8155

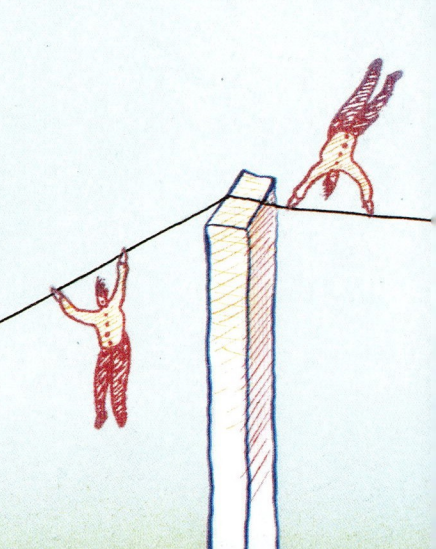

call for help!

CLAIRE BOOTH
MEDICAL ILLUSTRATION
212-768-1829

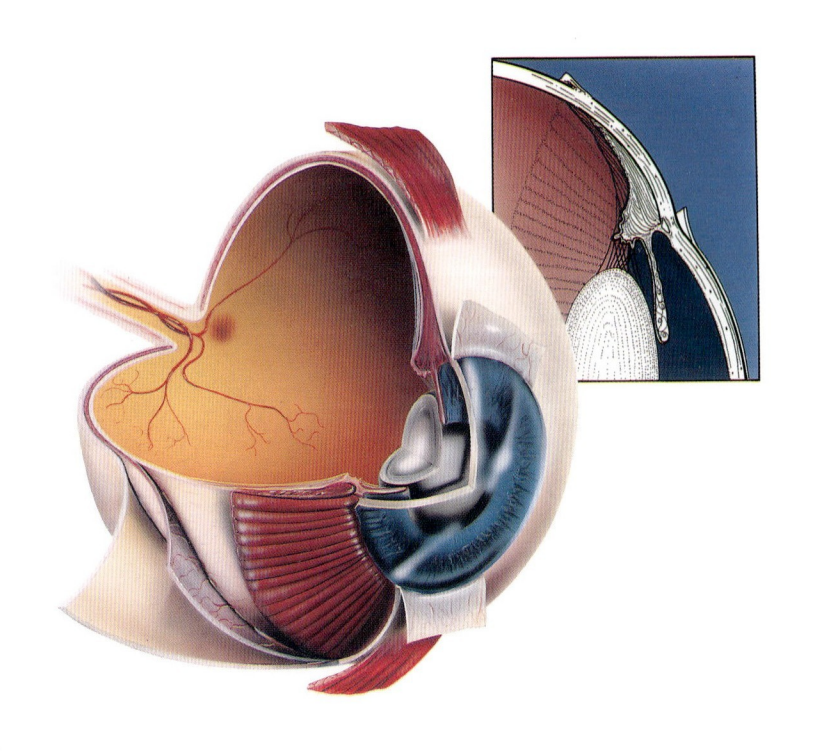

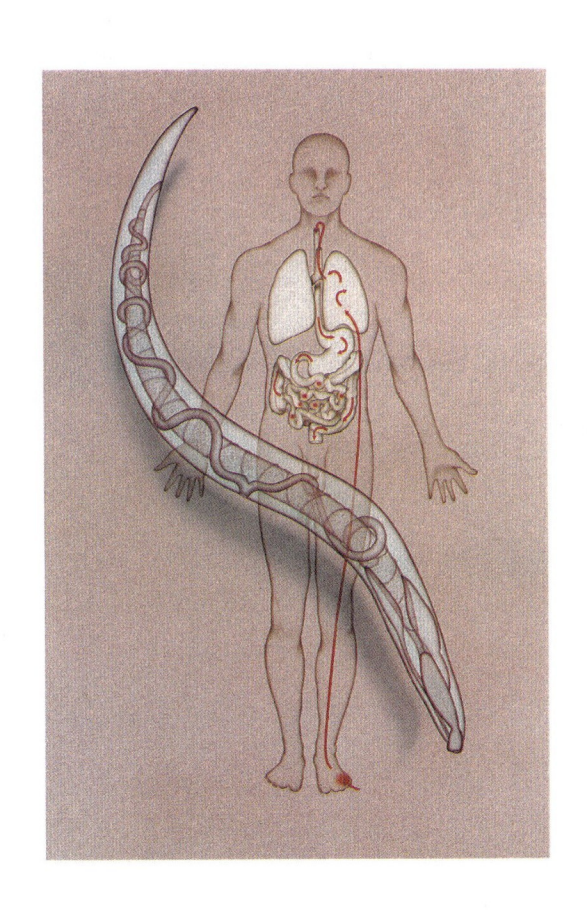

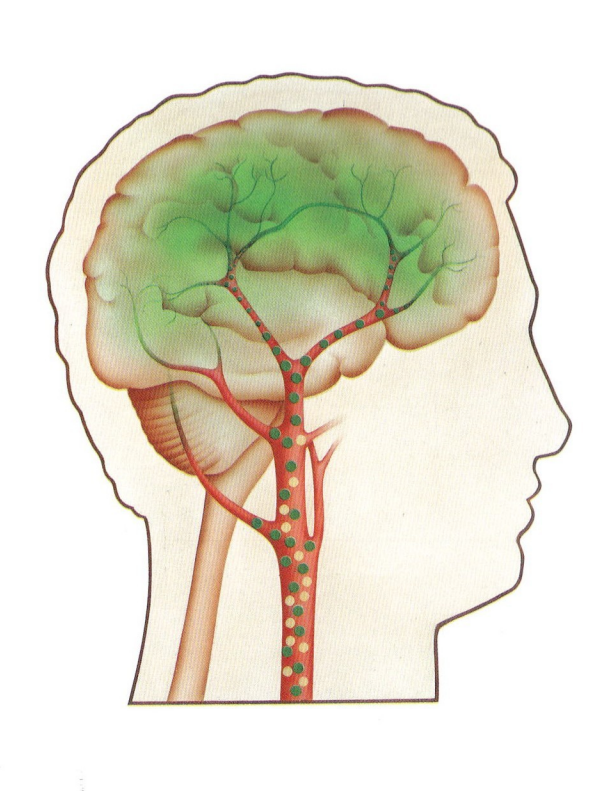

CLAIRE BOOTH MEDICAL ILLUSTRATION, AMI 2 WEST 46TH STREET, NEW YORK, NY 10036 212-768-1829

DAN BRENNAN
ILLUSTRATION

312 • 822 • 0887

CARLOS
3 0 5 · 6 5 1 · 9 5 2 4

CableVision Predicts Snow Tonight. Be Prepared.

Carlos Castellanos Illustration, Inc.
3 0 5 · 6 5 1 · 9 5 2 4
F A X I N S T U D I O

JON WEIMAN

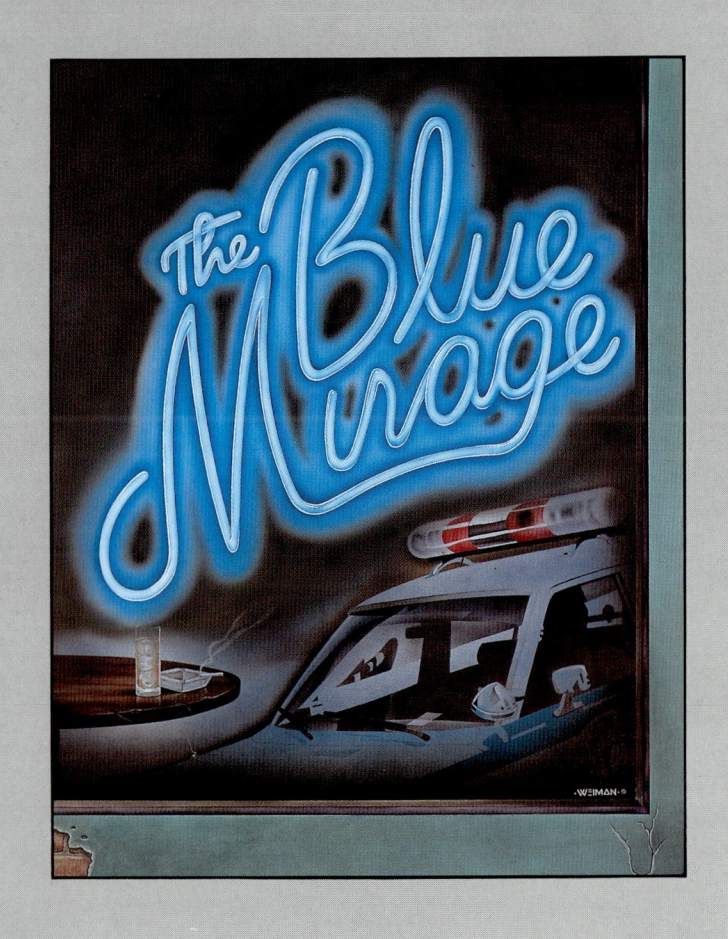

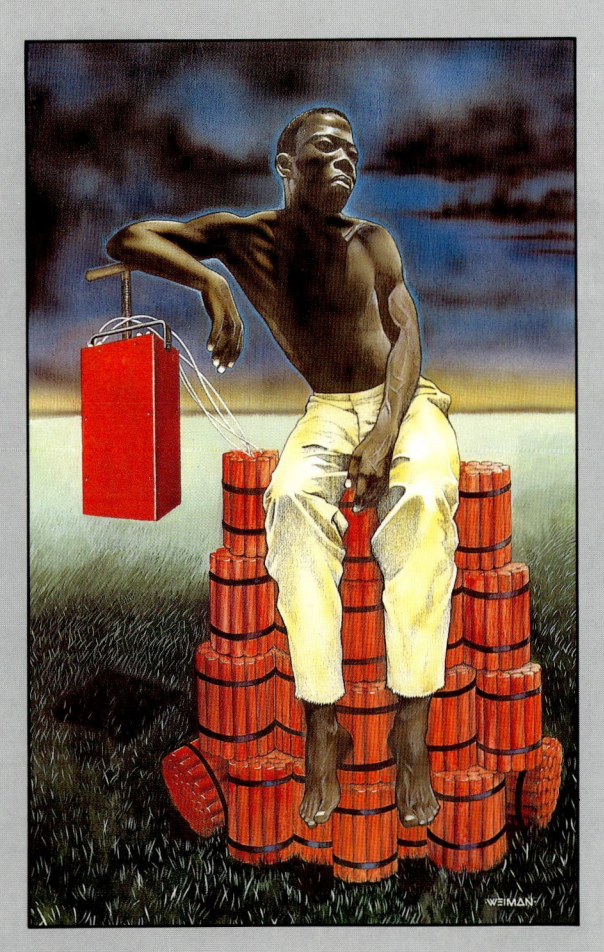

212 787·3184 2255 BROADWAY #306 NEW YORK, NY 10024

JAMES CHAFFEE

5400 COLUSA WAY
SACRAMENTO, CA 95841
(916) 348-6345

MEMBER SACRAMENTO ILLUSTRATORS GUILD

Jane Sterrett

160 FIFTH AVENUE NEW YORK NY 10010 (212) 929-2566

American Airlines • Annheuser Busch • ASK Computer Services • Atlantic Records • AT&T • Barnwell Industries • Benson & Hedges • Berlex Corp. • Bio-Medical World • Book of the Month Club • Booz-Allen & Hamilton • Consolidated Natural Gas • Continental Corporation • Datamation • Dell Bantam Doubleday • Dow B. Hickam • Encyclopaedia Britannica • E.P. Dutton • Exxon Corp. • Family Circle • Fortune • Hoechst Industries • I.B.M. • J.C. Penney Corporation • Macmillan • Mars Snickers • National Westminster Bank • New American Library • New Woman • Newsweek • The New York Times • Novell/NetWare • Page America/RCA • Paine Webber • J.C. Penney Corp. • Price-Waterhouse • Redbook • Sales & Marketing • The Salvation Army • Signature Magazine • Tylenol • Venture • Washington Post • Woman's Day

Guy Porfirio

Ceci Bartels Associates — Artists Representatives
(314) 241-4014 STL   (212) 912-1877 NY   (312) 786-1560 CHIC   (314) 241-9028 FAX

Ceci Bartels Associates ARTISTS REPRESENTATIVES

(314) 241-4014 STL   (212) 912-1877 NY   (312) 786-1560 CHIC   (314) 241-9028 FAX

Michael Halbert

SARA · SWAN

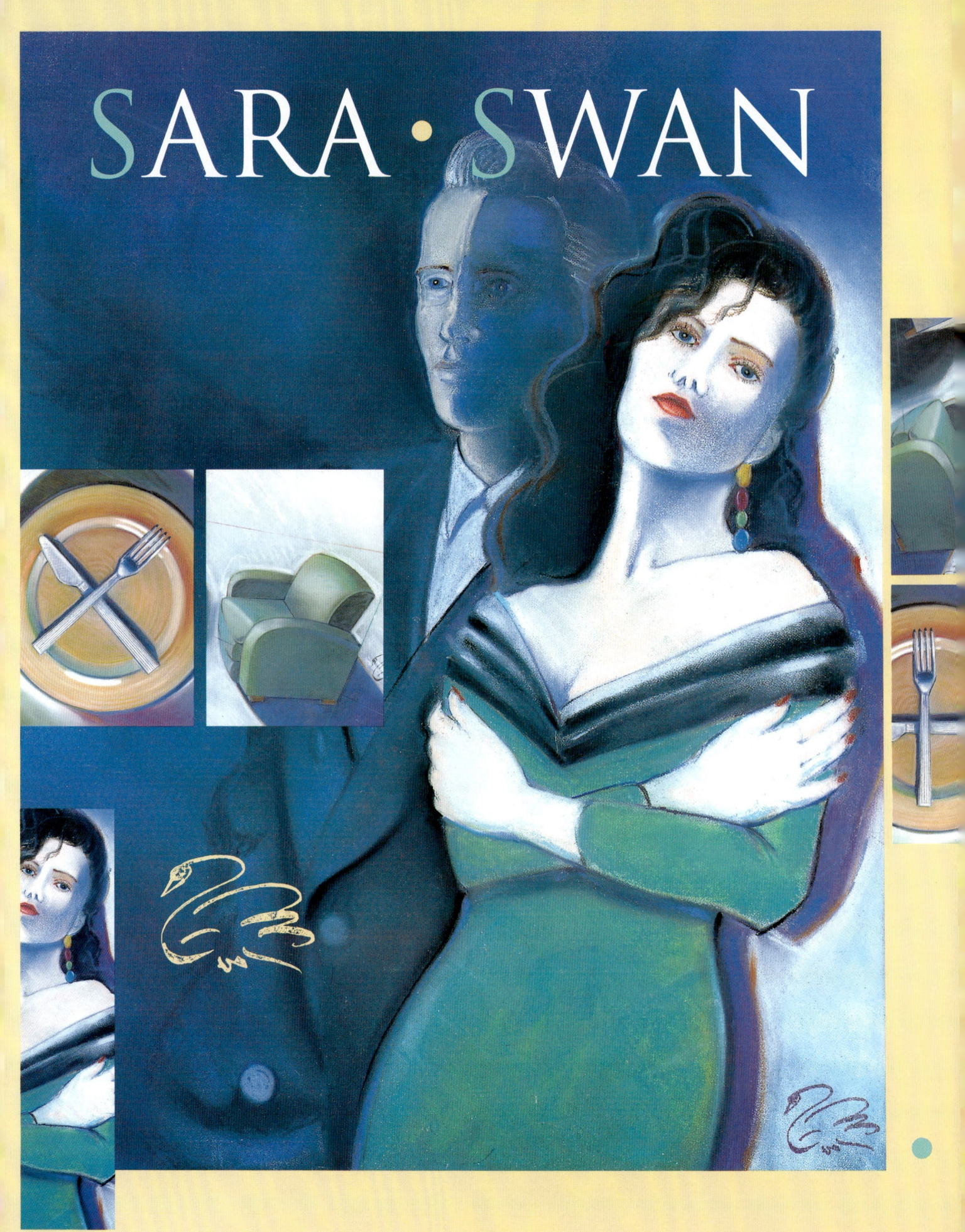

5904 W. 2ND STREET APT. B LOS ANGELES CA 90036 TELEPHONE (213)935-4781 FAX (213)935-5095

hanan yadin Technical Illustration

Hanan Yadin's full-color and black-and-white technical illustrations provide cutaway views that intrigue and captivate viewers. He renders diverse subjects—from cars, trucks and motorcycles to guns or high-tech products—in superb detail and three-dimensional perspective.

"Clients come to me for quality and precision," he says, "I never compromise the results." The play of light and unusual color mixtures also distinguishes these highly stylized technical illustrations. Yadin's metal and plastic surfaces appear almost luminescent.

A native of Israel, Hanan Yadin studied at the School of Graphic Arts in Tel Aviv and the Academy of Art and Design in Jerusalem. His unusual personal background includes serving as a sergeant in a combat division of the Israeli army, and challenging recreational pursuits such at mountain climbing, professional scuba diving and off-road jeep trips.

Clients include Daihatsu/ Continental Graphics, Guns & Ammo Magazine and Warren Miller Films/Boom Graphics. Member of Society of Illustrators Los Angeles and Art Directors Club of Los Angeles. Portfolio available upon request.

Represented by:

▶ OSTAN·PRENTICE·OSTAN·INC·
An Agency for Creative Talent

(213) 826-1332
Fax (213) 820-7518

HENRI BULTHUIS
932 FRANCISQUITO WEST COVINA, CA 91790 (818) 918 0755 CALL FOR FAX INFO.

Hedy Klein

111-56 76th Drive, #B3
Forest Hills, NY 11375
718-793-0246

Permanent records belong on an erasable medium like bearer bonds belong in a bus station locker.

Panasonic Office Automation OA

"That night at the Dilworthtown Inn, Barney speculated that George Washington could have dined at our very table. 'Why! Cornwallis could have eaten here, too!' I added. And Barney called me a Tory!"

Don't leave home without it.®

KAREN LEON

154-01 BARCLAY AVENUE, FLUSHING, N.Y. 11355 (718) 461-2050, (718) 463-3159.

ILLUSTRATION, HUMOR, & EDITORIAL CARTOONS, CARICATURES. **CLIENTS**: AMERICAN EXPRESS, KELLOGG'S, SEAGRAM'S, CRAIN'S NEW YORK BUSINESS, THOMAS PUBLISHING CO., OPPENHEIMER & CO., PANASONIC, FIRST MAGAZINE, PUBLIC RELATIONS SOCIETY OF AMERICA, BOOK-OF-THE-MONTH CLUB, EQUITABLE LIFE INSURANCE CO., WOMAN'S WORLD, THE ROCKPORT SHOE CO., NATIONWIDE INSURANCE CO., POLO MAGAZINE, FEDERAL EXPRESS

399

"It's done? You're a madman!"
-Richard Jackson, Orchard Books

"King of the overnighters!"
-Greg Scott, NYTimes Sports

"Hi, John, What are you doing this weekend?"
-Lois Erlacher, Cahners publications

John Ward. When you want it *yesterday*.
125 Maryland Ave., Freeport, N.Y. 11520   516·546·2906

See more work in the G.A.G. directory 6, RSVP 15, Print regional design annual, 1989 and CA Illustration annual '87.

MICHELE LAPORTE

PAMELA NEAIL

PAMELA NEAIL ASSOCIATES—27 BLEECKER STREET—NEW YORK, N.Y. 10012 ▪ 212 ▪ 673 ▪ 1600 ▪ FAX ▪ 212 ▪ 673 ▪ 7687   401

PETER MC CAFFREY

PAMELA NEAIL

PAMELA NEAIL ASSOCIATES—27 BLEECKER STREET—NEW YORK, N.Y. 10012 ▪ 212 ▪ 673 ▪ 1600 ▪ FAX ▪ 212 ▪ 673 ▪ 7687

LINDA RICHARDS

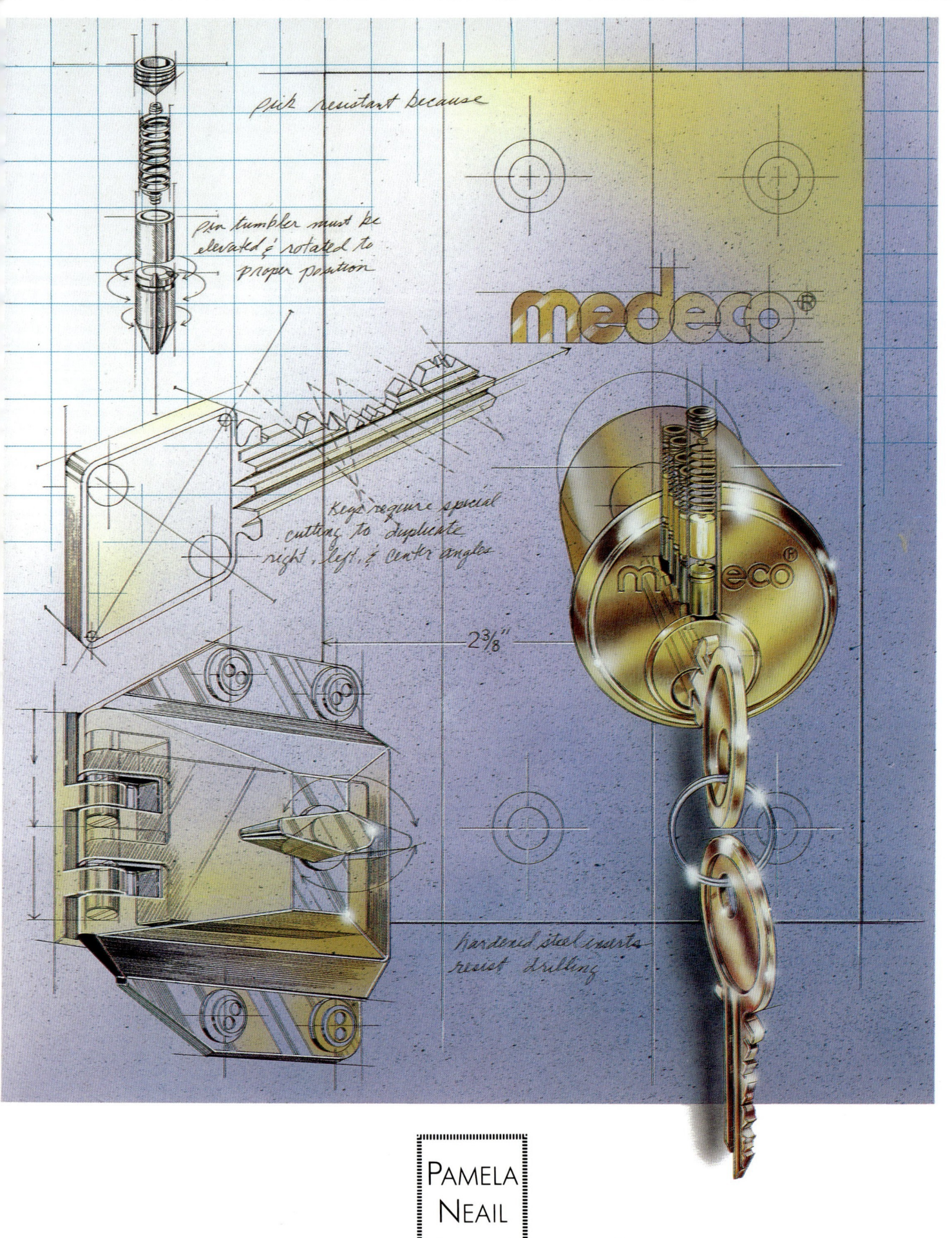

PAMELA NEAIL ASSOCIATES—27 BLEECKER STREET—NEW YORK, N.Y. 10012 ▪ 212 ▪ 673 ▪ 1600 ▪ FAX ▪ 212 ▪ 673 ▪ 7687

TONI HANZON-KURRASCH

SADE

213-474-7687

Pamela Neail

PAMELA NEAIL ASSOCIATES—27 BLEECKER STREET—NEW YORK, N.Y. 10012 • 212 • 673 • 1600 • FAX • 212 • 673 • 7687

C.B. MORDAN

PAMELA NEAIL

PAMELA NEAIL ASSOCIATES—27 BLEECKER STREET—NEW YORK, N.Y. 10012 ▪ 212 ▪ 673 ▪ 1600 ▪ FAX ▪ 212 ▪ 673 ▪ 7687

KEN SPENGLER

PAMELA NEAIL

PAMELA NEAIL ASSOCIATES—27 BLEECKER STREET—NEW YORK, N.Y. 10012 ▪ 212 ▪ 673 ▪ 1600 ▪ FAX ▪ 212 ▪ 673 ▪ 7687

CELESTE HENRIQUEZ

PAMELA
NEAIL

PAMELA NEAIL ASSOCIATES—27 BLEECKER STREET—NEW YORK, N.Y. 10012 ▪ 212 ▪ 673 ▪ 1600 ▪ FAX ▪ 212 ▪ 673 ▪ 7687   407

GENE REYNOLDS
ILLUSTRATOR
71 Thompson St., NYC, NY 10012

(212) 431-3072

Member Graphic Artists Guild

Just Raw Drawing.

Caricature has been with us forever. It's basically raw drawing with a slightly looser regard for actual precise facial and body ratios than do actually exist. Seemingly, a psychological insight to the subject reveals itself as a by-product in Good Caricatures.

Just look at Leonardo da Vinci's work. Thomas Rowlandson. Hogarth. Breugel the Elder. Sir John Tenniel. Perhaps even Hokusai. All these guys couldn't resist the urge to thrust an inky joust toward their fellow lusty, greedy, jealous, and envious co-inhabitants of this planet. After all, we're all in this together, aren't we? And no one's leaving alive, so don't kid yourself.

Over here on the left hand coast, (yeah, that's me in the fast lane cutting you off to make that Wilshire exit) we're up 3 hours later. Look at it as an extension of your New York minute. The FAX is on and the last Fed Ex plane leaves at 10 New York time. I'll be up, listening to Vin Scully and wondering why they let Sax get away.

ROBERT MYERS
213 • 396 • 7303

SHANNON JEFFRIES

PHONE
(718) 638-1132

FAX IN STUDIO

CLIENTS:

Sports Illustrated

Business Week

The New York Times

Money Magazine

Audio Magazine

Financial World

Colgate

CMP Publishing

Peterson Publishing

PC Magazine

Gillette

Ralston

Art Direction Magazine

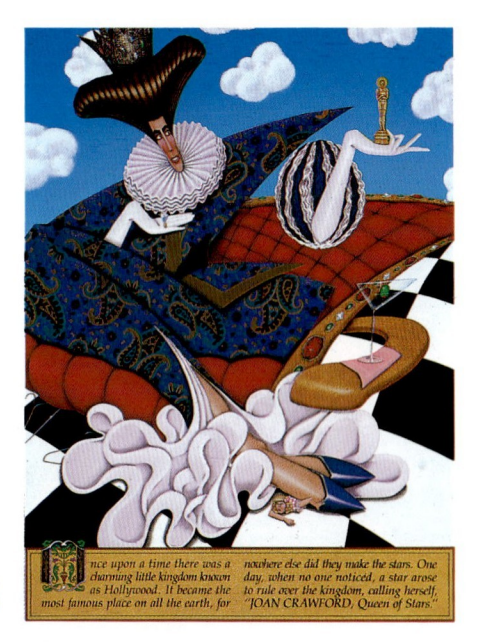

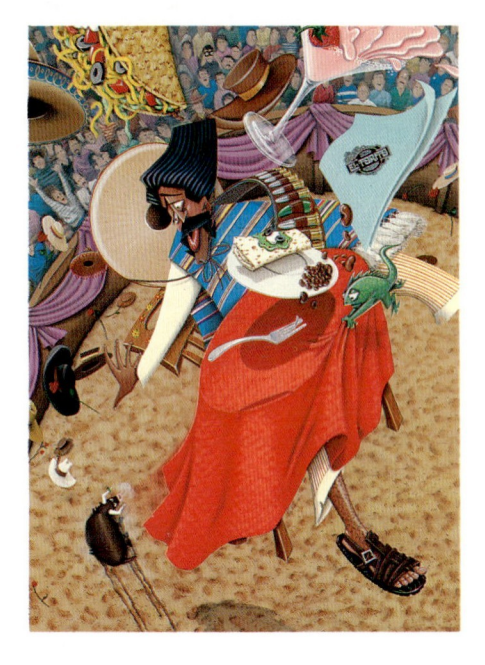

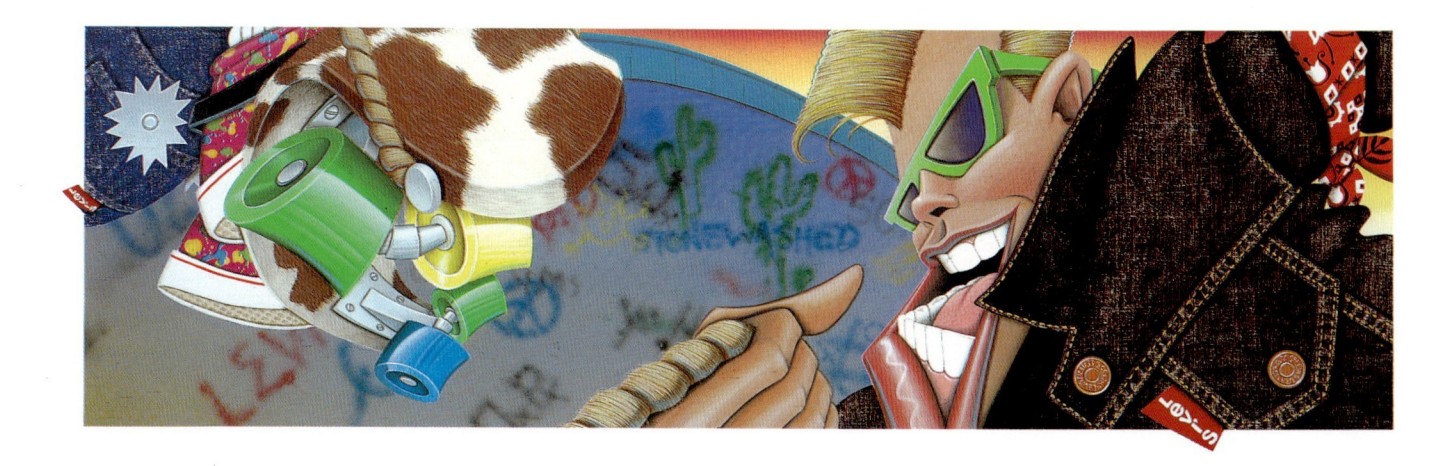

410

KYE CARBONE 718·802·9143
241 Union St. (3rd.fl.) Bklyn, N.Y. 11231

Clients include: Campbell·Mithun·Esty, Doremus & Co., Doubleday, Drackett & Lavidge, Forbes, Harper & Row, Newsday, N.Y. Times, Simon & Schuster, St. Martin's Press, U.S. News & World Report, Viking, Penguin

---

See: Full-page ad in THE CREATIVE ILLUSTRATION BOOK 1.

411

Steve McInturff (513) 834-3539
Studio   *Fax*Service
call for number

RICK LOVELL

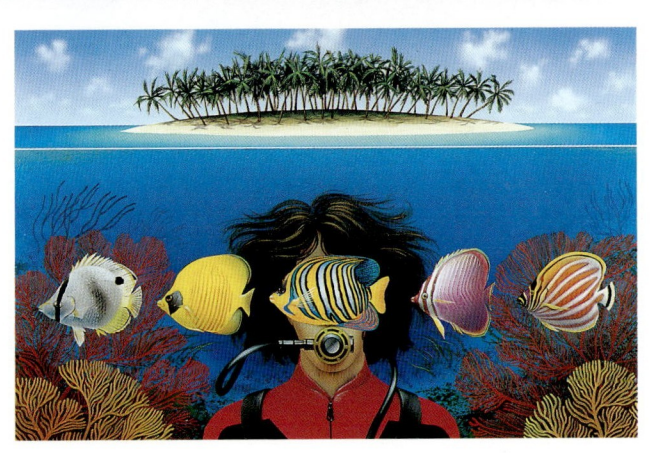

REPRESENTED BY

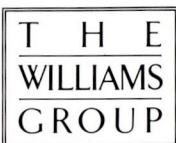

THE
WILLIAMS
GROUP

CONTACT PHIL WILLIAMS OR RICH COVENY
(404) 873-2287

IN NEW YORK, CONTACT TRICIA WEBER
(212) 799-6532

JOHN ROBINETTE

PAT MOLLICA

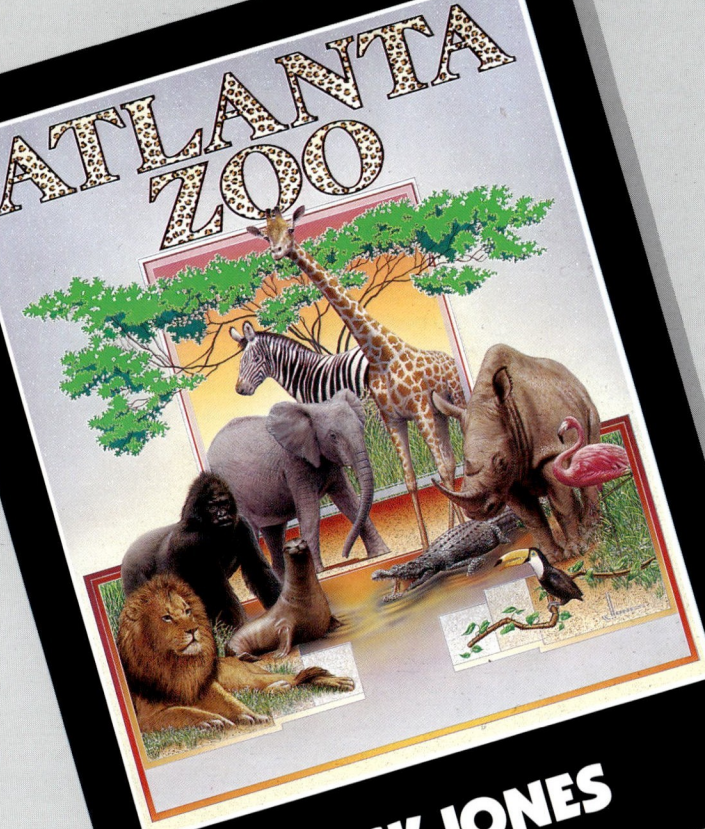

JACK JONES

DANNY SMYTHE

REPRESENTED BY

THE WILLIAMS GROUP

CONTACT PHILIP WILLIAMS OR RICH COVENY (404) 873-2287 · IN NEW YORK CONTACT TRICIA WEBER (212) 799-6532

DAVID McKELVEY · ILLUSTRATOR

REPRESENTED BY

T H E
WILLIAMS
GROUP

CONTACT PHILLIP WILLIAMS OR RICH COVENY
404 • 873 • 2287
IN NEW YORK CONTACT TRICIA WEBER
212 • 799 • 6532

Joe Rocco
(718) 492-4776
fax in Studio!

ROBIN WILLIAMS

Clients Include: L.A. Style, "D" Magazine, Spin Magazine, U.S.A. Film Festival, National Review, Outside Magazine, The Chicago Tribune, The Los Angeles Times, Joe Bob Briggs (Drive-In Movie Critic of Grapevine Texas), The Dallas Morning News, The Village Voice...!

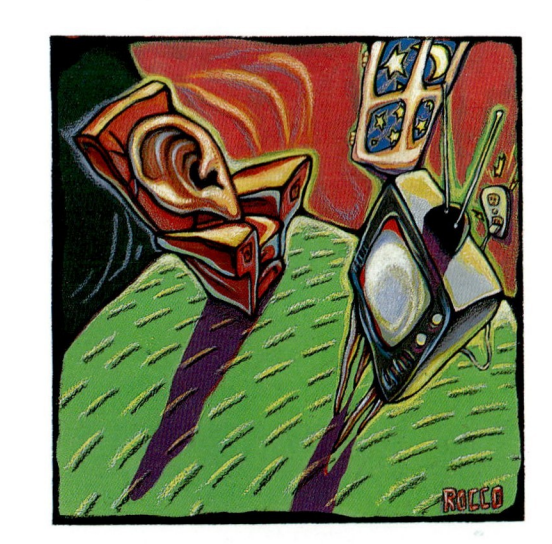

ILLUSTRATION

JANET HAMLIN

PHONE: (718) 492-4075
FAX: (718) 492-6269

CLIENTS INCLUDE:

Washington Post

Times Mirror

Revlon

Playboy

McGraw Hill

Diamandis Comm.

Chelsea House Pub.

Business Month

MD Publishing

US News & World Report

Essence

Beauty Magazine

417

smallish

CONTACT JIM HANSON AND TALENT   CHICAGO 312-337-7770   FAX 312-337-7112

REPRESENTED BY
DEBORAH WOLFE LTD
215-232-6666 FAX 215-232-6585

JIM HIMSWORTH III

DEBORAH DANILA

RAY DALLASTA

VERLIN MILLER

419

REPRESENTED BY
DEBORAH WOLFE LTD
215-232-6666 FAX 215-232-6585

LISA POMERANTZ

JENNY CAMPBELL

ANDY MYER

RICK BUTERBAUGH

REPRESENTED BY
DEBORAH WOLFE LTD
215-232-6666 FAX 215-232-6585

SKIP BAKER

SKIP BAKER

PATRICK GNAN

PATRICK GNAN

421

REPRESENTED BY
DEBORAH WOLFE LTD
215-232-6666 FAX 215-232-6585

MARIANNE HUGHES

PAT DUFFY

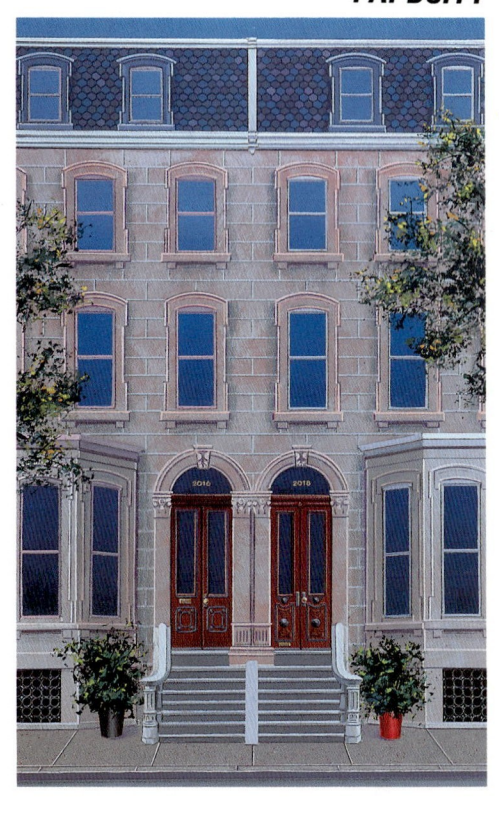

MICHAEL HOSTOVICH

JOHN PAUL GENZO

REPRESENTED BY
DEBORAH WOLFE LTD
215-232-6666 FAX 215-232-6585

NEAL HUGHES

NEAL HUGHES

JEFF FITZ-MAURICE

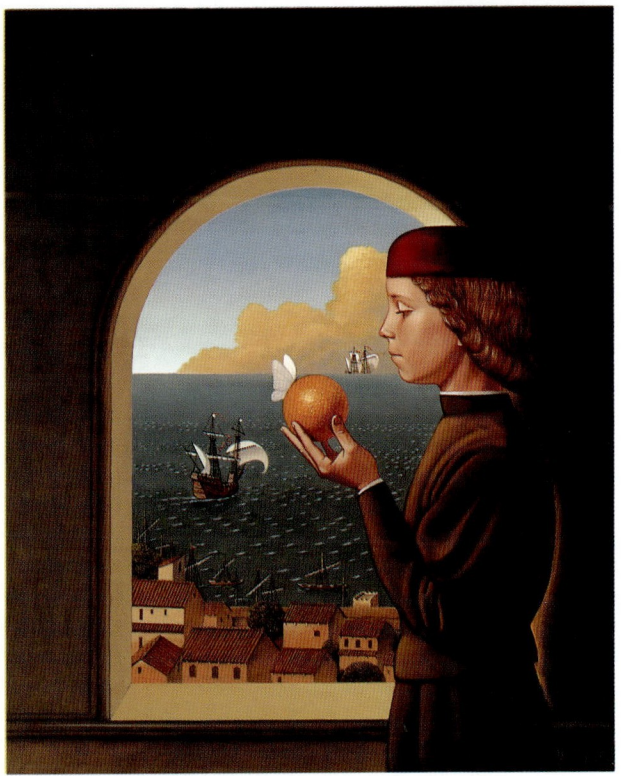

JEFF FITZ-MAURICE

McNEEL

RICHARD McNEEL

Sculptured Illustration

530 Valley Road
Apartment 2G
Upper Montclair, NJ 07043
201-509-2255 FAX 509-2253

Tungwai Chau
534 Richmar Drive
Nashville
Tennessee 37211
(615) 781-8607
FAX in Studio

Clients Include:
Country Music Hall of Fame
Jack Daniel's
1st American Bank
International Paper
United Savings of America
Tennessee Repertory Theatre
NESA
Bridgestone
K & N
Empire Pencil Company
Opryland Hotel
Service Merchandise
First National Bank & Trust
Outlet Ltd. Mall
HCA and many others.

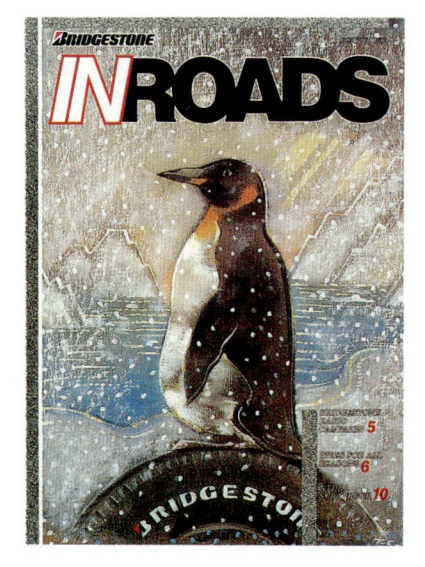

425

Chislovsky

CAROL CHISLOVSKY INC.

853 Broadway
New York, NY 10003
212-677-9100
FAX: 212-353-0954

TAYLOR BRUCE

STEVE GRAY

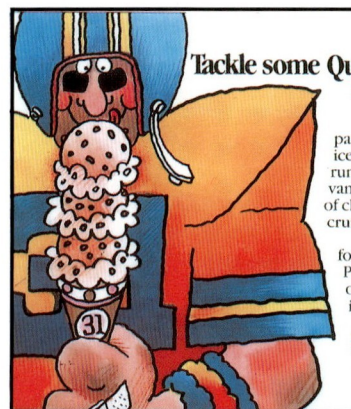

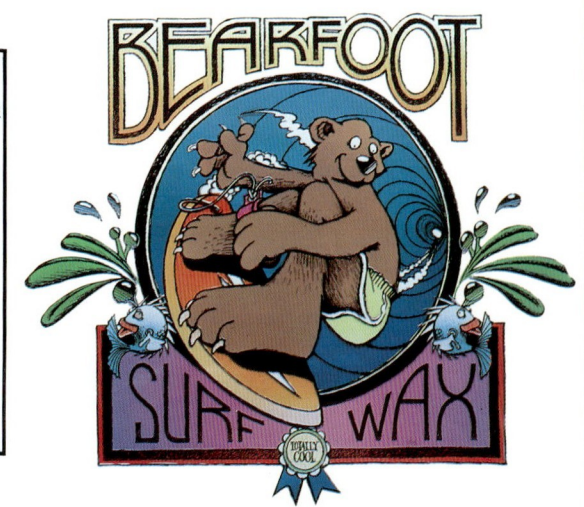

CHRIS GALL

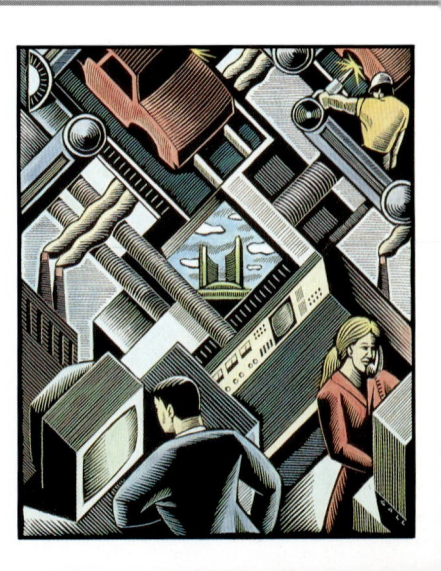

CAROL CHISLOVSKY INC.

853 Broadway
New York, NY 10003
212-677-9100
FAX: 212-353-0954

R.M. SCHNEIDER

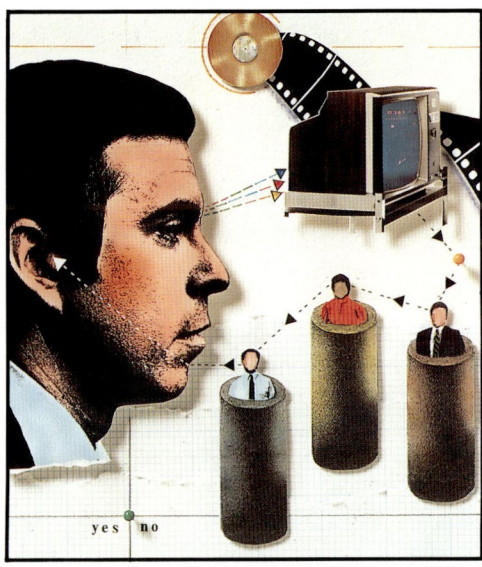

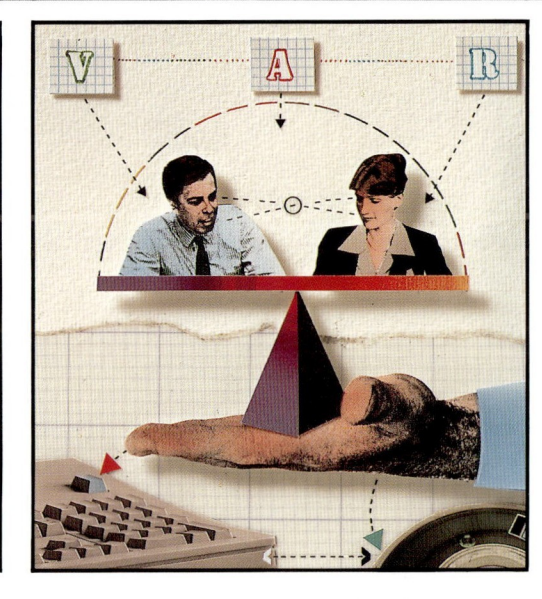

KAREN BELL

JIM COHEN

427

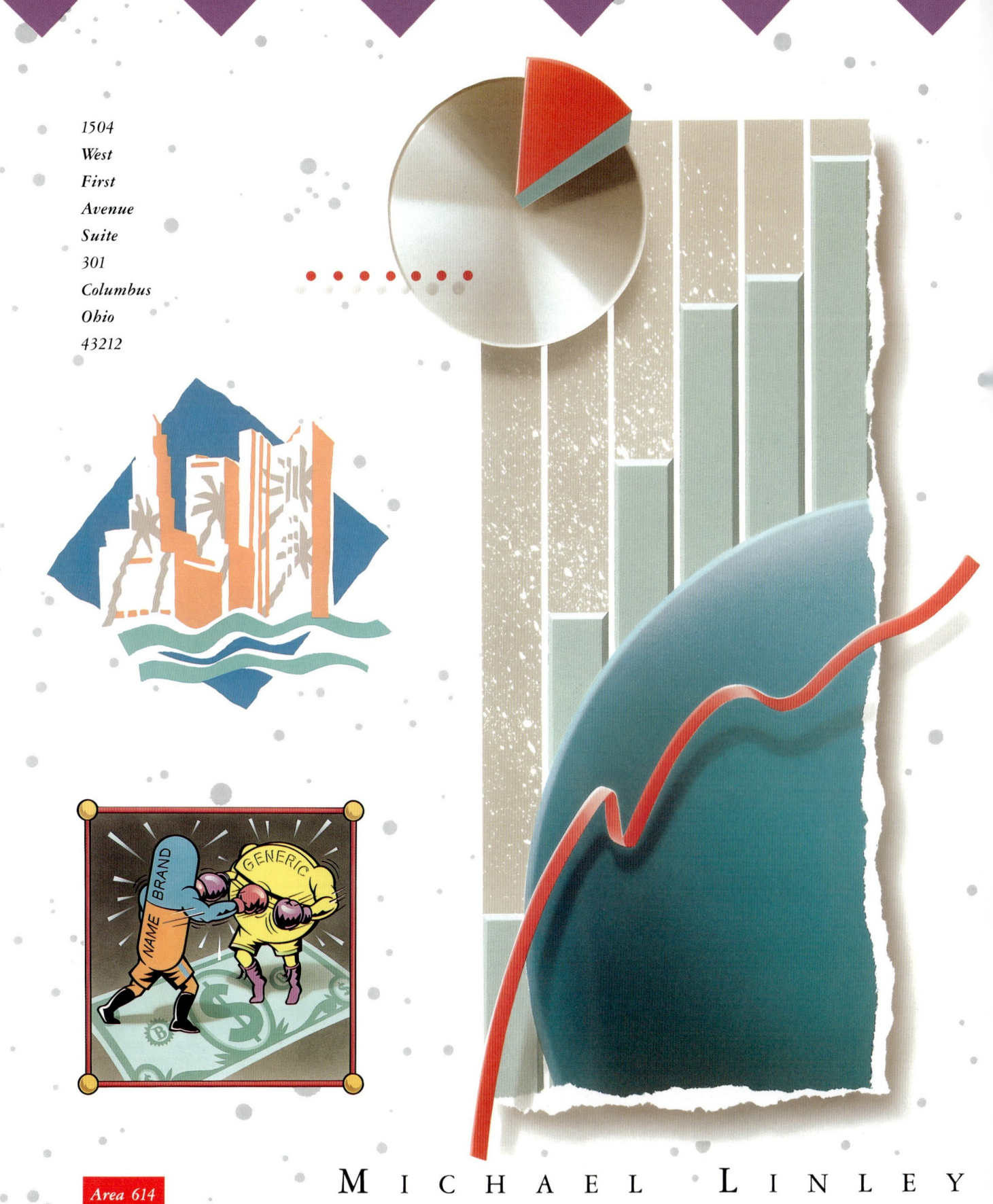

1504
West
First
Avenue
Suite
301
Columbus
Ohio
43212

Area 614
486-2921

MICHAEL LINLEY
ILLUSTRATION

Kurt Vargö

REPRESENTED BY PAMELA KORN • 321 EAST 12th STREET • NEW YORK, NY 10003 • **(212) 529•6389**

Jeff Moores

REPRESENTED BY PAMELA KORN • 321 EAST 12th STREET • NEW YORK, NY 10003 • **(212) 529•6389**

Brian Ajhar

REPRESENTED BY PAMELA KORN • 321 EAST 12th STREET • NEW YORK, NY 10003 • **(212) 529•6389**

KEVIN SPAULDING

REPRESENTED BY:

SAN FRANCISCO

BETSY HILLMAN

415-391-1181

NEW YORK CITY

BARNEY KANE & SID BUCK

212-221-8090

STUDIO

818-998-6091

DESIGN • STUDIO SERVICES

DESIGN • STUDIO SERVICES

LISTINGS

P A G E S   4 3 4 - 4 4 4

ADS

P A G E S   4 4 5 - 4 4 7

DESIGN • STUDIO SERVICES

A Matter of Design, Inc./165 Paramount Dr., Wood Dale .... (708) 860-0281
AB + Company Design/2606 W. Sunset Blvd., L.A. .... (213) 484-2084
ACT/36 E. 23rd St., NYC .... (212) 505-5510
AMG Marketing Resources/221 7E. Ninth St., Cleveland .... (216) 621-1835
ARIEL Computer Production, Inc./550 Queen St. E., Toronto .... (416) 863-9900
Abelleira, Aldo J./3546 Dakota Ave. S., Mpls. .... (612) 922-4474
Adams, Gaylord Design/401 E. 34th St., NYC .... (212) 684-4625
Adams, Marilyn/62 W. 45th St., NYC .... (212) 869-4170
Ade Skunta & Co., Inc./700 W. St. Clair Ave., Cleveland .... (216) 241-0730
Adesign Group, Inc./340 W. Butterfield Rd., Elmhurst .... (708) 530-0025
Adler, Stan Assoc., Inc./1140 Ave. of the Americas, NYC .... (212) 719-1944
Adler-Schwartz, Inc./Six N. Park Dr., Hunt Valley .... (301) 527-0600
Advance Design Center/2501 Oaklawn Ave., Dallas .... (214) 526-1420
Advertising & Design Services/14497 N. Dale Mabry Hwy., Tampa .... (813) 962-3221
Advertising Art Studios/710 N. Plankinton Ave., Milwaukee .... (414) 276-6306
Advertising Designers, Inc./818 N. La Brea Ave., L.A. .... (213) 463-8143
Aiese, Bob/60 Pineapple St., Brooklyn Heights .... (718) 596-2240
Albano, Chuck/192 N. Second St., Bethpage .... (516) 938-0821
Alison & Assocs./801 Broad St., Augusta .... (404) 724-3758
Alpert & Alpert, Inc./8357-B Greensboro Dr., McLean .... (703) 556-8901
Amberger Design Group/128 River Road, Lyme .... (603) 795-2645
American Art Studio/124 W. 24th St., NYC .... (212) 633-1466
Ampersand Studios Inc./3565 Piedmont Rd., Atlanta .... (404) 233-5789
Anagraphics/104 W. 29th St., NYC .... (212) 279-2370
Anderson, David/539 Linden Ave., Oak Park .... (708) 848-1020
Anderson, Jon/1465 Ellendale, Logan .... (801) 752-8936
Anderson, Lance/22 Margrave Pl., S.F. .... (415) 788-5893
Angel Studios/5677 Oberlin Dr., San Diego .... (619) 452-7775
Aniko Nemeth Graphics Enterprises/345 E. 73rd St., NYC .... (212) 794-1138
Another Color, Inc./1101 King St., Alexandria .... (703) 548-8980
Anspach Grossman Portugal, Inc./711 Third Ave., NYC .... (212) 692-9000
Anthony, Al/Ten Bradley St., Westport .... (203) 227-9386
Appelbaum Company, The/176 Madison Ave., NYC .... (212) 213-1130
Applequist Studio/5905 Golden Valley Rd., Mpls. .... (612) 545-2902
Archer Design Group/933 N. Kenmore St., Arlington .... (703) 528-0500
Arion, Katherine/L.A. .... (213) 654-6252
Arneal, Clark Graphics/1001 John St., Manhattan Beach .... (213) 376-6666
Arnold, Robert/149 W. 14th St., NYC .... (212) 989-7049
Art Commission, The, Inc./2287 Capehart Cr. N.E., Atlanta .... (404) 636-9149
Art Department, Inc./Two W. 46th St., NYC .... (212) 391-1826
Art Directions/812 Huron, Cleveland .... (216) 621-3697
Art Etc./316 W. Fourth St., Cincinnati .... (513) 621-6225
Art Media Services/7611 Slater Ave., Huntington Beach .... (714) 848-2861
Art Service Assoc., Inc./717 Liberty Ave., Pittsburgh .... (412) 391-0902
Art Staff, Inc./636 Eleventh Ave., NYC .... (212) 582-4700
Artfarm, Inc./3403 S.W. Corbett Ave., Portland .... (503) 241-2554
Artists Studios, Inc./668 Euclid Ave., Cleveland .... (216) 241-5355
Artline Graphics/3925 Peachtree Rd., Atlanta .... (404) 231-1004
Artworks, The/4020 Ponce de Leon Ave., Atlanta .... (404) 296-9835
Ashford Art/10235 W. Little York, Houston .... (713) 462-3358
Associated Industrial Designers, Inc./75 Livingston St., Brooklyn Heights .... (718) 624-0034
Attenzione Graphics/184 S. Goodman St., Rochester .... (716) 244-8028
Attiliis & Assocs./9710 Days Farm Dr., Vienna .... (703) 759-1519
August, Ray/149-41 Elm Ave., Flushing .... (718) 445-1792
Bailey, Stephen Ltd./474 Richmond St. W., Toronto .... (416) 862-1227
Barber, Ray/295 Washington Ave., Brooklyn .... (718) 857-2941
Barnard:Design/48 W. 21st. St., NYC .... (212) 627-1147
Barnes Design Office/680 N. Lake Shore Dr., Chicago .... (312) 951-0996

Barnes, Sue/1200 Broadway, NYC .... (212) 679-0086
Barry, James E./69 W. 68th St., NYC .... (212) 873-6787
Bartczak, Peter/Santa Cruz, CA/(408) 426-4247 .... **page 350**
Basevitz, Irv Inc./307 N. Michigan Ave., Chicago .... (312) 641-7272
Bass & Goldman, Inc./RD3 Gypsy Trail Rd., Carmel .... (914) 225-8611
Beatson Vermeer Design/Eight S. Hotel St., Honolulu .... (808) 523-2446
Becker/Hockfield Design Associates/35 E. 21st St., NYC .... (212) 505-7050
Bell, James Design/692 Washington Ave., Brooklyn .... (718) 638-8900
Bennett, Brad/2512 Oakwood Dr., Olympia Fields .... (312) 747-2095
Besalel, Ely/235 E. 49th St., NYC .... (212) 759-7820
Big Apple Sign Corp./247 W. 35th St., NYC .... (212) 575-0706
Big City Graphics/8270 S.W. 116th Ter., Miami .... (305) 235-4700
Bigelow & Eigel Creative Comm., Inc./2 Executive Park W., Atlanta .... (404) 320-7260
Biondo, Charles Design Assoc./389 W. 12th St., NYC .... (212) 645-5300
Black, Richard H./205 Foxridge Dr., Dayton .... (513) 293-9001
Blake, Hayward R./834 Custer Ave., Evanston .... (312) 864-9800
Blazing Messengers Inc./264 Ave. of the Americas, NYC .... (212) 475-8299
Bodenhamer, William S., Inc./7380 S.W. 121st St., Miami .... (305) 253-9284
Bogner, Douglas/1632 Barry Ave., L.A. .... (213) 207-2940
Bogusky Two/11950 W. Dixie Hwy., Miami .... (305) 891-3642
Bonder, Ronné Ltd./Five Main St., Southampton .... (516) 287-1746
Boss/Cies/Jones Partners in Design, Inc./1801 Broadway, Denver .... (303) 396-8989
Bossardt Design Ltd./82 Rue de Brésoles, Montréal .... (514) 849-3776
Boulevard Consulting Group, The/1626 N. Atlantic, Spokane .... (509) 328-7307
Bowlby Joseph Graphic Design Ltd./11 E. Hubberd, Chicago .... (312) 527-9009
Bowler, Tom Graphic Design & Adv./1133 Broadway, NYC .... (212) 691-1471
Boyd, Douglas Design & Mktg./6624 Melrose Ave., L.A. .... (213) 933-8383
Bradbury, Robert C. & Assocs./26 Halsey Ln., Closter .... (201) 768-6395
Brady & Paul Communications/134 Beach St., Boston .... (617) 350-0323
Brier, David/38 Park Ave., Rutherford .... (201) 896-8476
Briggs, Tom Design/257 Sidney St., Cambridge .... (617) 354-7444
Broom & Broom/99 Green St., S.F. .... (415) 397-4300
Broussard, Darrell/3515 Bellefontaine, Houston .... (713) 667-3216
Brown, Michael David, Inc./932 Hungerford Dr., Rockville .... (301) 762-4474
Buehner & Perlmutter Design Assoc./567 Coronation Dr., Franklin .... (508) 528-5788
Burgess Associates, Inc./90 Commandants's Way, Chelsea .... (617) 889-1088
Butler, Kosh, Brooks/940 N. Highland, L.A. .... (213) 469-8128
C.M.O. Graphics, Inc./223 W. Erie St., Chicago .... (312) 915-0001
Caggiano, Thom/8325 Dongan Ave., Elmhurst .... (718) 651-8993
Calderon, Jack Design Studios, Ltd./119 W. 57th St., NYC .... (212) 541-4848
Calnan, John/NYC .... (212) 727-2667
Calvello, Tony & Assocs./111 New Montgomery St., S.F. .... (415) 543-0271
Campbell, Tom Assocs., Inc./315 W. Ninth St., L.A. .... (213) 931-9990
Carlson & Albright/547 Oak Knoll Rd., Barrington Hills .... (708) 381-5614
Carnase, Inc./30 E. 21st St., NYC .... (212) 777-1500
Carter Design/555 Sutter St., S.F. .... (415) 781-7325
Cassady, Jack/Tampa .... (813) 264-4346
Cates, Ilona/1647 W. Fulton, Chicago .... (312) 666-4471
Chan Design/1334 Lincoln Blvd., Santa Monica .... (213) 393-3735
Chase, Margo/2255 Bancroft Ave., L.A. .... (213) 668-1055
Chermayeff & Geismar Assocs./NYC .... (212) 741-2539
Chevannes, Paul/362 Sixth Ave., Brooklyn .... (718) 788-3550
Cidonigraphics, Inc./122 E. 42nd St., NYC .... (212) 983-0339
Clichè Consultants Corp./Edison .... (201) 632-9747
Clownbank Studio/Santa Cruz, CA/(408) 426-4247 .... **page 350**
Cockerill, Bruce Designs/672 S. La Fayette Pk. Pl., L.A. .... (213) 382-2227
Coco, Raynes Graphics, Inc./35 Newbury St., Boston .... (617) 536-1499
Colliety, Ian/441 Park Ave. S., NYC .... (212) 889-6309
Colopy Dale, Inc./208 Pine St., Carnegie .... (412) 429-0400
Columbia Group, The, Inc./32 W. 40th St., NYC .... (212) 382-3790
Communication Design/435 N. Mulford Rd., Rockford .... (815) 397-3511
Communications Counselors/380 Essex Ave., Bloomfield .... (201) 743-9661
Comp Factory, The/4338 Roland Springs Dr., Baltimore .... (301) 366-4633

Comprehensive Packaging d.b.a. Compack/1575 Northside Dr., Atlanta . . . . (404) 351-0632
Computer Design & Publishing/179 Westmoreland Ave., S. White Plains . . . . (914) 949-4655
Condon, J&M, Inc./126 Fifth Ave., NYC . . . . (212) 242-7811
Condon, Norman Design/954 W. Washinston Blvd., Chicago . . . . (312) 226-3646
Cook & Shanosky Assoc., Inc./103 Carnegie Ctr., Princeton . . . . (609) 452-1666
Coopdesign Studio/313 E. Tenth St., NYC . . . . (212) 473-6028
Cooper & Garrett Associates/1250 Fifth Ave., NYC . . . . (212) 996-3827
Copeland Design, Inc./1151 W. Peachtree St. N.W., Atlanta . . . . (404) 892-3472
Copeland, Karen/322 W. 104th St., NYC . . . . (212) 864-1290
Corey Chaloner Millen/75 Varick St., NYC . . . . (212) 431-8490
Corey Design Studios/42 E. 23rd St., NYC . . . . (212) 529-7238
Cosgrove Assocs./223 E. 31st St., NYC . . . . (212) 889-7202
Crabtree & Jemison, Inc./1515 N. Court House Rd., Arlington . . . . (703) 525-7798
Crackerjack Studios/5901 Peachtree Dunwoody Rd. N.E., Atlanta . . . . (404) 396-6666
Creative Consulting/1376 W. Grand Ave., Chicago . . . . (312) 421-3739
Creative Graphics/318 Vanderbilt, Fairfax . . . . (319) 846-2534
Creative People, Inc./1700 Madison Rd., Cincinnati . . . . (513) 221-3213
Creative Resource Center, Inc./6321 Bury Dr., Eden Prairie . . . . (612) 937-6000
Creative Services, Inc./3925 Peachtree Rd. N.E., Atlanta . . . . (404) 262-7424
Cressy, Mike/L.A. . . . . (213) 937-4472
Crockett, David/114 E. 28th St., NYC . . . . (212) 889-6754
Cronan, Michael Patrick/One Zoe St., S.F. . . . . (415) 543-6745
Cross Assoc./3465 W. Sixth St., L.A. . . . . (213) 389-1010
Csoka/Benato/Fleurant, Inc./134 W. 26th St., NYC . . . . (212) 242-6777
Cullimore, M. Jack/1625 Hayford Rd., Spokane . . . . (509) 244-5015
Curtis Printing, Inc./533 Atlantic Ave., Freeport . . . . (516) 379-5404
Cygnus, Inc./1114 Ave. of the Americas, NYC . . . . (212) 391-1099
DaVinci Advertising & Design/Bayville . . . . (516) 628-1330
David, Judy B./1073 Lanier Blvd., Atlanta . . . . (404) 874-5678
David, Stuart/12 W. 95th St., NYC . . . . (212) 866-6089
De Felice, Robert & Assocs./152 Sylvan St., Danvers . . . . (508) 750-4400
De Olivera Creative, Inc./1750 Lafayette St., Denver . . . . (303) 837-8717
DeMarco & Associates/208 Fifth Ave., NYC . . . . (212) 725-5644
DeNapoli, Mike Studio, Inc./433 Park Ave. S., NYC . . . . (212) 576-1446
DeVault, Katherine/2400 Sunset Pl., Nashville . . . . (615) 269-0202
Dedini/Westport . . . . (203) 227-7806
DelliCarpini, Inc./118 E. 28th St., NYC . . . . (212) 684-3464
Dennard Creative, Inc./13601 Preston Rd., Dallas . . . . (214) 233-0430
Derrick & Love/676 Broadway, NYC . . . . (212) 777-3113
Design Art/3300 Henderson Blvd., Tampa . . . . (813) 879-3872
Design Center/12301 Whitewater Dr., Minnetonka . . . . (612) 933-9766
Design Four/4911 Aiken Ln., El Paso . . . . (915) 755-9179
Design Group 3, Inc./579 Mason St., Saugatuck . . . . (616) 857-2979
Design Group, The/Martin Luther King, Jr. Dr., Greensboro . . . . (919) 275-9944
Design Group/Dallas/13767 Littlecrest Dr., Dallas . . . . (214) 241-4085
Design Horizons/2523 W. Carriage Ln., Peoria . . . . (309) 692-0560
Design Ink/116 North Dale Mabry, Tampa . . . . (813) 875-9960
Design Research/Bangor . . . . (207) 825-3068
Design Shop, The/68 Winsor Pl., Glen Ridge . . . . (201) 743-5543
Design Solutions/5629 Carrollton Ave., Indpls. . . . . (317) 253-7284
Design Synergy, Ltd./500 Helendale Rd., Rochester . . . . (716) 288-8000
Design Vectors, Inc./408 Columbus Ave., S.F. . . . . (415) 391-0399
Design2/811 Barton Springs Rd., Austin . . . . (512) 474-5282
Design: Direction/1380 Filbert St., S.F. . . . . (415) 885-6729
DesignMarks Corporation/1462 W. Irving Park Rd., Chicago . . . . (312) 327-3670
Designed To Print & Assoc., Ltd./130 W. 25th St., NYC . . . . (212) 924-2090
Designers 3, Inc./25 W. 43rd St., NYC . . . . (212) 221-5900
Designworks/413 W. Hoover, Ann Arbor . . . . (313) 662-3579
Deutsch Design Inc./530 Broadway, NYC . . . . (212) 966-7710
Dever Design/7619 S. Arbory Ln., Laurel . . . . (301) 776-2812
Devlin, Bill/NYC . . . . (212) 889-3337
Di Spigna, Tony, Inc./215 Park Ave. S., NYC . . . . (212) 674-2647
Diamond Art Studio, Ltd./NYC . . . . (212) 685-6622

Dickens, Holly Design/612 N. Michigan, Chicago .... (312) 280-0777
Dicker, Debbie/765 Clementina St., S.F. .... (415) 621-0687
Dierksen, Jane Brunka/Duarte, CA/(818) 359-7745 .... page 245
Dodge, Sharon & Assocs./3033 13th Ave. W., Seattle .... (206) 284-4701
Doherty & Doherty Creative Services/74 Greenwich Ave., Greenwich .... (203) 629-2600
Donato & Berkley, Inc./386 Park Ave. S., NYC .... (212) 532-3884
Donovan's DreamMerchant Graphics/437 Engel Ave., Henderson .... (702) 564-3598
Doret, Michael/12 E. 14th St., NYC .... (212) 929-1688
Dorland, Sweeney, Jones/701 Market St., Phila. .... (215) 625-0111
Dougherty, Anne Design/7004 Clemson Dr., Alexandria .... (703) 765-5678
Downey, Weeks & Toomey/519 Eighth Ave., NYC .... (212) 564-8260
Dowson Design/7250 Beverly Blvd., L.A. .... (213) 937-5867
Drake & Boucher, Inc./857 Broadway, NYC .... (212) 242-4410
Drate, Spencer/160 Fifth Ave., NYC .... (212) 620-4672
Draw The Line Productions/144 Moody St., Waltham .... (617) 899-7914
Drebelbis, Marsha/8150 Brookriver Dr., Dallas .... (214) 951-0266
Droy, Brad/1873 S. Bellaire St., Denver .... (303) 691-5512
Dual Impressions/1518 N. St., N.W., Wash. D.C. .... (202) 293-2717
Dudash, Jim Graphics Service/7656 Fairview Ave., Mentor .... (216) 255-3225
Duffy Design Group/701 Fourth Ave. S., Mpls. .... (612) 339-3247
Dyer, Rod Group, Inc./8360 Melrose Ave., L.A. .... (213) 655-1800
Dynamic Graphics, Inc./6000 N. Forest Park Dr., Peoria .... (309) 688-8800
Dyographics, Inc./79 Walnut St., Belmont .... (617) 489-3505
Edelstein, Sy Design Studio/48 Brooks Ave., Venice .... (213) 399-3592
Egger Assoc., Inc./1032 Busse Hwy., Park Ridge .... (312) 296-9100
Ehlers, Lesley/NYC, NY/(212) 683-2773 .... pages 446-447
Eichenberger, David/228 Main St., Venice .... (213) 392-8781
El-Khadem-Howell, Mona/3820 Arroyo Sorrento Rd., San Diego .... (619) 481-6566
Elias/Savion Advertising, Inc./2424 CNG Tower, Pittsburgh .... (412) 642-7700
Elton Design Ltd./261 Broadway, NYC .... (212) 732-8726
Emerson, Wajdowicz Studios, Inc./1123 Broadway, NYC .... (212) 807-8144
Essex Partnership/116 S. Michigan Ave., Chicago .... (312) 630-4430
Faia Design/130 Camino Pacifico, Aptos .... (408) 662-8857
Falco & Falco/6 Auer Court, E. Brunswick .... (201) 390-0099
Falkins, Richard Adv. Design/15 W. 44th St., NYC .... (212) 840-3040
Fannell Studio/298A Columbus Ave., Boston .... (617) 267-0895
Farkas, Bob/1220 S. Bedford St., L.A. .... (213) 271-4909
Farmakis, Andreas/835 Third Ave., NYC .... (212) 758-5280
Feldman, Melissa/596 Broadway, NYC .... (212) 941-9568
Feldmeier Graphics/1138 Las Pulgas, Pacific Palisades .... (213) 454-6123
Finn/154 E. 64th St., NYC .... (212) 838-1212
First Nat'l. Braintrust & Co., Inc./Upper Montclair .... (201) 625-3250
Fisher, Hyman W., Inc./121 E. Northfield Rd., Livingston .... (201) 994-9480
Flat Lizard Graphics/26 Pinedale, Houston .... (713) 524-0579
Fleischer, Justin/85 Barrow St., NYC .... (212) 242-5299
Fogle, James/53 Pearl St., Brooklyn .... (718) 522-5724
Follis Design/2124 Venice Blvd., L.A. .... (213) 735-1283
Fossella, Gregory Assoc./451 D St., Boston .... (617) 951-2930
Fotografix/3309 E. Miraloma Ave., Anaheim .... (714) 528-2000
Franco/Richmond Hill, NY/(718) 441-0919 .... page 133
Frankfurt Gips Balkind/6135 Wilshire Blvd., L.A. .... (213) 965-4800
Freda, Tony/L.I.C. .... (718) 482-7455
Freelance Pool/Springfield .... (703) 451-5544
Freeman & Assoc./2194 S.W. Temple, Salt Lake City .... (801) 485-5721
Freeman, Carol Fox Assocs./5469 Ranier, Lisle .... (312) 971-3237
Freeman, Josh Design Office/8019½ Melrose Ave., L.A. .... (213) 653-6466
Friday Saturday Sunday, Inc./210 E. 15th St., NYC .... (212) 353-2060
Friedberg/ Feder/Ten E. 39th St., NYC .... (212) 532-5494
Froehlich, Dann/11012 Bermuda, Cerritos .... (213) 860-2677
Full Spectrum/2310 Fourth St., Santa Rosa .... (707) 578-3992
G.L. Graphics/333 N. Michigan Ave., Chicago .... (312) 782-4456
Gale Graphics/220 Pelham Rd., New Rochelle .... (914) 235-7648
Galit, Steve & Assocs./5105 Monroe Rd., Charlotte .... (704) 537-4071

Gampert, John/Kew Gardens, NY/(718) 441-2321 . . . . **page 163**
Gebhardt Assocs., Inc./2120 W. Grand Ave, Chicago . . . . (312) 944-6960
Georgopoulos/Imada Design, Inc./837 Traction Ave., L.A. . . . . (213) 972-0171
Gergin, Robert P. Assoc. Inc./11 E. 22nd St., NYC . . . . (212) 777-9500
Gillian/Craig Assoc., Inc./165 Eighth St., S.F. . . . . (415) 558-8988
Giosa, Sal/1123 Broadway, NYC . . . . (212) 260-8622
Glaser, Milton/NYC . . . . (212) 697-0858
Glassman Design, Inc./38 E. 29th St., NYC . . . . (212) 683-9466
Glazer and Kalayjian/301 E. 45th St., NYC . . . . (212) 687-3099
Glidden, Dan/26 Pinedale, Houston . . . . (713) 524-0579
Godbold Graphics Inc./3200 Gillham Rd., Kansas City . . . . (816) 753-4430
Goldstein, Howard Design/7031 Aldea Ave., Van Nuys . . . . (818) 987-2837
Goldstein, Stan Graphics,Co./Five Beekman St., NYC . . . . (212) 962-2845
Gonzer, L.J. Assoc./1225 Raymond Blvd., Newark . . . . (201) 624-5600
Good Design/Nice Pictures/1736 Columbia Rd., N.W., Wash. D.C. . . . . (202) 265-6608
Goodstadt, Sy/244-96 61st Ave., Douglaston . . . . (718) 423-8219
Goodwin, David Scott/Ashland, OR/(503) 488-2355 . . . . **page 305**
Gorbaty, Norman/14 East 38th St., NYC . . . . (212) 684-1665
Gorilla Graphics/ Adv. & Design/1053 Howard St., S.F. . . . . (415) 861-6661
Gorman, Chris Assocs./305 Madison Ave., NYC . . . . (219) 983-3375
Gorman, Cyd Kilbey/68 LaNell Dr., Stamford . . . . (203) 325-8833
Gould Graphics/800 Trust Bldg., Grand Rapids . . . . (616) 774-0510
Gournoe, M., Inc./60 E. Elm St., Chicago . . . . (312) 787-5157
Graca, James Design Group/5116 Sandpiper Way, Oxnard Shores . . . . (805) 985-6564
Graffito/601 N. Eutaw St., Baltimore . . . . (301) 837-0070
Graham Design Assocs./1825 K St. N.W., Wash. D.C. . . . . (202) 833-9657
Graham-Patterson, Inc./2915 Frankfort Ave., Louisville . . . . (502) 893-0240
Graphic Artist Associates/E. Burke . . . . (802) 626-5808
Graphic Design Centre/124 Galaxy Blvd., Toronto . . . . (416) 675-1999
Graphic Design Group/7500 Greenway Center Dr., Greenbelt . . . . (301) 220-1895
Graphic Ink/353 Church St., Clinton . . . . (508) 365-5205
Graphic Traffic Art Studio/309 N. Mandan St., Bismark . . . . (701) 258-3866
Graphic Workshop, Inc./80 Eighth Ave., NYC . . . . (212) 633-6333
Graphics Co., The/3411 First Ave. S., Seattle . . . . (206) 682-6351
Graphics International/555 Madison Ave., NYC . . . . (212) 688-0564
Graphics Plus Assoc./101 Smithfield St., Pittsburgh . . . . (412) 566-1010
Graphics Studio, The/811 N. Highland Ave., L.A. . . . . (213) 466-2666
Graphics by Nostradamus/250 W. 57th St., NYC . . . . (212) 581-1362
Graphicsgroup/6111 Peachtree Dunwoody Rd., Atlanta . . . . (404) 391-9929
Graphix, Inc./2675 Paces Ferry Rd. N.W., Atlanta . . . . (404) 433-0973
Grasch, Karen Design/405 N. Wabash, Chicago . . . . (312) 822-9632
Greco, Peter/813 Westbourne Dr., W. Hollywood . . . . (213) 657-5085
Greenebaum & Greenebaum/One South Ave., Natick . . . . (508) 657-8158
Greenfiled/Belser, Ltd./1818 N. St., Wash. D.C. . . . . (202) 775-0333
Greenspan, Sharon M./7301 Flower Ave. #1, Takoma Park . . . . (301) 270-6048
Greenwood, Rob Studio/Six Gracie Lane, Darien . . . . (203) 655-7269
Greif, Gene/270 Lafayette St., NYC . . . . (212) 966-0470
Greiman, April, Inc./620 Moulton Ave., L.A. . . . . (213) 227-1222
Grey Goose Design, Inc./100 Bella Vista Way, S.F. . . . . (415) 586-8644
Grimes, Don/3514 Oak Grove, Dallas . . . . (214) 526-0040
Gross, Ronald Design/366 Broadway, NYC . . . . (212) 227-8190
Group West, Inc./5455 Wilshire Blvd., L.A. . . . . (213) 937-4472
Guth, Marcy P./213 E. 34th St., NYC . . . . (212) 685-0734
Haan & Miskunas Adv./14 N. Second Ave., Lafayette . . . . (317) 423-5470
Hammond Design Assoc./206 W. Main St., Lexington . . . . (606) 259-3639
Hanson Graphic/301 N. Water St., Milwaukee . . . . (414) 347-1266
Harig, John H./6058 Wayside Ave., Cincinnati . . . . (513) 232-0261
Harmon, Richard Theatrical Design/167 W. 72nd St., NYC . . . . (212) 877-3405
Healy, David/49 Melcher St., Boston . . . . (617) 695-0006
Hecker, Jon Design/5140 N. College Ave., Indpls. . . . . (317) 283-2675
Heffron, Leslie/Gloucester . . . . (508) 281-6030
Held & Diedrich Design, Inc./703 E. 30th St., Indpls. . . . . (317) 926-6161
Hellman Assoc. Inc./1225 W. Fourth St., Waterloo . . . . (319) 234-7055

Henry & Peretti Studio/5810 Winsome, Houston	(713) 977-4959
Herbst Lazar Bell Inc./345 N. Canal St., Chicago	(312) 454-1116
Hernandez, Raymond/994 Ocean Ave., Brooklyn	(718) 462-9072
Hess, Milo/Forest Hills	(212) 975-2821
Higgins Group, The/87 N. Raymond Ave., Pasadena	(818) 793-1676
High, Richard/4500 Montrose, Houston	(713) 521-2772
Hill Theatre Studios/35 W. Broad St., Paulsboro	(609) 423-8910
Hilland, Earl E./6721 N. Sioux Ave., Chicago	(312) 774-3312
Hirsch, David Design Group Inc./205 W. Wacker Dr., Chicago	(312) 329-1500
Hirth, Russel/Valley Forge	(215) 964-0500
Hixo, Inc./1204 San Antonio, Austin	(512) 477-0050
Holst, Joni/204 W. 20th St., NYC	(212) 807-4194
Hommel, Dennis Assocs., Inc./3540 Middlefield Rd., Menlo Park	(415) 365-4565
Horizon Design/138 Chatsworth Ave., Larchmont	(914) 834-2388
Horn, Robert/Chicago/(312) 644-0058	**page 445**
Horvath, Steve Design, Inc./301 N. Water St., Milwaukee	(414) 271-3992
Houlé, Harrison/S.F., CA/(415) 871-9163	**page 112**
Houlé, Harrison/Sherman Oaks, CA/(818) 783-6563	**page 112**
Hubbard & Hubbard Design/815 N. First Ave., Phoenix	(602) 252-6463
Hubbard Studios/549 W. Randolph, Chicago	(312) 332-6298
Huckeba Design Studio/338 Apple Grove Lane, Santa Barbara	(805) 563-2389
HumanGraphic/CWA, Inc./4015 Ibis St., San Diego	(619) 299-0431
Hume, Kelly/912 S. Los Robles, Pasadena	(818) 793-8344
II & III D Design/944 Eighth Ave., NYC	(212) 265-1517
Icon Design/270 Lafayette St., NYC	(212) 431-5350
Identity Center/Schaumburg	(708) 843-2378
Illustration Design Group/1225 16th Ave., S., Nashville	(615) 327-8170
Image Communications, Inc./85 Fifth Ave., NYC	(212) 807-9677
Image Productions, Inc./727 N. Harbor Blvd., Fullerton	(714) 871-0191
Indiana Design Consortium, Inc./416 Main St., Lafayette	(317) 423-5469
Indigo Design/1050 Howard St., Omaha	(402) 341-8409
Innovations/182 Bernard St., S.F.	(415) 474-6385
Invisions, Ltd./4530 Wisconsin Ave. N.W., Wash. D.C.	(202) 362-4212
Irwin, Virginia/37 Jamaica St., Jamaica Plain	(617) 522-0736
It's In The Works, Inc./381 Park Ave. S., NYC	(212) 689-0371
JK Art Directions/200 N. Jefferson St., Milwaukee	(414) 273-8194
JK Designs/2717 S. Grant St., Arlington	(703) 548-5576
JMH Corporation/921 E. 66th St., Indpls.	(317) 255-3400
Jackson Gray Graphics, Inc./213 W. Institute Pl., Chicago	(312) 642-4727
Jacobs Fulton Design Group/745 Emerson St., Palo Alto	(415) 328-4669
Jaeger Design, Inc./2025 Eye St., N.W., Wash. D.C.	(202) 785-8434
Johnson, Dean Design, Inc./604 Fort Wayne Ave, Indpls.	(317) 634-8020
Johnson, Max/26 Strawberry Hill Ave, Stamford	(203) 323-1011
Jones, Brent A./328 Hayes St., S.F.	(415) 626-8337
Jones, Richmond A./2530 W. Eastwood Ave., Chicago	(312) 588-4900
Joy Street Studio, Inc./64 Long Wharf, Boston	(617) 742-8077
Kaeser & Wilson Design, Ltd./330 Seventh Ave., NYC	(212) 563-2455
Kaleidoscope International, Inc./16 Wilton Acres, Wilton	(203) 834-2700
Karo Design Resource/747 Bute St., Vancouver	(604) 688-9975
Karp, Michael Music, Inc./260 W. 39th St., NYC	(212) 840-3285
Katz Wheeler Design/1219 Spruce St., Phila.	(215) 985-0727
Kavelaras, Diane/2341 N. Cambridge Ave., Chicago	(312) 248-6798
Keig, Susan Jackson/860 N. Lake Shore Dr., Chicago	(312) 266-0329
Kellum, Ron/1133 Broadway, NYC	(212) 645-4370
Kennedy and Crew Inc../79 Bridle Trail, Ridgefield	(203) 431-6066
Kenney, Tim Design, Inc./1711 Connecticut Ave., Wash. D.C.	(202) 328-0353
Kessler, Leonard/Six Stoneham Ln., New City	(914) 354-2759
Kimmins, Geoffrey/123-60 83rd Ave., Kew Gardens	(718) 544-6124
Klaboe & Siwek Assoc./2315 Broadway, NYC	(212) 362-6666
Klim, Matt & Assoc., Inc./Avon Park N., Avon	(203) 678-1222
Klitsch, Libby Johnson/338 Iona Ave., Narberth	(215) 667-6805
Kneapler, John Design/48 W. 21st St., NYC	(212) 463-9774
Kollar, Candice/3856 21st St., S.F.	(415) 824-8240

Koppel & Scher/156 Fifth Ave., NYC .... (212) 627-9330
Kops, Debi, Inc./88 Lexington Ave., NYC .... (212) 683-6249
Kovach, Julianna/3498 Fairmount Blvd., Cleveland Hts. .... (216) 371-2526
Krent/Paffett Assoc., Inc./711 Atlantic Ave., Boston .... (617) 451-6301
Kristiansen Graphic Design/251 Kearny St., S.F. .... (415) 362-2448
Krudo Design Atelier Ltd./540 N. Lakeshore Dr., Chicago .... (312) 644-0737
Kulhanek, Paul/901 Dove St., Newport Beach .... (714) 752-8631
Kurtzman/ Slavin/ Linda, Inc./One Northfield Plz., Northfield .... (312) 822-0559
La Grone, Roy E./25 Indiana Rd., Somerset .... (201) 846-7959
Lance Studios/151 W. 46th St., NYC .... (212) 382-0290
Langdon, John/4529 Pine St., Phila. .... (215) 476-4312
Lange, Jim Design/320 N. Michigan, Chicago .... (312) 606-9313
Larson/Marvine/2524 N. Maplewood, Chicago .... (312) 772-7152
Laser Graphics, Inc./61 W. 23rd St., NYC .... (212) 929-0010
Latham Brefka Assocs./883 Boylston St., Boston .... (617) 536-8787
Laudicina, Rosario/3900 Montrose Blvd., Houston .... (713) 520-9639
Laughin, R. Bruce/156 W. 44th St., NYC .... (212) 921-9732
Lauren Assocs./Seven W. 22nd St., NYC .... (212) 463-8909
Lawrence Studio, Inc./444 Park Ave. S., NYC .... (212) 684-4122
Leah, Bonnie Lettering & Design/1801 Dove St., Newport Beach .... (714) 752-7820
Lebowitz, Mo/2599 Phyllis Dr., N. Bellmore .... (516) 826-3397
Lee Myles Assocs., Inc./Ten Cutter Mill Rd., Great Neck .... (516) 466-7814
Leick, Carl/3406 Rindge Ln., Redondo Beach .... (213) 370-9396
Leong, Russell Design/524-A Ramona St., Palo Alto .... (415) 321-2443
Les, LaMotte/3002 Keating Ct., Burnsville .... (612) 894-1879
Letterform Design/501 N. Orange Dr., L.A. .... (213) 932-1875
Levitt, Virginia/3905 Tyndall Rd., University Hts. .... (216) 321-6627
Lewis & Gace/One Bridge Plaza, Fort Lee .... (201) 461-9600
Liebert Studios, Inc./Six E. 39th St., NYC .... (212) 686-4520
Lion Arts, Inc./Southampton .... (516) 728-2430
Lipman Hearns, Inc./20 N. Michigan Ave., Chicago .... (312) 372-8910
Lipton Design M./392 Central Park W., NYC .... (212) 662-9292
Liska & Assoc./676 St. Clair, Chicago .... (312) 943-4600
Lister Butler, Inc./475 Fifth Ave., NYC .... (212) 951-6100
Logelman, Dick Design/1019 W Jackson, Chicago .... (312) 829-1290
Logowitz & Moore Design Assocs./70 Long Wharf, Boston .... (617) 227-2210
Loucks Atelier, Inc./2900 Weslayan, Houston .... (713) 877-8551
Loveless, Rick/St. Louis .... (314) 427-1787
Lowe, Robert I./1903 Colonial Ave., Norfolk .... (804) 622-9053
Loyd, Judy & Partners/28400 Hughes, St. Clair Shores .... (313) 259-6037
M Space/373 Ralcam Pl., Costa Mesa .... (714) 645-3139
Madsen & Kuester, Inc./81 S. Ninth St., Mpls. .... (612) 338-6030
Main Idea, The/345 Morgantown Rd., Reading .... (215) 376-4871
Maness, Michael/7658 Millbridge Dr., Southaven .... (601) 342-2348
Manhattan Design/47 W. 13th St., NYC .... (212) 620-0506
Manoogian, Michael/7457 Beck Ave., N. Hollywood .... (818) 764-6114
Manos, Michelle Inc./2220 Pennington Ct., Stockton .... (209) 473-4311
Marckrey Design Group, Inc./1201 34th Ave., L.I.C. .... (718) 204-0971
Marcks Grafik/46 Cole St., S.F. .... (415) 221-2776
Marco Assocs./370 Lexington Ave., NYC .... (212) 679-9270
Marker II Studio/222 Park Ave. S., NYC .... (212) 982-1390
Marketing Resources, Inc./3705 Whittle Springs Rd., Knoxville .... (615) 522-0455
Marr, Dan/26 Juanita Way, S.F. .... (415) 564-2096
Martinez, Glenn & Assocs./15 Third St., Santa Rosa .... (707) 526-3198
Massey, John/2131 N. Cleveland, Chicago .... (312) 871-5029
Masuda, Coco/NYC, NY (212) 727-1599 .... **page 105**
Matsuno Design Group/714 N. La Brea Ave., L.A. .... (213) 938-2050
May Bender Design Assoc./Seven Deer Park Dr., Monmouth Jct. .... (201) 329-8388
McAdams, The Larry McAdams Group/1400 Bristol St. N., Newport Beach .... (714) 833-8333
McCargar Design/2915A Red Hill Ave., Costa Mesa .... (714) 556-0908
McCollum, Sudi Design/3244 Cornwall Dr., Glendale .... (818) 243-1345
McCool & Co., Inc./701 Fourth Ave. S., Mpls. .... (612) 332-3993
McDonel, Phillip/2228 Union St., S.F. .... (415) 923-0700

McGuire Assoc./1234 Sherman Ave., Evanston ... (708) 328-4433
Meade Creative/219 W. Wayne St., Maumee ... (419) 666-1168
Meadesign Studio/170 Lexington Ave., NYC ... (212) 689-6778
Mechanical Men, Inc./3958 Ince Blvd., Culver City ... (213) 837-1904
MediaConcepts Corp./25 N. Main St., Assonet ... (508) 644-3131
Mediaworks Design/1909 S. George Masm Dr., Arlington ... (703) 998-8053
Meridian Design Studio, Inc./3590 N. Meridian St., Indpls. ... (317) 925-8333
Meriwether, Arthur, Inc./1529 Brook Dr., Downers Grove ... (312) 495-0600
Meth, Miriam & Saul/96 Greenwood Ln., White Plains ... (914) 592-3698
Michener, Kelly/Valley Forge ... (215) 964-0500
Middleberg Assocs./130 E. 59th St., NYC ... (212) 888-6610
Miller, Claudia Artist Unlimited/17 Rainbow Ln., Levittown ... (516) 731-1281
Miller, Doug/L.I.C. ... (718) 482-7455
Miller, Irving D./295 Nothern Blvd., Great Neck ... (516) 466-6585
Miller, Norman Assocs./17 E. 48th St., NYC ... (212) 752-4830
Miller, W./Westport ... (203) 227-7806
Mlicki Design, Inc./1847 W. Fifth Ave., Columbus ... (614) 486-0286
Modi & Beckler Design/19 W. 34th St., NYC ... (212) 695-1220
Moore, Hugh & Assocs./228 S.W. St., Alexandria ... (703) 548-4888
Moore, Larry/Orlando, FL/(407) 648-0832 ... **page 374**
Morning, John Design, Inc./866 United Nations Plz., NYC ... (212) 688-0088
Moscato Communications/7319 Giddings, Burr Ridge ... (708) 655-1453
Moss, Yamamoto, Inc./252 First Ave. N., Mpls. ... (612) 375-0180
Napoles Design Group/100 Upper Briar Rd., Kentfield ... (415) 461-1455
Nason Design Assoc., Inc./329 Newbury St., Boston ... (617) 266-7286
Naughton, Carol & Assocs., Inc./213 W. Institute Pl., Chicago ... (312) 951-5353
Neff, Glynda/76 Clifton Pl., Jersey City ... (201) 333-4716
Neilson Design Group, Inc./114 E. Front, Traverse City ... (616) 946-0925
Neuman, Virginia/451 Foothill Dr., Fillmore ... (805) 524-3718
Newman Design Associates, Inc./530 Whitfield St., Guilford ... (203) 453-9595
Nickels, Rich Design/130 W. Liberty, Wheaton ... (708) 653-2925
Niehaus, Don/2380 Malcolm Ave., L.A. ... (213) 279-1559
Nikosey, Tom/S.F. ... (415) 776-4247
Nolan & Co., Inc./8150 N. Central Pk., Skokie ... (708) 675-1360
Norrie Gordon Assoc., Inc./122 E. 25th St., NYC ... (212) 598-6900
North Side Studio/4221 Northgate Blvd., Sacramento ... (916) 927-5033
Northrop, Susan E./18 Imperial Place, Providence ... (401) 521-2389
O&J Design, Inc./Nine W. 29th St., NYC ... (212) 779-9654
Oaktree Graphics, Inc./570 Seventh Ave., NYC ... (212) 398-9355
Ollio Studios/1229 Fulton Bldg., Pittsburgh ... (412) 281-4483
Omni Studio, Inc./603 W. Franklin, Boise ... (208) 344-1332
Ong-Lee Design, Ltd./639-14th Ave., S.W., Calgary ... (403) 245-5200
Orit Design/27 W. 24th St., NYC ... (212) 727-1140
Osborn, Stephen & Assoc./710 Palo Alto Ave., Palo Alto ... (415) 326-2276
Osser, Stephanie Fleischer/150 Winding River Rd., Needham ... (617) 237-1116
Ovryn, Ken/638 Grace, Chicago ... (312) 525-2252
P.C. Assocs., Inc./105 E. Northfield Ave., Livingston ... (201) 535-6446
Page, Arbitrio & Resen, Ltd./305 E. 46th St., NYC ... (212) 421-8190
Paine Bluett Paine, Inc./4617 Edgefield Rd., Bethesda ... (301) 493-8445
Palsa, Joseph R. & Assocs./150 Green St., S.F. ... (415) 986-2022
Pan International, Inc./2016 Mt. Vernon Ave., Alexandria ... (703) 548-5535
Panton, Doug/341 Wellesley St. E., Toronto ... (416) 920-5612
Pantuse, Mike/350 E. 89th St., NYC ... (212) 534-3511
Parks Inc./226 Maple Ave. W., Vienna ... (703) 255-5500
Pasadena Production Studios/39 E. Walnut, Pasadena ... (818) 584-4090
Paslavsky, Ivan/510-7 Main St. N., NYC ... (212) 759-3985
Patterson, Margaret Co./234 Claredon St., Boston ... (617) 424-1236
Pearlman/Withers/305 E. 46th St., NYC ... (212) 935-2552
Pearson, Nancy/248 E. 31th St., NYC ... (212) 686-5754
Pease, Robert & Co., Inc./11 Orchard Ct., Alamo ... (415) 820-0404
Peckens, Ron/1250 Stephenson Hwy., Troy ... (313) 583-9200
Pedersen Design, Inc./141 Lexington Ave., NYC ... (212) 683-5450
Pelton & Assocs., Inc./36 14th St., Hermosa Beach ... (213) 376-8061

Pensare Design Group/1006 Thomas Jefferson St., N.W., Wash. D.C.	(202) 333-8401
Pentagram/620 Davis, S.F.	(415) 981-6612
Pentagram Design Services Inc./212 Fifth Ave., NYC	(212) 683-7000
Pentagraph, Inc./500 N. Clark, Chicago	(312) 661-0075
Perman, Norman, Inc./2238 Asbury Ave., Evanston	(312) 864-2786
Personal Touch, The/156 W. 56th St., NYC	(212) 752-2345
Peter T. Noble Assocs./305 Princehouse Ln., Encinitas	(619) 944-7626
Peterson, Gloria/Ten Aladdin Ter., S.F.	(415) 928-3033
Phase II/303 E. Wacker Dr., Chicago	(312) 565-0400
Photocom/2412 Converse, Dallas	(214) 428-8781
Picard Didier, Inc./13160 W. Burleigh St., Brookfield	(414) 783-7400
Pierre, Keith/1202 S.W. 82nd Ave., N. Lauderdale	(305) 726-0401
Pig Pen Studios/235 Carmelita Dr., Mountain View	(415) 961-5674
Pinkhaus Design Corporation/2424 S. Dixie Hwy., Miami	(305) 854-1000
Pinzke, Herbert Design, Inc./1935 N. Kenmore Ave., Chicago	(312) 528-2277
Pitt Studios of Ohio/1370 Ontario St., Cleveland	(216) 241-6720
Plataz, George Studios/Martin Bldg., Pittsburgh	(412) 322-3177
Podob, Al/370 Lexington Ave., NYC	(212) 697-6643
Pollard, Michelle/1231 State At., Santa Barbara	(805) 568-1113
Potts, Vickie/Chicago	(312) 631-0301
Pratt, Russell E./NYC, NY/(212) 685-7955	**page 140**
Pressley Jacobs Design, Inc./211 W. Wacker Dr., Chicago	(312) 263-7485
Printbox Graphics, Inc./25 W. 45th St., NYC	(212) 944-0055
Professional Art Studios, Inc./736 Lothrop, Detroit	(313) 875-2776
Projections Company/27 Warfield St., Upper Montclair	(201) 746-7265
Promedeus Arts, Inc./39 W. 14th St., NYC	(212) 989-7299
Prometheus Productions, Inc./110 E. 23rd St., NYC	(212) 677-2140
Publicom, Inc./1050 Waltham St., Lexington	(617) 863-2484
Punin, Nikolai/NYC, NY/(212) 727-7237	**page 166**
Qually & Company, Inc./30 E. Huron, Chicago	(312) 944-1510
Quon, Mike/NYC, NY/(212) 226-6024	**page 225**
R.H. Graphics, Inc./23 E. 22nd St., NYC	(212) 505-5070
RMR Portfolio/7701 Normandale Rd, Mpls.	(612) 835-6039
Rabil & Assocs./806 W. Diamond Ave., Gaithersburg	(301) 670-9355
Raess Design/424 N. Larchmont Blvd., L.A.	(213) 461-9206
Ray, Bert Studio/43 E. Ohio, Chicago	(312) 944-0651
Rayfield, Robert Corporate Design/5072 Peck Hill Rd., Jamesville	(315) 446-5216
Rebechini Studios/1390 Howard St., Elk Grove	(312) 437-9030
Rebel With A Cause/4515 Van Nuys Blvd., Sherman Oaks	(818) 986-4822
Redline Illustrations, Inc./L.I.C.	(718) 482-7455
Redmond, Patrick Design/757 Raymond Ave., St. Paul	(612) 224-7155
Reetz, Al/1813 Linden Ave., Waukegan	(312) 662-2411
Regn/Califano, Inc./330 W. 42nd St., NYC	(212) 239-0380
Renaissance Communications, Inc./7835 Eastern Ave., Silver Spg.	(301) 587-1505
Renfro, Ed/250 E. 83rd St., NYC	(212) 879-3823
Richards Design Group, Inc./4722 Old Kingston Pike, Knoxville	(615) 588-9707
Richman, Micheal/50 Greene St., NYC	(212) 925-2182
Richmond Studio, The/508 Richmond St. E., Toronto	(416) 366-0049
River City Studio/116 W. Third, Kansas City	(816) 474-3922
Robbins, Ira Design/157 Luquer St., Brooklyn	(718) 624-5194
Roessner & McMillin Graphic Designers/57 Main St., Pluckemin	(201) 658-9898
Rogers Seidman Design Team/20 W. 20th St., NYC	(212) 741-4687
Rohr, Dixon/430 W. 34th St., NYC	(212) 268-6907
Romanoff Design/156 Fifth Ave., NYC	(212) 807-0236
Rosler, Philip Associates, Inc./North Babylon	(516) 321-6273
Ross Culbert Holland & Lavery/15 W. 20th St., NYC	(212) 206-0044
Ross, Phillip Assocs., Ltd./213 Hancock Ave., Lake Bluff	(312) 234-4484
Rossin Creative Group, Inc./639 Atlantic St., Stamford	(203) 325-1133
Roth, Randall R./531 Forestview Ave, Chicago	(708) 823-4785
Roto Litho, Inc./1827 E. 16th St., L.A.	(213) 749-7551
Rousso & Assoc., Inc./2060 Mt. Paran Rd. N.W., Atlanta	(404) 239-0810
Rouya, Es/45-19 42nd St., L.I.C.	(718) 392-5887
Royter Snow Design/145 Pierpont Ave., Salt Lake City	(801) 328-0112

Rubin-Cordaro Design/115 N. First St., Mpls. ... (612) 343-0011
Ruenitz & Co./50 Washington St., Norwalk ... (203) 855-8281
Rupert, Paul/708 Montgomery, S.F. ... (415) 391-2966
Russell, Anthony & Assoc./584 Broadway, NYC ... (212) 431-8770
S.E. Graphics Ltd./795 King St. E., Hamilton ... (416) 545-8484
SMP Graphic Service Center/26 E. 22nd St., NYC ... (212) 254-2282
Sackett Design Assoc./864 Fulson St., S.F. ... (415) 543-1590
Saiki & Assoc., Inc./154 W. 18th St., NYC ... (212) 255-0466
Saloutos, Alex Graphic Design/20½ E. Mifflin St., Madison ... (608) 258-8933
Salvato & Coe Assocs., Inc./2015 W. Fifth Ave., Columbus ... (614) 488-3131
Samata Associates/101 S. First St., Dundee ... (312) 428-8600
Samerjan/ Edigraph, George/45 Cantitoe, Katonah ... (914) 232-3725
Sargent, Claudia Karabaic/15-38 126th St., College Point ... (718) 461-8280
Savlin/Petertil/1335 Dodge, Evanston ... (708) 328-3366
Schema/258 W. Escalones, San Clemente ... (714) 361-2349
Schlatter Group, The/40 E. Michigan Mall, Battle Creek ... (616) 964-0898
Schoenfeld Design/Six Colony Ct., Parsippany ... (201) 263-1635
SchommerGraphics/Newfane ... (802) 365-7777
Schraad, Mark Design/Graphics/Ten E. Ninth, Lawrence ... (913) 842-0265
Schulman, Robert/Wash. D.C. ... (202) 453-8315
Seid, Eva/85 South St., NYC ... (212) 825-1984
Seidman Design/20 W. 20th St., NYC ... (212) 645-6160
Service Art Studio, Inc./49 W. 45th St., NYC ... (212) 398-1212
Sevelle & Sevelle/96 E. Lincoln St., Columbus ... (614) 291-8838
Shapiro, Deborah Designs/150 Bentley Ave., Jersey City ... (201) 432-5198
Sheibley, Thomas Design/320 N. Kensington, LaGrange Pk. ... (312) 354-2094
Sherman, Linda Design, Inc./9825 Cannal Rd., Gaitherburg ... (301) 590-0604
Shimokochi /Reeves Design/4465 Wilshire Blvd., L.A. ... (213) 937-3414
Sigalos, Alex Design/400 W. Erie, Chicago ... (312) 787-5767
Sizemore, Lillian Design/3125 W. Palmer Sq., Chicago ... (312) 252-0284
Skolnick, Arnold/211 W. 20th St., NYC ... (212) 243-7808
Slaughter/Hanson & Assoc. Advertising/2100 Morris Ave., Birmingham ... (205) 252-9998
Smallkaps Assoc., Inc./40 E. 34th St., NYC ... (212) 683-0339
Smith Art Direction and Design Assoc./205 Thomas St., Glen Ridge ... (201) 429-2177
Smith Dawson, Inc./29 Bear Mtn. Rd., Ridgefield ... (203) 798-2526
Smith, Tyler/127 Dorrance St., Providence ... (401) 751-1220
Smudin Studios, Inc./210 W. Washington Sq., Phila. ... (215) 925-9901
Sobel, Phillip Eric/Jackson Hts. ... (718) 476-3841
Soileau & Assocs./4545 Bissonnet, Bellaire ... (713) 666-1380
Soo Hoo, Patrick Designers/8800 Venice Blvd., L.A. ... (213) 836-8800
Sosin, Bill/415 W. Superior, Chicago ... (312) 751-0974
Sparkman & Bartholomew/1120 Connecticut Ave. N.W., Wash. D.C. ... (202) 785-2414
Spector Design/350 Hudson St., NYC ... (212) 929-4008
Spectrum Design/4041 Mac Arthur Blvd., Newport Beach ... (714) 752-5738
Speulda, William/363 Diamond Bridge Ave., Hawthorne ... (201) 427-6661
Staada & Koorey, Inc./Hackettstown ... (201) 852-4949
Staebler, Tom/680 N. Lake Shore Dr., Chicago ... (312) 751-8000
Starr, James M./Dallas ... (214) 369-6990
Stevens, Phyllis/112 E. Tenth St., NYC ... (212) 674-0496
Stillerman, Robbie/52 Prospect Ave., Sea Cliff ... (516) 671-5815
Strandell Design, Inc./218 Ontario, Chicago ... (312) 661-1555
Streetworks Studio/1414 S. Pollard St., Arlington ... (703) 521-6227
Structural Graphics, Inc./80 Plains Rd., Essex ... (213) 767-2661
Studio & Co./13353 Sorrento Dr., Largo ... (813) 595-2275
Studio 225/225 N. Michigan Ave., Chicago ... (312) 861-8555
Studio Specialties/1040 N. Halsted, Chicago ... (312) 337-5131
Studiographix/350 Phelps Ct., Irving ... (214) 541-1001
Sullivan, Timothy/1015 Battery St., S.F. ... (415) 788-4555
Svolos, Maria Design/1936 W. Estes, Chicago ... (312) 338-4675
Symbol Group Design, Inc./10308 Broom Ln., Seabrook ... (301) 794-4435
Synthesis Concepts, Inc./360 N. Michigan Ave., Chicago ... (312) 609-1111
TAB Graphics Design Studio/303 E. 17th Ave., Denver ... (303) 830-2416
TSI Communications, Inc./16 W. 46th St., NYC ... (212) 869-8787

Tanenbaum Graphic Design, Inc./4701 Sangamne Rd., Bethesda . . . . (301) 229-1135
Tangram Design Group, Inc./323 Park Ave. S., NYC . . . . (212) 473-8330
Taub, Morris/165 W. 20th St., NYC . . . . (212) 627-6678
Taylored Art/725 N. Western Ave., L.A. . . . . (213) 466-5663
Teller, Ira & Co./519 N. Maple, Beverly Hills . . . . (213) 274-8917
Tercovich, Douglas Assoc./575 Madison Ave., NYC . . . . (212) 838-4800
The Best Graphics Group/1648 Flower St., Glendale . . . . (818) 507-8730
Third Image/389 Campbell Ave., West Haven . . . . (203) 932-5856
Thirst/855 W. Blackhawk, Chicago . . . . (312) 951-5251
Thompson, Brian/7032 E. 33rd St., Tulsa . . . . (918) 663-1862
Thomson, Pamela/2915 Redhill Ave., Costa Mesa . . . . (714) 557-6274
Tocquigny Design/1601 E. Seventh St., Austin . . . . (512) 477-5565
Toothaker, Kimberly/119 S. Maple Ln., E. Peoria . . . . (309) 383-4227
Town Studios, Inc./717 Liberty Ave., Pittsburgh . . . . (412) 471-5353
US Design/853 Broadway, NYC . . . . (212) 505-1454
UVG & N, Inc./4415 W. Harrison St., Hillside . . . . (708) 449-1500
Ulrich, Mark/NYC . . . . (212) 989-9325
Ultragraphics/228 Main St., Venice . . . . (213) 399-3666
Urban, Taylor & Assocs./12250 S.W. 131st Ave., Miami . . . . (305) 238-3223
Van Hamersveld, John/St. Louis . . . . (314) 231-6800
Vanides Graphics, Inc./1202 Norwood St., Melrose Park . . . . (708) 681-0022
Vermont, Hilary Designs/218 E. 17th St., NYC . . . . (212) 674-3845
Vernon Design/468 S.E. 14th St., Dania . . . . (305) 654-8852
Victore, James B./146 E. 46th St., NYC . . . . (212) 682-3734
Viscom Ltd./99 Sumach St., Toronto . . . . (416) 366-6400
Visualgraphics Design/1211 N. Westshore Blvd., Tampa . . . . (813) 289-9308
Von Brincken, Maria/28 Village Rd., Sudbury . . . . (508) 443-4540
Vrabec Design/630 Busse Highway, Park Ridge . . . . (708) 518-8812
W/C Studio, Inc./241 Central Ave., St. Petersburg . . . . (813) 821-9050
WRK/602 Westport Rd., Kansas City . . . . (816) 561-4189
Walton, Tony/NYC . . . . (212) 787-9162
Warshaw/Blumenthal, Inc./400 E. 56th St., NYC . . . . (212) 759-7171
Watts Design, Inc./444 N. Wells, Chicago . . . . (312) 321-0191
Waxworks, The, Inc./124 N. Harrison St., Barrington . . . . (312) 381-0011
Weed, Eunice Assoc., Inc./303 Fifth Ave., NYC . . . . (212) 725-4933
Weiss, Jack Assocs./409 Custer Ave., Evanston . . . . (708) 866-7480
Weller Institute, The/1398 Aerie Dr., Park City . . . . (801) 649-9859
Wesolosky, Robert Graves/1250 Stephenson Hwy., Troy . . . . (313) 583-9200
Westgate Graphic Design, Inc./1111 Westgate, Oak Park . . . . (312) 848-8323
Weymouth Design/332 Congress St., Boston . . . . (617) 542-2647
Wiggin Design, Inc./23 Old Kings Hwy., Darien . . . . (203) 655-1920
Wilder-Fearn & Assoc., Inc./644 Linn St., Cincinnati . . . . (513) 621-5237
Williams, John Design/330 Fell St., S.F. . . . . (415) 621-0330
Wilson, Lisabet/2570 Tokalon Ct., San Diego . . . . (619) 276-1091
Wise, Thomas and Cheryl/146 Endslow Rd., Marietta . . . . (717) 426-1344
Wiseman Design/1530 Menard, St. Louis . . . . (314) 241-4442
Witus, Edward Design/634 W. Knoll Dr., W. Hollywood . . . . (213) 854-6514
Wolfe, Jack, Inc./25 W. Long Lake Rd., Bloomfield Hills . . . . (313) 642-0997
Wong, Fran Mechanicals/574 Pacific Ave., S.F. . . . . (415) 981-2250
Wong, Steve & Assoc./1447 Lombard St., S.F. . . . . (415) 673-3303
Wood, Alan Graphic Design/57-22 163rd St., Flushing . . . . (212) 889-5195
Wrobleski Design/8960 E. Navajo Ct., Prescott Valley . . . . (602) 772-7016
Xenoworks, Inc./280 Daines, Birmingham . . . . (313) 647-0100
Yamashita, Taro Hiroshi/211 E. 53rd St., NYC . . . . (212) 753-3242
Yankee Doodles/1101 30th St., Wash. D.C. . . . . (202) 944-5225
Yazzetta, Tony, Inc./1150 Foothill Blvd., La Canada . . . . (818) 790-0198
Young & Laramore/310 E. Vermont St., Indpls. . . . . (317) 264-8000
Young, Doyald/13957 Valley Vista Blvd., Sherman Oaks . . . . (818) 788-5562
Zahor & Bender, Inc./200 E. 33rd St., NYC . . . . (212) 532-7475
Zahra/Lout Adv. Designers, Inc./2811 McKinney Ave., Dallas . . . . (214) 855-5353
Zaslavsky, Morris/228 Main St., Venice . . . . (213) 399-3666
Zavesky Productions, Inc./8990 Shepard Rd., Macedonia . . . . (216) 467-5917

ROBERT HORN DESIGN ENSEMBLE

110 WEST KINZIE CHICAGO ILLINOIS 60610 PHONE 312 644 0058 FAX 312 644 3992

445

LESLEY EHLERS DESIGN

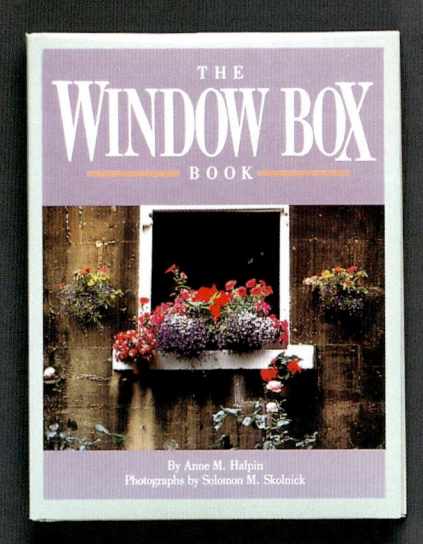

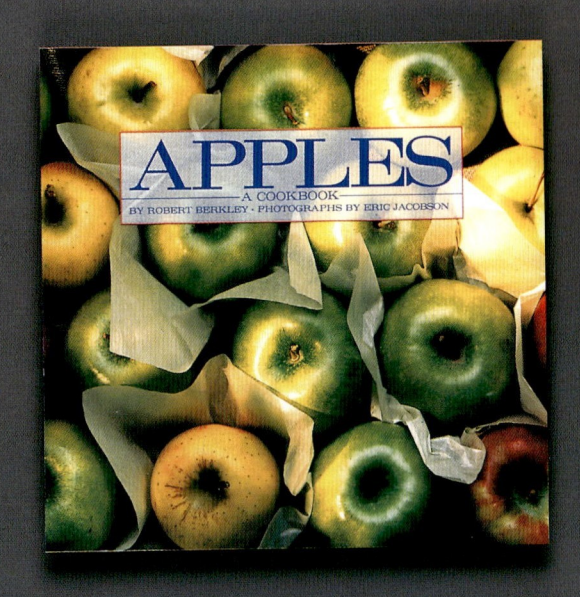

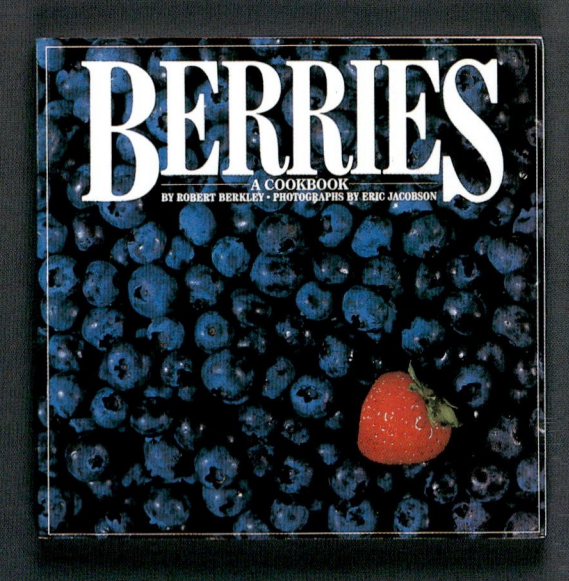

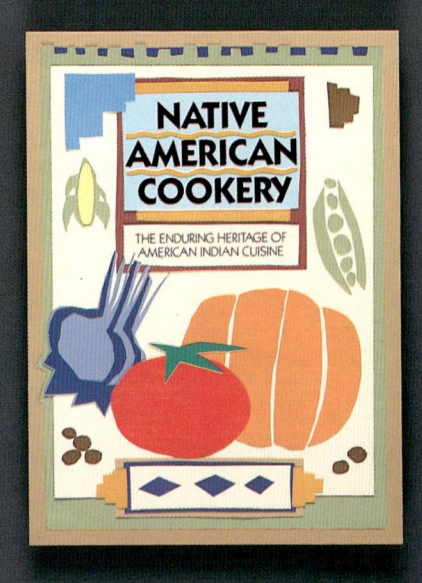

244 FIFTH AVENUE
NEW YORK CITY 10001
(212) 683-2773

LESLEY EHLERS DESIGN

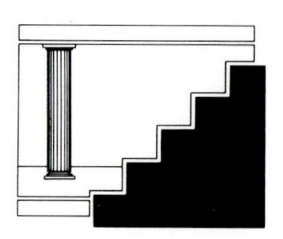

SUSAN COHEN INTERIOR DESIGN

Phoebe

244 FIFTH AVENUE
NEW YORK CITY 10001
(212) 683-2773

BOOK DESIGN · IDENTITY PROGRAMS · ILLUSTRATION · BROCHURES · PACKAGING

INDEXES

ALPHABETICAL INDEX

PAGES 451 - 453

REGIONAL INDEX

PAGES 454 - 458

REPRESENTATIVES & TALENT INDEX

PAGES 459 - 463

ALPHABETICAL INDEX

Abraham, Daniel, 226
Adams, Jeanette, 186
Airbrush Ink Studio, 315
Ajhar, Brian, 431
Aldridge Reps, Inc., 339
Alexander/Pollard, 300-304
Alper, A.J., 213
Alterio, Caroline, 197
American Artists, 115-132, 212, 240
Armes, Steve, 291
Asbaghi, Zita, 76
Bailey, Pat, 71
Baker, Skip, 421
Baradat, Sergio, 275
Barnes, Suzanne, 196
Bartczak, Peter, 350
Bartels, Ceci Assocs., 394-395
Bartholomew, Caty, 150
Baseman, Gary, 113
Batcheller, Keith, 120
Bates, Harry G., Jr., 75
Baumann, Karen, 253
Bell, Karen, 427
Belliveau, Allison, 244
Bennett, Gary, 269
Benny, Mike, 351
Benoît, 247
Bergendorff, Roger, 123
Berglund, Cindy, 154
Bernal, Richard, 384
Bernstein & Andriulli, 53-73
Biegel, Michael David, 352
Björkman, Steve, 322
Blakey, Paul, 342
Boies, Alex, 156
Boll, Maxine, 178
Booth, Claire, 388
Bramhall, William, 247
Brennan, Dan, 389
Brennan, Neil, 355
Bridy, Dan, 203
Brindle, Carolyn & Partner, 168-169
Brody, Sam, 97, 198
Brooks, Nan, 187
Brown, Rick, 59
Bruce, Taylor, 426
Bruckstein, Donald, 248-266
Brun, Robert, 88
Brusca, Jack, 251
Bryant, Amy, 314
Buck, Sid & Kane, Barney, 171, 290, 432
Bulthuis, Henri, 397
Burn, Ted, 347
Burnett, Lindy, 300-301
Burton, Caroline, 316

Buterbaugh, Rick, 420
Butler, Chris, 129
Call, Ken, 290
Campbell, Jenny, 420
Caporale, Wende, 233
Carbone, Kye, 411
Carbone, Lou, 237
Carver, Steve, 363
Cashwell, Charles, 280
Castellanos, Carlos, 390
Chaffee, James, 392
Chau, Tungwai, 425
Chichoni, Oscar, 263
Chirko, Gail, 338
Chislovsky, Carol Inc., 426-427
Chodos-Irvine, Margaret, 135
Clayton, Elaine, 246-247
Clegg, Dave, 268
Clownbank Studio, 350
Codarcea, Daniela, 265
Cohen, Jim, 427
Collier, Jan, 113, 331
Collingnon, Daniele, 331
Collins, Britt Taylor, 278
Conner, Mona, 294
Consani, Chris, 115
Cook, John, 337
Cooper, Bob, 282
Cooper, Cheryl, 303
Corkery, Eddie, 172
Courtney Studios, 266
Coveny, Rich, 413-415
Covington, Neverne, 157
Cozzolino, Paul, 215
Crawford, Denise Chapman, 314
Creative Capers, 58
Creative Freelancers, Inc., 223, 230-236
Creative Source, 82
Curran, Don, 386
Dale, Robert, 365
Dallasta, Ray, 419
Daniels, Sid, 83
Danila, Deborah, 419
Davidson, Dennis, 250
Davis, Allen, 255
de Barros, A. Martins, 264
De Cerchio, Joe, 236
De Luz, Tony, 288
De Muth, Roger T., 237
De Vito, Grace, 310
de la Houssaye, Jeanne, 89
DeLapine, Jim, 144
Dean, Glenn, 327
Degen, Paul, 246
Demarest, Chris, 247
Detrich, Susan, 289

Dierksen, Jane Brunkan, 245
Dininno, Steve, 230
Doktor, Patricia, 148
Dolobowsky, Mena, 237
Downs, Bob, 93
Drexler, Sharon, 100
Dryden, Jim, 155
duCharme, Tracy, 373
DuPont, Lane, 127
Duffy, Pat, 422
Dykes, John S., 387
Dzedzy, John, 235
Edwards, Karl, 308
Effler, Jim, 119
Ehlers, Lesley, 446-447
Einsel, Naiad, 237
Ellis, Jon, 65
Elmer, Richard, 79
Eloqui, 158
Enik, Ted, 261
Ericksen, Marc, 273
Evans, Robert, 272
Faria, Jeff, 340-341
Farrell, Russ, 125
Feldman, Ken, 97
Fernandez, Laura, 357
Filip, Traian Alexandru, 179
Filippo, Judy, 114
Fisher, Jeffrey, 246
Fitz-Maurice, Jeff, 423
Fleck, Tom, 338
Fleishman, Michael, 381
Fleming, Ron, 68
Flood, Richard, 147
Floyd, Walt, 86
Foty, Tom, 200
Franco, 133
French, Martin, 311
Frisari, Frank, 92
Fujisaki, Tuko, 238
Fuka, Ted, 307
Gaadt, David, 285
Gaadt, George, 117
Gadino, Victor, 56
Gall, Chris, 426
Gampert, John, 163
Garé, m., 243
Garns, Allen, 360
Garrow, Dan, 326
Geng, Maud, 196-197
Genzo, John Paul, 422
Gergely, Peter, 167
Giguere, Ralph, 362
Gilbert, Jim, 329
Glasgow & Assocs., 276-277
Glasgow, Dale, 276-277
Glick, Ivy & Assocs., 311-313
Gnan, Patrick, 421

Gomberg, Susan, 353-367
Gonzalez, Thomas, 339
Goodwin & Friends, Inc., 305
Goodwin, David Scott, 305
Graham, Tom, 241
Grandstaff, Chris, 164
Grant, Mel, 252
Gray, Steve, 426
Greenberg, Sheldon, 180
Grinnell, Derek, 313
Grossman, Myron, 237
Grove, David, 160-161
Guitteau, Jud, 323
Gulick, Dorothy, 319
Gustafson, Glenn, 106
Hackett, Pat, 311
Haefele, Steve, 260
Hahn, Holly, 187
Halbert, Michael, 395
Hallgren, Gary, 243
Hamagami, John, 126
Hamlin, Janet, 417
Hanson, Jim and Talent, 107, 331, 418
Hanzon-Kurrasch, Toni, 404
Hardiman, Miles W., 221
Harrington, Stephen, 274
Harris, Leslie, 330
Harrison, William, 321
Harwood, John, 61
Hauser, Barb, 97, 212
Havlicek, Karel, 130
Henriquez, Celeste, 407
Herbert, Jonathan, 94-95
Hilliard, Fred, 97
Hillman, Betsy, 432
Himsworth, Jim III, 419
Hines, Norman, 372
Hogan, Barb, 344
Hogarth, Paul, 246-247
Holladay, Reggie, 82
Holmberg, Irmeli, 166, 202-207, 349
Holmes, Matthew, 312
Hong, Min Jae, 80-81
Hoover, Sherry, 258
Horn, Robert, 445
Hostovich, Michael, 422
Houlé, Harrison, 112
Hughes, Marianne, 422
Hughes, Neal, 423
Huhn, Tim, 192
Hul, Jon Jr., 332
Hull, John, 131
Humphries, Michael, 194
Independent Pencil Co., 88
Inouye, Carol, 184
Jackson, Barry, 149
Jacobson, Rick, 356
Janovsky, Paul, 193
Jarvis, David, 171
Jaz & Jaz, 135
Jeffries, Shannon, 410

Johnson, Lonni Sue, 102
Jones, Jack, 414
Jorgensen, Donna, 97
Kabaker, Gayle, 380
Kaczman, James, 152
Kane, John, 96
Kanelous, George, 328
Kasper, Robert, 196
Katz, Les, 100
Klein, David G., 229
Klein, Hedy, 398
Klimt, Bill & Maurine, 211
Knaff, Jean-Christian, 196
Knutsen, Jan, 137-139
Korn, Pamela & Associates, 429-431
Kozmiuk, Michael, 116
Krejca, Gary, 307
LaFleur, Dave, 383
LaPorte, Michele, NYC, NY, 401
Laden, Nina, 208-209
Laney, Ron, 369
Langley, Sharon, 172-173
Lasher, Mary Ann, 54
Le-Tan, Pierre, 246
Lebo, Narda, 182-183
Leedy, Jeff, 367
Leff, Jerry Assocs., Inc., 370
Leiner, Alan, 124
Lengyel, Kathy, 304
Leon, Karen, 399
Leonard, Richard, 254
Lesh, David, 376-377
Lester, Mike, 188-189
Levine, Bette, 64
Lewis, Maurice, 240
Ligresti, Roberto, 298-299
Linden, Tamara, 338
Lindlof, Ed, 212
Linley, Michael, 428
Little, Ed, 190-191
Littmann, Barry, 375
Livingston, Francis, 370
Llewellyn, Sue, 202
Lloyd, Jeff, 237
Loehle, Don, 346
Losey, Brenda, 279
Lovell, Rick, 413
Lundeen, Cathy, 153
Lunia Blue Graphics, 165
Lynch, Larry & Andrea, 106, 314
Macanga, Steve, 87
Mahan, Benton, 368
Mahoney, Ron, 121
Maioresco Deca, Wanda, 185
Manasse, Michèle, 174-184
Manyum, Wallop, 174
Marden, Phil, 104
Margulies, Robert, 195
Mark, Steve, 138
Martin, Lyn, 218
Martinez, Sergio, 248

Mason, Marietta, 106
Masuda, Coco, 105
Mateu, Franc, 257
Matthews, Lu, 205
Mattingly, David B., 134
Mayer, Bill Inc., 108-109
McCaffrey, Peter, 402
McClure, Tim, 336
McGovern, Preston, 318
McGowan, Dan, 364
McGurl, Michael, 101
McIntosh, Jon, 197
McInturff, Steve, 412
McKelvey, David, 415
McKissick, Stewart, 159
McLennan, Constance, 271
McLoughlin, Wayne, 325
McNeel, Richard, 424
Mehalko, Donna, 169
Meisel, Paul, 246-247
Melrath, Susan, 223
Mendola Ltd., 371
Messi, Enzo, 358
Meyer, Gary, 270
Miller, Dave, 118
Miller, Verlin, 419
Milnazik, Kimmerle, 146
Mollica, Pat, 414
Moore, Chris, 55
Moore, Larry, 374
Moores, Jeff, 430
Mordan, C.B., 405
Morgan, Jacqui, 110
Morgan, Wendy, 308-309
Morrow, J.T., 84
Morse, Bill, 73
Moses, David, 283
Mowry, Scott, 293
Mueller, Pete, 70
Mull, Christy, 345
Myer, Andy, 420
Myers, Robert, 409
Najaka, Marlies Merk, 91
Nakamura, Carl, 224
Neail, Pamela Assocs., 401-407
Nelson, Craig, 69
Neski, Peter, 317
Network Studios, 308-309
New York Airbrush, 141
Newman, Carole & Assocs., 190-194
Ng, Michael, 231
Nishinaka, Jeff, 66
O'Connor, Cathy Christy, 181
O'Donnell, Billy, 385
O'Neill, Fran, 222
Olson, Richard A., 78
Ortega, José, 103
Ostan•Prentice•Ostan, Inc., 397
Oudekerk, Doug, 137
Ovies, Joseph M., 338
Palulian, Dickran, 378
Palulian, Joanne, 376-380

Paperny, Vladimir, 194
Parkinson, Jim Lettering, 246-247
Parrish, George I. Jr., 328
Parry, Ivor, 267
Parton, Steve, 262
Passerelli, Charles A., 338
Pasternak, Robert, 320
Pembroke, Richard, 122
Penca, Gary, 211
Peterson, Cheryl, 246-247
Phillips, Laura, 60
Pinkney, Deborah, 204
Pittman, Jackie, 284
Polenghi, Evan, 227
Pomerantz, Lisa, 420
Pomilla, Joseph, 315
Porazinski, Rob, 107
Porfirio, Guy, 394
Potts, Carolyn & Assocs., 346
Pratt, Russell E., 140
Pritchett, Karen, 207
Pritchett, Tom, 328
Punin, Nikolai, 166
Quon, Mike, 225
Radigan, Bob, 349
Ramin, Linda, 384-386
Reed, Mike, 306
Reid, Glenn Robert, 196
Renard Represents, 312, 321-327
Repertoire, 106, 314
Reynolds, Bill, 139
Reynolds, Gene, 408
Richards, Kenn, 141
Richards, Linda, 403
Riley Illustration, 246-247
Robinette, John, 414
Rocco, Joe, 416
Roman, Helen Assocs., Inc., 237
Rosales, Melodye, 256
Rose, Drew, 281
Rosenbaum, Tina, 334
Rosenthal Represents, 82, 295, 349
Rosenthal, Elise, 295
Rosenthal, Marc, 151
Rosner, Meryl, 234
Roth, Robert G., 216-217
Roth, Roger, 176-177

Rotoloni, Dave, 173
Rudnak, Theo, 324
Ruiz, Art, 249
Rush, John, 77
Ryan, Terry, 328
S.I. International, 248-266
Saffold, Joe, 145
Salk, Larry, 228
Sandler, Neil, 295
Sands, Trudy, 334-337
Sasaki, Goro, 57
Schaffer, Amanda, 382
Schmidt, John F., 239
Schmidt, Urs, 358
Schneider, R.M., 427
Schrier, Fred, 309
Schuna, Frank, 153-157, 306
Schuna, JoAnne, 153-157, 306
Schweigert, Carol, 136
Scott, Freda, 370
Sell Inc., 147
Sempé, J.J., 246
Shaw, Ned, 170
Shohet, Marti, 366
Sipp, Geo, 214
Sirrell, T., 199
Skillins, Gunar, 72
Small, David, 247
Smallish, Craig, 418
Smallwood, Steve, 143
Smith, Roy, 386
Smith, Vicki, 197
Smythe, Danny, 414
Sours, Michael, 335
Spaulding, Kevin, 432
Spear, Charles, 74
Spector, Joel, 201
Spengler, Ken, 406
Spiers, Herbert, 248-266
Stallard, Peter, 62
Starr, David, 104
Sterrett, Jane, 393
Stillman, Whit & Iréné, 246-247
Stokes, Fiona, 193
Story, Michael, 99
Stubbs, Tommy, 348
Stutzman, Mark, 158
Sullivan, Suzánne Hughes, 142
Sumpter, Will & Assocs., 278-287
Swan, Sara, 396

Talaro, Lionel, 232
Taleporos, Plato, 333
Tamara Inc., 338
Tate, Clarke, 287
Taylor, C. Winston, 111
Taylor, David, 292
Teach, Buz Walker, 220
Tedesco, Michael, 296
Tenud, Tish, 210
Tessler, John, 165
Thorn, Dick, 128
Timmons, Bonnie, 379
Traynor, Elizabeth, 302
Tughan, James, 361
Turner, Clay, 67
Unruh, Jack, 343
Van Seters, Kim, 90
Vargö, Kurt, 429
Viviano, Sam, 98
Von Schmidt, Eric, 242
Wagoner, Jae, 331
Wall, Pam, 63
Ward, John, 400
Warnick, Elsa, 198
Warter, Fred, 219
Wasserman, Randie, 206
Watts, Sharon, 168
Watts, Stan, 132
Weakley, Mark, 359
Weber, Tricia, 413-415
Weiman, Jon, 391
Weller, Don, 331
Wells, Susan, 342-349
Wende, Philip, 286
Wenzel, Paul, 259
Whitney, Jack, 386
Whitney, Mike, 386
Widener, Terry, 175
Williams Group, The, 413-415
Williams, Phillip, 413-415
Williams, Tim, 162
Wimmer, Mike, 371
Wolfe, Deborah Represents, 419-423
Yadin, Hanan, 397
Yamada, Kenny, 295
Yee, Terry, 85
Yesawich & Welsh, 82
Young, Eddie, 192
Zwolak, Paul, 297

REGIONAL INDEX

NORTHEAST

Abraham, Daniel, NYC, NY, 226
Adams, Jeanette, NYC, NY, 186
Airbrush Ink Studio, Ronkonkoma, NY, 315
Ajhar, Brian, NYC, NY, 431
Alper, A.J., NYC, NY, 213
Alterio, Caroline, Boston, MA, 197
American Artists, NYC, NY, 115-132, 212, 240
Asbaghi, Zita, Forest Hills, NY, 76
Bailey, Pat, NYC, NY, 71
Baker, Skip, Phila., PA, 421
Baradat, Sergio, NYC, NY, 275
Barnes, Suzanne, Boston, MA, 196
Bartels, Ceci Assocs., NYC, NY, 394-395
Bartholomew, Caty, Brooklyn, NY, 150
Baseman, Gary, Brooklyn, NY, 113
Batcheller, Keith, NYC, NY, 120
Bates, Harry G., Jr., Brooklyn, NY, 75
Baumann, Karen, NYC, NY, 253
Bell, Karen, NYC, NY, 427
Benoît, NYC, NY, 247
Bergendorff, Roger, NYC, NY, 123
Bernstein & Andriulli, NYC, NY, 53-73
Biegel, Michael David, Allendale, NJ, 352
Björkman, Steve, NYC, NY, 322
Boll, Maxine, NYC, NY, 178
Booth, Claire, NYC, NY, 388
Bramhall, William, NYC, NY, 247
Brennan, Neil, NYC, NY, 355
Bridy, Dan, NYC, NY, 203
Brindle, Carolyn & Partner, NYC, NY, 168-169
Brody, Sam, NYC, NY, 97, 198
Brown, Rick, NYC, NY, 59
Bruce, Taylor, NYC, NY, 426
Bruckstein, Donald, NYC, NY, 248-266
Brun, Robert, Newburyport, MA, 88

Brusca, Jack, NYC, NY, 251
Buck, Sid & Kane, Barney, NYC, NY, 171, 290, 432
Burton, Caroline, Jersey City, NJ, 316
Buterbaugh, Rick, Phila., PA, 420
Butler, Chris, NYC, NY, 129
Campbell, Jenny, Phila., PA, 420
Caporale, Wende, NYC, NY, 233
Carbone, Kye, Brooklyn, NY, 411
Carbone, Lou, NYC, NY, 237
Carver, Steve, NYC, NY, 363
Chichoni, Oscar, NYC, NY, 263
Chislovsky, Carol Inc., NYC, NY, 426-427
Clayton, Elaine, NYC, NY, 246-247
Codarcea, Daniela, NYC, NY, 265
Cohen, Jim, NYC, NY, 427
Collignon, Daniele, NYC, NY, 331
Conner, Mona, Brooklyn, NY, 294
Consani, Chris, NYC, NY, 115
Courtney Studios, NYC, NY, 266
Cozzolino, Paul, NYC, NY, 215
Creative Capers, NYC, NY, 58
Creative Freelancers, Inc., NYC, NY, 223, 230-236
Dale, Robert, NYC, NY, 365
Dallasta, Ray, Phila., PA, 419
Daniels, Sid, NYC, NY, 83
Danila, Deborah, Phila., PA, 419
Davidson, Dennis, NYC, NY, 250
Davis, Allen, NYC, NY, 255
de Barros, A. Martins, NYC, NY, 264
De Cerchio, Joe, NYC, NY, 236
De Luz, Tony, Boston, MA, 288
De Muth, Roger T., NYC, NY, 237
De Vito, Grace, Stamford, CT, 310
DeLapine, Jim, Lindenhurst, NY, 144

Dean, Glenn, NYC, NY, 327
Degen, Paul, NYC, NY, 246
Demarest, Chris, NYC, NY, 247
Detrich, Susan, Brooklyn, NY, 289
Dininno, Steve, NYC, NY, 230
Doktor, Patricia, NYC, NY, 148
Dolobowsky, Mena, NYC, NY, 237
Drexler, Sharon, NYC, NY, 100
DuPont, Lane, NYC, NY, 127
Duffy, Pat, Phila., PA, 422
Dykes, John S., Westport, CT, 387
Dzedzy, John, NYC, NY, 235
Effler, Jim, NYC, NY, 119
Ehlers, Lesley, NYC, NY, 446-447
Einsel, Naiad, NYC, NY, 237
Ellis, Jon, NYC, NY, 65
Elmer, Richard, NYC, NY, 79
Eloqui, Mt. Lake Park, MD, 158
Enik, Ted, NYC, NY, 261
Faria, Jeff, Hoboken, NJ, 340-341
Farrell, Russ, NYC, NY, 125
Fernandez, Laura, NYC, NY, 357
Filip, Traian Alexandru, NYC, NY, 179
Filippo, Judy, Brookline, MA, 114
Fisher, Jeffrey, NYC, NY, 246
Fitz-Maurice, Jeff, Phila., PA, 423
Fleming, Ron, NYC, NY, 68
Franco, Richmond Hill, NY, 133
Frisari, Frank, Richmond Hill, NY, 92
Gaadt, George, NYC, NY, 117
Gadino, Victor, NYC, NY, 56
Gall, Chris, NYC, NY, 426
Gampert, John, Kew Gardens, NY, 163
Garé, m., NYC, NY, 243
Garns, Allen, NYC, NY, 360
Garrow, Dan, NYC, NY, 326
Geng, Maud, Boston, MA, 196-197
Genzo, John Paul, Phila., PA, 422
Gergely, Peter, Highland Falls, NY, 167
Giguere, Ralph, NYC, NY, 362

Gnan, Patrick, Phila., PA, 421
Gomberg, Susan, NYC, NY, 353-367
Graham, Tom, Brooklyn, NY, 241
Grant, Mel, NYC, NY, 252
Gray, Steve, NYC, NY, 426
Greenberg, Sheldon, NYC, NY, 180
Grossman, Myron, NYC, NY, 237
Guitteau, Jud, NYC, NY, 323
Haefele, Steve, NYC, NY, 260
Hallgren, Gary, Mastic Beach, NY, 243
Hallgren, Gary, NYC, NY, 243
Hamagami, John, NYC, NY, 126
Hamlin, Janet, Brooklyn, NY, 417
Harrington, Stephen, Norwalk, CT, 274
Harrison, William, NYC, NY, 321
Harwood, John, NYC, NY, 61
Havlicek, Karel, NYC, NY, 130
Henriquez, Celeste, NYC, NY, 407
Herbert, Jonathan, NYC, NY, 94-95
Himsworth, Jim III, Phila., PA, 419
Hogarth, Paul, NYC, NY, 246-247
Holmberg, Irmeli, NYC, NY, 166, 202-207, 349
Hong, Min Jae, NYC, NY, 80-81
Hoover, Sherry, NYC, NY, 258
Hostovich, Michael, Phila., PA, 422
Hughes, Marianne, Phila., PA, 422
Hughes, Neal, Phila., PA, 423
Hull, John, NYC, NY, 131
Independent Pencil Co., Newburyport, MA, 88
Inouye, Carol, NYC, NY, 184
Jackson, Barry, NYC, NY, 149
Jacobson, Rick, NYC, NY, 356
Jeffries, Shannon, Brooklyn, NY, 410
Johnson, Lonni Sue, NYC, NY, 102
Johnson, Lonni Sue, New Milford, CT, 102
Kabaker, Gayle, NYC, NY, 380
Kaczman, James, Watertown, MA, 152
Kane, John, New Hope, PA, 96
Kanelous, George, NYC, NY, 328

Kasper, Robert, Boston, MA, 196
Katz, Les, NYC, NY, 100
Klein, David G., Brooklyn, NY, 229
Klein, Hedy, Forest Hills, NY, 398
Klimt, Bill & Maurine, NYC, NY, 211
Knaff, Jean-Christian, Boston, MA, 196
Korn, Pamela & Associates, NYC, NY, 429-431
Kozmiuk, Michael, NYC, NY, 116
LaPorte, Michele, NYC, NY, 401
Lasher, Mary Ann, NYC, NY, 54
Le-Tan, Pierre, NYC, NY, 246
Lebo, Narda, NYC, NY, 182-183
Leedy, Jeff, NYC, NY, 367
Leff, Jerry Assocs., Inc., NYC, NY, 370
Leiner, Alan, NYC, NY, 124
Leon, Karen, Flushing, NY, 399
Leonard, Richard, NYC, NY, 254
Levine, Bette, NYC, NY, 64
Ligresti, Roberto, NYC, NY, 298-299
Little, Ed, Bridgewater, CT, 190-191
Littmann, Barry, Hackettstown, NJ, 375
Llewellyn, Sue, NYC, NY, 202
Lloyd, Jeff, NYC, NY, 237
Macanga, Steve, Roseland, NJ, 87
Mahoney, Ron, NYC, NY, 121
Maioresco Deca, Wanda, NYC, NY, 185
Manasse, Michèle, NYC, NY, 174-184
Manyum, Wallop, NYC, NY, 174
Marden, Phil, NYC, NY, 104
Margulies, Robert, NYC, NY, 195
Martinez, Sergio, NYC, NY, 248
Masuda, Coco, NYC, NY, 105
Mateu, Franc, NYC, NY, 257
Matthews, Lu, NYC, NY, 205
Mattingly, David B., Hoboken, NJ, 134
McCaffrey, Peter, NYC, NY, 402
McGovern, Preston, NYC, NY, 318
McGowan, Dan, NYC, NY, 364
McGurl, Michael, Brooklyn, NY, 101
McIntosh, Jon, Boston, MA, 197

McLoughlin, Wayne, NYC, NY, 325
McNeel, Richard, Upper Montclair, NJ, 424
Mehalko, Donna, NYC, NY, 169
Meisel, Paul, NYC, NY, 246-247
Mendola Ltd., NYC, NY, 371
Messi, Enzo, NYC, NY, 358
Miller, Dave, NYC, NY, 118
Miller, Verlin, Phila., PA, 419
Milnazik, Kimmerle, Drexel Hill, PA, 146
Moore, Chris, NYC, NY, 55
Moores, Jeff, NYC, NY, 430
Mordan, C.B., NYC, NY, 405
Morgan, Jacqui, NYC, NY, 110
Morgan, Wendy, Northport, NY, 308-309
Morse, Bill, NYC, NY, 73
Mowry, Scott, Charlestown, MA, 293
Mueller, Pete, NYC, NY, 70
Myer, Andy, Phila., PA, 420
Najaka, Marlies Merk, NYC, NY, 91
Neail, Pamela Assocs., NYC, NY, 401-407
Nelson, Craig, NYC, NY, 69
Neski, Peter, NYC, NY, 317
Network Studios, Northport, NY, 308-309
New York Airbrush, E. Northport, NY, 141
Ng, Michael, NYC, NY, 231
Nishinaka, Jeff, NYC, NY, 66
O'Connor, Cathy Christy, NYC, NY, 181
O'Neill, Fran, Boston, MA, 222
Olson, Richard A., NYC, NY, 78
Ortega, José, NYC, NY, 103
Palulian, Dickran, NYC, NY, 378
Palulian, Joanne, NYC, NY, 376-380
Parkinson, Jim Lettering, NYC, NY, 246-247
Parrish, George I. Jr., NYC, NY, 328
Parry, Ivor, NYC, NY, 267
Parton, Steve, NYC, NY, 262
Pasternak, Robert, NYC, NY, 320
Pembroke, Richard, NYC, NY, 122
Peterson, Cheryl, NYC, NY, 246-247
Phillips, Laura, NYC, NY, 60

Pinkney, Deborah, NYC, NY, 204
Polenghi, Evan, Brooklyn, NY, 227
Pomerantz, Lisa, Phila., PA, 420
Pomilla, Joseph, Ronkonkoma, NY, 315
Pratt, Russell E., NYC, NY, 140
Pritchett, Karen, NYC, NY, 207
Pritchett, Tom, NYC, NY, 328
Punin, Nikolai, NYC, NY, 166
Quon, Mike, NYC, NY, 225
Reid, Glenn Robert, Boston, MA, 196
Renard Represents, NYC, NY, 312, 321-327
Reynolds, Gene, NYC, NY, 408
Richards, Kenn, E. Northport, NY, 141
Richards, Linda, NYC, NY, 403
Riley Illustration, NYC, NY, 246-247
Rocco, Joe, Brooklyn, NY, 416
Roman, Helen Assocs., Inc., NYC, NY, 237
Rosales, Melodye, NYC, NY, 256
Rosenthal, Marc, Malden Bridge, NY, 151
Rosner, Meryl, NYC, NY, 234
Roth, Robert G., Kings Park, NY, 216-217
Roth, Roger, NYC, NY, 176-177
Rudnak, Theo, NYC, NY, 324
Ruiz, Art, NYC, NY, 249
Ryan, Terry, NYC, NY, 328
S.I.International, NYC, NY, 248-266
Sasaki, Goro, NYC, NY, 57
Schmidt, Urs, NYC, NY, 358
Schneider, R.M., NYC, NY, 427
Schrier, Fred, Northport, NY, 309
Schweigert, Carol, Boston, MA, 136
Sempé, J.J., NYC, NY, 246
Shohet, Marti, NYC, NY, 366
Skillins, Gunar, NYC, NY, 72
Small, David, NYC, NY, 247
Smallwood, Steve, Fort Lee, NJ, 143
Smith, Vicki, Boston, MA, 197
Spear, Charles, Hoboken, NJ, 74
Spector, Joel, NYC, NY, 201
Spengler, Ken, NYC, NY, 406
Spiers, Herbert, NYC, NY, 248-266
Stallard, Peter, NYC, NY, 62
Starr, David, NYC, NY, 104
Sterrett, Jane, NYC, NY, 393
Stillman, Whit & Iréné, NYC, NY, 246-247
Stutzman, Mark, Mt. Lake Park, MD, 158
Sullivan, Suzánne Hughes, NYC, NY, 142
Talaro, Lionel, NYC, NY, 232
Taleporos, Plato, NYC, NY, 333
Tedesco, Michael, Brooklyn, NY, 296
Thorn, Dick, NYC, NY, 128
Timmons, Bonnie, Phila., PA, 379
Tughan, James, NYC, NY, 361
Turner, Clay, NYC, NY, 67
Van Seters, Kim, Wayne, NJ, 90
Vargö, Kurt, NYC, NY, 429
Viviano, Sam, NYC, NY, 98
Wall, Pam, NYC, NY, 63
Ward, John, Freeport, NY, 400
Wasserman, Randie, NYC, NY, 206
Watts, Sharon, NYC, NY, 168
Watts, Stan, NYC, NY, 132
Weakley, Mark, NYC, NY, 359
Weber, Tricia, NYC, NY, 413-415
Weiman, Jon, NYC, NY, 391
Wenzel, Paul, NYC, NY, 259
Widener, Terry, NYC, NY, 175
Williams Group, The, NYC, NY, 413-415
Wolfe, Deborah Represents, Phila., PA, 419-423
Zwolak, Paul, Toronto Ontario, 297

MIDWEST

Bartels, Ceci Assocs., Chicago., IL, 394-395
Bartels, Ceci Assocs., St. Louis, MO, 394-395
Bennett, Gary, Louisville, KY, 269
Berglund, Cindy, Mpls., MN, 154
Bernal, Richard, St. Louis, MO, 384
Boies, Alex, Mpls., MN, 156
Brennan, Dan, Chicago, IL, 389
Brooks, Nan, Wilmette, IL, 187
Call, Ken, Chicago, IL, 290
Corkery, Eddie, Villa Park, IL, 172
Covington, Neverne, Mpls., MN, 157
Creative Source, Chicago, IL, 82
Curran, Don, St. Louis, MO, 386
Dryden, Jim, Mpls., MN, 155
Eloqui, Mt. Lake Park, MD, 158
Feldman, Ken, Chicago, IL, 97
Fleishman, Michael, Yellow Spring, OH, 381
Flood, Richard, Chicago, IL, 147
Foty, Tom, Minnetonka, MN, 200
Fuka, Ted, Chicago, IL, 307
Gilbert, Jim, Toledo, OH, 329
Gustafson, Glenn, Westmont, IL, 106
Hahn, Holly, Chicago, IL, 187
Halbert, Michael, St. Louis, MO, 395
Hanson, Jim and Talent, Chicago, IL, 107, 331, 418
Horn, Robert, Chicago, IL, 445
Knutsen, Jan, Bloomington, MN, 137-139
LaFleur, Dave, Derby, KS, 383
Laney, Ron, St. Louis, MO, 369
Langley, Sharon, Chicago, IL, 172-173
Lesh, David, Indpls., IN, 376-377
Linley, Michael, Columbus, OH, 428
Loehle, Don, Chicago IL, 346
Lundeen, Cathy, Mpls., MN, 153
Mahan, Benton, Chesterville, OH, 368
Mark, Steve, Bloomington, MN, 138
Mason, Marietta, Mpls., MN, 106
McInturff, Steve, Mechanicsburg, OH, 412
McKissick, Stewart, Columbus, OH, 159
O'Donnell, Billy, St. Louis, MO, 385
Oudekerk, Doug, Bloomington, MN, 137
Porazinski, Rob, Chicago, IL, 107
Porfirio, Guy, St. Louis, MO, 394
Potts, Carolyn & Assoc., Chicago, IL, 346
Ramin, Linda, St. Louis, MO, 384-386
Reed, Mike, Mpls., MN, 306
Reynolds, Bill, Bloomington, MN, 139

Rotoloni, Dave, Chicago, IL, 173
Rush, John, Evanston, IL, 77
Schuna, Frank, Mpls., MN, 153-157, 306
Schuna, JoAnne, Mpls. MN, 153-157, 306
Sell, Inc., Chicago, IL, 147
Shaw, Ned, Bloomington, IN, 170
Sirrell, T., Bartlett, IL, 199
Smallish, Craig, Chicago, IL, 418
Smith, Roy, St. Louis, MO, 386
Taylor, David, Indpls., IN 292
Whitney, Jack, St. Louis, MO, 386
Whitney, Mike, St. Louis, MO, 386

WEST

Alper, A.J., L.A., CA, 213
Bartczak, Peter, Santa Cruz, CA, 350
Belliveau, Allison, Pasadena, CA, 244
Benny, Mike, Sacramento, CA, 351
Bulthuis, Henri, W. Covina, CA, 397
Chaffee, James, Sacramento, CA, 392
Chodos-Irvine, Margaret, Seattle, WA, 135
Clownbank Studio, Santa Cruz, CA, 350
Collier, Jan, S.F., CA, 113, 331
Dierksen, Jane Brunkan, Duarte, CA, 245
Downs, Bob, Littleton, CO, 93
duCharme, Tracy, Venice, CA, 373
Edwards, Karl, Nevada City, CA, 308
Ericksen, Marc, S.F., CA, 273
Evans, Robert, S.F., CA, 272
French, Martin, Redmond, WA, 311
Fujisaki, Tuko, San Diego, CA, 238
Glick, Ivy & Associates, S.F., CA, 311-313
Goodwin & Friends, Inc., Ashland, OR, 305
Goodwin, David Scott, Ashland, OR, 305
Grinnell, Derek, S.F., CA, 313
Grove, David, S.F., CA, 160-161
Gulick, Dorothy, Whittier, CA, 319
Hackett, Pat, Seattle, WA, 311
Hanzon-Kurrasch, Toni, L.A., CA, 404
Hardiman, Miles W., Littleton, CO, 221
Hauser, Barb, S.F., CA, 97, 212
Hilliard, Fred, Bainbridge Is., WA, 97
Hillman, Betsy, S.F., CA, 432
Hines, Norman, W. Sacramento, CA, 372
Holmes, Matthew, Carmichael, CA, 312
Houlé, Harrison, S.F., CA, 112
Huhn, Tim, Santa, Monica, CA, 192
Hul, Jon Jr., N. Hollywood, CA, 332
Humphries, Michael, Santa Monica, CA, 194
Janovsky, Paul, Santa Monica, CA, 193
Jaz & Jaz, Seattle, WA, 135
Jorgensen, Donna, Seattle, WA, 97
Krejca, Gary, Tempe, AZ, 307
Livingston, Francis, San Anselmo, CA, 370
Lunia Blue Graphics, Sacramento, CA, 165
McLennan, Constance, Rocklin, CA, 271
Meyer, Gary, Woodland Hills, CA, 270
Morrow, J.T., Pacifica, CA, 84
Myers, Robert, Santa Monica, CA, 409
Nakamura, Carl, L.A., CA, 224
Newman, Carole & Assocs., Santa Monica, CA, 190-194
Ostan • Prentice • Ostan, Inc., L.A., CA, 397
Paperny, Vladimir, Santa Monica, CA, 194
Rosenthal, Represents, L.A., CA, 82, 295, 349
Rosenthal, Elise, L.A., CA, 295
Salk, Larry, L.A., CA, 228
Sandler, Neil, L.A., CA, 295
Schaffer, Amanda, Ramona, CA, 382
Scott, Freda, S.F., CA, 370
Spaulding, Kevin, Chatsworth, CA, 432
Stokes, Fiona, Santa Monica, CA, 193
Swan, Sara, L.A., CA, 396
Taylor, C. Winston, Granada Hills, CA, 111
Teach, Buz Walker, Sacramento, CA, 220
Tenud, Tish, Sacramento, CA, 210
Tessler, John, Sacramento, CA, 165
Von Schmidt, Eric, Glendale, CA, 242
Wagoner, Jae, L.A., CA, 331
Warnick, Elsa, Portland, OR, 198
Warter, Fred, Sherman Oaks, CA, 219
Weller, Don, Park City, UT, 331
Yadin, Hanan, L.A., CA, 397
Yamada, Kenny, Berkeley, CA, 295
Yee, Terry, Mesa, AZ, 85
Young, Eddie, Santa Monica, CA, 192

SOUTH

Aldridge Reps, Inc., Atlanta, GA, 339
Alexander/Pollard, Atlanta, GA, 300-304
Armes, Steve, Irving, TX, 291
Bennett, Gary, Louisville, KY 269
Blakey, Paul, Marietta, GA, 342
Bryant, Amy, Dallas, TX, 314
Burn, Ted, Marietta, GA, 347
Burnett, Lindy, Atlanta, GA, 300-301
Cashwell, Charles, Atlanta, GA, 280
Castellanos, Carlos, Hialeah, FL, 390
Chau, Tungwai, Nashville, TN, 425
Chirko, Gail, Atlanta, GA, 338
Clegg, Dave, Cumming, GA, 268
Collins, Britt Taylor, Atlanta, GA, 278
Cook, John, Dallas, TX, 337
Cooper, Bob, Atlanta, GA, 282
Cooper, Cheryl, Atlanta, GA, 303
Coveny, Rich, Atlanta, GA, 413-415
Crawford, Denise Chapman, Houston, TX, 314
de la Houssaye, Jeanne, New Orleans, LA, 89
Fleck, Tom, Atlanta, GA, 338
Floyd, Walt, Atlanta, GA, 86
Gaadt, David, Atlanta, GA, 285
Glasgow & Assocs., Woodbridge, VA, 276-277

Glasgow, Dale, Woodbridge, VA, 276-277
Gonzalez, Thomas, Atlanta, GA, 339
Grandstaff, Chris, Woodbridge, VA, 164
Harris, Leslie, Atlanta, GA, 330
Hogan, Barb, Atlanta, GA, 344
Holladay, Reggie, Lauderhill, FL, 82
Jarvis, David, Cocoa Beach, FL, 171
Jones, Jack, Atlanta, GA, 414
Laden, Nina, Atlanta, GA, 208-209
Lengyel, Kathy, Atlanta, GA, 304
Lester, Mike, Atlanta, GA, 188-189
Lewis, Maurice, Houston, TX, 240
Linden, Tamara, Atlanta, GA, 338
Lindlof, Ed, Austin, TX, 212
Loehle, Don, Atlanta, GA, 346
Losey, Brenda, Atlanta, GA, 279
Lovell, Rick, Atlantic, GA, 413
Lynch, Larry & Andrea, Dallas, TX, 106, 314
Martin, Lyn, Knoxville, TN, 218

Mayer, Bill Inc., Decatur, GA, 108-109
McClure, Tim, Dallas, TX, 336
McKelvey, David, Atlanta, GA, 415
Melrath, Susan, W. Palm Beach, FL, 223
Mollica, Pat, Atlanta, GA, 414
Moore, Larry, Orlando, FL, 374
Moses, David, Atlanta, GA, 283
Mull, Christy, Atlanta, GA, 345
Ovies, Joseph M., Atlanta, GA, 338
Passerelli, Charles A., Atlanta, GA, 338
Penca, Gary, Coral Springs, FL, 211
Pittman, Jackie, Atlanta, GA, 284
Radigan, Bob, Atlanta, GA, 349
Repertoire, Dallas, TX, 106, 314
Robinette, John, Atlanta, GA, 414
Rose, Drew, Atlanta, GA, 281
Rosenbaum, Tina, Dallas, TX, 334
Saffold, Joe, Atlanta, GA, 145
Sands, Trudy, Dallas, TX, 334-337
Schmidt, John F., Springfield, VA, 239

Sipp, Geo, Atlanta, GA, 214
Smythe, Danny, Atlanta, GA, 414
Sours, Michael, Dallas, TX, 335
Story, Michael, Columbia, SC, 99
Stubbs, Tommy, Atlanta, GA, 348
Sumpter, Will & Assocs., Atlanta, GA, 278-287
Tamara Inc., Atlanta, GA, 338
Tate, Clark, Atlanta, GA, 302
Traynor, Elizabeth, Atlanta, GA, 302
Unruh, Jack, Atlanta, GA, 343
Wells, Susan, Atlanta, GA, 342-349
Wende, Philip, Atlanta, GA, 286
Williams Group, The, Atlanta, GA, 413-415
Williams, Phillip, Atlanta, GA, 413-415
Williams, Tim, Alpharetta, GA, 162
Wimmer, Mike, Norman, OK, 371
Yesawich & Welsh, Orlando, FL, 82

REPRESENTATIVES & TALENT INDEX

ALDRIDGE REPS, INC.
ATLANTA, GA
339
    Gonzalez, Thomas, 339

ALEXANDER/POLLARD
ATLANTA, GA
300-304
    Burnett, Lindy, 300-301
    Cooper, Cheryl, 303
    Lengyel, Kathy, 304
    Traynor, Elizabeth, 302

AMERICAN ARTISTS
NYC, NY
115-132, 212, 240
    Batcheller, Keith, 120
    Bergendorff, Roger, 123
    Butler, Chris, 129
    Consani, Chris, 115
    DuPont, Lane, 127
    Effler, Jim, 119
    Farrell, Russ, 125
    Gaadt, George, 117
    Hamagami, John, 126
    Havlicek, Karel, 130
    Hull, John, 131
    Kozmiuk, Michael, 116
    Leiner, Alan, 124
    Lewis, Maurice, 240
    Lindlof, Ed, 212
    Mahoney, Ron, 121
    Miller, Dave, 118
    Pembroke, Richard, 122
    Thorn, Dick, 128
    Watts, Stan, 132

BARTELS, CECI ASSOCS.
ST. LOUIS, MO
394-395
    Halbert, Michael, 395
    Porfirio, Guy, 394

BERNSTEIN & ANDRIULLI
NYC, NY
53-73
    Bailey, Pat, 71
    Brown, Rick, 59
    Creative Capers, 58
    Ellis, Jon, 65
    Fleming, Ron, 68
    Gadino, Victor, 56
    Harwood, John, 61

    Lasher, Mary Ann, 54
    Levine, Bette, 64
    Moore, Chris, 55
    Morse, Bill, 73
    Mueller, Pete, 70
    Nelson, Craig, 69
    Nishinaka, Jeff, 66
    Phillips, Laura, 60
    Sasaki, Goro, 57
    Skillins, Gunar, 72
    Stallard, Peter, 62
    Turner, Clay, 67
    Wall, Pam, 63

BRINDLE, CAROLYN & PARTNER
NYC, NY
168-169
    Mehalko, Donna, 169
    Watts, Sharon, 168

BRODY, SAM
NYC, NY
97, 198
    Hillard, Fred, 97
    Warnick, Elsa, 198

BUCK, SID & KANE, BARNEY
NYC, NY
171, 290, 432
    Call, Ken, 290
    Jarvis, David, 171
    Spaulding, Kevin, 432

CHISLOVSKY, CAROL INC.
NYC, NY
426-427
    Bell, Karen, 427
    Bruce, Taylor, 426
    Cohen, Jim, 427
    Gall, Chris, 426
    Gray, Steve, 426
    Schneider, R.M., 427

COLLIER, JAN
S.F. CA
113, 331
    Baseman, Gary, 113
    Weller, Don, 331

COLLIGNON, DANIELE
NYC, NY
331
    Weller, Don, 331

CREATIVE FREELANCERS, INC.
NYC, NY
223, 230-236
    Caporale, Wende, 233
    De Cerchio, Joe, 236
    Dininno, Steve, 230
    Dzedzy, John, 235
    Melrath, Susan, 223
    Ng, Michael, 231
    Rosner, Meryl, 234
    Talaro, Lionel, 232

CREATIVE SOURCE
CHICAGO, IL
82
    Holladay, Reggie, 82

DREXLER, SHARON, NYC, NY, 100
    Katz, Les, 100
    FELDMAN, KEN
    CHICAGO, IL
    97Hilliard, Fred, 97

GENG, MAUD
BOSTON, MA
196-197
    Alterio, Caroline, 197
    Barnes, Suzanne, 196
    Kasper, Robert, 196
    Knaff, Jean-Christian, 196
    McIntosh, Jon, 197
    Reid, Glenn Robert, 196
    Smith, Vicki, 197

GLICK, IVY & ASSOCIATES
S.F., CA
311-313
    French, Martin, 311
    Grinnell, Derek, 313
    Holmes, Matthew, 312

GOMBERG, SUSAN
NYC, NY
353-367
    Brennan, Neil, 355
    Carver, Steve, 363
    Dale, Robert, 365
    Fernandez, Laura, 357
    Garns, Allen, 360
    Giguere, Ralph, 362
    Jacobson, Rick, 356
    Leedy, Jeff, 367
    McGowan, Dan, 364
    Messi, Enzo, 358
    Schmidt, Urs, 358
    Shohet, Marti, 366
    Tughan, James, 361
    Weakley, Mark, 359

HACKETT, PAT
SEATTLE, WA
311
    French, Martin, 311

HAHN, HOLLY
CHICAGO, IL
187
    Brooks, Nan, 187

HANSON, JIM AND TALENT
CHICAGO, IL
107, 331, 418
    Porazinski, Rob, 107
    Smallish, Craig, 418
    Weller, Don, 331

HAUSER, BARB
S.F., CA
97, 212
    Hilliard, Fred, 97
    Lindlof, Ed, 212

HILLMAN, BETSY
S.F., CA
432
    Spaulding, Kevin, 432

HOLMBERG, IRMELI
NYC, NY
166, 202-207, 349
    Bridy, Dan, 203
    Llewellyn, Sue, 202
    Matthews, Lu, 205
    Pinkney, Deborah, 204
    Pritchett, Karen, 207
    Punin, Nikolai, 166
    Radigan, Bob, 349
    Wasserman, Randie, 206

JAZ & JAZ
SEATTLE, WA
135
    Chodos-Irvine, Margaret, 135

JORGENSEN, DONNA
SEATTLE, WA
97
    Hilliard, Fred, 97

KLIMT, BILL & MAURINE
NYC, NY
211
    Penca, Gary, 211

KNUTSEN, JAN
BLOOMINGTON, MN
137-139
    Mark, Steve, 138
    Oudekerk, Doug, 137
    Reynolds, Bill, 139

KORN, PAMELA & ASSOCIATES
NYC, NY
429-431
    Ajhar, Brian, 431
    Moores, Jeff, 430
    Vargö, Kurt, 429

LANGLEY, SHARON
CHICAGO, IL
172-173
    Corkery, Eddie, 172
    Rotoloni, Dave, 173

LEFF, JERRY ASSOCS., INC.
NYC, NY
370
    Livingston, Francis, 370

MANASSE, MICHÈLE
NYC, NY
174-184
    Boll, Maxine, 178
    Filip, Traian Alexandru, 179
    Greenberg, Sheldon, 180
    Inouye, Carol, 184
    Lebo, Narda, 182-183
    Manyum, Wallop, 174
    O'Connor, Cathy Christy, 181
    Roth, Roger, 176-177
    Widener, Terry, 175

MASON, MARIETTA
MPLS., MN
106
    Gustafson, Glenn, 106

MENDOLA LTD.
NYC, NY
371
    Wimmer, Mike, 371

NEAIL, PAMELA ASSOCS.
NYC, NY
401-407
    Hanzon-Kurrasch, Toni, 404
    Henriquez, Celeste, 407
    LaPorte, Michele, 401
    McCaffrey, Peter, 402
    Mordan, C.B., 405
    Richards, Linda, 403
    Spengler, Ken, 406

NETWORK STUDIOS
NORTHPORT, NY
308-309
    Edwards, Karl, 308
    Schrier, Fred, 309

NEWMAN, CAROLE & ASSOCS.
SANTA MONICA, CA
190-194
    Huhn, Tim, 192
    Humphries, Michael, 194
    Janovsky, Paul, 193
    Little, Ed, 190-191
    Paperny, Vladimir, 194
    Stokes, Fiona, 193
    Young, Eddie, 192

OSTAN • PRENTICE • OSTAN, INC.
L.A., CA
397
    Yadin, Hanan, 397

PALULIAN, JOANNE
NYC, NY
376-380
    Kabaker, Gayle, 380
    Lesh, David, 376-377
    Palulian, Dickran, 378
    Timmons, Bonnie, 379

POTTS, CAROLYN & ASSOC.
CHICAGO, IL
346
    Loehle, Don, 346

PRITCHETT, TOM
NYC, NY
328
    Kanelous, George, 328
    Parrish, George, I. Jr., 328
    Ryan, Terry, 328

RAMIN, LINDA
ST. LOUIS, MO
384-386
    Bernal, Richard, 384
    Curran, Don, 386
    O'Donnell, Billy, 385
    Smith, Roy, 386
    Whitney, Jack, 386
    Whitney, Mike, 386

RENARD REPRESENTS
NYC, NY
312, 321-327
    Björkman, Steve, 322
    Dean, Glenn, 327
    Garrow, Dan, 326
    Guitteau, Jud, 323
    Harrison, William, 321
    Holmes, Matthew, 312
    McLoughlin, Wayne, 325
    Rudnak, Theo, 324

REPERTOIRE
DALLAS, TX
106, 314
    Bryant, Amy, 314
    Crawford, Denise Chapman, 314
    Gustafson, Glenn, 106

RILEY ILLUSTRATION
NYC, NY
246-247
    Benoît, 247
    Bramhall, William, 247
    Clayton, Elaine, 246-247
    Degen, Paul, 246
    Demarest, Chris, 247
    Fisher, Jeffrey, 246
    Hogarth, Paul, 246-247
    Le-Tan, Pierre, 246
    Meisel, Paul, 246-247
    Parkinson, Jim Lettering, 246-247
    Peterson, Cheryl, 246-247
    Sempé, J.J., 246
    Small, David, 247

ROMAN, HELEN ASSOCS., INC.
NYC, NY
237
    Carbone, Lou, 237
    De Muth, Roger T., 237
    Dolobowsky, Mena, 237
    Einsel, Naiad, 237
    Grossman, Myron, 237
    Lloyd, Jeff, 237

ROSENTHAL REPRESENTS
L.A., CA
82, 295, 349
    Holladay, Reggie, 82
    Radigan, Bob, 349
    Yamada, Kenny, 295

S.I. INTERNATIONAL
NYC, NY
248-266
    Baumann, Karen, 253
    Brusca, Jack, 251
    Chichoni, Oscar, 263
    Codarcea, Daniela, 265
    Courtney Studios, 266
    Davidson, Dennis, 250
    Davis, Allen, 255
    de Barros, A. Martins, 264
    Enik, Ted, 261
    Grant, Mel, 252
    Haefele, Steve, 260
    Hoover, Sherry, 258
    Leonard, Richard, 254
    Martinez, Sergio, 248
    Mateu, Franc, 257
    Parton, Steve, 262
    Rosales, Melodye, 256
    Ruiz, Art, 249
    Wenzel, Paul, 259

SANDS, TRUDY
DALLAS, TX
334-337
    Cook, John, 337
    McClure, Tim, 336
    Rosenbaum, Tina, 334
    Sours, Michael, 335

SCHUNA, FRANK
MPLS., MN
153-157, 306
    Berglund, Cindy, 154
    Boies, Alex, 156
    Covington, Neverne, 157
    Dryden, Jim, 155
    Lundeen, Cathy, 153
    Reed, Mike, 306

SCHUNA, JOANNE
MPLS., MN
153-157, 306
    Berglund, Cindy, 154
    Boies, Alex, 156
    Covington, Neverne, 157
    Dryden, Jim, 155
    Lundeen, Cathy, 153
    Reed, Mike, 306

SCOTT, FREDA
S.F., CA
370
    Livingston, Francis, 370

SELL, INC.
CHICAGO, IL
147
    Flood, Richard, 147

STARR, DAVID
NYC, NY
104
    Marden, Phil, 104

SUMPTER, WILL & ASSOCS.
ATLANTA, GA
278-287
    Cashwell, Charles, 280
    Collins, Britt Taylor, 278
    Cooper, Bob, 282
    Gaadt, David, 285
    Losey, Brenda, 279
    Moses, David, 283
    Pittman, Jackie, 284
    Rose, Drew, 281
    Tate, Clarke, 287
    Wende, Philip, 286

TAMARA INC.
ATLANTA, GA
338
    Chirko, Gail, 338
    Fleck, Tom, 338
    Ovies, Joseph M., 338
    Passerelli, Charles A., 338

WAGONER, JAE
L.A., CA
331
    Weller, Don, 331

WELLS, SUSAN
ATLANTA, GA
342-349
    Blakey, Paul, 342
    Burn, Ted, 347
    Hogan, Barb, 344
    Loehle, Don, 346
    Mull, Christy, 345
    Radigan, Bob, 349
    Stubbs, Tommy, 348
    Unruh, Jack, 343

WILLIAMS GROUP, THE
ATLANTA, GA
413-415
    Jones, Jack, 414
    Lovell, Rick, 413
    McKelvey, David, 415
    Mollica, Pat, 414
    Robinette, John, 414
    Smythe, Danny, 414

WOLFE, DEBORAH REPRESENTS
PHILA., PA
419-423
    Baker, Skip, 421
    Buterbaugh, Rick, 420
    Campbell, Jenny, 420
    Dallasta, Ray, 419
    Danila, Deborah, 419
    Duffy, Pat, 422
    Fitz-Maurice, Jeff, 423
    Genzo, John Paul, 422
    Gnan, Patrick, 421
    Himsworth, Jim III, 419
    Hostovich, Michael, 422
    Hughes, Marianne, 422
    Hughes, Neal, 423
    Miller, Verlin, 419
    Myer, Andy, 420
    Pomerantz, Lisa, 420

YESAWICH & WELSH
ORLANDO, FL
82
    Holladay, Reggie, 82